Global Environmental Governance and Desertification

About the Author

Dr. A. Kannan is presently working as Assistant Professor at the Department of Public Administration and Development Management, Wollega University, Nekemte, Ethiopia. He completed his M.A. (Public Administration) from Madras Christian College, Chennai. He did his M.Phil. and Ph.D. at the Centre for West Asian and African Studies, School of International Studies, Jawaharlal Nehru University, New Delhi. He published research Articles in a number of leading journals and also presented research papers in national and international Seminars and Conferences. His areas of interest include Natural Resources Management, Desertification, Global Environmental Governance and Multilateral Environmental Agreements.

Global Environmental Governance and Desertification

A Study of Gulf Cooperation Council Countries

Dr. A. Kannan
Assistant Professor
Dept. of Public Admn. and Development Management
Wollega University
Nekemte (Ethiopia)

CONCEPT PUBLISHING COMPANY PVT. LTD.,
NEW DELHI-110059

ISBN-13 : 978-81-8069-848-4

First Published 2012

Published and Printed by

Concept
Since 1974

Concept Publishing Company Pvt. Ltd.
A/15-16, Commercial Block, Mohan Garden
New Delhi-110059 (India)
T: 25351460, 25351794, *F*: 091-11-25357109
E: publishing@conceptpub.com, W: www.conceptpub.com
Editorial Office: H-13, Bali Nagar, New Delhi-110 015, India.

Cataloging in Publication Data--*Courtesy:* D.K. Agencies (P) Ltd. <docinfo@dkagencies.com>

Kannan, A., ***Dr.***
Global environmental governance and desertification : a study of Gulf Cooperation Council countries / A. Kannan.
p. cm.
Includes bibliographical references (p.) and index.
ISBN 9788180698484

1. Desertification—Control—Political aspects—Persian Gulf Region. 2. Environmental policy—Persian Gulf Region. I. Title.

DDC 333.73609174927 23

Dedicated
to
The People of Africa

Preface

Global environmental problems are increasingly becoming complex and dynamic. Environmental problems experienced at any given political level frequently have their origins at locations other than where their impact is most acutely felt. These trans-boundary and cross-border nature of environmental issues are rightly called as 'problems without passports'. Among them, desertification is considered as one of the greatest environmental and development problems of the 21st century.

Desertification is potentially the most threatening ecosystem change impacting livelihoods of the poor. It is a detrimental process that brings about a gradual and an unnoticed reduction in the productive capacity of land over a period of years which in turn leads to the formation of a complete wasteland incapable of producing anything useful. Desertification is a problem of global magnitude with major environmental and socio-economic consequences. It is a complex issue, arises not from a single, identifiable cause, but from complex interactions among physical, biological, political, social, cultural and economic factors. The countries most seriously affected by desertification usually are developing countries.

The unprecedented scale and magnitude of environmental problems appear to signal the demand not only for cooperation among governments, but also for cooperation among others including civil society. No crisis in history has so clearly demonstrated the interdependence of nation states as the environmental crisis. Growing recognition of the complexity, pervasiveness, and mutual interdependence of environmental problems is reshaping environmental regulation and natural resource management. Environmental logic demands broad-based international cooperation and coordination of policies, and requires the international community to evolve effective global environmental policies. This demand for new forms of governance is increasingly being met by Global Environmental Governance (GEG) framework.

The traditional models of administration failed to address many global problems. In the emerging web of transnational links, old forms of collective decision-making are weakened and new forms become possible. Governance, broader than government is a new process of governing or the new method by which society is governed. It consists of formal institutions and informal arrangements. As a comprehensive and inclusive concept, governance is an all-encompassing, highly participatory, dynamic and engaging process. It seeks solutions to problems through dialogue and communicative action.

Today the policy formulation and implementation processes are made up of these diverse, overlapping and integrated networks which comprise varying relational geometries of States, markets and associational sectors. These actors bring their own specific sets of powers, roles and responsibilities as determined by values, skills and organizational resources into the network arena.

Global environmental governance is the establishment and operation of a set of rules of conduct that define practice, assign roles and guide interaction so as to enable State and non-State actors to address environmental problems across national boundaries. Growing recognition of the complexity, pervasiveness, and mutual interdependence of environmental problems reshaped environmental regulation and natural resource management.

Global Environmental Governance emerged in a significant way, however, only in the late 1960s and 1970s, as part of a growing concern about environmental problems. The Stockholm Conference in 1972 launched global efforts to protect, preserve and enhance the environment. International environmental accords, treaties and agreements were central components of these collective efforts. These global environmental instruments, collectively known as Multilateral Environmental Agreements (MEAs) are the legal framework for international environmental governance.

The United Nations Convention to Combat Desertification (UNCCD) is the newest link in the evolving international system for environmental governance. In linking a serious environmental concern with development issues, this Convention can be viewed as an important step towards building a multilateral framework for sustainable development. The Convention recognizes desertification primarily as a problem of sustainable development, poverty and human well-being, and environmental preservation. Therefore, it is a much more comprehensive treaty than earlier efforts to combat desertification.

Standing at the intersection between domestic, international, and global pressures, the State is the preeminent institution with requisite political authority and steering capacity to tackle ecological problems through MEAs and domestic regulations of natural resources management. Over the past few decades governments adopted a large number of MEAs. With intensified use of international treatises as a means to address global environmental problems, concerns expressed are being regarding the compliance of States with commitments to which they agreed.

Basically the global environmental agreements are only as effective as the parties make them. Effectiveness is the result not only of how the government implements accords (the formal legislation or regulations that countries adopt) but also of compliance (the observance of these regulations and commitments contained in the international instruments). In other words compliance goes beyond implementation. However, implementation is generally considered as an essential predicate for compliance. This study analyses the implementation of UNCCD in the Gulf Cooperation Council (GCC) countries and their compliance with the same.

The GCC countries are situated in extremely arid zones. The source, nature and intensity of environmental degradation differentiate this region from the rest of the world. This is not because of the interaction between man-made and natural environmental problems but because of the magnitude and speed with which this interaction takes place. The unprecedented levels of industrialization, inefficient use of limited resources, unplanned urbanization, large-scale consumption, higher population growth and lack of regulatory mechanisms produced a critical environmental situation in the GCC countries.

The scarcity of water and land resources is the most pressing. Deterioration of the marine and coastal environment, loss of biodiversity, increasing industrial pollution and poor management of hazardous wastes also threaten the sustainable development of this region. Most land is either desertified or vulnerable to desertification. These serious environmental problems including desertification must be addressed immediately because failure to act now will greatly compound the cost and complexity of later remedial efforts.

The administrative system in these countries, although simple until recently, is being steadily inflated due to an unclear vision of future objectives and the abundance of financial resources. It suffers from structural and behavioural defects of both external and internal origin.

Even though all the GCC countries signed and ratified the UNCCD and, subsequently initiated several measures to implement the same, their compliance with this significant global treaty remains poor and inadequate. The efforts made by the GCC countries to implement the Convention and to comply with the same are analyzed within the framework of Global Environmental Governance.

This study begins with the following hypotheses:

1. The large-scale socio-economic developmental activities and the harsh climatic conditions accelerated the intensity and magnitude of desertification in the GCC countries.
2. Political and economic issues remain top on the agenda of the governments rather than environmental issues.
3. Administrative machineries are not adequately equipped to tackle environmental problems in general and desertification in particular.
4. Only limited provisions of the UNCCD have been implemented in these countries.
5. Lack of effective mechanism for people's participation is a major constraint in addressing the desertification problem in the GCC countries.
6. In the GCC countries radical reform measures are required in the areas of recruitment, training and administrative procedures.

This book consists of seven chapters. The first chapter analyses the concept of desertification and the controversies related with its definition. It examines the global status of desertification and its far-reaching consequences on climate change and food security. It traces the emergence of global environmental governance as a tool to address the complex nature of contemporary environmental problems. The place of UNCCD within the framework of GEG is briefly explained.

The second chapter examines the causes and consequences of

environmental problems in GCC Countries. It also analyses the various dimensions of desertification in the GCC Countries. Besides these, this chapter also explores the linkages between desertification and other developmental issues such as agriculture, water resources, urbanization, population growth, deforestation and industrialization.

The third chapter examines the role of the State in environmental protection and sustainable development. It analyses the administrative system in the GCC Countries with emphasis on its rapid expansion and functions. It also traces the evolution of environmental administration in the GCC Countries and its relationships with regional and international environmental institutional arrangements.

The efforts of international community to protect environment especially since the Stockholm Conference are examined in the fourth chapter. This chapter also reviews the emergence of MEAs as a mechanism to address global environmental problems. It further explores the evolution of UNCCD with emphasis on the outcome of Nairobi Conference the 1977, Rio Summit 1992 and the deliberations of Intergovernmental Negotiation Committee on Desertification (INCD). It finally analyses the structure of UNCCD including its administrative and financial aspects.

The fifth chapter analyses the various measures taken by the GCC Countries to combat desertification including the implementation of Plan of Action (PoA) of Nairobi Conference, 1977. This chapter in detail studies the initiatives undertaken by the GCC Countries under UNCCD and surveys the implementation of West Asia Sub-regional Action Programme and its pilot projects. It also investigates the role of GCC Countries in executing UNCCD at the regional level.

The sixth chapter underlines the importance of compliance with an international treaty, besides elucidating the difference between implementation and compliance with respect to MEAs. The efforts of GCC Countries to comply with the provisions of UNCCD are critically analyzed in this chapter. It examines the various indicators used to measure the effective compliance with UNCCD with reference to GCC Countries. The seventh chapter concludes with important findings.

While it is observed that most States comply with most international treaties most of the time, there are reasons to believe that national implementation of and compliance with international accords is not only imperfect but often inadequate. However there are only a few systematic studies of factors affecting compliance with international environmental accords into which countries are already entered. Among them, there are even fewer studies that focus on factors at the national level that affect compliance. This work analyses the implementation of the UNCCD by the GCC countries and their compliance with global environment-development treaty. In this context, this book attempts to fill the knowledge gap which exits in analyzing the compliance of MEAs especially in developing countries.

Dr. A. Kannan

Acknowledgements

I express my deepest gratitude to Prof. Gulshan Dietl for her guidance and constant encouragement. I am grateful to Prof. Girijesh Pant, Prof. A.K. Pasha, Prof. P.R. Kumaraswamy and Prof. Anwar Alam for their guidance and moral support. I am greatly indebted to Dr. N. Janardhan and Mrs. Meena Janardhan for their support during my field study in Bahrain and the United Arab Emirates.

I extend my sincere thanks to Dr. Ahmad Ghosn, West Asia Regional Coordinator (UNCCD) for his expert comments. I am grateful to Prof. Asma Ali Abahussain, Arabian Gulf University, Manama for her valuable suggestions. I am thankful to Shri K.P. Fabian, Former Indian Ambassador to Qatar and Prof. A.K. Ramakrishnan for their valuable comments. Also I sincerely acknowledge the scholarly support of a number of authors and researchers whose views and opinions have significantly shaped this work.

I am deeply and for ever indebted to many of my teachers in the past including Mr. Thiruvarangam, Mr. Sangara Narayanan, Mrs. Julia Mary, Mrs. Thilakambal, Mrs. K. Pakkiam, Dr. Ramesh Sunder and Dr. P. Kingsley Chandrasekhar for their guidance. I wish to extend my warm thanks to an endless number of my friends including Ms. Chitra, N. and A.G. Selam for their moral support.

My deepest gratitude goes to my family for their unflagging support. Sincere thanks are due to the Concept Publishing Co. Pvt. Ltd., New Delhi who have made meticulous efforts to ensure that the publication becomes a quality one.

Nekemte (Ethiopia) **Dr. A. Kannan**
November 2010

Contents

List of Tables

Abbreviations

ACSAD	Arab Centre for the Study of Arid Zones and Dry Lands
AFESD	Arab Fund for Economic and Social Development
ALESCO	Arab League Education, Scientific and Cultural Organization
AMCEN	African Ministerial Conference on the Environment
AOAD	Arab Organization for Agriculture Development
API	Arab Planning Institute
ARCEL	Arab Regional Centre for Environmental Law
CAME	Centre for the Affairs of Man and the Environment
CAMRE	Council of Arab Ministers Responsible for the Environment
CBD	Convention on Biological Diversity
CEDARE	Centre for Environment and Development in the Arab Region and Europe
CGDC	Consultative Group on Desertification Control
CIESIN	Centre for International Earth Science Information Network
CITES	Convention on International Trade in Endangered Species of Wild Fauna and Flora
CITET	Centre for Environmental Technology
COPs	Conference of Parties
CRIC	Committee for the Review of the Implementation of the Convention
CSD	Commission on Sustainable Development
DFID	UK Department For International Development
EPA	Environment Public Authority
ESCWA	Economic and Social Commission for Western Asia
FAO	Food and Agriculture Organization of the United Nations

FEA	Federal Environment Agency
GATT	General Agreement on Tariffs and Trade
GACGÇ	German Advisory Council on Global Change
GCC	Gulf Cooperation Council
GCCFAE	GCC Framework Agreement on Environment
GDP	Gross Domestic Products
GEF	Global Environmental Facility
GEG	Global Environmental Governance
GEO	Global Environmental Outlook
GGI	Gulf Green Initiatives
GHG	Green House Gas
GLASOD	Global Assessment of Human Induced Soil Degradation
GM	Global Mechanism
GRC	Gulf Research Centre
ICARDA	International Centre for Agricultural Research in Dry Areas
IDB	Islamic Development Bank
IFAD	International Fund for Agricultural Development
IMF	International Monetary Fund
INCD	Intergovernmental Negotiation Committee on Desertification
JCEDAR	Joint Committee for Environment and Development in the Arab Region
JIU	Joint Inspection Unit
JLG	Joint Liaison Group
LADA	Land Degradation Assessment in Drylands Project
LAS	League of Arab States
MEA	Multilateral Environmental Agreement
MEDRC	Middle East Desalinization Research Centre
MENA	Middle East and North Africa
NAP	National Action Plan for implementation of UNCCD activities
NCBs	National Coordination Bodies
NEAP	National Environmental Action Plan
NES	National Environmental Strategy
NFPs	National Focal Points
NGOs	Non-Governmental Organizations
NSDAP	National Sustainable Development Action Plan
NSDS	National Sustainable Development Strategy

OECD	Organization for Economic Cooperation and Development
OIC	Organization of Islamic Conference
OPEC	Organization of Petroleum Exporting Countries
PAAET	Public Authority for Applied Education and Training
PACD	Plan of Action to Combat Desertification
PERSGA	Programme for the Environment of the Red Sea and Gulf of Aden
PoA	Plan of Action
POPs	(Stockholm Convention on) Persistent Organic Pollutants
PRSP	Poverty Reduction Strategy Paper
RAP	Regional Action Programme
RCEDC	Regional Centre for Environmental Disasters and Crises
RCU	Regional Coordination Unit
ROPME	Regional Organization for the Protection of the Marine Environment
ROWA	Regional Office for West Asia
SALAM	Sustainable Arid Land Management
SDFP	Sustainable Development Focal Point
SRAP	Sub-Regional Action Programme
TPNs	Thematic Programme Networks
UNCCD	United Nations Convention to Combat Desertification
UNCED	United Nations Conference on Environment and Development
UNCSD	United Nations Commission on Sustainable Development
UNDP	United Nations Development Programme
UNEP	United Nations Environment Programme
UNESCO	United Nations Educational, Scientific and Culture Organization
UNFCCC	United Nations Framework Convention on Climate Change
WANA	West Asia and North Africa
WB	World Bank
WHO	World Health Organization
WMO	World Metrological Organization
WSSD	World Summit on Sustainable Development
WTO	World Trade Organization

I

Introduction: Desertification and Global Environmental Governance

The Millennium Ecosystem Assessment[1] describes desertification as "potentially the most threatening ecosystem change impacting livelihoods of the poor."[2] Desertification is a detrimental process that brings about a gradual and an unnoticed reduction in the productive capacity of land over a period of years. The end point of the process would be the formation of a complete wasteland incapable of producing anything useful. "Desertification is one of the greatest environmental and development problems of the 21st century. Some two billion people live in the world's drylands, whose biological productivity is under threat from the progressive degradation of soils and other natural resources. Desertification can trigger a vicious circle of environmental degradation, impoverishment, migration and conflicts, often also putting the political stability of the affected countries and regions at risk. It is estimated that about half of all armed conflicts present environmental causal factors characteristic of drylands."[3]

"Already today, environmental refugees[4]—refugees fleeing desertification—greatly outnumber those fleeing from war, ethnic confrontation and persecution. Growing desertification will only worsen this trend."[5] It is in fact the "(f)ood insecurity caused by the loss of productive land creates a spiral of poverty, forced migration and social and political conflict. By 2020, it is estimated (that) 60 million people will have to move from sub-Saharan Africa towards North Africa and Europe."[6]

Although desertification occurs all around the world, only

developing countries in the world's arid and semi-arid regions are severely affected by its severe consequences.[7] Developing countries in "Asia, Africa, and South America have the larger population living in drylands, both in numbers and percentage: 1.4 billion, 268 million, and 87 million people, or 42, 41, and 30 per cent of each region's population, respectively."[8] According to the United Nations Convention to Combat Desertification (UNCCD), "desertification arises not from a single, identifiable cause, but from complex interactions among physical, biological, political, social, cultural and economic factors. The manifestations and causes of desertification are believed to vary from place to place and with climatic and human contexts."[9] Desertification costs are often borne by the poorest of subsistence farmers and herders.

> Waging an effective fight against the spread of desertification is one of the greatest challenges in development politics today. The worst environmental changes brought on by desertification are happening in the poorest countries of the world. They affect first and foremost the most destitute of social groups. An estimated 40 per cent of all Africans and Asians live in areas threatened by desertification; in Latin America, it is 30 per cent of the population.[10]

"The annual loss of income as a result of land degradation is estimated at US$ 65 billion annually, and this does not include the difficult to measure but extremely important costs incurred in social and environmental terms to the current and future generations."[11] The costs of land degradation and desertification are most often measured in terms of lost productivity. This could mean reduced crop yields, grazing intensities, etc. Secondary costs include loss of ecosystem services, and indirect costs are those associated with mitigating desertification.[12] Recent extensive and in depth evaluations, such as the Millennium Ecosystem Assessment completed in 2005, "clearly demonstrate that there are no signs that the desertification trends are abating on a global scale."[13]

Global environmental problems are increasingly becoming complex and dynamic, do not conform to the boundaries of political and administrative jurisdiction. Kofi Annan rightly calls these trans-boundary and cross-border nature of environmental issues as "problems without passports."[14] It is impossible for an individual nation alone to effectively address these intricate and complicated problems. Global Environmental Governance (GEG) which consists of a number of actors and institutions provides a framework to address global environmental issues.

Keeping in view of its far reaching consequences on sustainable development and food security, concerted efforts are being made by the international community to address desertification through the United Nations Convention to Combat Desertification (UNCCD) within the framework of GEG.

"Perhaps more than any other MEA (Multilateral Environmental Agreement), the UNCCD promotes action at the intersection of environmental protection, economic development and social development."[15] Because of this UNCCD is considered as "a sustainable development treaty rather than as an environmental treaty in the narrow sense..... Indeed, poverty eradication—a policy objective central to developing countries—is prominently anchored in the convention as an essential precondition for the 'combat' against desertification to be effective."[16] Therefore, the UNCCD is viewed "as much a developmental as an environmental agreement."[17] Focused essentially on developing countries, UNCCD "offers a platform for effective environmental governance at national, regional and international levels. And if properly...(implemented), it could be a powerful weapon in the war against poverty and hunger."[18] UNCCD is often called as the "convention of the poor."[19]

> "Yet UNCCD has been plagued by lack of implementation and underfunding. The text of the Convention lacks teeth and a feasible work plan. Despite UNCCD's ratification by the Parliaments of more than 190 countries and over $100 million invested by member countries so far, progress is hard to discern and, in some countries, disillusionment has started set in."[20]

In this context, this chapter analyses the concept of desertification and the controversies related with its definition. It examines the global status of desertification and its far-reaching consequences on climate change and food security. It also traces the emergence of global environmental governance as a tool to address the complex nature of contemporary environmental problems. Besides it also briefly explains the place of UNCCD within the framework of GEG.

I. Concept of Desertification

Land is a natural component of an ecosystem. It is composed of several elements describable in terms of biophysical characteristics, including soil, water, flora and fauna, microclimate and physiography. Land serves many purposes of human kind, i.e. agriculture, forests and pastures, and infrastructure development. Besides these economic uses, land also performs environmental regulatory or ecological functions. These include controlling global warming and acting as a sink for many harmful chemicals. Since soil, in turn, is a component of land, its use and functions form a significant part of those attributed to land. Desertification is land degradation in arid, semi-arid and dry sub-humid areas resulting from various factors including climatic variations and human activities.

The main "issues related to land in the developing world include increasing degradation and desertification, together with inappropriate and inequitable land tenure systems, which have played a major role in exacerbating degradation. Other widespread problems include a decline in soil fertility, soil contamination, land management and conservation, gender imbalance in land tenure, and conversion of land habitat to agricultural or urban uses."[21]

i. Meaning of Desertification

Desertification is a "term that has not only generated long-lasting debate in the scientific community charged with its accurate definition, measurement, and monitoring, but has also exercised the minds and actions of policymakers in dryland nations."[22] The word desertification has a Latin origin: *fication*, which means the action of doing (or creating) comes from *fieri*, the passive form of the verb *facere*, to do, while desert is derived from both the adjective *desertus*, meaning uninhabitated, and the noun *desertum*, a desert area. In a wider sense, desertification can signify an environmental crisis which produces desert-like conditions or desert like landscapes in any ecosystem.[23] Therefore "desertification is not the natural expansion of existing deserts but the degradation of land in arid, semi-arid, and dry sub-humid areas."[24] It is a gradual process of soil productivity loss and the thinning out of the vegetative cover because of human activities and climatic variations. It occurs because dryland ecosystems, which cover over one-third of the world's land area, are extremely vulnerable to over-exploitation and inappropriate land use.

Desertification is a slow process by which the productivity of land is reduced over a period of time. It is also going through several stages before reaching the final one, which is an irreversible change. Natural threshold changes exist-historical events as well as current geo-socio-economic changes—which constantly intensify the desertification process.[25] Desertification also differs from drought. Drought is a general term meaning a sustained period of significantly sub-normal water or soil moisture supply.[26] Basically "drought is a temporary phenomenon occurring when precipitation falls below normal or when near normal precipitation is made less effective by other climate parameters such as high temperature, low humidity and strong winds."[27] According to Article 1(c) of UNCCD, drought is the naturally occurring phenomenon that exists when precipitation has been significantly below normal recorded levels, causing serious hydrological imbalances that adversely affect land resource production systems. "Manifestations (of drought) include: annual rainfall less than normal; month/season rainfall less than normal; reduced river flow; reduced groundwater availability."[28] Incidents of drought prevail in all climate zones of the world, but its impacts are acutely felt in the drylands.[29] Drought plays a part in desertification, usually worsening it.[30]

ii. Definition of Desertification

Since the United Nations Conference on Desertification (1977) "brought the world's attention to land degradation in the drylands, there has been a multitude of definitions and interpretations of the term desertification."[31] It also "triggered a great deal of scientific interest—and controversy. A heated and ongoing desertification debate has raged after this conference, reflected in a plethora of literature and the existence of more than a hundred definitions of desertification."[32]

Desertification has a multidimensional interpretation. More than 100 formal definitions of desertification are proposed by the experts in the literature. These definitions cover a gamut of issues, involve a multitude of spatial and temporal scales of concerns and often connote disparate meanings and interpretations. In general, these various definitions of desertification differ in their emphasis on the three distinct dimensions of the problem: ecological, meteorological and human.[33]

The phenomenon of desertification is very old, but national and international awareness of it and the efforts to address it are very recent. Some researchers consider desertification to be a process of change, while others view it as the end result of a process of change.[34] When considered to be a process, desertification is generally viewed as a series of incremental changes in biological productivity in arid, semi-arid, and sub-humid ecosystems. When considered as an end result, desertification refers to the prevalence of desert-like conditions in areas once green.

The "term desertification...was first coined in 1927 by the French scientist and explorer Louis Lavauden and first popularized in 1949 by the French forester Andre Aubreville. The latter (is) generally considered as the father of the term."[35] "The first use of the word desertification by an International Agency was in 1962 by FAO (Food and Agriculture Organization)."[36] Lavauden, who studied grazing lands in arid southern Tunisia, "did not expressly define the term but used it in referring to the low grazing productivity of land surrounding a protected 3,500 ha ranch near Maknassy (Tunisia)."[37] Aubreville, too, "did not define desertification in his book. He described the eroded land as being like a desert, abandoned and useless."[38]

Early experts on desertification promoted the idea of the 'encroaching desert', 'moving desert' or 'advancing desert' to illustrate desertification. This "expansion of the desert" theory culminated in the assertion by Lamprey that the Sahara was marching at a rate of 5.5 km/year.[39] "During the French occupations in West Africa, colonial foresters and administrators perceived clear signs of indigenous environmental mismanagement and subsequent advance of desert. In 1907, a forestry mission lead by J. Vuillet, chief of *Service de l' Agriculture* in the colony *Haut-Senegal et Niger*, stated: it is indeed true. The Sahara progresses towards, the South; and that (is) because of Man's action."[40] The "encroachment of the Saharan desert into fertile lands to the south, burning of the land, and apparent malpractices and overutilization of grazing areas were prime concerns."[41] This idea of advancing deserts was later regularly supported by colonial administrative reports, research documents and travel accounts.[42] Subsequent studies proved conclusively that no threat from expanding deserts existed.[43]

In 1937, the French and British colonial administrations in West Africa set up a Joint Forestry Commission to investigate reports of severe dryland degradation in south of the Sahara. The bilateral character of this commission reflected the possibility that dryland degradation could be a transnational problem against which France and Britain might join forces. The Commission did not use standardised measures or indicators of desertification or global maps or any other reliable documents. Relying instead on first-hand observations and the accounts of local inhabitants, the Commission ultimately rejected a framing of dryland degradation as a transnational problem. In particular, they refuted claims by some researchers that the Sahara desert was advancing southward thereby posing a threat against which the French and British should join forces. However, the Commission agreed with the research findings on extensive deforestation due to shifting cultivation, a farming method allegedly popular among Africans.[44]

Aubreville[45] was the first one to explain desertification as "not an extension of the existing desert. Desertification was not the result of the Sahara spreading outward but of localized activity that could begin anywhere."[46] He described desertification as the transformation of productive land into an ecological desert due to the ruinous act of erosion, often impelled by man-made deforestation.[47] "Aubreville was quite clear in his conclusion that desertification in tropical Africa was due to man's activity and that (there) had been no significant climatic change during the past thousand or more years. Most of that destructive activity has occurred within recent historic time by the action of agricultural populations."[48]

Almost 30 years after Aubreville published his treatise on desertification, the United Nations Conference on Desertification (UNCOD) was held at Nairobi, in 1977. This Conference was the reaction to a severe drought that befell the Sahel and other parts of Africa beginning in the late 1960s and continuing through much of the 1970s. The UNCOD "specifically refuted the idea that desertification principally involves the spreading of deserts, though some people still do not accept this and so question its existence when evidence of advancing deserts is not found."[49]

The definition of desertification agreed upon in 1977 at UNCOD[50] is as follows: "desertification is the diminution or destruction of the biological potential of land, and can lead ultimately to desert-like conditions. It is an aspect of the widespread deterioration of ecosystems, and has diminished or destroyed the biological potential, i.e. plant and animal production, for multiple use purposes at a time when increased productivity is needed to support growing populations in quest of development."[51] "This definition raises various points of debate-questions of causation (climatic or land use induced), timescales (short or long term), mensuration (what indicators can be measured) and degree of reversibility." [52]

The UNCOD description did not clearly identify the target area of applicability of the term desertification. In other words, there was "no reference to the climatic zones in which desertification occurs."[53] This definition was found inadequate and not sufficiently operational when attempts started in different parts of the world to implement various practical recommendations of the PACD and to undertake the quantitative assessment of desertification.[54] "A new, more precise definition was required to distinguish between desertification and other problems of climatic change."[55]

In February 1990 UNEP, based on special studies and extensive discussions and aware of the danger of inflationary definitions of the term desertification, formed an *ad hoc* Committee for the Global Evaluation of the Desertification: State and Methods of Investigation.[56] This technical committee "produced a new definition that equated desertification with land degradation and specified the climate zones to which the term applies."[57] It suggested the following definition: "desertification is land degradation in arid, semi-arid and dry sub-humid areas resulting from adverse human impact."[58]

Again this 1990 UNEP's new definition, which identified the human activities as the sole factor for desertification, was heavily criticised as being over simplistic and ignoring the role of climate factors. Against this background, the Panel of Senior Consultants, convened by UNEP in Geneva from 25th to 27th April, 1991, to discuss the first draft of a revised PACD (Plan of Action to Combat Desertification of Nairobi Conference, 1977), considered the desertification concept as well. "It was pointed out that the new document should more clearly spell out the likely impacts of natural climatic conditions, particularly of recurrent drought, on desertification; it would be necessary to note that in certain instances desertification might not only be human-induced but climate-induced as well."[59]

Accordingly the Governing Council of UNEP, at its 16th session in May 1991, also considered this dimension. By its decision 16/22, it underlined the need for further refinement of the definition of the concept of desertification, taking into account recent findings and new knowledge acquired in the course of detailed area-specific studies, surveys and assessments about the influence of climate fluctuations and about the resilience of soils.[60] In a recent study in China by Wang, Xunming *et al.*, it was found that "human activity may not be principally responsible for the rapid desertification."[61] According to Wang, Xunming *et al.*, "(n)evertheless, the proxies... used for human activity did not clearly support the hypothesis that human activities are principally responsible for desertification or rehabilitation in this region."[62]

During preparations for the United Nations Conference on Environment and Development (UNCED) popularly known as the Earth Summit, held at Rio in June 1992, the definition of desertification was further disputed. After extensive consultations, an amended formulation developed for inclusion in *Agenda 21*. Accordingly the 1990 UNEP definition was only partially accepted at Rio Summit 1992 which suggested the following revised definition: "desertification is land degradation in arid, semi-arid and dry sub-humid areas resulting from various factors including climatic variations and human activities."[63] This definition is now widely regarded to be the authoritative definition of desertification.

The United Nations Convention to Combat Desertification (UNCCD) 1994 also adopted the Earth Summit's definition on desertification.[64] The UNCCD explains land degradation as "reduction or loss.... of the biological or economic productivity and complexity of rainfed cropland, irrigated cropland, or range, pasture, forest and woodlands resulting from land uses or from a process or combination of processes, including processes arising from human activities and habitation patterns."[65] These include soil erosion caused by wind and/or water, deterioration of the physical, chemical and biological or economic properties of soil and long-term loss of natural vegetation.[66]

The inclusion of climatic factors as a partial cause of desertification in the UNCCD's definition was "intended to soften the political consequences of a definition that places all responsibility on human activity."[67] There are broader definitions in use. For example, the Global Environment Facility (GEF) definition includes deforestation as a form of land degradation. "Nonetheless, the definition of desertification adopted in the Convention has scientific relevance and is perhaps justified in the context of current concerns over the impacts of anthropogenically-induced global warming and its impacts on semi-arid and desert margin environments."[68]

The main difference between the above two definitions (UNCOD and UNCCD) lies in the latter's explicit inclusion of climate as a major cause. There are several implications of accepting the latter definition. First, it reduces the emphasis in the first definition on human activities as being primarily responsible for desertification. Secondly, it opens up the possibility of countries suffering from desertification being able to claim that responsibility lies also with those countries, which have provoked climatic change by undertaking unprecedented level of industrialization process at the global level, that is, those of the developed countries. Accepting such causality could lead to claims for compensation to be paid to those affected by desertification process.[69]

However, this definition excluded the hyper-arid zones, representing the inner core of the desert where processes leading to desertification as such are less likely to make it more desert-like. This is because "they are presumed to be so dry that human degradation is severely limited unless irrigation is practiced"[70] and are "incapable of supporting human occupancy dependent upon plants, directly or indirectly, for food."[71] Whether to include reversible (affordable) land degradation to describe desertification or not, is another major point of contention. "Since the UNCCD is restricted to (arid, semi-arid and sub-humid) drylands, it only partially covers global land degradation, having come into being in the aftermath of the large-scale droughts in the Sahel and the failed 1977 Plan of Action to Combat Desertification."[72]

In order to have a better understanding, it will be necessary to adopt quantitative and qualitative indices for each of the key elements constituting a definition. Among all the definitions on desertification, the one given by the UNCED, 1992 is the clearest and most straightforward in intent and substance. However, it does not distinguish whether the desertification is a 'process' (a natural phenomenon marked by regular changes that lead towards a particular result), or a 'condition' (a state of being) created by land degradation. The answer to this key issue will shift the focus of combating strategies from ameliorating the effect to containing the cause. The UNCED definition does not quantify the degree of land degradation that signifies desertification or distinguish between degradation that is reversible or not.[73]

iii. Drylands and Aridity Index

The drylands are a vital part of the Earth's human and physical environments. These ecosystems play a major role in global biophysical processes by reflecting and absorbing solar radiation, and maintaining an effective balance of atmospheric constituents. Desertification takes place in drylands where the earth is especially fragile, rainfall is meagre and the climate is harsh. In drylands "over the long term, natural moisture inputs (precipitation) are counterbalanced by moisture losses through evaporation from surfaces and transpiration by plants (evapotranspiration). This potential water deficit affects the production of crops, forage, and other plants and has great impacts on sustainable development of people in these regions."[74]

The rapidly changing socio-economic conditions—along with the potential for climate change pose serious challenges to many drylands areas in the world. The result is the destruction of topsoil followed by the loss of land's ability to sustain crops, livestock or human activities. In the past, drylands recovered easily following long drought and dry periods. Under modern conditions, however, they tend to lose their biological and economic productivity quickly unless they are sustainably managed.

Drylands are not uniform. However they differ in the degree of water limitation they experience. The UNEP classified drylands into sub-humid, semi-arid, arid, and hyper-arid—based on an increasing level of aridity or moisture deficit. This was based on a global coverage of mean annual precipitation and temperature data collected between 1951 and 1980. The level of aridity typical for each of these sub-types is given by the ratio of its mean annual precipitation to its mean annual evaporative demand, expressed as potential evapotranspiration. The long-term mean of this ratio is termed the aridity index. The UNCCD, although excluding the hyper-arid drylands from its consideration, adopted the UNEP classification.[75] Even the World Bank considers drylands by excluding hyper-arid regions.[76]

Drylands occur on all continents and collectively comprise nearly half of the global landmass. However, these drylands are not spread equally between poor and rich countries: 72 per cent of the global dryland area occurs within developing countries and only 28 per cent within industrial ones. Similarly, the proportion of drylands occupied by developing countries increases with increasing aridity (from dry sub-humid to hyper-arid) and it reaches almost 100 per cent for the hyper-arid areas. In other words, nearly 100 per cent of hyper-arid areas are in developing countries and for arid regions it is more than 90 per cent. Consequently, the majority of dryland people live in developing countries.[77]

Table 1.1: Proportion of Drylands Affected by Various Processes of Soil Degradation

Sl. No.	*Process of degradation*	*Soil area affected (in %)*
1.	Water erosion	45
2.	Wind erosion	42
3.	Chemical erosion	10
4.	Physical erosion	3

Source: Nasr, M., "Assessing Desertification and Water Harvesting in the Middle East and North Africa: Policy Implications", Policy Paper no. 10, Centre for Development Research, Bonn University, Germany, 1999, p. 17.

Desertified lands are also categorized into four classes according to their degree of desertification (slight, moderate, severe, and very severe). Land categorized as slightly desertified shows little or no degradation (less than 10 % loss in potential yield), moderately desertified land shows 10-25 per cent, severely desertified land 25-50 per cent, and very severely desertified land over 50 per cent degradation.[78]

Aridity of a region is categorized by the ratio of Mean Annual Precipitation (P) to Mean Annual Potential Evapotranspiration (PE). As per this, the aridity zones are classified as given in Table 1.2.

Table 1.2: Classification of the Regions on the Basis of Aridity Index

Sl. No.	*Climatic Zone*	*P/PE* Ratio*	*Percentage of World Covered*
1.	Hyper-arid	<0.05	7.5
2.	Arid	0.05-0.20	12.5
3.	Semi-arid	0.21-0.50	17.5
4.	Dry sub-humid	0.51-0.65	9.9
5.	Humid	>0.65	39.2
6.	Cold	>0.65	13.6

*P = Mean Annual Precipitation and PE = Mean Annual Potential Evapotranspiration.

Source: Ministry of Environment and Forest, Government of India, *National Action Programme to Combat Desertification*, (New Delhi: 2002), p. 4.

Annual precipitation in drylands is quite low. Rainfall often consists of high intensity events that occur over short periods of time. It is highly variable throughout the year and there is high overland runoff.

Most, if not all, of the annual precipitation is lost from the system via evapotranspiration (evaporated from soil or transpired by plants) rather than via drainage to groundwater or surface runoff. This is due to the high evaporative demand of the atmosphere resulting from high air temperatures, low humidity and abundant solar radiation, i.e. the potential for evapotranspiration is high.[79]

II. Global Status of Desertification

The assessment of the current status of desertification "throughout the world shows that there is a lack of hard, precise data that allows conclusions to be drawn regarding the extent and rate of desertification in various parts of the world."[80] The global assessments of the status and rate of desertification conducted by the UNEP in 1977, 1984 and 1991 revealed insufficient basic knowledge of desertification processes. The capacity of existing international, regional and national institutions, particularly in developing countries, to generate and exchange relevant information is limited. Adequate worldwide systematic observation systems will facilitate for the formulation and implementation of effective measures to combat desertification.[81]

Drylands account for roughly 47 per cent of the global landmass or approximately 5.2 billion ha.[82] It is now widely, but not exclusively, accepted that desertification is a problem that occurs in the world's drylands. Occasionally the term desertification is used in a broader spatial context, applied to any environment where land degradation is occurring. It is a global phenomenon affecting about one-fifth of the world population, 70 per cent of all dry lands (3.6 billion ha) and one-quarter of the total land area of the world. Every year an additional 200,000 km sq of productive lands are lost due to desertification.[83]

Sixty four per cent of all drylands are found in Africa and Asia (32% each). Another 12 per cent are found in North America, 11 per cent in Australia, and 9 per cent in South America. Though these regions may appear to have less drylands, they nevertheless make up important proportions of their landmasses (e.g. over 75 per cent of the Australian continent).[84] Desertification occurs to some extent on

30 per cent of irrigated lands, 47 per cent of rain-fed agricultural lands, and 73 per cent of rangelands. Annually, an estimated 1.5 to 2.5 million hectares (3.7 to 6 million acres) of irrigated land, 3.5 to 4.0 million hectares (8.6 to 9 million acres) of rain-fed agricultural land, and about 35 million hectares (86 million acres) of rangeland lose all or part of their productivity due to desertification.[85]

The amount of land susceptible to desertification (areas known as tension zones) also is increasing. Currently, 7.1 million km sq. (2.7 million square miles) of land face low risk of human-induced desertification, 8.6 million sq km (3.4 million square miles) are at moderate risk, 15.6 million sq km (6.2 million square miles) are at high risk, and 11.9 million sq km (4.6 million square miles) are at very high risk.[86]

Over 30 per cent of the land in the United States is affected by desertification. In Spain, one-fifth of the land is at risk of turning into deserts. In China, since the 1950s, sand drifts and expanding deserts have taken a toll of nearly 700,000 hectares of cultivated land, 2.35 million hectares of rangeland, 6.4 million hectares of forests, woodlands and shrub lands.[87]

Table 1.3: Extent and Distribution of Susceptible Drylands by Continent

Sl. No.	*Regions*	*Area (m. ha)*	*Percentage of Total*
1.	Africa	1,286	43
2.	Asia	1,672	39
3.	Australia	663	>75
4.	Europe	300	31
5.	North America	732	33
6.	South America	516	29
	World Total	5,169	40

Source: Ministry of Environment and Forest, Government of India, *National Action Programme to Combat Desertification*, (New Delhi: 2002), p. 10.

The irrigated lands are affected by various degradation processes, mainly waterlogging, salinisation and alkalinisation. The rain-fed croplands are mostly affected by soil erosion through water and wind, depletion of nutrients and physical deterioration. The rangelands are affected by degradation of vegetation, which is accompanied by soil degradation consisting, mainly of erosion.[88]

i. Issues in Desertification Assessment

The shortage of adequate and "reliable national and global data on the extent and rate of change of desertification has been a persistent problem since the 1970s. It results from both a limited monitoring effort and inadequate monitoring procedures, and contrasts with the wealth of localized evidence of widespread and substantial dryland degradation, e.g. in East Africa."[89] Darkoh argues that "(e)xisting data, even at the national level, are not based on quantitative measures, but are best-guess estimates at a high level of generality, which means that they cannot be used as a baseline against which to measure change."[90]

> The complexity of the causes of desertification and the diversity of its effects make it difficult to evaluate accurately its magnitude. Estimates of the areas lost to or threatened by desertification are a matter of controversy because of the complexity and variety of the forms of desertification, and also due to the different notions of irreversibility in terms of the time-scales considered.[91]

Despite the global importance of addressing the problem of desertification, the available data on the extent of land degradation in drylands are limited. To date, there are only two studies with global coverage and both have considerable weakness. But in the absence of anything better they were widely used as a basis for national, regional, and global environmental assessments.[92]

The best known study is the Global Assessment of Soil Degradation (GLASOD). Intended as an exploratory study, it did not include any remote sensing or field measurements and was based on expert opinion only. A more detailed assessment—Soil Degradation in South and Southeast Asia—also relied heavily on expert opinion. A more thorough, measurement-based global follow-up has not been conducted. Additionally, these studies only considered soil degradation and placed a strong emphasis on erosion, which is extremely hard to measure. These studies also formed the basis of the data and maps presented in the World Atlas of Desertification. A reported 20 per cent of the world's drylands (excluding hyper-arid areas) suffer from soil degradation, mainly caused by water and wind erosion, which is presented as the prime cause for 87 per cent of the degraded land.[93]

The second study with global coverage is that of Dregne and Chou, which covers both soil and vegetation degradation. It was based on secondary sources. It was reported that "(t)he information base upon which the estimates in this report were made is poor. Anecdotal accounts, research reports, travellers' descriptions, personal opinions, and local experience provided most of the evidence for the various estimates."[94]

This study reported that some 70 per cent of the world's drylands (excluding hyper-arid areas) were suffering from desertification (soil plus vegetation degradation). All these assessments have their weaknesses. Due to the poor quality of the information sources, Dregne and Chou's numbers are most likely an overestimation.

Perceptions of the severity of desertification are to a large extent self-confirming, but have a scarcity of scientific base. Relatively detailed studies were done in certain areas, for example attempts to estimate present rates of water and wind erosion and land salination in the Nile Basin.[95] Understanding of the extent and rates of desertification were also clouded by definitional confusion and various myths, such as the "the myth of the marching desert," which sometimes served to further the objectives of international development agencies rather than clarify the nature of the problem.[96]

According to Orone, "the accuracy, meaning, and practical usefulness of these estimates of global desertification trends are increasingly questioned, particularly given the difficulty of determining the causal relationships of such complex processes."[97] Others suggest that there is a need to move beyond such global estimates by undertaking localized studies and on-the-ground measurements. The shortage of reliable national and global data on the extent and rate of change of desertification has been a persistent problem since the 1970s. The main reasons for considerable lack of clarity about the extent, nature and causes of desertification are due to the complexities and scientific uncertainties involved."[98]

The Action Plan of UNCOD "gave each country the task of making its own assessment (partly due to sovereignty issues) but most failed to do so. UNEP created a spatial database of desertification but acknowledged that their assessments were based mainly on expert opinion and guesswork."[99] During the earlier stages of negotiations of UNCCD, "there was hope that a high priority would be assigned to assessing and monitoring desertification. The hope has disappeared. The UNCCD had a unique opportunity to initiate research on the status of land degradation, coordinate data collection procedures, and achieve international cooperation on the process. The tragic shortage of data continues, for the most part."[100]

"The lack of precise, agreed estimates of the extent of desertification opens the door to misusing the concept. For instance, figures portraying a dramatic image of desertification have proved very popular among politicians seeking to attract international funds."[101] Therefore "as long as the true effect of desertification...in Africa and elsewhere are not documented according to scientific standards, there is a risk that the desertification issue will become a political and developmental fiction rather than a scientific fact."[102] Given the potential relevance of combating desertification in ensuring sustainable development, "it is surprising that there is no consensus on the proper way to assess it."[103]

ii. Remote Sensing Technologies and Desertification Assessment

There is a growing interest in the application of remote sensing technologies to the protection of the global environment and preservation of natural resources. Remote Sensing (RS) technologies may prove "extremely beneficial in the creation of environmental commitments. Defining the scope and characteristics of an environmental problem with greater accuracy will help potential parties to an MEA better define necessary and feasible political responses."[104]

A number of national, regional and international research institutes are actively involved in improving data collection and analysis, thanks to the use of remote sensing[105] and Geographic Information Systems (GISs). Besides the use of satellite images and powerful data-processing technologies, efforts were made on broadening the scope of action of the alert systems, so as to take into account the food security concerns.[106]

A better understanding of the incidence, causes, and trends in dryland degradation requires the interpretation of data collected over a period of years. Such an analysis needs to be carried out at a micro-level.[107]

> The first satellite to be launched successfully was the Soviet SPUTNIK, which went into orbit in 1957. Today, almost 10,000 satellites are being used to serve the earth and/or study

> the environment. The spatial resolution of satellites ranges from high-resolutions capable of imaging objects only five metres in size to low resolutions covering tens of kilometres. The temporal resolution ranges between geo-stationary satellites and those that cover a certain strip of area every 10-16 days. The spectral resolution ranges between long-wave Infra Red (IR) and Ultra shortwave [UV (Ultra Violet)].[108]

No monitoring system will be effective if its resolution is inappropriate to the phenomenon being observed. The resolution of satellite remote sensing techniques has so far been too low to monitor desertification effectively on a large scale. Basically desertification is a spatially complex, fine-grained phenomenon that mainly consists of dispersed, patch-like degradation, not the frontier expansion of desert fringes of popular imagination. A UNEP expert panel called for the use of high resolution remote sensing data to produce 'geographically explicit and precise assessments of dryland resources.'[109]

Systematic data on the extent of desertification problem based on actual observation are few and limited. Despite the use of satellite remote sensing over several decades, data are still lacking on the extent of land degradation on a global scale.[110] Current data deficiencies are due to the limited number of databases, and to the fact that these data have a limited temporal scale and mainly reflect biophysical conditions. The socioe-conomic dimensions are derived from simple overlay techniques (man/land ratios, human population carrying capacity), and no systematized and global data sets exist on human causes. A new direction would be to link biophysical and socio-economic properties such as, for example, soil properties (physical, chemical, biological) with landscape or ecosystem dynamics, which in turn are linked to land-use practices (land tenure, livestock, wealth, etc.).[111]

Therefore, the future studies of desertification will need to rely on combinations of satellite observations of climate and land cover, coupled with ground-based assessments of human activities and soils, to be able to draw firm conclusions about trends and severity.[112]

An integrated and coordinated information and systematic observation system based on appropriate technology and embracing global, regional, national and local levels is essential for understanding the dynamics of desertification and drought processes. It is also important for developing adequate measures to deal with desertification and drought and improving socio-economic conditions.

iii. Climate Change and Desertification

Both climate and desertification interact at a variety of scales through a complex and still only partially understood series of feedback loops. Climate has an important but often subtle influence on desertification processes through its impact on drylands soils and vegetation.[113] Climate change is a major global challenge. The impacts of this phenomenon are already evident, and changes in water availability, food security and sea-level rise are expected to dramatically affect millions of people. Climate change is defined as a "local, regional or large-scale change in the long term average regime of temperature, precipitation, circulation and related variables characterizing the climate."[114]

Climate change and desertification remain inextricably linked. Climate change might exacerbate desertification through alteration of spatial and temporal patterns in temperature, precipitation, solar insolation, and winds. The conditions of desertification are dictated by climatic factors since the process occurs mainly in arid, semi-arid and dry sub-humid regions. The reduction in moisture availability would both increase aridity of existing drylands and progressively shift the boundaries of areas susceptible to desertification.[115]

Conversely, desertification induces climate change through the release of CO_2 from cleared and dead vegetation and reduction of the carbon sequestration potential of desertified land.[116] Climate change could worsen the effects of desertification. According to the United Nations Framework Convention on Climate Change, "countries with arid and semi-arid areas or areas liable to floods, drought and desertification... are particularly vulnerable to the adverse effects of climate change."[117]

The Green House Gas (GHG) emissions (principally CO_2) are the main drivers of change. It is estimated that the Earth's average temperature increased by approximately 0.74°C over the past century. The impacts include sea-level rise and increasing frequency and intensity of heat waves, storms, floods and drought. The best estimate for warming over this century is projected by the Inter-Governmental Panel on Climate Change (IPCC) to be between a further 1.8 and

4°C. This will intensify the impacts, leading to potentially massive consequences, especially for the most vulnerable, poor and disadvantaged people on the planet.

There is increasing concern about the likelihood of changes in rainfall patterns and water availability thereby affecting food security. Major changes are projected for regions, such as Africa, that are least able to cope. Sea-level rise threatens millions of people and major economic centres in coastal areas and the very existence of small island states. Even though the cycles of drought years and climatic changes can contribute to the advance of desertification, it is mainly caused by changes in the ways people use the natural resources, mainly by over-grazing, land clearance, over-cropping cultivated land and wood formations and more generally using land in a way that is inappropriate for the local conditions.

Natural climate variations can strongly affect drought patterns. Currently the best understood link between global climate variability and drought involves sea-surface temperature patterns. For example, the El Niño-Southern Oscillation, events are associated with a warming of the Eastern Equatorial Pacific. They were especially frequent in the 1980s and early 1990s and occurred in tandem with widespread drought in Southern Africa and elsewhere. Efforts to strengthen predictions are an important part of national action programmes to combat desertification and will help dryland farmers and herders to prepare better for drought.

Scientists cannot yet predict how rising atmospheric levels of GHG will affect the global rate of desertification. However, it was established that changes in temperature, evaporation, and rainfall will vary from region to region. As a result, desertification is likely to be aggravated in some critical areas but eased in other places.

Desertification may temporarily affect climate change. Land degradation tends to reduce surface moisture. Because less water is available for the sun's energy to evaporate, more energy is left over for warming the ground. Meanwhile, wind erosion in drylands releases dust and other particulates into the atmosphere. By absorbing the sun's rays or reflecting them back out into space, they may help to cool the Earth's surface. However, the energy which they absorb heats the lower atmosphere. Finally, the periodic burning of arid and semi-arid grasslands, often associated with unsustainable slash-and-burn agriculture, emit greenhouse gases.

Overall the extent of impact of desertification on climate as a very complex phenomenon is not fully understood. The changes in vegetative cover due to various human-induced changes can influence the solar radiation and thus the energy balance of both the surface and atmosphere of the earth. The global community already acknowledged the causes and effects of desertification and climate changes.

> "The single biggest impediment to quantifying the interactions between desertification and climate stems from the variable quality of the data relating to the extent, severity and trends of the various forms of dryland degradation collectively contained within the general term desertification. There is a particular and increasingly urgent need for uniform and objective methods of data collection relating to the characteristics and status of dryland ecosystems, soils, water resources, salinity and microclimates, and for the evaluation and dissemination of such data on an integrated basis."[118]

"Desertification is already integral to assessments of the potential for mitigating global climate change by restoring degraded lands to sequester surplus carbon from the atmosphere."[119] However, substantial efforts need to be initiated in the areas of Research and Development (R&D) to equip the developing countries to cope with serious consequences of climate change and desertification.

iv. Food Security and Desertification

By impoverishing the natural potential of the ecosystems, desertification reduces agricultural yields making them more unpredictable. Therefore, it affects the food security of the people living in these areas.[120] The steady and unprecedented "increase in human populations and periodic droughts in many areas around the developing world have caused food shortages, put stress on the resource base and have jeopardized the long term sustainability of these agricultural production systems."[121]

> "With 852 million chronically hungry people in the world today and world population expected to grow by an additional 2 billion people by 2030, feeding this growing population and reducing hunger will only be possible if agricultural yields can be increased significantly."[122]

Desertification is considered a major global environmental issue largely because of the link between drylands degradation and food production. Desertification is "a serious threat to food security, rural incomes, and rural livelihoods in many parts of the world. The food gap (the difference between what is produced and what is needed to maintain minimal per capita consumption needs) is widening in 66 low-income developing countries, most in Africa. This is occurring as food needs are increasing as fast as or faster than food production increases because of population growth, lower rates of new land being put into production, and declining yields."[123]

"The conversion of fragile marginal drylands to agriculture, as well as improper agricultural, pastoral, and land management techniques are two of the most important drivers of land degradation and desertification worldwide. Several regions of the world experience stagnating or even declining agricultural yields due to land degradation."[124]

A nutritionally adequate diet for the world's growing population implies tripling food production over the next 50 years. This will be difficult to achieve even under favourable circumstances. If desertification is not stopped and reversed, food yields in many affected areas will decline. Malnutrition, starvation, and ultimately famine may result. The relationship between soil degradation and crop yields, however, is seldom straightforward. Productivity is affected by many different factors, such as the weather, disease and pests, farming methods, and external markets and other economic forces.[125]

Providing enough food for the world's poor is a continuing challenge. According to the International Food Policy Research Institute, by 2020 world population will reach at least 8 billion. Most of this growth will take place in the developing countries and will account for about 85 per cent of the increase in demand for cereals and meat. Already, almost one billion people live in poverty and suffer chronic hunger. The United Nations Population Division also made similar projections.[126] And "(d)esertification is strongly correlated to poverty because it is directly associated with declining agricultural yields. For example, per capita agricultural production increased by about 40 per cent between 1980 and 2001 in developing countries, but fell by about 5 per cent in Sub-Saharan Africa over the same period, due in large part to land degradation and low access to modern agricultural inputs and technology."[127]

Therefore, one of today's urgent problems, requiring immediate, all-out action, is the need to increase world food production and agricultural productivity. The shortage of cropland, together with falling productivity, is a significant factor contributing to global food shortages and associated human malnutrition and hunger.[128]

Drylands play a vital role as a source and in maintaining biomass and biological diversity. "These drylands are a critical source of food and account for about a fifth of the world's food production."[129] Many of the world's most important foodgrains—including wheat, barley, millet and sorghum—originated in the drylands. Furthermore, wildlife, including large mammals and migratory birds, depend on them for their habitat. However, "(w)orldwide 90 per cent of original dryland ecosystems have been converted to pasture, agriculture, or urban settlements. The expansion of cultivated area through land conversion is often associated with deforestation and loss of biodiversity, as well as with increased wind and water erosion that leads to land degradation."[130]

Drylands typically have a number of distinguishing ecological characteristics that largely contribute to their susceptibility to disturbance and ultimately to desertification. The natural vegetation is composed of various mixtures of grasslands, scrublands and savannas with trees either scattered or concentrated along watercourses. Since vegetation cover is usually relatively sparse, much of the soil is exposed directly to rain, sunlight and wind.

Degradation of these drylands led to profound implications for agriculture production given both the time scales and spatial coverage over which soil processes can operate. Significant decline in agricultural productivity in many developing countries especially in Africa will increase the food insecurity. Unfortunately, most of the vulnerable developing countries are already troubled by crucial imbalances between rapidly growing populations and existing constraints in increasing food production capabilities.

Combating desertification is essential to ensuring the long-term productivity of inhabited drylands. It greatly stresses the world's food producing capacity. A Food and Agriculture Organization (FAO) study on population change and environment linkages in the Arab States region, considers population growth to play an unquestionable role in land degradation's impact on food insecurity. According to this study, "land degradation...has much to do with accelerated agricultural intensification and the pressure of an increasing population combined with the scarcity of cultivable land, leading farmers to ask more of the land than it can yield. And the pressure increases all the more rapidly as the spatial growth of human settlements, especially cities, takes a direct toll on the surrounding land resources."[131]

Over the past few centuries, the rate of increase in arable area slowed down, although population growth has not. For instance, the relative increase in arable land was 103 per cent from 1700 to 1850, and only 28 per cent from 1950 to 1980. However, population growth continued unabated. Against the nine-fold surge in population from 0.7 billion in 1700 to 6 billion in 1996, the arable area has spread only about five-fold. Accordingly, per capita cropland availability fell from 0.39 ha to 0.22 ha.[132] Opportunities for adding cropland area are shrinking fast, so the rate of cropland expansion is expected to fall further in the future. The present growth rate of arable land (0.2%) is only one-seventh of the growth rate in population.[133]

The arable land in the drylands is being degraded at an astonishing rate (10 million hectares a year lost) while the world's population growth continues unabated (1.67% per year, or an expected global population of 10 billion by 2050).

The decline in per capita cropland availability will be particularly sharp in the developing countries, where 94 per cent of the future population growth (74 out of 78 million each year) will occur. In Sub-Saharan Africa, for instance, land holding per capita of 1.6 ha in 1990 will drop to 0.63 ha in 2025. With humanity's need for food increasing, declining per capita cropland availability will lead to intensified use of already stressed resources in the developing countries, which include more than 80 per cent of the countries suffering from desertification.[134]

The increase in world population means that pressures on land will continue to be acute, particularly in Africa and Asia. The increased needs for food and other agricultural products must be met mainly by raising and sustaining crop and livestock yields and by more intensive land use. This has to be accompanied by more efficient harvesting and processing of products so as to reduce post-production losses. However, current projections also assume an expansion of the arable area in developing countries.

By 2030, FAO estimates suggest that an additional 57 million ha will be brought into cultivation in Africa, and 41 million ha in Latin America, increases of 25 per cent and 20 per cent respectively. This expansion must necessarily come either from further conversion of forest and woodland, or by bringing into cultivation fragile areas of the semi-arid zone, both of which raise serious environmental concerns. Meeting these challenges will stretch the limited resources currently allocated to agricultural research and development, and may call for reallocation of the scarce funding available. It will, in addition, require good governance, land and soil policies, and continued[135] efforts to achieve sustainable use of land resources.

In exceptionally fragile ecosystems, such as those on the desert margins, the loss of biological productivity through the degradation of plant, animal, soil and water resources can easily become irreversible, and permanently reduce their capacity to support human life.

A prerequisite is the adequate support by governments for national land resource institutions, and for building up the capacities of land resource planners, farmers and managers at local and national levels. Maintenance or improvement of the productive potential of land resources to meet the needs of present and future populations, while at the same time sustaining the vital ecosystem functions and other multiple uses of land, is a fundamental requirement for sustainability.

Implementation of the UNCCD, in letter and spirit will go a long way in ensuring a hunger-free world. Appropriate technologies and resources need to be transferred to the developing countries to achieve the sustainable development objectives underlined in the UNCCD.

III. Global Governance

"The notion of global governance departs from traditional state-centred politics in accepting a host of non-state entities as new influential actors in transnational relations."[136] Over the past few decades, social scientists observed significant changes in the role of government in relation to socio-economic changes. These include a shift from government defined strictly by the nation state to a more inclusive concept of governance that recognizes the contributions of various levels of government (global, transnational, regional, local) as well as the roles of the private sector, non-governmental actors, and civil society. In other words, "global governance describes world politics that is no longer confined to nation states, but characterized by increased participation of actors that have so far been largely active at the sub-national level."[137] The emergence of these new forms of governance can be attributed to the need for new institutions to address the more complex problems of present-day society, among which global environmental risks figure prominently.[138]

> Environmental issues have come to exemplify most starkly the complexity and interconnectedness of the contemporary world. They have evolved over time from minor nuisances (emissions from the local factory) to serious health hazards (the smog across the industrialized world) to global concerns (transboundary air and water pollution, deforestation, fisheries depletion, biodiversity loss, and climate change). Contemporary environmental problems, therefore, require not only specialized knowledge about specific issues but also coordination and cooperation among close to two hundred countries.[139]

Widespread concern about the need for global action for the protection of the natural environment is a relatively recent phenomenon. General public awareness of the problems relating to the global environment and the need for coordinated multilateral action to address these problems was not evident even a few decades ago. With the wider dissemination of information relating to the ever increasing environmental challenges, international concern grew steadily over the years.

Global environmental governance consists of diverse institutional arrangements which include "national governments, regional and multilateral institutions and agencies established by national governments, cooperative regimes and also non-governmental organizations—in some of which governments are nevertheless direct or indirect participants. Binding the structure together is a body of agreements and arrangements, ranging from unofficial expression of national interest to firm treaty commitments under international law."[140]

i. Government and Governance

Governance is "a word characterised more by its widespread use than its clarity or singularity of meaning."[141] The core of State and administration persists in the broader sense of continuity. At the same time, major changes have been occurring as a consequence of globalization that alters the nature and character of state and public administration.[142] "The traditional models of governing and governments have failed to address many problems of the economy and the environment."[143] The concepts of governance "arose in recognition that there are other ways of dealing with divergent interests and collective action problems than government by the state and its agencies. This is something of a departure from the habit not only of this century, but also of most of the three centuries that preceded it."[144] In the emerging web of transnational links, old forms of collective decision-making are weakened and new forms become possible. The striking growth in numbers and influence of transnational non-governmental organizations is one example of these developments.[145]

Globalization changes the conditions for governance. There is a pervasive, shared, global perception of governance as a topic far broader than government. Governance is seen as a "new process of governing, or a changed condition of ordered rule; or the new method by which society is governed."[146] Governance includes "all of the ways that individuals and institutions plan and manage their common affairs and consists of formal institutions and informal arrangements."[147]

Kooiman rightly explains governance as "a pattern or structure that merges in socio-political systems as a common result or outcome of the interacting intervention efforts of all the involved actors. This pattern cannot be reduced to one actor or groups of actors in particular. No single actor, public or private has all the knowledge and information required to solve complex, dynamic and diversified problems; no actor has sufficient overview to make the application of particular instruments effective; no single actor has sufficient action potential to dominate unilaterally in a particular governing model."[148] Therefore "....effective governance in an era of globalisation is not achieved by any one rule, institution or economic policy but requires a multi-faceted and multi-disciplinary approach." [149]

Today the policy formulation and implementation processes are "now made up of these diverse, overlapping and integrated networks which comprise varying relational geometries of the state, market and associational sectors. The actors from each sector bring their own specific sets of power portions, roles and responsibilities as determined by values, skills and organisational resources into the network arena."[150] Governance at all levels (local, national, regional and global) is mutually reinforcing.[151] As a comprehensive and inclusive concept, governance is an all-encompassing, highly participatory, dynamic and engaging process. It seeks solutions to problems through dialogue and communicative action, engagement through the interactions of citizens and Non-Governmental Organizations (NGOs), and Governmental Institutions.[152]

However governance does not reduce the importance of a government since it's the government which still holds the regulatory powers and the majority of the fiscal responsibilities and its normative and political legitimacy helps to create and sustain the structures that encourage to act together.[153] On the other hand it has been acknowledged that the role of governments have been refined to the "one of seeking to coordinate or manage policy networks through facilitation and negotiation."[154]

These new patterns of interactions between government and society can be observed in areas such as social welfare, environmental protection, education and physical planning. These are apparently aimed at discovering other ways of coping with new challenges or of creating new possibilities for governing[155] the emerging issues of global scale and complex nature. Global Environmental Governance has emerged as the best response to address the interconnected and dynamic issues of global environmental problems. It has also become an important tool for preserving the natural resources and ensuring sustainable development.

ii. Global Environmental Governance

Global Environmental Governance (GEG) is the establishment and operation of a set of rules of conduct that define practice, assign roles and guide interaction so as to enable State and non-State actors to grapple with collective environmental problems across State boundaries.[156] GEG "involves the clear articulation of values, the identification of interests, the negotiation of environmental management plans for realising those values in areas of great environmental significance and the creation of environmental governance regimes to make those plans a reality."[157]

'Global' in the context of governance, likewise is different from inter-governmental and international. While inter-governmental treats the official affairs between and among governments, international, in addition to considering the relationship among governments, also includes the common contacts and dealings of their citizens. The term 'global' signifies far broader meaning by which it embraces the official and unofficial activities of a long list of institutions including governments, businesses, Non-Governmental Organizations (NGOs), universities, research centres and foundations.

Significantly the "(u)se of global acknowledges that a large number of institutions inside and outside government and across national and institutional boundaries are responsible for much of the administration and management of our planet."[158] Today, global environmental governance "takes place predominantly within numerous independent institutional arrangements. A study conducted for the UN Conference on Environment and Development in Rio de Janeiro identified more than 125 separate international environmental regimes."[159] Within these institutional arrangements, "Multilateral Environmental Agreements (MEAs)... have become an important component of environmental governance."[160]

> "Institutions for global environmental governance have not only grown in numbers, they have also over the years metamorphosed from performing the more modest roles of data acquisition and preservation of endangered species to high profile and more sensitive roles such as resource allocation, as in the case of the United Nations Conferences on the Law of the Sea; burden sharing, as in the case of the Climate Change regime; and regulation of trade, as in the case of the Basel Convention on the Transboundary Movements of Hazardous Wastes and their Disposal."[161]

The unprecedented "growth of institutions for environmental co-operation can easily be described as one of the most prominent features of international politics in the last three decades or so."[162]

The earth is the only planet that is known to support a vast diversity of life. For millennia a natural balance is maintained among all organisms, which sustained each other and performed their task in complete harmony. Then the evolutionary forebears of modern human beings appeared on the earth. They "exploited the earth's natural resources and modified the environment for thousands of years, but in the last two centuries human impact has increased hugely in part because of population growth, in part because of technological changes and partly as a consequence of the way that development has been allowed to proceed."[163] The continuing and accelerating deterioration of the earth's ecological base has posed a major threat to humanity.

Environmental problems are increasingly understood to play an important role in increasing human vulnerability and insecurity, undermining livelihoods and human well-being, creating instability, and potentially generating or exacerbating violent conflict. Principal concerns are the depletion of water resources, over-fishing, degradation of arable land, decimation of forests, and alteration of natural cycles and ecosystems.[164]

Environmental problems are characteristically complex and dynamic, do not conform to the boundaries of political jurisdiction. For many issues it has became clear that national action alone would not successfully address the environmental problems. "No matter how much nations try to protect, there is no avoiding the fact that the national sovereignty—the ability of States to control events within their territory—is undermined in a world where borders are routinely breached by pollution..."[165]

Secondly, "the idea developed that more than 70 per cent of the biosphere lying outside national boundaries—the oceans, the polar regions, the atmosphere—and even outer space are not *res nullius,* to be abused at will, but rather *res communis*, a commons of man land requiring protection."[166] For this a unified, comprehensive framework of international environmental laws, and machinery for developing such laws and coordinating environmental resources were needed.

Finally, the multi-dimensional problems to the human environment necessitated response in kind, both in terms of legal instruments as well as effective institutional structures. Since the formation of the United Nations, there has been a significant proliferation in the number of new States on the international scene. This has put its own pressure in terms of addressing the environmental issues.

"Growing recognition of the complexity, pervasiveness, and mutual interdependence of environmental problems is reshaping environmental regulation and natural resource management, both within the nation state and internationally."[167] The unprecedented scale and magnitude of environmental problems "appear to signal the demand not only for cooperation among governments, but also for cooperation among sectors, as well as among different scales of policy-making, exemplified for instance by the "global anticipatory governance" on biosafety. This demand for new forms of governance is increasingly being met by "coalitions of the willing" that on one occasion may comprise a number of states and on another occasion business corporations collaborating with civil society groups at different governance levels."[168]

"Environmental logic demands broad-based international

cooperation and coordination of policies, and requires the international community to evolve effective global environmental policies. Given the magnitude of the problems, and their profound implications, there is no place for exclusive national responses in addressing most of these challenges."[169]

It was in the late 1960s; the gravity of the situation became imminent which "sharpened the perception of ecological imperatives among many national leaders as well as the people—who, on an unprecedented scale, are beginning to mobilize for protecting and restoring the environment domestically and globally."[170] And public pressure was mounted to bring governmental response to environmental crisis. To control pollution and its further occurrences, legislation was introduced and administrative machinery was set up.[171] International environmental law began to emerge in a significant way in the late 1960s and 1970s, as part of a growing concern about environmental problems in many developed countries and their growing awareness of the global nature of environmental issues. During this period, States negotiated conventions on the protection of the marine environment from oil pollution, trade in endangered species, dumping of hazardous wastes at sea, wetlands, and world heritage sites, in some cases with significant involvement by international organizations and Non-Governmental Organizations (NGOs).[172]

The resulted institutional arrangements of international environmental cooperation "not only encompasses a much wider range of concerns, but it also involves an increasingly complex array of actors. States, international institutions, individuals, NGOs, business, and technical experts—these categories only begin to capture the rich variety of actors"[173] and the constructive cooperation of these actors "must be obtained in defending the integrity of the earth."[174]

Contemporary environmental governance addresses not a single problem, but instead, a complex set of issues including pollution control, natural resource management, and human health and safety.[175] Thus Global Environmental Governance (GEG) is currently an intricate web of environment-related institutions, treaties, conventions and agreements. The mosaic of actors that make up the *de facto* system of global environmental governance is both rich and diverse and includes multiple institutional entities, although not all have equal influence on the system. The State, of course, remains the primary subject of as well as the essential actor in global governance, because the effectiveness of the UN and its specialized agencies depend upon the support and the cooperation of national governments to implement their policies and programmes.[176]

Within this complex web of institutions, the United Nations, through, in particular, the United Nations General Assembly (UNGA), the Economic and Social Commission, and the Commission on Sustainable Development, plays a significant coordinating role. The UNGA, for example, convened the three major environmental Summits—Stockholm Conference (1972), Rio Summit (1992) and Johannesburg Summit on Sustainable Development (2002)—and established the UNEP. These Summits played an instrumental role in generating political consensus on the issues to be addressed in international law and policy.[177]

However, GEG is composed of at least four additional entities, each of which is influenced by and can impact the behaviour of States.[178] The first category is international environmental organizations—including, for example, the United Nations Environmental Programme (UNEP), the Commission on Sustainable Development (CSD), the Global Environmental Facility (GEF), and the Secretariats to various multilateral environmental agreements and conventions. These UN environmental specialized agencies perform a catalytic role in problem identification, and in the negotiation and further development of environmental regimes. In problem identification, these agencies provide forums for coordinating scientific research. They support the development and implementation of international environmental treaties by hosting the secretariats for negotiating conferences and for the Multilateral Environmental Agreements (MEAs).[179]

The second category includes a broader set of related international organizations whose primary mandate is not environmental but which can have significant impacts in addressing environmental problems. The World Bank and the United Nations Development Programme (UNDP), which are direct interlocutors in environmental governance through, for example, the GEF and also wield inordinate influence through their portfolios of development interventions, are important examples.[180] Increasingly, the World Trade Organization (WTO) is becoming a nexus of influence because of the overarching impacts of international trade, its direct regulatory intrusions and its powerful dispute resolution mechanism.[181]

The third category, non-State actors, is not only the largest category but has probably had the largest impact on environmental governance. This category would include the vast number of Non-Governmental Organizations (NGOs)—from multinational to small community based organizations. This category, however, has to be broader than just NGOs of all variety and would also include business, academia, science and the mass media, all of which can influence how global environmental governance is conceived and implemented.[182] For example, the Non-Governmental Organizations "provide major inputs into the formation of public opinion about environmental problems and the need to solve them. They care most about the differential environmental impact of different activities, they have an interest in being at the forefront of those seeking new ways to produce goods and services that are not environmentally damaging."[183] Today, therefore, the important challenge for GEG is "to create the institutional space to allow non-state actors to realize their full potential."[184]

The fourth and final category spans public concern and action for the global environment. This becomes the basis and driver of action of the other categories and is a powerful trigger of domestic political pressure, which, in turn, can dictate the behaviour of international organizations. At the same time, public concern is nurtured through the opinions of civil society and the decisions of international organizations. However, it can also be a direct actor, for example, through consumer activism that can result in product boycotts, product preference and other forms of *de facto* standard setting.

Together, these above-mentioned components of international environmental governance are supposed to set priorities and facilitate steps to protect the environment and further sustainable development. Most of these steps must be implemented by individual nations themselves. From legislation to regulation to enforcement, it is the actions taken by nations at the domestic level that ultimately count most for success at the global level. But international organizations like United Nations Development Programme (UNDP), UNEP, and the World Bank also play major roles in implementation. Bilateral aid agencies and civil society groups also participate in important ways, as does the private sector.

The UNEP remains on the top of this loose hierarchical structure of GEG. Many of the institutions and activities within this loose structure address fundamentally similar, and often related, issues. The Environment Ministry of each country and its field organizations form the subsequent level in this order. Along with these institutions, a number of Non-Governmental Organizations (NGOs) and Research Institutions are working closely at different levels to protect the environment. Besides these institutions, a number of environment-related treaties, agreements and conventions form the other significant component of GEG. In other words, GEG is "the sum of organizations, policy instruments, financing mechanisms, rules, procedures and norms that regulate the processes of global environmental protection."[185]

This intricate environmental governance system clearly reflects the complexity and diversity of environmental issues themselves. This also indicates the dynamic nature of environmental concerns which span a huge range, touching almost every aspect of human existence. Similarly the immense growth of GEG "signifies the world's growing appreciation of the scope and scale of the problems."[186]

As international environmental regimes, institutions, and tribunals have proliferated, some have expressed concern about threats to the coherence of international arrangements. But the emergence of new approaches to standard setting and compliance could be viewed, instead, as an entirely appropriate response to the distinctive characteristics of international environmental problems. These problems are not only political but also physical and involve a great deal of technical complexity. They are highly uncertain and rapidly changing. All of these factors mean that, to address international environmental problems, there is an urgent need of complex regulatory regimes, which involve more flexible and dynamic standard-setting processes, and there is a need to take a pragmatic and forward-looking approach.[187]

IV. Desertification and Global Environmental Governance

Combating desertification is also one of the action fields for global governance.[188] Increasing rates of desertification are being experienced in many regions, as demonstrated by the degradation and depletion of natural resources, the shortage and poor quality of water, the fall in the productivity and the settlement expansion. Desertification appears also through sand dune movements and deterioration of vegetation cover.[189]

A severe drought in the Sahel region of Africa from 1969 to 1973 did catastrophic damage to grazing land vegetation, livestock, and eventually, refugees from the devasted land. The deterioration of productive ecosystem is an obvious and serious threat to human progress.

> It was the severe and protracted drought that menaced the Sahel countries of Africa (1968-1972) that triggered worldwide concern. Aid and relief resources were rushed in attempt to save people and their livestocks. Governments of menaced countries formed a heads-of-states Inter-State Committee for Control of Drought in the Sahel (CILSS), the donor community (mostly OECD), formed the Sahel Club to mobilize and coordinate assistance to drought-stricken territories, the UN created a United Nations Sahelian Office (UNSO) to coordinate the contributions of the UN System. Later drought spread eastward menacing the whole Sudano-Sahelian belt of countries extending from the Atlantic to the Red Sea and the African Horn. By 1984, 20 African countries were in a state of famine.[190]

Because of the global magnitude of desertification and its potential effects on populations, the UN has taken a leading role in providing an international framework for studying and resolving this problem. In 1974, the United Nations General Assembly through Resolution 3202 recommended that the international community must undertake speedy measures to arrest desertification and to plan for economic development of the affected areas. The Governing Councils of the United Nations Economic and Social Council (UNESCO), the United Nations Development Programme (UNDP), and the UNEP also emphasized the need for initiating effective steps to check desertification. In view of the intensity of the problem, the UN General Assembly passed a resolution initiated by Burkina Faso to convene a Conference on desertification.[191]

In accordance with this decision, the UN Conference on Desertification (UNCOD) was held in Nairobi (Kenya) between 29th August and 9th September, 1977. Approximately 100 countries participated enthusiastically in a Conference that convened to address one of the most important environmental threats to the well-being of humanity. Out of Nairobi came a Plan of Action (PoA) to combat desertification, which recommended 28 measures that national, regional and international institutions could take to halt land degradation around the world.

In 1984, the UNEP evaluated the implementation of the UNCOD's Plan of Action. This included sending a questionnaire to 91 countries with lands at risk. To the UNEP's dismay, no country was able to provide data on its desertification assessment (UNEP, 1984). A second attempt to assess the general status and trend of desertification was undertaken by UNEP and FAO in 1984. The third assessment of the world status of desertification was done by the UNEP in preparation for the 1992 Rio Summit. In 1991, the UNEP concluded that the problem of land degradation in arid, semi-arid and dry sub-humid areas had intensified, although there were a few local examples of success.

African Environment Ministers met in December 1991 in Abidjan in order to prepare a common position to the 1992 Earth Summit. In particular, they were unanimous in requesting that a new convention to combating desertification should be a specific recommendation to be included in Agenda 21. They also enjoyed the support of many other countries facing similar problems of desertification.[192]

The Earth Summit held in Rio (Brazil) in 1992 reviewed the progress in this regard. The Conference supported a new, integrated approach to the problem. The Conference asked the UN to adopt a Convention, an action framework designed to establish programmes to counter the threat of drylands degradation throughout the world, particularly in arid, semi-arid and dry sub-humid regions. The General-Assembly acted swiftly and established the International Negotiating Committee through Resolution 47/188. The Committee met five times and was able to complete the final draft of the Convention in time for the June 1994 deadline. The United Nations Convention to Combating Desertification (UNCCD) was adopted in Paris on 17th June, 1994 and opened for signature there on 14th to 15th October, 1994. A notable implication pertaining to the post-Rio emergence of the UNCCD is that it was framed as a sustainable development treaty rather than as an environmental treaty in the narrow sense.[193] The fourth chapter discusses the UNCCD in details.

The UNCCD "provides a code of good practices for dryland management for governments of affected countries and donors as well as offering for cooperation between local land users, NGOs, governments, international organizations, funding agencies and northern donor countries."[194]

Therefore, "UNCCD is a multi-layered legally-binding cooperation instrument and establishes a framework for the development of NAPs,

SRAPs and RAPs and international cooperation which are mutually reinforcing instruments. It also offers the opportunity to establish synergies or linkages with other major environmental and socio-economic treaties including the United Nations Framework Convention on Climate Change (UNFCCC) and the Convention on Biological Diversity (CBD) as well as with regional agreements."[195]

After several years of negotiations, States set up an international institutional framework, including a decision-making body, the Conference of the Parties (COP), a permanent regime secretariat, and a number of committees, which follow-up the activities and prepare future COPs. In addition, compliance and sanctioning mechanism is specified. A Committee on Science and Technology also ensures a serious input from scientists in the operation of the regime.[196]

Typical for the functioning of international environmental regimes and policy-making is also that the goals and principles included in the UNCCD are determined at the level of the COP and then translated into practice at the national policy level (National Action Plans in the case of the UNCCD) and, specifically for the UNCCD also at the regional level (Regional Action Plans). This regional level forms a key strategic planning and operational level for the convention.

Based on the above, the Desertification Convention can be described very much as a "normal, standard" regime. However, in addition to this fairly straightforward institutional set-up, the Desertification Convention also makes ample use of the newer international policy discourses of participatory policy-making and implementation, decentralization as a fundamental policy goal, and the use of local knowledge as an explicit "good". The sustainable development concept forms the overarching umbrella for these discourses, which represent—at least in policy practices—a fairly recent dimension in international environmental policy-making. In fact, the UNCCD could be considered as the first of a new generation of post-Rio regimes, which could be labelled "sustainable development regimes".[197]

The Convention provides a detailed and comprehensive roadmap for combating desertification. The Convention is considered significant for two reasons. First, the importance and the complementary role of the administrative system were well recognized. Secondly, it also gives a broad outline and a new strategy for improving the performance of the administration in dealing with the desertification.

The countries affected by desertification are implementing the Convention by developing and carrying out national, sub-regional and regional action programmes. These programmes are the core of the Convention. The action programmes are being developed through consultations among the affected countries, inter-governmental organizations and non-governmental organizations. These processes will improve effective coordination in implementing the programmes. All the GCC countries are members in this programme. The activities within the SRAP will focus on two main areas: water resources and vegetation cover. An operational structure was finalised and agreed at the Dubai meeting in 2000.

National Action Programme (NAP) constitutes the conceptual and legal framework for implementing the Convention at national and local levels. Article 10 of the Convention speaks about the objectives, formulation and implementation of the NAPs. The main purpose of the programme is to identify the factors contributing to desertification and practical measures necessary to combat desertification. The NAPs shall specify the respective roles of government institutions, local communities and land users. Article 10(e) spells out the need for introducing radical reform in the administrative machinery, which will enable administration to cooperate and work with a number of other agencies. Article 10 (f), mandates the government to create an appropriate mechanism, which will ensure people's participation in planning, implementation and evaluation of desertification-related programmes.

The Convention recognizes the need for effective partnership between the government and the people in addressing the issue. It means that the administrative machinery should work along with people at different levels to combat desertification. The GCC countries have a major stake in the implementation of UNCCD given the proportion of land areas subject to arid, semi-arid and dry sub-humid conditions, their exposure to desertification risks, and their long history of devising indigenous technologies to mitigate the effects of desertification.

All the GCC countries signed the Convention and subsequently ratified the same. However, ratification of or accession to an international instrument is not sufficient in itself to achieve the objective of the Convention. These countries must also adopt and implement appropriate measures including legislative and institutional arrangements to give effect to the Convention. The fifth chapter reviews the measures taken by the GCC countries to implement the UNCCD. The sixth chapter examines the GCC countries' compliance with UNCCD.

V. Administrative System in Combating Desertification

Prime resources—fertile topsoil, vegetation cover, and healthy crops—are the first victims of desertification. The people themselves begin to suffer when food and water supplies become threatened. In the worst cases, they endure famine, mass migration, and colossal economic losses. Combating desertification assumes greater significance in view of its far-reaching consequences on food security and sustainable development. Feeding the world's growing population while preserving the natural resources on which it depends presents a real challenge. The rapid reduction of the arable land due to various developmental activities created serious concern among the policy makers.

Two important components are involved in addressing the issue of desertification. These are the scientific and technical knowledge of the problem and the administrative system to plan and execute the desertification-related programmes. Both are complementary in addressing this issue, because the policy-makers need sufficient data about the problem. On the other hand, without proper implementing agencies, these data become meaningless. Though the first step towards addressing the problem was taken in 1977 by UNCOD, no substantial progress was made in this regard. The poor performance of the administration in planning and implementation is considered as the reason for this failure.

> Despite all efforts, however, there is no doubt that the processes of desertification is accelerating, with millions of hectares of arable land being lost every year.... Ten years later, the cause of desertification remain unaddressed... the tools to bring it to an end lie around us unused... The administrative dimension still remains inadequate to the nature of the problem.... (T)he scientific or limitation was not the constraint.[198]

To understand the causes and the consequences of the problem, a large number of studies and projects were undertaken which were mainly technical in nature. But the criticism was that the administrative system did not respond positively in converting these reports into a plan of action.[199]

The gap between the scientific community and the administrative system has been confirmed by a number of studies including the UNESCO's (1979), Munro (1983), Johnels (1983), World Bank (1986) and the World Commission on Environment and Development (1987)[200]. For example Munro argues that the "[g]overnments and international organisations have been much less successful in converting the new scientific knowledge and insights into...effective national and international policies and programmes."[201] Baker also says it is "not solely a matter of organisation, but organisation is still a major factor."[202]

The administrative system is a backbone of a nation. "Among the many reasons that might explain the inability of a nation to fulfil its commitments, administrative inadequacy is perhaps the most common."[203] Therefore the administrative "institutional arrangements have (a) profound impact on the environmental performance of a country."[204]

Traditionally the administrative system had limited functions. But the advancement of technology, rapid growth of population, concept of welfare State and State's intervention in economic activities dramatically changed the role and function of the administrative machineries. In developing countries the increasing responsibilities affected the quality of service. It leads to the "administrative lag" which means the gap between the people's expectation and the performance of the administrative system.

State is much more interventionist for a variety of reasons. Consequently, the State apparatus particularly in the 1960s and 1970s became increasingly involved directly in production and distribution in addition to their traditional functions. It never went beyond these functions. Environmental management and sustainable development hardly found a place in the agenda of the administrative machineries. The sudden eruption of environmental problems literally created confusion and led to inefficiency and poor performances of the administration. Governments' response to the speed and scale of global changes were inadequate.[205] The case is made that there is a considerable dysfunction between the nature of ecological problems and the problem-solving structures within the public area. This dysfunction is termed as "administrative trap."[206] Now the challenge is how to integrate environmental consideration into decision-making in a more systematic, focused and coordinated way.

Administrative systems in the GCC countries are highly centralized. Limited and inefficient mechanism for coordination, evaluation and follow up, lack of human resources and overlapping functions are the other major problems faced by the administrative system in these countries. Even the Environment Ministries are not having adequate staff members to deal with the problem. In all the GCC countries, the national planning focuses excessively on large-scale projects rather than on the institutions and programmes needed for sustainable development. Even these projects are approved without proper environmental clearance.

Lack of people's participation in plan formulation as well as implementation of government programmes has affected the effectiveness of the administrative system and its programme implementation. Considering the gravity of the problem and nature of administration, it becomes inevitable to undertake radical administrative reform measures in these countries. The administrative reforms are required in at least four major areas. These are administrative functions, administrative structures, administrative procedures and skills and training.

The legal and institutional capacities to cope with the challenging tasks of achieving a cleaner environment and the integration of development and environment are often either lacking or inadequate in GCC countries. In these countries there is no proper policy-making body for environmental problems in general and desertification in particular. The administrative machineries are not adequately and professionally equipped to plan and implement the programmes. Even though the governments have signed a number of international Conventions including the UNCCD, their implementation is not adequate. This study will take the strategy outlined by the Convention 1994 as a standard or a base in the planning and the implementation of desertification programmes by the administrative system in GCC countries. The third chapter discusses in detail about the environmental administration in the GCC countries.

Conclusion

Desertification is one of the greatest environmental and development problems of the 21st century. It is a detrimental process that brings about a gradual and an unnoticed reduction in the productive capacity of land over a period of years. The end point of the degradation process would be the formation of a complete wasteland incapable of producing anything. Although it does occur all-around the world, only developing countries in the world's arid and semi-arid regions are severely affected by its consequences. Despite the global importance of desertification, the available data on the extent to land degradation in drylands are limited.

Keeping in view of its far reaching consequences on food security, climate change and sustainable development, concerted efforts are being made to address desertification within the framework of global environmental governance. Global environmental governance consists of diverse institutional arrangements which include national governments, regional and multilateral institutions. Binding the structure together is a body of agreements and arrangements, ranging from unofficial expression of national interest to firm treaty commitments under international law. Within this institutional framework, the national administrative arrangements play a greater role in combating desertification.

References

1. The Millennium Ecosystem Assessment (MA) established by the United Nations in 2000 involving some 1,360 scientists and experts worldwide, was a four-year international scientific assessment of the condition of the Earth's ecosystems, the potential impacts of changes to ecosystems on their ability to meet human needs and policies, technologies, and tools to improve their management. The MA is designed to enhance economic and environmental decisions by improving the information used by decision-makers and the public and strengthening the institutions involved in ecosystem assessments (United Nations Environment Programme (UNEP), *UNEP Annual Report 2000* (Nairobi: UNEP, 2000), p .6. and GEF and GM, *Resource Mobilization and the Status of Funding of Activities Related to Land Degradation*, Report prepared for the Global Environment Facility (GEF) and the Global Mechanism of the United Nations Convention to Combat Desertification (UNCCD), (Washington, DC, 2006), p. i.
2. Diallo, Hama Arba, "Seizing the Chance", *Our Planet* (the Magazine of the United Nations Environment Programme), vol. 17, no. 1, p. 10.
3. Federal Foreign Office (Government of Germany), *Desertification: A Security Threat? Analysis of Risks and Challenges* (Berlin: Technische Zusammenarbeit (GTZ), 2007), p. 3.
4. "Environmental refugees are people who leave the area in which they have traditionally settled or lived because natural or human-induced environmental crises have made their lives far more difficult or have even threatened their very survival. Desertification destroys natural

life-support systems permanently, and is thus the main long-term cause of environmentally-induced displacement." (German Advisory Council on Global Change, (GACGC) *World in Transition: Fighting Poverty through Environmental Policy*, (London: Earthscan, 2005), p. 60.
5. Töpfer, Klaus, "Controlling Desertification: An Essential Element of Global Governance", in Federal Ministry for Economic Cooperation and Development, FMECD (Germany), *The Role of Governance in Combating Desertification*, (Berlin: GTZ Haus, 2007), p. 11.
6. Diallo, n. 2, p. 10.
7. Bauer, Steffen, Per-Olof Busch and Bernd Siebenhüner, "Administering International Governance: What Role for Treaty Secretariats?", Global Governance Working Paper No. 29, (Amsterdam: Vrije Universiteit, Global Governance Project, 2006), p. 17.
8. GEF and GM, *Resource Mobilization and the Status of Funding of Activities Related to Land Degradation*, Report prepared for the Global Environment Facility (GEF) and the Global Mechanism of the United Nations Convention to Combat Desertification (UNCCD), (Washington, DC, 2006), p. 7.
9. Martello, Marybeth Long, "Expert Advice and Desertification Policy: Past Experience and Current Challenges," *Global Environmental Politics*, (MIT Press), vol. 4, no. 3, 2004, p. 86.
10. Stather, Erich "Germany's Engagement" in FMECD, n. 5, p. 5.
11. Adeel, Zafar, "Overcoming One of the Greatest Environmental Challenges of Our Times: Rethinking Policies to Cope with Desertification", A Policy Brief based on the Joint International Conference on Desertification and the International Policy Imperative Algiers, Algeria, 17-19 December, 2006, p. 5.
12. Sherbinin, Alex de., *A CIESIN Thematic Guide to Land-use and Land-cover Change,* (New York: Centre for International Earth Science Information Network (CIESIN), Columbia University, 2002), p. 28.
13. Adeel, n. 11, p. 5.
14. Lugt, Cornis van der, "Thirty Years After Stockholm: What Role for State Sovereignty?", in Biermann, Frank, Rainer Brohm and Klaus Dingwerth, eds., *Global Environmental Change and the Nation State*, (Potsdam, Germany: Potsdam Institute for Climate Impact Research, 2002), p. 227.
15. Bassett, Charles and Joana Talafre, "Implementing the UNCCD: Towards a Recipe for Success", *Reciel*, vol. 12, no. 2, 2003, p. 133.
16. Bauer, n. 7, p. 17.
17. World Bank, *New Opportunities for Development: The Desertification Convention*, (Washington D.C.: World Bank, 1998), p. v.
18. FMECD, n. 5, p. 3.
19. Cowie, Annette, *et al.*, "Potential Synergies between existing Multilateral Environmental Agreements in the Implementation of

Land-use, Land-use change and Forestry Activities", *Environmental Science and Policy*, vol. 10, 2007, p. 338.

20. FMECD, n. 5, p. 4.
21. UNEP, *Success Stories in the Struggle against Desertification: A Holistic and Integrated Approach to Environmental Conservation and Sustainable Livelihoods* (Nairobi: UNEP, 2002), p. iii.
22. Batterbury, S.P.J., *et al.*, "Responding to Desertification at the National Scale: Detection, Explanation, and Responses", in Reynolds, J.F., and D.M. Stafford Smith, eds., *Global Desertification: Do Humans Cause Deserts*? (Dahlem University Press, 2002), p. 358.
23. Alexander, David, E. and Rhodes W. Fairbridge, eds. *Encyclopaedia of Environmental Science*,(Dordrexche the Netherlands): Kluwer Academic Publishers, 2001), p. 125.
The word desert originated as an Egyptian hieroglyph pronounced, *tesert,* meaning a place that was forsaken or left behind. From this came the Latin verb *desere,* to abandon. From the latter came *desertum,* waste place or wilderness, and *desertus,* meaning abandoned or relinquished. This in itself implies that desert had once been a better place. In it there was life—in some places teeming life. There was much vegetation, grasses and trees, many animals and human beings. Then something happened, and the place became a wasteland; it was deserted.
24. UNCCD Secretariat, "Frequently Asked Questions," [Online: web] Accessed on 23rd June, 2008 URL http://www.unccd.int/knowledge/faq.php#answer0.
25. Odingo, R.S., "Review of UNEP's Definition of Desertification and its Programmatic Implications", in Odingo R., ed., *Desertification Revisited: Proceeding of an Ad Hoc Consultative Meeting on the Assessment of Desertification*, (Nairobi: UNEP, 1990), p. 24.
26. Amin, Ammar A., "The Extent of Desertification on Saudi Arabia", *Environmental Geology*, vol. 46, 2004, p. 22.
27. El-Tantawi, Attia Mahmoud Mohamed., *Climate Change in Libya and Desertification of Jifara Plain: Using Geographical Information System and Remote Sensing Techniques*, Dissertation submitted in der Johannes Gutenberg-Universität in Mainz (Germany), 2005, p. 3. According to Le Hou′erou, "(d)rought, being a normal feature of arid climates, is typically of a temporary nature usually leaving little permanent aftermath. It affects production, not productivity in the long-term. Desertification is the opposite; it has a long lasting effect with permanent and sometimes irreversible consequences on production potential, i.e. on the ability of the environment to maintain its long-term productivity" (Le Hou′erou, Henry N., "Climate change, Drought and Desertification," *Journal of Arid Environments*, vol. 34, 1996, p. 158).
28. Kassas, M., "Desertification: A General Review", *Journal of Arid Environments*, vol. 30, 1995, p. 119.

29. *Ibid.*
30. United Nations Non-Governmental Liaison Service, "The International Convention to Combat Desertification in Countries Experiencing Serious Drought and/or Desertification, Particularly in Africa", *The Sustainable Development Treaty Series,* vol. I, no. 1, 1994, p. 1.
31. Dregne, H.E., "Land Degradation in the Drylands", *Arid Land Research and Management*, vol. 16, 2002, pp. 124-125.
32. Herrmann, S.M., and C.F. Hutchinson, "The Changing Contexts of the Desertification Debate," *Journal of Arid Environments*, vol. 63, 2005, p. 539.
33. Reynolds, James F., "Desertification" in Levin, Simon Asher, ed., *Encyclopaedia of Biodiversity*, (London: Academic Press, 2001), p. 70.
34. Glantz, M.H., and Orlovsky, N.S., "Desertification: A Review of the Concept", *Desertification Control Bulletin*, (Nairobi), vol. 9, 1983, p. 4.
35. Darkoh, M.B.K., "The Nature, Causes and Consequences of Desertification in the Drylands of Africa" in Darkoh, Michael and Apollo Rwomire, *Human Impact on Environment and Sustainable Development in Africa* (Aldershot: Ashgate Publishers, 2003), p. 199. Darkoh, in another place says it was Aubreville who coined the term desertification first in 1949 (Darkoh, M.B.K., "The Nature, Causes and Consequences of Desertification in the Drylands of Africa", *Land Degradation and Development*, vol. 9, 1998, p. 1).
36. Amin, n. 26, p. 22.
37. Dregne, H.E., n. 31, p. 100.
38. *Ibid.*
39. Lamprey, H.F., "Report on the Desert Encroachment Reconnaissance in Northern Sudan, 21st October to 10th November, 1975", *Desertification Control Bulletin*, vol. 17, 1975, pp. 1-7.
40. Adger, W. Neil., *et al.* "Advancing Political Ecology of Global Environmental Discourses", *Development and Change*, vol. 32, 2001, p. 689.
41. Nielsen, T.T. and H.K. Adriansen, "Government Policies and Land Degradation in the Middle East", *Land Degradation and Development*, vol. 16, 2005, p. 151.
42. Adger, n. 40, p. 689. Mainguet points out that "(t)he theory of an encroaching desert, which has now been scientifically rejected, is still a fixed idea in the minds of governments, donors, and journalists." (Quoted in Agnew, Clive and Andrew Warren, "A Framework for Tackling Drought and Land Degradation", *Journal of Arid Environments*, vol. 33, 1996, p. 312).
43. Katyal, Jagdish C. and Paul L.G. Vlek, "Desertification—Concept, Causes and Amelioration", Discussion Papers on Development Policy, Centre for Development Research, Bonn, October 2000, p. 7. Similarly Nicholson, S.E. *et al.*, supports this with an example of extensive studies

carried out by scientists of Lund University (Sweden) in Sudan to test some of the tenets of desertification. Scientists "showed through a combination of fieldwork and analysis of satellite photos that there was neither a systematic advance of the desert or other vegetation zones, nor a reduction in vegetation cover, although degradation and replacement of forage with woody species was apparent. There was no evidence of a systematic spread of desertified land around villages and waterholes or of reduced crop yield due to cultivation of marginal or vulnerable areas. On the other hand, they clearly demonstrated that changes took place in response to drought, with full recovery of the land productivity at the end of the drought." (Nicholson, S.E. *et al.*, "Desertification, Drought, and Surface Vegetation: An Example from the West African Sahel," *Bulletin of the American Meteorological Society*, vol. 79, n. 5, 1998, pp. 818-19.)

44. Martello, n. 9, p. 92.
45. Aubreville, a perceptive and well informed Botanist and Ecologist, published a book entitled: *Climate, Forests, et Desertificatiom de l Afrique Tropicale* in 1949.
46. Dregne, H.E., *Desertification of Arid Lands,* (London: Harwood Academic Publishers, 1983), p. 4. "As the 'advancing deserts' narrative faded in the absence of convincing data, attention shifted towards human actions that were demonstrably degrading lands, such as deforestation, over-cultivation, over-grazing, and salinity-inducing irrigation practices, frequently aggravated by droughts." [Winslow, M., *et al.*, "Desertification, Drought, Poverty and Agriculture: Research Lessons and Opportunities", (Aleppo, Syria: Centre for Agricultural Research in the Dry Areas, (ICARDA), 2004), p. 4].
47. Katyal, n. 43, p. 7.
48. Dregne, n. 46, p. 4.
49. Grainger, Alan, *et al.*, "Desertification and Climate Change: The Case for Greater Convergence" *Mitigation and Adaptation Strategies for Global Change,* vol. 5, 2000, p. 362.
50. Extensive preparations were made for this Conference through a number of technical studies, surveys and workshops. Details of this can be found elsewhere in this book.
51. Dregne, H.E., "Desertification: Problems and Challenges", *Annals of Arid Zone* (Jodhpur), vol. 34, no. 3, 2000, p. 365.
52. Glenn E., *et al.*,"On Our Failure to Control Desertification: Implications for Global Change Issues, and a Research Agenda for the Future", *Environmental Science and Policy*, vol. 1, 1998, p. 74.
53. Rechkemmer, Andreas, *Global Environmental Governance: the United Nations Convention to Combat Desertification,* (Berlin: Wissenschaftszentrum Berlin für Sozialforschung (WZB), 2004), p. 55.
54. UNEP, *The Status of Desertification and Implementation of the United Nations Plan of Action to Combat Desertification*, (Nairobi: UNEP, 1992) p. 13.

55. Nasr, M., "Assessing Desertification and Water Harvesting in the Middle East and North Africa: Policy Implications", Pol'cy Paper no. 10, Center for Development Research, Bonn University, Germany, 1999, p. 5.
56. UNEP, n. 54, p. 13.
57. Dregne, *et al.*, "A New Assessment of the World Status of Desertification", *Desertification Control Bulletin,* vol. 19, 1991, p. 12.
58. Mainguet, Monique, *Aridity: Droughts and Human Development*, (New York: Springer, 1999), p. 252.
59. UNEP, n. 54, p. 13.
60. *Ibid.*, p. 14. and also Nasr, n. 55, p. 6.
61. Wang, Xunming, *et al.*, "The Relative Role of Climatic and Human Factors in Desertification in semi-arid China." *Global Environmental Change*, vol. 16, 2006, p. 55.
62. *Ibid.* p. 54.
63. Mainguet, n. 58, p. 252.
64. Martello, n. 9, p. 86. On the other hand Le Hou'erou argues that UNCED definition was retained "although many scientists would have preferred to have connotations to irreversibility and desert landscapes included in the definition. Many specialists consider them to be the result of political compromises whose goals are not scientific. Under this meaning, desertification may be equated with land degradation under arid to dry sub-humid climates. Many scientists prefer to use the latter terms because, unlike desertification, *the expression 'land degradation' does not have emotional connotations,"* (emphasis added), (Le Hou'erou, Henry, N., "Climate Change, Drought and Desertification," *Journal of Arid Environments*, vol. 34, 1996, p. 137).
65. Article 1(f) of UNCCD, UNCCD Secretariat, "The United Nations Convention to Combat Desertification" [Online: web] Accessed on 23rd June, 2008 URL: http://www.unccd.int/convention/text/convention.php.
66. *Ibid.*
67. Corell, Elisabeth., "Drylands Degradation-Africa's Main Environmental Challenge" in Chaytor, Beatrice and Kevin R. Gray, eds., *International Environmental Law and Policy in Africa,* (London: Kluwer Academic Publishers, 2003), p. 4.
68. Thomas, David S.G., "Science and the Desertification Debate", *Journal of Arid Environments,* vol. 37, 1997, p. 605. According to Clive Agnew and Andrew Warren, "(d)ifferent definitions are inevitably attached to different stake holders. The resulting conflicts and confusions have produced constantly shifting sets of definition, between definitions that exclude climatic deterioration and emphasise mismanagement, and those that put the emphasis the other way around. Needless to say, the confusion of definition has had a major role in the inability of

institutions to respond to the problems concerned."(Agnew, Clive and Andrew Warren, "A Framework for Tackling Drought and Land Degradation", *Journal of Arid Environments*, vol. 33, 1996, p. 312).

69. Toulmin, Camilla, "Combating Desertification: Encouraging Local Action within a Global Framework", in Helge Ole Bergesen and Georg Parmann, eds, *Green Globe Yearbook of International Co-operation on Environment and Development,* (Oxford: Oxford University Press, 1994), p. 79.
70. UNEP, *Report on Millennium Ecosystem Assessment,* (UNEP: Nairobi, 2006), p. 208.
71. Katyal, n. 43, p. 10.
72. German Advisory Council on Global Change (GACGC) *New Structures for Global Environmental Policy,* (London: Earthscan, 2001), p. 75.
73. Katyal, n. 43, p. 10.
74. UNEP, n. 70, p. 626.
75. *Ibid.*
76. World Bank, n. 17, p. 5.
77. UNEP, n. 70, p. 626.
78. Nasr, n. 55, p. 17.
79. Reynolds, n. 33, p. 62.
80. Nasr, n. 55, p. 41. "...the extent of affected lands has been exaggerated and the issue of desertification has become a controversial one, suffering from a dearth of data and rigorous scientific study."(Nicholson, S.E. *et al.*, "Desertification, Drought, and Surface Vegetation: An example from the West African Sahel," *Bulletin of the American Meteorological Society*, vol. 79, no. 5, 1998, p. 815).
81. UNEP, *The United Nations Conference on Environment and Development: Agenda 21*, Chapter 12, paragraph 12.5, (Nairobi: UNEP, 1992).
82. Sherbinin, n. 12, p. 26.
83. Abahussain, *et al.*, "Desertification in the Arab Region: Analysis of Current Status and Trends", *Journal of Arid Environments,* vol. 51, 2002, p. 522.
84. Sherbinin, n. 12, p. 26.
85. UNEP, *One Planet and Many People: Atlas of Our Changing Environment,* (UNEP: Nairobi, 2006), p. 29.
86. *Ibid*, p. 30.
87. UNCCD Secretariat, *the Basic Facts Sheet,* available at www.unccd.org accessed on 18th November, 2006.
88. UNEP, n. 54, p. 34.
89. Grainger, n. 49, p. 364.
90. Darkoh, M.B.K., "The Nature, Causes and Consequences of Desertification in the Drylands of Africa", *Land Degradation and Development*, vol. 9, 1998, p. 13. "A lack of data meant that the best that could be done was an 'educated guess' at the true extent of the problem." (E. Symeonakis, and N. Drake, "Monitoring Desertification

and Land degradation over Sub-Saharan Africa," *International Journal of Remote Sensing,* vol. 25, no. 3, 2004, p. 573).

91. Abahussain, n. 83, p. 529.
92. UNEP, n. 70, p. 637.
93. UNEP, n. 70, p. 637. "Since few countries had sufficient quantitative data on land degradation, the GLASOD estimates were mainly based on expert judgments that were necessarily subjective." (Winslow, M., *et al.*, "Desertification, Drought, Poverty and Agriculture: Research Lessons and Opportunities", [Aleppo, Syria: Centre for Agricultural Research in the Dry Areas (ICARDA),2004], p. 7. According to Clive Agnew and Andrew Warren, "(t)here is no consensus at present concerning the status of desertification in the world as a whole or in its various regions". However "this has not stopped the publication of numerous data on the global threat of desertification." And they further says that the "UNEP data on desertification have been repeatedly criticised as being too loosely defined and collected to be of anything but publicity value." (Agnew, Clive and Andrew Warren, "A Framework for Tackling Drought and Land Degradation", *Journal of Arid Environments*, vol. 33, 1996, pp. 311-12).
94. UNEP, n. 70, p. 637.
95. Adams, William Mark, *Green Development: Environment and Sustainability in the Third World* (New York: Routledge, 2001), p. 181.
96. Sherbinin, n. 12, p. 27.
97. *Ibid.*, p. 26.
98. Humphreys, David and Susan Carr, "Land Degradation and Sustainable Resource Management in an African Context" in Thomas, Alan, *et al.*, (eds.), *Environmental Policies and NGO Influence: Land Degradation and Sustainable Resource Management in Sub-Saharan Africa* (London: Routledge, 2001), p. 26.
99. Glenn E., *et al.*, n. 52, p. 74.
100. Dregne, n. 31, pp. 124-125.
101. Vero'n, S.R. *et al.*, "Assessing Desertification", *Journal of Arid Environments,* vol. 66, 2006, p. 752.
102. Humphreys, n. 98, p. 26.
103. Vero'n, n. 101, p. 752. In the 1980s, the importance of using indicators to monitor desertification at local, regional and global scales was recognized by the FAO and the UNEP, by developing a total of 22 indicators. Researchers who used these indicators in Kenya concluded that most of the indicators proposed by UNEP could only be used at the local scale, because the costs at the regional scale would be prohibitive and the process of data collection time-consuming. They also concluded that the use of remotely sensed data was necessary to monitor desertification over large areas. Thus, remote sensing-derived indicators provide an attractive way to map and monitor the desertification processes (Symeonakis, E. and N. Drake, "Monitoring

desertification and land degradation over sub-Saharan Africa," *International Journal of Remote Sensing*, vol. 25, no. 3, 2004, p. 575).

104. Kline, Karen and Kal Raustiala, "International Environmental Agreements and Remote Sensing Technologies", Background paper prepared for the Workshop on Remote Sensing and Environmental Treaties: Building More Effective Linkages, December 4-5, 2000, sponsored by the Socio-economic Data and Applications Centre (SEDAC), Centre for International Earth Science Information Network, Columbia University, New York, p. 28.

105. Remote Sensing (RS) refers to the collection of atmospheric, terrestrial, marine, or social data from a platform located above the surface of the earth, including satellites, airplanes (manned and unmanned) and the Space Shuttle. Recent advances in RS technologies allow the collection of a wide array of hitherto unavailable data that are relevant to global environmental policy and the number and variety of RS instruments in the sky at any given time keeps increasing. RS data has several attractive qualities. It is generally accurate and objective. It can have globally-consistent coverage. It can be tuned to ecological regions of widely varying scales. Since it is sensed from space, it can present a wide range of relevant data synoptically and without legally infringing national sovereignty.

    RS. data also has limitations. It must be interpreted by people with sufficient technical expertise and therefore the process of interpretation is still subject to subjective biases. It is equally expensive to obtain especially for developing and underdeveloped countries, and will not eliminate core political obstacles to environmental protection. On balance, however, RS data has many positive features in the context of environmental agreements that require data about both human behaviour and environmental change. From the late 1960s to the mid-1980s there was substantial opposition to the legality of remote sensing. But in 1986 RS proponents succeeded in this debate and the right to collect environmental data from space was affirmed. (Kline, no. 104, p. 1).

106. UNCCD, Committee for the Review of the Implementation of the Convention, *Review of the report on enhanced implementation of the obligations of the Convention,* Fourth Session Nairobi, 18-21 October 2005, p. 18.

107. Toulmin, n. 69, p. 81.

108. Nasr, n. 55, p. 22.

109. Grainger, n. 49, p. 365.

110. Adams, n. 95, p. 181.

111. Sherbinin, n. 12, p. 26.

112. *Ibid.*, p. 27.

113. Williams, Martin A.J., "Interactions of desertification and climate:

Present understanding and future research imperatives", *Arid Lands News letter*, vol. 49, May/June 2001, p. 2.
114. Levin, n. 33, p. 314.
115. El-Tantawi, n. 27, p. 189.
116. *Ibid.*, p. 4.
117. Mun, Ted, *Encyclopedia of Global Environmental Change* (Chichester: John Wiley & Sons, 2002), p. 452.
118. Williams, n. 113, p. 4.
119. Grainger, n. 49, p. 363.
120. Abahussain, n. 83, p. 535.
121. Sivakumar, M.V.K., *et al.*, "Agrometeorology and Sustainable Agriculture" *Agricultural and Forest Meteorology*, vol. 103, 2000, p. 24.
122. Diouf, Jacques, "Thirsty Land: Untapped Opportunity", *Our Planet* (the Magazine of the United Nations Environment Programme), vol. 17, n. 1, p. 8.
123. GEF and GM, no. 8, p. 11.
124. Mayrand, Karel, *et al.* "Agricultural Trade Liberalization, Poverty, and Desertification in Rural Drylands: The Role of UNCCD", (Unisféra International Centre, 2005), p. 6.
125. UNCCD Secretariat, "Fact Sheet," [Online: web] Accessed on 23rd June, 2008 URL:http://www.unccd.int/publicinfo/factsheets/showFS.php?number=3.
126. "Sustainable Agriculture in Developing Countries", *Bio.org* [Online: web] Accessed on 23rd June, 2008 URL:http://www.bio.org/foodag/background/developingc.asp.
127. Mayrand, n. 124, p. 6.
128. UNEP, n. 85, p. 28.
129. Speth, James and Peter M. Haas, *Global Environmental Governance* (London: Islander Press, 2006), p. 32.
130. Mayrand, n. 124, p. 6.
131. Rechkemmer, n. 53, p. 66.
132. Katyal, n. 43, p. 20.
133. *Ibid.*
134. Katyal, n. 43, p. 20.
135. UNEP, *Global Environmental Outlook 2002* (Nairobi: UNEP, 2002), p. 68.
136. Biermann, Frank, "Global Environmental Governance: Conceptualization and Examples", Global Governance Working Paper No. 12, (Amsterdam: Vrije Universiteit, Global Governance Project, 2004), p. 9. The then UN General Secretary, Kofi Annan, in his report to the Millennium Assembly of the United Nations, said "the very notion of centralizing hierarchies is itself an anachronism in our fluid, highly dynamic and extensively networked world—an outmoded remnant of nineteenth century mindsets." Instead, he provided the UN vision of global governance as being dependent on:

"[g]reater participation coupled with accountability. Therefore, the international public domain—including the United Nations—must be opened up further to the participation of the many actors whose contributions are essential to managing the path of globalization." Malabed, Rizalino Noble, *Global Civil Society and the Environmental Discourse,* [Tokyo: UNU/Global Environmental Outreach Centre (GEOC),2000], p. 34. Former President of Brazil, Fernando Henrique Cardoso, points out that the "[c]ontemporary global order is increasingly the outcome of multiple, interlocking patterns of transnational interaction shaped both by state and non-state actors." (Fisher, Dana R. and Jessica F. Green, Understanding Disenfranchisement: Civil Society and Developing Countries' Influence and Participation in Global Governance for Sustainable Development, *Global Environmental Politics*, vol. 4, no. 3, 2004, p. 65).

137. *Ibid*, p. 8.
138. Sathaye, J., *et al.*, "Sustainable Development and Mitigation", in Metz, B. *et al.* (eds.), *Climate Change 2007: Mitigation*, Contribution of Working Group III to the Fourth Assessment Report of the Inter-governmental Panel on Climate Change (Cambridge: Cambridge University Press, 2007), p. 708. "The failure of state-centred international regimes to address many of the most pressing global problems successfully prompted a search for new institutions, partnerships, and governance mechanisms A more inclusive global environmental governance paradigm holds the promise not only of innovative governance strategies, but also of expanded cooperation among social actors that may have been previously outside the policy process." (Lemos, Maria Carmen and Arun Agrawal, "Environmental Governance," *Annual Review of Environment Resources*, vol. 31, 2006, p. 301).
139. Ivanova, Maria and Jennifer Roy, "The Architecture of Global Environmental Governance: Pros and Cons of Multiplicity" in Swart, Lydia and Estelle Perry, *Global Environmental Governance: Perspectives on Current Debates* (New York: Centre for UN Reform, 2007), p. 48.
140 Caldwell, Lynton Keith, *Environment Policy: From the Twentieth to Twenty-First Century* (London: Duke University, 1996), p. 122.
141. Sampford, Charles., "Environmental Governance for Biodiversity", *Environmental Science and Policy*, vol. 5, 2002, p. 79.
142. Farazmand, Ali, "Globalization and Governance: A Theoretical Analysis" in Farazmand, Ali, ed, *Sound Governance: Policy and Administrative Innovations* (Westport: Praeger/Greenwood, 2004), p. 30.
143. Farazmand, Ali, "Building Partnerships for Sound Governance" in Farazmand, n. 142, p. 78.
144. Sampford, n. 141, p. 80.
145. Sjoberg, Helen, "The Challenge of Global Environmental Governance" in Rolen, Mats, *et. al*, eds., *International Governance on Environmental Issues*, (Dordrecht, the Netherlands: Kluwer Academic

Press, 1997), p. 8. The Commission on Global Governance defines governance as "the sum of many ways individuals and institutions, public and private, manage their common affairs. It is a continuing process through which conflicting or diverse interests may be accommodated and co-operative action may be taken. It includes formal institutions and regimes empowered to enforce compliance, as well as informal arrangements that people and institutions either have agreed to or perceive to be in their interest." (Commission on Global Governance, *Our Global Neighborhood,* The Report of the Commission on Global Governance, (New York: Oxford University Press, 1995), p. 2.

146. Ewalt, Jo Ann G., "Alternative Governance Structures of Welfare Provider Networks" in Ingraham, Patricia W. and Lawrence E. Lynn, Jr., eds., *The Art of Governance: Analyzing Management and Administration*, (Washington D.C., Gorgetown University Press, 2004), p. 49. "Governance is not the same as government. It includes the actions of the state and, in addition, encompasses actors such as communities, businesses, and NGOs" (Lemos, Maria Carmen and Arun Agrawal, "Environmental Governance," *Annual Review of Environment Resources*, vol. 31, 2006, p. 298). According to Rosenau, Governance is "a more encompassing phenomenon than government. It embraces governmental institutions, but it also subsumes informal, non-governmental mechanisms whereby those persons and organizations within its purview move ahead, satisfy their needs, and fulfil their wants." (Rosenau, J.N., "Governance, Order, and Change in World Politics" in Rosenau, James N. and Ernst-Otto Czempiel, eds., *Governance without Government: Order and Change in World Politics*, (Cambridge: Cambridge University Press, 1992), p. 4.
147. Saunier, Richard E and Richard A. Meganck, *Dictionary and Introduction to Global Environmental Governance* (London: Earthscan, 2007), p. 3.
148. Vogler, John and Andrew Jordan, "Governance and Environment" in Berkhout, Frans, *et al.*, eds, *Negotiating Environmental Change: New Perspectives from Social Science* (Cheltenham, JK: Edward Elger, 2003), p. 143.
149. Sampford, n. 141, p. 81.
150. Lovan, W. Robert, *et al.*, "Participatory Governance in a Changing World" in Lovan, W. Robert, *et al., Participatory Governance: Planning, Conflict Mediation and Public Decision Making in Civil Society* (Aldershot (UK): Ashgate Publishing Ltd, 2004), p. 3.
151. Steiner, Achim, *et al.*, "Global governance for the environment and the role of Multilateral Environmental Agreements in conservation", *Oryx*, vol. 37, n. 2, 2003, p. 227.
152. Farazmand, n. 143, p. 78.
153. Saunier, no. 147, p. 3. For example, "NGO inclusion does not come

at the expense of state power or centrality. The participation of NGOs enhances the ability, in both technocratic and political terms, of states to regulate through the treaty process." (Raustiala, Kal, "States, NGOs and International Environmental Institutions", *International Studies Quarterly*, vol. 41, 1997, p. 736).

154. Lovan, n. 150, p. 3.
155. Kooiman, Jan, "Social-Political Governance: Introduction" in Kooiman, J., ed., *Modern Governance: New Government-Society Interactions*, (New Delhi: Sage Publications, 1993), p. 1.
156. Baker, Susan, *Sustainable Development* (New York: Routledge, 2006), p. 53. Environmental governance also defined as "the set of regulatory processes, mechanisms and organizations through which political actors influence environmental actions and outcomes." (Lemos, Maria Carmen and Arun Agrawal, "Environmental Governance," *Annual Review of Environment Resources*, vol. 31, 2006, p. 298.)
157. Sampford, n. 141, p. 89. According to Yohei Harashima, "(s)ince the mid-1980s, the emergence of global environmental problems such as climate change and ozone depletion has coincided with new thinking about governance. Today the core issue of environmental governance is the way societies deal with environmental problems. It concerns interactions among formal and informal institutions and actors within society that influence how environmental problems are identified and framed." (Harashima, Yohei, "Environmental Governance in Selected Asian Developing Countries", *International Review for Environmental Strategies*, vol. 1, no. 1, 2000, p. 194).
158. Saunier, n. 147, pp. 3-4.
159. Oberthur, Sebastian and Thomas Gehring, "Reforming International Environmental Governance: An Institutionalist Critique of the Proposal for a World Environment Organisation", *International Environmental Agreements: Politics, Law and Economics*, vol. 4, 2004, p. 360.
160. Steiner, n. 151, p. 231.
161. Okereke, Chukwumerije, "Global environmental sustainability: Intragenerational equity and conceptions of justice in multilateral environmental regimes", *Geoforum*, vol. 37, 2006, pp. 726-27.
162. Low, N., Gleeson, B., "The Ethical Challenge of Environmental Governance", in Gleeson, B. and, Low, N. eds., *Governing for the Environment: Global Problems, Ethics and Democracy*, (London: Palgarve, 2001), p. 1.
163. Barrow, CJ, *Developing the Environment: Problems and Management*, (London: Longman, 1995), p. xi. "Modem technology and an exploding population enable man to set in motion forces that threaten the quality of his life, perhaps his survival. There is growing evidence that our existing social institutions, especially our legal institutions, are inadequate to come to grips with the problem." (Ottinger, Richard

L., "Legislation and the Environment: Individual Rights and Government Accountability", *Pace Law Faculty Publications*. Paper 538, 1970, p. 666.)

164. Renner, Michael "Environmental Security: the Policy Agenda", *Conflict, Security and Development*, vol. 4, no. 3, 2004, p. 314.
165. Hilary F. French, "Strengthening Global Environmental Governance" in *State of the World 1992*, World Watch Institution Report on Progress Toward A Sustainable Society (Horizon India Books: New Delhi: 1992), p. 157.
166. Mark Allan Gray, "The United Nations Environment Programme: An Assessment", *Journal Environmental Law*, vol. 20, no. 2, 1990, p. 21.
167. Karkkainen, Bradley C. "Post-Sovereign Environmental Governance: The Collaborative Problem-Solving Model" in Biermann, no. 14, p. 207. "The most important contemporary environmental challenges involve systems that are intrinsically global (e.g., climate change) or are tightly linked to global pressures (e.g., timber production for the world market) and that require governance at levels from the global all the way down to the local."(Dietz, Thomas, *et al.*, "The Struggle to Govern the Commons", *Science*, vol. 302, 2003, p. 1908).
168. Biermann, Frank and Klaus Dingwerth, "Global Environmental Change and the Nation State", *Global Environmental Politics*, vol. 4, no. 1,2004, p. 11. "The emergence of these hybrid forms of environmental governance is based upon the recognition that no single agent possesses the capabilities to address the multiple facets, interdependencies, and scales of environmental problems that may appear at first blush to be quite simple." (Lemos, Maria Carmen and Arun Agrawal, "Environmental Governance," *Annual Review of Environment Resources*, vol. 31, 2006, p. 311.)
169. Untawale, Mukund G., "Global Environmental Degradation and International Organizations", *International Political Science Review*, vol. 11, no. 3, 1990, p. 382.
170. *Ibid.*, p. 372.
171. Dwivedi, O.P., "Environmental Administration in Canada", *International Review of Administrative Sciences*, 1973; 39; p. 149.
172. Bodansky, Daniel, *et al.*, "International Environmental Law: Mapping the Field" in Bodansky, Daniel, *et al.*, (eds.), *The Oxford Handbook of International Environmental Law*, (Oxford: Oxford University Press, 2007), p. 3.
173. *Ibid.*, p. 16.
174. Caldwell, Lyndon K., *International Environmental Policy: Emergence and Dimensions*, (New Delhi: Affiliated East West Press Private Limited: 1991), p. 94.
175. Dunoff, Jeffrey L., "Levels of Environmental Governance" in Bodansky, no. 172, p. 87.
176. Caldwell, Lynton K., "Management of Resources and Environment:

A Problem in Administrative Coordination", *International Review of Administrative Sciences*, vol. 38, 1972, p. 115.
177. Bodansky, n. 172, p. 18.
178. Najam, Adil, Ioli Christopoulou, and William R. Moomaw, "The Emergent "System" of Global Environmental Governance", *Global Environmental Politics*, vol. 4, no. 4, 2004, p. 12.
179. Bodansky, n. 172, p. 18.
180. Tolba, M.K., *Global Environmental Diplomacy: Negotiating Environmental Agreements for the World, 1973-1992,* (Cambridge, MA: MIT Press, 1998), p. 67.
181. Najam, Adil, and Nick Robins, "Seizing the Future: The South, Sustainable Development and International Trade", *International Affairs*, vol. 77, no. 1, 2001, pp. 93-94.
182. Lipschutz, Ronnie, and Judith Mayer, *Global Civil Society and Global Environmental Governance: The Politics of Nature from Place to Planet,* (New York: State University of New York, 1996), p. 56.
183. Sampford, n. 141, p. 88.
184. Najam, Adil, *et al, Global Environmental Governance: A Reform Agenda*, (Winnipeg: International Institute for Sustainable Development, 2006), p. 16.
185. *Ibid*, p. 3.
186. *Ibid*, p. v.
187. Bodansky, n. 172, p. 24.
188. Holtz, Uwe, "The United Nations Convention to Combat Desertification (UNCCD) and its Political Dimension", Paper was prepared for the Fifth Parliamentary Round Table in the context of the implementation of the United Nations Convention to Combat Desertification (UNCCD), (Bonn, 26th May, 2003), p. 8.
189. El-Tantawi, n. 27., p. 161.
190. Kassas, M., n. 28, p. 123. "The African Sahel stretches from the Atlantic Coast of Senegal and Mauritania to the Red Sea coast of Sudan and Eritrea. It forms the southern margin of the Sahara desert, or, alternatively, the northern margin of the region influenced by the northern summer African monsoon. It is a semi-arid environment, characterized by a highly variable climate, with an intense rainy season, centred on August and no more than 4 months long, and a prolonged dry season." (Giannini, Alessandra, "A Climate Model-based Review of Drought in the Sahel: Desertification, the Re-greening and Climate Change", *Global and Planetary Change*, vol. 64, 2008, p. 119). "Four major droughts have occurred in the West African Sahel this century, during the 1910s, 1940s, 1970s and 1980s...The last was the most severe, affecting, for example, at least half of Sudan's population.... by 1990 the cumulative impact of drought in the Sahel would have resulted in the deaths of hundreds of thousands of people with millions more displaced.... 'after a 20 year series of droughts, the Sudano-

Sahelian region remained the most permanently vulnerable area and desertification had adversely affected the well-being of some 80-85 per cent of the population of the region'"(Agnew, Clive and Andrew Warren, "A Framework for Tackling Drought and Land Degradation", *Journal of Arid Environments,* vol. 33, 1996, p. 309).

191. Rechkemmer, n. 53, p. 54.
192. Chasek, Pamela, "The Convention to Combat Desertification: Lessons Learned for Sustainable Development", *Journal of Environment and Development*, vol. 6, no. 2, 1997, p. 150.
193. Bauer, n. 7, p. 17.
194. Corell, n. 67, p. 11.
195. Holtz, n. 188, p. 8.
196. Chasek, Pamela S., and Elisabeth Corell, "Addressing Desertification at the International Level: The Institutional System" in J.F. Reynolds and D.M. Stafford Smith, eds., *Global Desertification: Do Humans Cause Deserts?*, (Dahlem: Dahlem University Press, 2002), p. 278.
197. Corell, Elisabeth, *The Negotiable Desert: Expert Knowledge in the Negotiations of the Convention to Combat Desertification,* (Linköping: Department of Water and Environmental Studies, Linköping University, 1999), p. 20.
198. Baker, R., "Institutional Innovations, Development and Environment: An Administrative Trap Revisited", *Public Administration and Development,* vol. 9, nos. 1 and 2, 1989, p. 32.
199. *Ibid.*
200. UNESCO, *Trends in Research and Application of Science and Technology for Arid Zone Development* (Paris: UNESCO, 1979), Munro, R.D., "Environmental Resources and Management for the 1980s" *Ambio*, vol. 12, no. 1, 1983, pp. 60-61, Johnels, A., "Conference on Environmental Resources and Management for the 1980s", *Ambio*, vol. 12, no. 1, 1983, pp. 58-59, Report of World Commission on Environment and Development (Oxford: Oxford University Press, 1987).
201. Baker, R., n. 198, pp. 32-33.
202. *Ibid*, p. 33.
203. Caldwell, n. 176, p. 118.
204. Desai, Uday, "Institutions and Environmental Policy in Developed Countries" in Desai, Uday, ed, *Environmental Politics and Policy in Industrial Countries*, (London: MIT Press, 2002), p. 7.
205. Report of World Commission on Environment and Development, *Our Common Future,* (Oxford: Oxford University Press, 1987), p. 9.
206. Baker, R., "The Administrative Trap", *The Ecologist, vol.* 6, no. 7, 1976, p. 248.

II

Desertification in the GCC Countries

Historically, the Gulf region played a significant role in fostering a maritime trading culture, linking Arabia and Africa with Europe and Asia. It is bound on three sides by four water bodies: the Arabian Sea, the Gulf of Oman, the Red Sea and the Arabian Gulf, making it home to rich marine biodiversity. The Gulf Cooperation Council (GCC) countries[1] are cemented by a number of common characteristics related to its distinct climate, ecology, history, language and culture, which permeate its social fabric, development aspirations, and quest for a meaningful future. These geographically contiguous States have similar political orientations and an economic system based on the rentier State.[2] The classic formulation of Gulf Arab rentierism is put forward by Giacomo Luciani, who states:

> A state that economically supports society and is the main source of private revenues through government expenditure, while in turn supported by revenue accruing from abroad, does not need to respond to society. On the contrary, a state that is supported by society, through taxes levied in one form or another, will in the final analysis be obliged to respond to societal pressure.[3]

The GCC countries are "detached from their local socio-economic realm by virtue of rent. They have acquired relative autonomy from society, which gives them the ability to pursue national goals without accountability."[4]

The GCC countries are endowed with abundant natural resources in the form of combined oil and natural gas reserves, but they are less fortunate in the critical resources of productive land and accessible renewable water resources. For example in Saudi Arabia, "(t)he area of the suitable agricultural lands is estimated to be about 29 million hectares representing 14.5 per cent of the total area of the Kingdom."[5] It is even 2.4 per cent in the United Arab Emirates (UAE).[6] Oil and natural gas resources in the region play an important role not only as primary exports, but also as feeding inputs for energy-intensive, value-added industries that are proliferating throughout the region. This poses a serious challenge for sustainable development.

The GCC countries witnessed major socio-economic transformation and demographic change including substantial agricultural and industrial development, since oil was discovered at the beginning of the 20th century. These countries are also facing a number of major environmental issues. The source, nature and intensity of environmental threats differentiate this region from the rest of the world. This is not because of the interaction between man-made and natural environmental problems but because of the magnitude and speed with which this interaction takes place. The unprecedented levels of industrialization, inefficient use of limited resources, unplanned urbanization, large-scale consumption, higher population growth and lack of regulatory mechanisms produced a critical environmental situation in the GCC countries.

The scarcity of water and land resources is the most pressing. Deterioration of the marine and coastal environment, loss of biodiversity, increasing industrial pollution and poor management of hazardous wastes also threaten the socio-economic development of this region. Desertification has been a serious problem over the past decade, and the region's rangelands—important for food security—are deteriorating. Most land is either desertified or vulnerable to desertification. These serious environmental problems including desertification must be addressed immediately because failure to act now will greatly compound the cost and complexity of later remedial efforts.

This chapter examines the causes and consequences of environmental problems in the GCC countries. It analyses the status and various dimensions of desertification in the GCC countries. Besides these, it also explores the linkages between desertification and other developmental issues such as agriculture, water resources, urbanization, population growth, deforestation and industrialization.

I. Environmental Problems in the GCC Countries

The GCC countries are situated in extremely arid zones. The region is mostly a desert with the exception of narrow coastal areas and mountain ranges. The average annual rainfall ranges from 70 to 130 mm except in the coastal zone along the Red Sea in southwestern Saudi Arabia and along the Gulf of Oman on the Eastern shore, where orographic rainfall reaches more than 500 mm. The total annual evaporation rate ranges from 2,500 mm in the coastal areas to more than 4,500 mm inland. With this harsh climatic and hydrological condition, the GCC countries have an extremely poor endowment of water resources. The amount of renewable aquifer volume is insignificant and shallow alluvial aquifers provide some renewable groundwater only in those limited coastal strips. Large deep aquifers are present in the region, which contain non-renewable supplies of fossil water, but have a finite life and quality limitations. Only Saudi Arabia possesses substantial amounts of non-renewable groundwater resources in deep aquifers.[7]

The discovery of oil in the early 1930s heralded a new economic and environmental chapter in the region's history. The eastern areas of the Arabian Peninsula and northern Iraq emerged as the main sources of fossil fuel (oil and gas) in the world. The surplus oil revenue brought a period of rapid socio-economic development in these countries. These trends intensified during the past 30 years. This reliance on oil, abetted by the aridity of the region produced a distinct pattern of environmental problems.

The first discovery of oil on the Eastern shore of the Gulf took place on the Island of Bahrain in 1932 and this was the prelude to extensive and successful exploration in adjacent areas. In 1938 oil was discovered in Kuwait and at Dammam in Saudi Arabia, while in the following years oil was found in Qatar. Kuwait, Saudi Arabia, Bahrain and Qatar were all significant oil producers by the early 1950s, while Abu Dhabi and Dubai, which were to become the UAE, did not commence large scale exports until a decade later. Throughout the 1950s, 1960s, and 1970s, many new oilfields were discovered onshore, while offshore exploration in the Gulf also revealed large oil and gas accumulations.[8]

In the GCC countries, oil contributes about one-third to total Gross Domestic Product (GDP) and three-fourths to annual government revenues and exports. Together, these countries account for about 45 per cent of the world's proven oil reserves and 25 per cent of crude oil exports (Saudi Arabia is the world's largest oil exporter), and possess at least 17 per cent of the proven global natural gas reserves (Qatar is the fourth-largest exporter of liquefied natural gas).[9] The dynamics of the international oil market gives the GCC countries a decisive say in determining the production and pricing of these strategic commodities through the mighty oil cartel called the Organization of Petroleum Exporting Countries (OPEC).[10]

Over the past few decades, all the GCC countries witnessed an unprecedented economic and social transformation. The oil income created modern physical and social infrastructures and substantially raised the standard of living of the population. The huge oil revenue enabled the governments to provide extensive services to its people. The "offerings included the provision of such expensive services as health care, education from nursery to university, subsidized housing, food, electricity, petroleum, and a wide range of other important services, a high-tech infrastructure, and subsidized consumer goods, as well, of course, as employment."[11]

Water supply and sanitation services were made accessible to a large percentage of the population. Life expectancy increased by about 10 years during the period 1980-2000, and reached 74 years by 2000, which is among the highest in the world. Literacy rates rose from 20 per cent to about 80 per cent over the same period.[12] Similarly in the health sector "there was only one hospital in Qatar in 1945 and two in Kuwait in 1949, and prior to the establishment of the UAE in 1971, health service existed only in the cities of Abu-Dhabi and Dubai. By the end of the twentieth century, however, the indigenous GCC population enjoyed one of the top health services worldwide, with health centres spread throughout the area, including hospitals with the most advanced facilities."[13]

These unprecedented levels of socio-economic transformation coupled with limited natural resources created a number of major environmental issues. "Desertification, resource degradation, soil erosion, water-logging and salinity are examples of environmental developments at work in the...region. Some of these developments are of a natural origin, but many changes are man-made."[14] Scarcity of water, arid and harsh nature of the environment are the natural problems due to the geographical location of the region. But the pattern in which industrial activities were undertaken, the nature and speed of exploitation of natural resources and urbanisation and the scale of migration are some of the man-made problems.

Inefficient use of water for agricultural and industrial purposes is widespread in the GCC countries. "Greater quantities of water are lost through inefficient irrigation systems such as flood irrigation of fields, unlined or uncovered canals, and evaporation from reservoirs behind dams. Pollution from agriculture, including fertilizers and pesticides runoff and increased salts, added to increasing amounts of industrial and toxic waste and urban pollutants, combine to lower the quality of water."[15]

Indigenous plants and animals in this region are under increasing threat due to the impact of development. "Overfishing, pollution, and destruction of habitat (from land reclamation and filling in of wetlands) have all had a negative impact on marine biodiversity. As a result, declining fish and shrimp harvests have become a common feature in the Persian Gulf region"[16]

Fertile agricultural land around major cities was lost to urbanization, industrial establishments and transportation infrastructure. Similarly the "(d)eterioration of rangeland and farm productivity is forcing farmers to abandon agricultural land and migrate to cities, increasing pressure on services and infrastructure."[17]

Marine biodiversity in the GCC countries is under severe stress, primarily from oil spillage. "The region is the oil tanker highway of the world—approximately 25,000 tankers carrying about 60 per cent of total oil exports navigate through it."[18] War caused "extensive damage to the marine environment of the Persian Gulf. The Iran/Iraq war, which lasted eight years, targeted refineries, oil terminals, offshore oil fields and tankers. However, the war over Kuwait exceeded all other environmental disasters of the past four decades. Several million barrels of oil were released into the marine environment. Fallout from burning oil products produced a sea surface microlayer that was toxic to plankton and the larval stages of marine organisms. The long-term impacts of these wars on fisheries and the marine environment in general have yet to be assessed."[19]

With regard to environmental problems, two important factors warrant an analysis of these countries as a group. "First, because it shapes the economic behaviour, economic policies, and the socio-economic transformations (including urbanisation patterns), oil has an important implication for the quality of the environment... Secondly, the aridity of land and the scarcity of water play significant roles in the region's environmental profile. The interaction between these two factors produces a pattern of environmental degradation that is unique to the region."[20] Even though these countries are facing numerous environmental challenges, the problem of desertification has greater implication for the sustainable development and food security of this region.

II. Desertification in the GCC Countries

Land resources are finite, fragile and non-renewable. Besides forming a basis for life support systems and agricultural production, land ensures the preservation of terrestrial biodiversity, regulation of the hydrological cycle, carbon storage and recycling, and other ecosystem services. Land degradation has natural (or biophysical) and human-induced components. It is sometimes difficult to determine where the biophysical factors leave off and the socio-economic drivers begin. "The complex of socio-economic and biophysical causal factors involved in land degradation has differing levels of influence in different regions of the world and at different times."[21]

Desertification is a common problem in the GCC countries "resulting both from natural environmental factors and from the misuse of land. Periodic droughts along with extensive pressure from overgrazing, uncontrolled cultivation, fuelwood gathering, wind-blown soil materials, inappropriate use of irrigation water, uncontrolled urbanization, and sand encroachment have all contributed to the process of land degradation in the region."[22]

Therefore, desertification is caused by a combination of factors that change over time and vary by location. The underlying causes of the phenomenon of desertification in the GCC countries are directly related to unsustainable human activities and harsh and arid environment. The important drivers of desertification include excessive use of groundwater for agriculture, urbanization, population growth, deforestation and industrialization.

These factors put a tremendous pressure on the limited natural resources of these countries. These resources are degenerating and in some cases disappearing as a result of their unsustainable exploitation and management and the increasing imbalance between the limited supply and the increasing demand.

> "The information base on the current magnitude of and trends in desertification in the world, particularly in the MENA region, is very poor... There is no comprehensive

> assessment of the degradation of irrigated land, rainfed cropland, or rangeland in the region. There are no time-series data available on the development of desertification in the region."[23]

However, the available data on desertification shows that due to the socio-economic and climatic factors, the percentages of desertified land are high in the GCC countries ranging from 89 per cent in Oman to 100 per cent in Bahrain, Kuwait, UAE and Qatar.[24] In fact, large parts of the Arabian Peninsula can be classified as hyper-arid. "Most (62%) of the MENA region is hyper-arid. Five North African countries (Egypt, Libya, Tunisia, Algeria, and Morocco) and twelve countries of the Middle East (Bahrain, Iraq, Israel, Jordan, Kuwait, Lebanon, Oman, Qatar, Saudi Arabia, Syria, the United Arab Emirates, and Yemen) lie entirely in arid areas. Over half of Saudi Arabia is hyper-arid."[25] However, the hyper-arid zones do not fall within the scope of UNCCD based on the argument that deserts are naturally low in productivity. Hyper-arid zones are "presumed to be so dry that human degradation is severely limited unless irrigation is practiced. So there can be no desertification."[26] This would leave a large part of the GCC countries outside the scope of the UNCCD. But the experts argue that "even hyper-arid areas have measurable levels of service provision and land and vegetation degradation is possible in such areas."[27]

> A study by Shakhatra reported in 1987 that almost 100 per cent of the land in Bahrain, Qatar, Kuwait and UAE was desertified. Shakhatra's study also indicated that in the case of Oman, about 89 per cent of the land was already desertified, with another 8 per cent vulnerable to desertification, while in the case of Saudi Arabia around 92 per cent of the land was desertified and the remaining land area was vulnerable to desertification.[28]

In the Arab region, "(o)vergrazing is responsible for about 26 per cent of the desertification that is taking place, whereas 21 per cent of the total area is threatened by desertification due to forest/shrub clearing operations, compared to 2 per cent and 1 per cent of the total area lost annually due to salinization and urban expansion respectively."[29] Depletion of groundwater table, increase of soil salinity, loss of the agricultural lands and vegetative cover, soil erosion, sand encroachment and rangelands degradation are the important manifestations of desertification in the GCC countries. (See Table 2.1).

Table 2.1: Manifestation of Desertification in the GCC Countries

Sl. No.	*Country*	*Manifestation of Desertification*
1.	Bahrain	Depletion of groundwater table
		Increase of soil salinity
		Loss of agricultural land
		Loss of vegetative cover
		Soil erosion by wind
2.	Kuwait	Sand encroachment, Soil erosion
		Increase of soil salinity
3.	Oman	Land degradation due to overgrazing (especially in the Dhofar mountains areas)
		Wind erosion
		Water erosion
		Sand encroachment
4.	Qatar	Decrease of the level of groundwater
		Degradation of irrigated lands
		Rangelands degradation and sand encroachment
5.	Saudi Arabia	Constant movement of sand
		Deterioration of plant cover and forests
		Depletion of groundwater resources
6.	U.A.E.	Grazing of local plants
		Depletion of groundwater resources
		Decrease of plant cover

Source: Compiled from UNEP/Regional Office for West Asia, *The State of Desertification in the Arab World*, (Manama: UNEP/ROWA, 2004, pp. 9-17.

i. Forms of Desertification in the GCC Countries

The degree and type of desertification varies from one country to another within the region.[30] There are several forms of desertification prevalent in the GCC countries and it should be noted that two or more land degradation processes might interact in the same area.[31] These are wind erosion, water erosion, chemical degradation and physical degradation.

A. Wind Erosion

Wind erosion is considered the most common environmental problem in the GCC countries. Soil erosion under the action of wind is the one of the major forms of land degradation which in turn leads to desertification. Soil erosion in this region "results from the uprooting of shrubs, which leads to the destruction of the soil structure and thus to accelerated erosion of the soil by wind and water. Soil infiltration of rainwater decreases, and surface runoff increases."[32]

The Food and Agriculture Organization (FAO) studies in 1992 indicated that in Saudi Arabia alone, approximately 50 million ha was affected by wind erosion.[33] The area affected by wind erosion is gradually increasing because of the extensive and intensive cultivation of marginal lands and the movement of sand dunes towards agricultural land and rangelands and owing to the loss of precious vegetation cover, which binds together the soils particles. Similarly, it leads to the loss of fertile top soils in arable lands.[34] Removal of vegetation cover from an arid environment "aggravates the magnitude of wind erosion and sand movement, thus endangering the life of the surrounding people, because vegetation removal increases not only the rate of water evaporation from the soil surface, but also minimizes rainwater conservation."[35] In Oman, "Sand drifting represent serious problems especially over areas adjacent to Wahiba Sands and in the plains and *wadis* of Dakhliya, Wusta and Janubiya Regions."[36]

In Qatar, for example, it was found that "the sand dunes encroach 8 metres/year towards the south and south-east, which is in the dominant wind directions. In the eastern part of the country sand dunes movement varies from 7.9 to 20.7 m/year. This is due to the size of sand dune, sand dune slope, and moisture content especially along the coast. In addition to the sand dune movement, there are sand storms-dust storms and clay storms. These lead to deposition of soil particles on plant leaves and on civil constructions."[37]

In comparison with other types of soil erosions, "all that is required for wind erosion to occur is a minimum wind shear stress that can detach and force the movement of naturally held soil particles from their place. Evidently, soils with smooth dry and loose surfaces offer the least resistance to blowing wind and are particularly vulnerable to wind erosion. Hence wind erosion is most pervasive in arid regions."[38] Wind erosion is the dominant form of land degradation in the GCC countries. See Table 2.2.

Table 2.2: Land Degradation in the GCC Countries (in '000 ha)

Sl. No.	*Country*	*Chemical degradation*	*Physical degradation*	*Water erosion*	*Wind erosion*	*Other inundated lands*
1.	Bahrain	—	—	—	—	—
2.	Kuwait	40	—	—	281	—
3.	Oman	167	—	2772	3653	123437
4.	Qatar	18	—	—	191	—
5.	Saudi Arabia	2647	—	212	49445	99781
6.	UAE	49	—	118	1070	1665

Source: Ali Abahussain, no. 34, p. 528.

B. Water Erosion

Land degradation due to water erosion is very serious in mountainous areas particularly in Oman and Saudi Arabia. Although the rainfall is often higher, due to their inaccessibility mountainous areas tend to be the most isolated and marginalised areas. The complex landscape of the mountainous region consists of steep slopes, terraced croplands, sloping rangelands, and scattered patches of shrubs and trees. The degradation of these areas includes severe soil erosion by water run-off on unprotected slopes, which in extreme cases can lead to silting of *wadis* and loss of agricultural land downstream, degradation of natural vegetation and depletion of biodiversity.[39]

Areas devoid of vegetation cover tend to have poor soil structure due to paucity of rooting systems and organic matter, resulting in poor permeability and increased runoff. Runoff and erosion further results in leakages of nutrients to adjacent landscape components.[40] "The hydro-transmission characteristics of a soil profile or cloddiness of the soil and the slope of the surface determine the onset and subsequent intensity of erosion. Soils resisting the infiltration and percolation of water are more susceptible to water erosion, while soils with a non-cloddy, pulverized surface are vulnerable to wind erosion."[41] For example in Qatar, "shallow profile soils (approximately 136,000 ha) are said to be susceptible to water erosion due to the occurrence of erratic rainstorms."[42]

Water harvesting plays a major role in combating desertification in mountainous areas suffering from water erosion and its subsequent adverse impact on soil resource and vegetation cover.[43] "Due to rising costs for maintaining past benching and terracing conservation and other runoff control structures on the slopes, vast areas have been completely degraded and abandoned, resulting in great loss in land and water resources."[44]

C. Chemical Degradation

The main indicator of degradation in the region's irrigated areas is salinity, combined with waterlogging.[45] The chemical degradation of land in the GCC countries involves salinisation[46] and alkalisation, the loss of soil nutrients and soil and water pollution. In drylands, irrigation is the key to overcome the adverse effects of arid conditions and recurrent droughts and it is also vital to ensure food security for a growing population. However poor management and inefficient use of water for irrigation resulted in salinisation, alkalinisation, waterlogging and nutrient depletion in large areas of these countries.

About 2 million ha of irrigated land area in Saudi Arabia and 33.6 per cent of the cultivated land of Bahrain are moderately salinised.[47] For example in Qatar around 30 per cent of irrigated agriculture land is salinised.[48] Similarly "(a)bout 68 farms went out of production due to salinization (in Qatar). The yield in state farms decreased by 30 per cent or about 1500 ha from irrigated soil degraded due to salinization."[49]

The extensive use of fertilizers and pesticides in irrigated agricultural areas cause soil and water pollution in the region. "The development of waterlogging and salinity/alkalinity is an outstanding example of man's role in inducing land degradation in areas that did not pose any problem earlier."[50] Despite today's understanding and the availability of preventive and remedial technologies, the problems of waterlogging and salinity continue to spread. As a result, the productivity of land and water resources is steadily declining and sustainability is at risk, if not already collapsed, as indicated by land abandonment and migration to nearby cities.[51]

D. Physical Degradation

The physical degradation of the land in the form of soil structure deterioration resulting from cementation, the accumulation of gypsum power and the formation of soil crusts are also prevalent in these countries. The physical consequence of land degradation is the expansion of deserts and desert-like landscapes in areas where this did not occur previously, the generation of shifting sand dunes, expanding sand-seas and the crusting of bare soils. For instance, in northwestern Kuwait, the areas subjected to severe soil disruptions are invaded by mobile sand sheets, which support minimal natural vegetation.[52]

III. Dimension of Desertification in the GCC Countries

"Since desertification is a complex process, involving a mix of conflicting definitions, causes and effects, no single indicator alone can adequately reflect the interaction of its several components."[53] "Although climate change, overcultivation, overgrazing, poor irrigation management, and deforestation are considered to be directly responsible for desertification, they usually are exacerbated by a number of underlying social, economic, and political realities in the drylands."[54] Accordingly the UNCCD recognises the interlinkages among sustainable development, climate change, biological diversity, water resources, energy sources and food security.[55] Therefore, it is necessary to analyse the complex character of desertification and its various dimensions in detail.

Unsustainable agricultural practices, scarcity of water, increasing urbanisation, growing population, rapid industrialisation and declining vegetation cover are the important factors which need to be discussed in the context of their role in accelerating the process of desertification in the GCC countries.

i. Agricultural Practices

Agricultural activity has significant environmental impacts and constitutes the important form of land-use. Globally, poor water management has "resulted in the salinization of 20 per cent of the world's irrigated land, with an additional 1.5 million hectares affected annually, significantly reducing crop production."[56]

The conversion of fragile drylands to agriculture, as well as improper land management techniques are the most important drivers of desertification worldwide. "Until the advent of oil production in the region, the net export of raw materials derived from agriculture had accounted for the largest part of economic activity. Today the 'food gap', whereby the region cannot produce enough from agriculture to feed its population, has made the area 'the least food self-sufficient region' in the world."[57]

In West Asia traditionally, grazing and subsistence farming were the main forms of agriculture but, by the middle of this century, modern agricultural systems were introduced to increase food production. Marginal and rangelands were put under cultivation to cope with the increasing food demand.[58] In the past, nomadic tribes practiced a number of rangeland protection techniques (known as the *Al-hema, Hamiyah* and *Sann* systems). These systems set aside large tracts of rangeland to be used as reserves. During the 1950s, two major events caused many nomads to abandon their traditional grazing systems: new land-use laws were introduced in several countries which designated rangelands as public property; and agricultural machinery was widely introduced, with some rangelands being ploughed up for cereal farming, particularly barley. As a result of these and other trends, rangelands are deteriorated throughout the region.[59]

In the GCC countries agriculture accounts for a small portion of the GDP and does not constitute an important source of employment, except in Oman and, to a lesser extent, Saudi Arabia.[60] However "(g)eopolitical instability in and around the countries of West Asia has persuaded governments to adopt policies aimed at achieving national food security. These policies have been accompanied by agricultural protectionism, the erection of trade barriers and government subsidies for agricultural inputs."[61]

Table 2.3: Agricultural Sector in the Total GDP of the GCC Countries (2002)

Sl. No	*GCC Countries*	*Agriculture Labour Force (1,000)*	*Agricultural GDP (million US $)*	*Agricultural contribution to Total GDP (%)*
1.	Bahrain	3	54	0.7
2.	Kuwait	14	142	0.4
3.	Oman	358	650	3.3
4.	Qatar	4	70	0.4
5.	Saudi Arabia	680	9612	5.1
6	UAE	71	2555	3.6

Source: Bazza, no. 60, p. 3.

The government provided subsidies in several forms, including wells, fuel, energy, inputs, price support programmes, trade protection, and free access to unlimited amounts of groundwater most of which is non-renewable. In Qatar "(s)upport in the field of marketing had been made, since (1991) and cash funds support was also discussed."[62]

The low rainfall has always meant that agriculture is only possible with irrigation. Consequent to the food self-sufficiency policies adopted by the GCC countries, the irrigated areas as well as agricultural production increased manifold. For example, Saudi Arabia heavily invested in agricultural projects. These include new irrigation schemes using water from deep wells, as well as modernization of the existing irrigation system.

In the GCC countries, areas under irrigation increased by 5 per cent per year up until 1990, then by 1.2 per cent per year thereafter. The areas of most crops increased steadily between 1980 and 1999 in most countries, although there were marked declines in cereals in Saudi Arabia and the UAE between 1990 and 2003.[63] "The first well was drilled in Bahrain in 1924. The number increased to 165 in 1940, 325 in 1955, and shot up to 1020 in 1979. Besides these wells, there were 1200 hand-dug wells. As of 1997, there were about 2000 wells in Bahrain."[64] In Qatar "(a)griculture ... was confined to a few farms and date gardens during the period prior to the late 1950s. From about 1958 onwards the number of farms increased steadily to reach a total of over 1300 by now (2000)."[65]

From the 1950s through the 1970s, changing food consumption habits, as well as the increasing salinity of the aquifers that served as irrigation sources, led to a gradual decline in date cultivation. By the 1980s, a significant number of palm groves were replaced by new kinds of agricultural activities, including vegetables, gardens, nurseries for trees and flowers, poultry production, and dairy farms.[66]

The net irrigated areas increased in all GCC countries by around 100-300 per cent. In the case of the UAE, Kuwait, Qatar and Bahrain, new irrigation projects have been initiated by the governments with the provision of various forms of subsidies. Advanced irrigation systems, including dripper and greenhouses, have been built to cultivate high value cash crops.[67]

"Without exception, all of the GCC countries are extracting groundwater resources in an unsustainable manner. In Oman, Bahrain, Kuwait, Qatar, and the UAE, this represents a level of extraction in excess of the natural recharge of the aquifers. In the case of Saudi Arabia, this represents the accelerated extraction of non-renewable resources without adequate knowledge of the finite life of water supplies within the aquifers." [68] Over-extraction of water resources affected the quantity and quality of groundwater. This led to seawater intrusion along the shoreline, causing salinization of coastal agricultural lands. For example, in Qatar "(a)bout 98 per cent of groundwater withdrawal (amounts to 244 million cubic metres in 1997) is made for agricultural purposes creating an imbalance between the sustainable supply and demand, which also resulted in both an annual deficit (39 mcm) and an accumulated deficit in the range of (1000 mcm)."[69]

For example, the main area of concentrated vegetation cover in Oman is in "the Batinah coastal plain, which is 10-30km wide and extends towards west from the capital Muscat to the border with the United Arab Emirates for a distance of some 300km. Intensive agriculture is practised in the Batinah, drawing water largely from groundwater resources. These groundwater resources are fed by the Jebel Akhdar mountains inland from the Batinah coast but, because of both more spatially extensive and more intensive agriculture, the groundwater is becoming more saline."[70]

Similarly, "(i)n Saudi Arabia water levels declined by more than 70 metres in the Umm Er Radhuma aquifer from 1978 to 1984 and this decline was accompanied by a salinity increase of more than 1000 milligrams per litre."[71]

As a result, many farms were abandoned in all countries and several aquifers were either depleted or highly polluted. As a result, agricultural production reduced, and some arable land, such as the Batinah coastal plain of Oman, completely lost. Again in Oman "(i)n areas near to the sea, salt accumulation is observed and the agricultural activities in some farms have been abandoned. This has pushed farmers to search for new farm lands towards the inland area in a search for good soils for agriculture. Accumulation of salt in soils near the sea has been attributed to the intrusion of seawater."[72] Salinity of both irrigation water and cultivated soils has increased to an extent of damaging crops of coastal farms. Abandonment of agricultural activities in coastal farms of Batinah region in Oman represents a real threat.[73]

Likewise in Bahrain it is estimated that the saline interface between the sea and groundwater advances at an annual rate of 75-130 metres.[74] In all these projects the emphasis was on high technology and little attentions were paid to the cost-effective nature of the scheme.[75] From the economic standpoint, the subsidies distorted costs and revenues and many of the agricultural activities were financially profitable only because of government subsidies and incentives.[76]

Table 2.4: Area under Irrigation in GCC Countries, 1965-2002 ('000 ha)

Sl. No.	*Country*	*Year*								
		1965	*1970*	*1975*	*1980*	*1985*	*1990*	*1995*	*2000*	*2002*
1.	Bahrain	1	1	1	1	1	2	4	4	4
2.	Kuwait	0	1	1	1	2	3	5	10	13
3.	Oman	23	29	34	38	41	58	62	62	62
4.	Qatar	1	1	1	3	5	6	13	13	13
5.	Saudi Arabia	353	365	375	600	1150	1600	1620	1620	1620
6.	U A E	35	45	50	53	58	63	68	76	76
	GCC Countries	413	442	462	696	1257	1732	1772	1785	1788

Source: Bazza, no. 60, p. 3.

"The net productivity of agriculture increased two-and-half folds between 1980 and 2000. It increased steadily in Oman and very rapidly in the UAE, but declined in Saudi Arabia reflecting the abandoning of some areas where groundwater resources have been exhausted and because of declining prices for some crop products. A severe drop in agricultural productivity in the UAE occurred between 2000 and 2004; it is also attributed to the depletion of groundwater resources and the consequent change in agricultural policy."[77]

> One of the primary reasons for the unsustainable exploitation of groundwater resources has been the provision of direct and indirect subsidies to well excavation, pumps, fuel and other inputs as well as price support programmes and trade protection in some GCC countries. This has resulted in distorted costs and revenues as well as misallocation of resources by artificially attracting investment to the sector that have obscured the high opportunity cost of groundwater for municipal and industrial uses, and have created a disincentive for the rational use of this resource. While the governments intend to redistribute oil revenues for citizens, given that most of the employment in the agriculture sector is provided by expatriates, employment generation is not an objective of agricultural policy in GCC countries.[78]

With respect to employment in the field of agriculture the "young Omanis show unwillingness to work in agriculture because of misconception of prestige, hard working conditions or long day work and for these reasons the number of foreign agricultural workers have increased, many of them have no experience before and after they gain experience they usually return to their home countries."[79] Similar trend prevails in other GCC countries also.

All the GCC countries are in the process of adopting water saving techniques and practices. In an extraordinary move, Saudi Arabia decided to abandon its 30-year programme to grow wheat that achieved self-sufficiency but depleted Saudi Arabia's scarce water resources. The government will start reducing purchases of wheat from local farmers by 12.5 per cent per year from 2008. Saudi Arabia aims to rely entirely on imports by 2016.[80]

Similarly Bahrain, "in spite of limited financial sources, has attempted to implement several measures through formulating

Table 2.5: Groundwater Irrigation and Agriculture

Sl No.	Country	1990			2000			1990-2000
		Irrigation water (mcm/year)	Groundwater extraction (mcm/year)	Share of irrigation water in total groundwater extraction (%)	Irrigation water (mcm/year)	Groundwater extraction (mcm/year)	Share of irrigation water in total groundwater extraction (%)	Groundwater irrigation increase in volume (%)
1.	Bahrain	120	167	72	137	195	70	14
2.	Kuwait	80	143	56	221	393	56	176
3.	Oman	1150	1204	95	1124	1240	91	-2
4.	Qatar	109	111	98	270	270	100	148
5.	Saudi Arabia	14600	15505	94	18300	19680	93	25
6.	U.A.E.	950	1148	83	2162	2673	81	128
	Total	17009	18278	93	22214	24415	91	31

Source: Adapted from World Bank, no. 7, p. 20.

Table 2.6: Agriculture Net Productivity Index in the GCC Countries, 1965-2004

Sl. No.	*Country*	*Year*								
		1965	*1970*	*1975*	*1980*	*1985*	*1990*	*1995*	*2000*	*2004*
1.	Bahrain	44.1	45.0	79.2	141.4	100.3	87.8	101.0	103.2	110.2
2.	Kuwait	14.4	19.8	23.1	44.4	64.9	53.0	55.0	91.0	124.6
3.	Oman	13.6	15.4	21.5	35.0	53.5	59.3	66.7	97.5	91.1
4.	Qatar	16.6	23.2	10.9	23.6	30.6	63.4	103.5	111.7	143.9
5.	Saudi Arabia	15.4	18.6	30.5	26.5	56.6	104.0	87.2	93.0	108.2
6.	UAE	3.1	4.5	5.7	10.1	15.2	21.3	41.8	140.9	53.4
	GCC Countries	107.2	126.6	171.0	280.9	321.0	388.8	455.2	637.2	631.4

Source: Bazza, o. 60, p. 4.

legislation, improving irrigation methods, replacing high-irrigation requirement crops with others, introducing tariffs for using the underground water, using the TSE (Treated Sewage Effluent) for irrigation, constructing land drainage, zoning of agricultural land, improving agricultural research activities, enhancing agricultural extension services, and supporting agricultural inputs by limited levels of subsidies." [81]

Equally Omani Government provides financial subsidies to farmers to purchase modern irrigation equipments. Recent years Oman also adopts proactive sustainable development policies which encourage farmers to introduce improved irrigation methods aiming at rationalization of water consumption in the agriculture sector. Modern irrigation methods, i.e. sprinkle, pivot, drip and bubbler are introduced to some newly established farms and have achieved higher productivity. Shortage of capital, awareness and adequate technical knowledge delay the acquaintance of these irrigation methods by many of the Omani farmers and/or landlords.[82]

Likewise in Qatar, the Department of Agricultural and Water Resources is "normally encouraging local population... (to) enhance their participation in all activities taken by its various sections through agricultural extension efforts among farmers. It also realizes the importance of agricultural mass communication, which was indicated by the very recent appointment of a Mass Communication Specialist."[83]

ii. Depletion of Water Resources

Sustainable management of water resources is "a must as water scarcity is becoming more and more a development constraint impeding the socio-economic development of the GCC countries."[84] However in these countries the "*way water* is being used at present does not give the impression that people have fully realised the scarcity and limited availability of water resources."[85] An adequate and dependable supply of fresh water is essential for human health, agriculture production and economic development. But only 3 per cent of Earth's water is salt-free, or fresh water. Moreover, nearly 70 per cent of fresh water is locked in glaciers and icebergs, and is not available for human use. The fresh water that is available comes from rain or from rivers, lakes, springs, and some groundwater reserves, such as aquifers.

Water is the most precious and limited natural resource in the GCC countries. This region is one of the most water-stressed areas in the world, and its long-term water situation is becoming increasingly alarming and uncertain. The GCC countries have similar physiographic characteristics, including extremely arid climates, sparse natural vegetation, and fragile soil conditions. This region is also characterised by large variability in rainfall, limited renewable groundwater resources, problems related with increasing groundwater salinity, and the absence of rivers and lakes. The natural water resources of these countries consist of limited quantities of run-off resulting from floods, groundwater in the alluvial aquifers, and extensive groundwater reserves in the deep sedimentary aquifers. The supplementary non-conventional sources include desalination of sea and brackish water, and treated wastewater.

Basically the availability of water is governed by rainfall distribution in time and space, in relation to topographic and geological features that influence water movement and storage. In Saudi Arabia, "the loss in runoff water is estimated at 60 per cent of the total runoff water, due to high evaporation, traditional irrigation systems application and absent of proper areas for water storage. Because the rainfall in Saudi Arabia is very low and unpredictable, runoff is irregular and generally speaking rainfall alone is insufficient to meet the needs of agriculture."[86] In order to capture the surface runoff, Saudi Arabia "has built about 200 dams with a total storage capacity of around 800 million m^3, of which the Jizan and Ajran dams are the most important with 86 and 56 million m^3 capacity respectively. The capacity of the Jizan dam was reduced by about 70 million m^3 on account of siltation and needs occasional dredging. The dam, like others in Saudi Arabia, is exposed to a high evaporation rate."[87]

The widening gap between supply and demand for water in the GCC countries can be "attributed to limited available surface water, high population growth and urbanization development, deficient institutional arrangements, poor management practices, water depletion and deterioration of quality, especially in shallow groundwater aquifers."[88]

> The increased use of fixed water resources in response to rising water demands is not only reducing its availability but

Table 2.7: Water Availability in the GCC Countries

Sl. No.	*Country*	*Conventional water resources (mcm)*			*Non-conventional water resources (mcm)*			*Total (mcm)*
		Surface water	*Ground water*	*Sub-total*	*Desalination*	*Agriculture drainage reuse*	*Sub-total*	
1.	Bahrain	0.2	100	100.2	75.0	17.5	92.5	192.7
2.	Kuwait	0.1	160	160.1	388.0	30.0	418.0	578.1
3.	Oman	918.0	550	1468.0	47.3	21.5	68.8	1536.8
4.	Qatar	1.4	50	51.4	131.0	33.0	164.0	215.4
5.	Saudi Arabia	2230.0	3850	6080.0	795.0	131.0	926.0	7006.0
6.	U.A.E.	185.0	130	315.0	405.0	108.0	513.0	828.0

Source: Compiled from Al-Weshah, Radwan, "The Role of UNESCO in Sustainable Water Resources Management in the Arab World", *Desalination*, vol. 152, 2002, p. 5.

also jeopardizing its quality, both having direct impact on accelerating the desertification process in the region.[89]

From an economic perspective, the burden of adjustment to increasingly scarce and limited water must fall on the agricultural sector since the economic value of water in much lower in farming than for domestic or industrial use.

A. Sectoral Distribution of Water in the GCC Countries

Owing to rapid increase in population and urbanisation, domestic water and industry needs are escalating at rates with which available water resources cannot keep pace. Throughout history, the unavailability of adequate water in these countries affected the sustainable development. During the last few decades, water demand in all sectors increased dramatically as a result of socio-economic transformation, high population growth, the availability of modern water pumping and irrigation technology, as well as rapid urbanisation and the expansion of agricultural activities which placed tremendous pressures on both the quality and the quantity of water resources.

1. Agricultural Sector

Domestic and industrial water requirements of the GCC countries are satisfied through desalination and a limited amount of groundwater from both shallow and deep aquifers. However, agricultural requirements of these countries are met through abstraction of water from shallow alluvial aquifers located in the coastal strips and inland basins. In Saudi Arabia, rapid expansion of agricultural activities resulted in substantial increases in water demand, leading to extensive mining of the deep aquifers. Likewise, agricultural water demand sharply increased in the other GCC countries, where groundwater reserves are being mined. Agriculture sector is accounting for nearly 82 per cent of the total water consumed compared to 10 per cent and 8 per cent for the domestic and industrial sectors respectively. The major cause of the increasing demand for water is rapid population growth. Domestic water demand has been rising due to an increase in per capita consumption.[90]

The intensive use of groundwater resources from shallow and deep aquifers to meet the rising demand for agriculture led to further

Table 2.8: Water Resource Endowment in the GCC Countries

Country	*Area (km^2)*	*Average annual rainfall (mm)*	*Groundwater recharge (mcm/year)*	*Non-Renewable Reserve (mcm)*
Bahrain	652	30-140	110	Negligible
Kuwait	17,818	30-140	160	n/a
Oman	212,460	80-400	900	102,000
Qatar	11,610	20-150	50	negligible
Saudi Arabia	2,149,690	30-550	3,850	428,400
UAE	83,600	80-160	190	n/a

Source: World Bank, no. 7, p. 3.

exploitation of water resources in excess of natural renewability and contributed towards water quality deterioration, especially in the coastal zones. Increasing demand also brings about an entirely new progression of environmental concerns and their associated socio-economic development costs.

Table 2.9: Water Demand Increase of the GCC Countries (mcm)

Country	*Years (mcm)*		
	1980	*1990*	*2000*
Bahrain	138	223	269
Kuwait	186	383	993
Oman	665	1236	1303
Qatar	110	194	433
Saudi Arabia	2362	16300	20800
UAE	789	1490	3506
Total	6230	19826	27304

Source: World Bank, no. 7, p. 5.

Groundwater resources in the GCC countries are in a critical condition because the volumes withdrawn far exceed natural recharge rates. In the region as a whole, groundwater is extracted much faster than its renewal rate. As a result, water levels in the shallow aquifers are continually declining. In the past Bahrain was called the green spot of the Arabian Gulf. But over pumping of groundwater resources led to the drying of most of the natural springs and the deterioration of their water quality and this led to land degradation as well as salinization of several regions due to low water quality.[91] In UAE, the "annual consumption of groundwater is more than thousand million cubic metre, therefore, the static groundwater depth level is increasing about 2m per year."[92]

Furthermore unregulated pumping, absence of or minimal irrigation water tariffs, lack of enforcement measures against unlawful drilling and poor irrigation practices resulted in excessive use. Intensive agriculture and large-scale application of agro-chemicals also contributed to the contamination of water resources. Excessive use of groundwater has resulted in a sharp decline of the groundwater levels and the quality due to seawater intrusion.

2. Industrial Sector

Industrial activities in the GCC countries are limited and have contributed to only small increases in total water requirements, when compared with the domestic and agricultural sectors. Industrial water use (4% on the average in all countries) relies for 94 per cent on groundwater (of which 80% is non-renewable) and 6 per cent on desalination (Kuwait and Qatar). However, treated wastewater is not used, despite its suitability for some industries. Excluding Saudi Arabia and Oman, the ratio of industrial water consumption becomes 7 per cent in the other 4 States.[93]

Major industries in Saudi Arabia, UAE and Oman consist of petrochemicals, cement, and limited food and beverage production. Countries with relatively well-established petrochemical industries and refineries are Saudi Arabia, Kuwait, and Bahrain. Most industrial activities are confined to major urban centres, requiring competition with the domestic sector to satisfy water requirements. In most of the GCC countries, field development and petro-chemical industries are considered to be water-use intensive, and rely on groundwater supplemented with surface water, desalination, and a limited amount of recycled water.[94]

3. Domestic Water Supply

Domestic water use relies on both desalination and good quality groundwater (usually fossil) with the exception of Saudi Arabia where surface water is available to some extent. Another striking feature with respect to municipal water use is that GCC countries have the highest per capita consumption in the world, in contrast with being the least endowed with renewable water resources. Potable water demand is around 70 per cent higher than in rich countries considered to be high

Table 2.10: Sectoral Water Use Changes between 1990 and 2000

Country	*Sectoral water use (mcm/year)*						*Growth rate (%)*		
	1990			*2000*					
	Municipal water	*Agriculture water*	*Total*	*Municipal water*	*Agriculture water*	*Total*	*Municipal water*	*Agriculture water*	*Total*
Bahrain	103	120	223	132	137	269	128	114	121
Kuwait	303	80	383	772	221	993	255	276	259
Oman	86	1,150	1,236	179	1,124	1,303	208	98	105
Qatar	85	109	194	163	270	433	192	248	223
Saudi Arabia	1,700	14,600	16,300	2,500	18,300	20,800	147	125	128
UAE	540	950	1,490	1,344	2,162	3,506	249	228	235
Total	2,817	17,009	19,826	5,090	22,214	27,304	181	131	138

Source: World Bank, no. 7, p. 6.

Table 2.11: Critical Issues in Water Management in the GCC Countries

Sl. No.	*Problem*	*Evidence*	*Causes*	*Importance*
1.	Limited water resources	Depletion of available water per capita over time	Arid region with frequent drought cycles Growing population Food self-sufficiency policies	Socio-economic development slows down
2.	Inefficient water use	Irrigation losses up to 45% Excessive leakage from supply networks Wasteful water use	Extensive traditional irrigation practice Old water supply networks Lack of awareness Lack of realistic pricing Lack of stringent regulation	Excessive losses of available water
3.	Internal water allocation conflicts	Increasing competition among sectoral users	Growing water demand Limited water resources	Increasing water scarcity
4.	Deteriorating water quality	Contamination of surface water Sea water intrusion Groundwater depletion Loss of agricultural lands	Discharge of untreated domestic and industrial effluents into water courses Over-exploitation of groundwater Lack of strict penalties Irrational water demand Insufficient studies	Water-related diseases Soil damage Complicated groundwater problems Negative impact on environment
5.	Weak institutions	Duplication of efforts Inefficient water management	Undefined responsibilities Lack of coordination Inadequate technical capacity and training	Poor water development Inefficient services

Source: Dawoud, no. 88, p. 192.

users of water such as the United States of America or Australia. Inadequate demand management and inefficient service delivery are believed to be the main reasons behind this situation.[95]

B. Desalination

The growing advanced technology of desalination is currently providing enormous quantities of water to meet the escalating needs for domestic and industrial sectors in the GCC countries. Since good quality water is not available or is extremely limited, desalination[96] of sea water is commonly used to solve the problems of water supply for municipal and industrial uses in the GCC countries.[97] The GCC countries are considered to be the world leaders in desalination. The bulk of the total installed capacity of all desalination plants[98] in the world is in the Gulf region. "Desalination has become the main source of potable water in all the GCC states, where the annual demand rose from 1,500 million m^3 in 1980 to 6,000 million m^3 in 2000. Desalination is expected to provide an additional 5000 million m^3 per year by 2015."[99]

Table 2.12: Desalination Capacity of the GCC Countries (mcm/year)

Sl. No.	*Country*	*1990*	*2000*
1.	Bahrain	75	104
2.	Kuwait	318	522
3.	Oman	55	60
4.	Qatar	112	178
5.	Saudi Arabia	950	1278
6.	U.A.E.	502	1081
	Total	2012	3223

Source: World Bank, no. 7, p. 13.

All the GCC countries have an established policy of providing the principal municipal/industrial supply of water from desalination of water diverted from the sea. A significantly large share of drinking water is supplied by desalination plants in these countries. In particular, Qatar and Kuwait almost entirely rely on desalination plants for drinking water supply. UAE rapidly increased its share by building several large-scale desalination plants to meet ever-increasing urban water demands. Saudi Arabia is by far the largest desalination of water supplier for its citizens. The amount of desalination production of water is around 1 billion m^3 equivalent to about 40 per cent of the total urban water demand.[100]

"A major environmental problem of water desalination is the production of a flow of brine containing the salts removed from the intake water and that needs to be disposed. In addition, this brine may be polluted. This brine represents a significant fraction of the intake water flow. Seawater desalination typically yields a brine flow of 50-65 per cent of the intake water flow, with about twice the initial concentration."[101]

Given the high consumption rate from the desalination sources and its high production cost, a serious effort must be made to implement comprehensive conservation measures to reduce the consumption and invest in Research and Development to reduce the costs through improved design and operation features. At the administrative level, development of a water policy and effective strategies in each country for stressing the sustainable water resources management and optimising allocation of water in accordance with market value, conservation, pollution control and cooperation among water involved institutions is very important. Manpower development and training are also essential aspects.[102]

Oman developed "a long range National Water Resources Master Plan which includes strong measures, including restriction of the irrigated area, to reduce groundwater extraction to sustainable levels. The Plan also calls for the development of surface water storage and groundwater recharge systems to enhance usable groundwater supplies."[103] Similarly in Bahrain "(l)egislation to strictly monitor the use of groundwater and drilling of wells is in place with effect from 1997. Besides, the Amiri Decrees in respect of organizing date palm protection and land drainage system are effective to protect the state infrastructure to combat the menace of shrinking agricultural land."[104]

Two major steps were taken in the GCC countries that will enhance regional cooperation in the field of water resource management. The first one is the setting up of the GCC Water Cooperation Committee in 2002, which consists of all the Water Ministers. The important function of this committee is to ensure the integration and harmonization of the water policies in the region. The second one was strengthening coordination in Research and Development (R&D) in the field of desalination. The GCC have more than 60 per cent of the total world desalination capacity with major investments in this sector, and desalinated water represents the principal source for providing drinking water to its urban centres. It is expected that this coordinated research will help in acquiring and indigenizing desalination technology in the region. More importantly it will facilitate in reducing the unit production cost of desalination and treatment and modify per capita freshwater share in the domestic sector in the region."[105]

An increasing vegetation cover in the GCC countries will stabilize the hydrological balance in the dryland areas and maintain land productivity. Prevention of not yet degraded land and rehabilitation of moderate and severely degraded drylands can be achieved through the introduction of environmentally sound, socially acceptable, fair and economically feasible land-use systems. This will enhance the land carrying capacity and maintenance of biotic resources in fragile ecosystems.

iii. Population Growth

Population size, rate of change, distribution, age structure and migration are the critical aspects of demography. Population size to a great extent governs demand for natural resources and material flows. Population growth creates the challenge of improving living standards and providing essential services, including housing, transport, sanitation, health, education, jobs and security. The increasing demand for services put tremendous pressure on the environment.

> The increase in the population....has put considerable pressure on limited arable land and water resources of the region. This along with the changing life styles and consumption patterns, and the increasing food demand combined with the aridity of the environment accelerated the rate of land degradation. The unprecedented rate of demographic changes have led to losses of land to urbanisation and the diminishing of per capita share of cultivated land in these countries.[106]

One of the main reasons for rapid population growth over the last 200 years is the declining mortality rate due to improved sanitation, health care, medicine, shelter and nutrition. These same led to dramatic increases in life expectancy.

Rapid population growth not only pushes up demand for food,

Table 2.13: Population Growth in the GCC Countries

Country	*Population in millions*						
	1970	*1980*	*1990*	*2000*	*2010*	*2020*	*2030*
Bahrain	0.2	0.3	0.5	0.7	0.8	0.9	1.0
Kuwait	0.7	1.4	2.1	2.2	2.8	3.2	3.5
Oman	0.7	1.1	1.6	2.4	3.0	3.7	4.2
Qatar	0.1	0.2	0.5	0.6	0.7	0.8	0.8
Saudi Arabia	5.7	9.4	15.8	20.7	27.4	35.5	42.5
UAE	0.2	1.0	1.8	3.2	3.5	3.9	4.2
Total	7.8	13.5	22.3	29.8	38.1	47.9	56.2

Source: World Bank, no. 3, p. 4.

but leads to overexploitation and conversion of arable land for residential, infrastructure, and industrial uses. In many developing countries, with limited prospects of bringing additional land into production, intensification will be required to enable higher productivity.[107]

The common perception on the relation between population dynamics and desertification is that population pressures lead to the intensification of agriculture activities which further resulted in decline of productivity. Similarly, the increasing demands of growing population needs to be met by converting arable lands into urban centres, shelters, etc. Indeed research findings and evidence from several developing countries support this notion. [108] These observations show that the connection between population dynamics and desertification is complex and that always other contributing factors (socio-economic and natural) must be taken into account.[109]

During the period 1978-1988, the population of the GCC countries grew rapidly. The upsurge in growth rates was mainly due to the increasing numbers in the non-national labour force entering these countries. However, between 1988 and 1998, the GCC countries except Bahrain witnessed a downward trend in the rate of population growth. In the GCC countries rapid economic growth and massive public investment in infrastructure development in the 1970s and 1980s produced labour shortage which was met by importing large numbers of workers.[110]

In these countries the percentage of expatriates in the total labour force varied from 90 per cent of the workforce in the U.A.E. (1994), to 83 per cent in Kuwait (1997) and 46 per cent in Oman (1993). The participation rate among nationals of the GCC countries is significantly lower that of other countries in the region ranging between 20 per cent for the U.A.E. and 32 per cent in Bahrain. This is because of the early retirements in response to generous social security schemes for nationals and the extremely low female labour force participation.[111]

The UNCCD is the first global environmental treaty to recognize the link between environmental degradation and migration. It is also the first to incorporate provisions for addressing the adverse impact of this phenomenon.[112] The available data does not support making a direct link between desertification and population growth. However, there are enough well established evidences to support the link between desertification and other developmental indicators including industrialization and urbanization. In fact this produces an indirect link between population growth and desertification, since population growth is an important factor in industrialization and urbanization.

iv. Urbanization

Urbanisation means an increase in the proportion of the urban population to the total population over a period of time. Urbanization is a consequence of economic growth, which is also associated with population growth rate as well as industrialization.[113] Nearly half of the world's population live in towns and cities. Between 1975 and 2000, urban population increased from 1,500 million to over 2,800 million, or about 45 per cent of the world's population.[114]

Urbanization is inextricably linked with the economic transition that is taking place in the region from agrarian and nomadic societies to one that is based on manufacturing and services. Economic development brought dramatic improvement in the well-being of the West Asian people including longer life expectancies, higher incomes and decreased child mortality rates. Urbanization significantly redistributed the population geographically and sharply decreased the percentage of people engaged in agriculture.

As urban areas expand, they often encroach into agricultural lands. In developing countries, this resulted in the conversion of nearly 500,000 hectares (1235,526 acres) of arable land annually. China, for example, lost around one million hectares of arable land between 1987 and 1995, due to construction.[115] However, urbanization currently covers only about two to four per cent of the Earth's land surface. As a result, researchers argue that land lost to urbanization will not threaten global food production in the foreseeable future. Nevertheless, rapid urban expansion frequently takes away prime agricultural land out of production.[116]

Though the extent of urban areas is not that large when compared with other land uses such as agriculture or forestry, their environmental impact is significant. This is due not only to the large concentrations of population in cities, but because these are centres of political, cultural and economic influences.[117] Urban areas rely on vast hinterlands for food, raw materials for industry, energy, water supplies, construction materials, recreational areas and a myriad of other goods and services.[118] The environmental consequences of urban growth are considerable and it has a clear link with the process of desertification.

> Urban areas consume natural resources from both near and distant sources. Cities encroach onto agricultural lands, where the urban fringes and peripheries grow faster than the cities and spontaneous or squatter settlements do it even faster. This uncontrolled growth lead to rapidly increasing amounts of wastes (solid and liquid) causing pollution of land and water resources and aggravate the desertification problem. Intensification of agricultural production to meet urban demand for food lead to heavy, concentrated use of fertilizers and pesticides causing pollution of land and water resources. This along with the fast growing industrialization near urban centres add(s) to the active desertification process.[119]

In addition to agriculture, the urbanization process brings change in the landscape. Historically, forests and grasslands were converted to cropland. Increasingly, cropland is being converted to urban areas. Millions of hectares of cropland in the industrial world have been paved to create roads and parking lots. The average car requires 0.07 hectares (0.17 acres) of paved land for roads and parking space.[120]

The transport, industrial and energy sectors produce major air-pollution problems which has substantial adverse effects on human health. The use of leaded gasoline, in a fleet of aging vehicles, inefficient use of fossil fuels in power generation, and industrial emissions of particulates and sulphur oxides are some of the important sources of urban pollution.[121] Urbanization also generated most of the greenhouse gases that cause global climate change.[122]

Urbanization in coastal areas often leads to the destruction of sensitive ecosystems and can also alter the hydrology of coasts and their natural features such as mangrove swamps, reefs and beaches that serve as barriers to erosion and form important habitats for species. Pollution from urban run-off, sewage and untreated discharges of industries has adversely affected many water bodies, leaving many cities with unsafe water supply.

Three crucial factors shaped the urban landscapes of the region.[123] The 1970s oil boom and the sharp fluctuations of oil revenues during

Table 2.14: Urban Population Growth in the GCC Countries (1970-2000) (in thousands)

Sl. No.	*Country/Year*	*1970*	*% of total population*	*1980*	*% of total population*	*1990*	*% of total population*	*2000*	*% of total population*
1.	Bahrain	173	78.7	279	80.5	429	87.6	570	92.2
2.	Kuwait	579	77.8	1240	90.2	2054	95.8	1919	97.6
3.	Oman	83	11.4	356	31.5	1109	62.1	2282	84
4.	Qatar	89	79.9	196	85.6	436	89.9	554	92.5
5.	Saudi Arabia	2796	48.7	6325	65.9	12602	78.5	18572	85.7
6.	UAE	127	57.2	726	71.5	1554	80.9	2099	85.9

Source: ESCWA, no. 24, pp. 189-190.

the following two decades. The large-scale movement of people within the region because of armed conflict and civil strife; and the forces of globalization that have played and continue to play a vital role since the beginning of the early 1990s, integrating West Asian nations into the global economy and increasing the role of information technology.

Urbanization in the GCC countries was rapid and sudden, and occurred within the past four decades as GDP and revenues from oil increased. In the GCC countries "the revenues from this boom have resulted in a phase of urbanization and development which has possibly been unequalled in world history and it has completely changed the urban fabric of these small towns."[124] The most dramatic increase was experienced in Oman, where the share of the urban population increased from 11 per cent to 82 per cent between 1970 and 1999[125] which has required significant restructuring by urban centres to absorb new residents. On a positive note, secondary cities tended to grow faster than larger cities in the region during the 1990s,[126] signalling better distribution of populations among urban centres.

In the GCC countries, urbanization is fuelled by international and regional labour migration, as well as by natural growth. These factors, along with rural-to-urban migration, contribute to urban expansion outside the Gulf.[127] The impact of rural migration on urban centres is measured by the: (1) intensity of the migratory movement; (2) ability of rural migrants to adapt to urban life; and (3) capacity of cities to absorb rural migrants.[128] Modern urban infrastructure was created featuring new municipal and government buildings, new industries, and health and educational services.

Between 1972 and 1980, the total urban population increased from 17.8 million (44.7 per cent of the total population) to 27 million (55.8 per cent of the total population). The average annual growth rate of the urban population in this period was 5.6 per cent, substantially more than that of the general population, which was 3.6 per cent. In 2002, almost the entire population of Kuwait (96.1%), Qatar (93%) and Bahrain (92.7%) lived in urban areas, while the level of urbanization was also high in the others—Saudi Arabia (87%), the UAE (87.5%) and Oman (77%).[129]

Such a scale of population growth and urbanisation led to "the conversion of agricultural and grazing lands and coastal areas for development of roads, industry and housing, with the associated loss of biodiversity. Continued encroachment of agricultural lands lead to the cultivation of marginal lands, which further intensifies the desertification process."[130]

For instance, Manama, grew from 3.3 sq. km in 1951 to 24.4 sq. km in 2000; 53 per cent of this increase came at the expenses of fertile agricultural lands, while remaining 47 per cent was accomplished through the reclamation of control areas. The area of Dubai city increased from 6.5 sq. km in 1970 to 605 sq. km at present and more expansion is planned. Similarly, the area of Sharjah city increased from 0.5 sq. km in 1960 to more than 100 sq. km at present.[131]

Uncontrolled urban sprawl generates urban stress, which impacts on the limited available of natural resources as well as socio-economic development. This trend imposes tremendous pressures on housing, healthcare, education, sanitation, transport, infrastructure and other public services. A related manifestation in the GCC countries is the "coastalisation" of urban movements whereby population migrates not only between rural and urban centres, but also between inland and coastal areas. This has doubled the functions of public authorities, i.e. to effectively manage the coastal zones and marine ecosystems along with the traditional urbanisation challenges (air quality, water and sanitation services). The continuous discharge of partially treated industrial and municipal wastewater from many coastal cities into regional seas has also become problematic for marine environment of the GCC countries.[132]

In addition to urban sprawl along coastlines, dredging and land reclamation projects are expanding cities into the sea. This is transforming the natural landscape of coastal cities such as Dubai and Manama. These projects also impact marine habitats, coral reefs and coastal depositions, which in turn increases soil erosion and the loss of nursing grounds for fish and marine life.[133]

Urban air pollution is emerging as a serious environmental problem facing not only major but also many medium size cities in the GCC countries. These cities are experiencing air pollution at such levels often exceeding the WHO guidelines. The main sources of air pollution in these countries are energy and industrial production and vehicular emissions, which tend to expand with economic growth. Vehicle emission is considered the most prevailing source of air pollution amounting to 90 per cent of CO emission, due to poor maintenance of vehicles, aged cars, low quality fuels and poor traffic management and road conditions. Stationary sources, such as outdated power generation stations, refineries, fertilisers' plants, cement manufacturing, and thermal water desalination and power plants also significantly contribute to urban air quality deterioration, especially where low fuel quality power is used.[134]

Urban air pollution is significantly high in the GCC countries. "(t)he number of registered motor vehicles in the GCC countries has steadily increased since the mid-1980, doubling and even tripling in some countries. The increase in scale has important effect on air quality, health, and land-use. Average vehicle concentration per capita for the region now exceeds the world average. High levels are particularly evident in Kuwait, Qatar and Saudi Arabia. Bahrain has by far the highest vehicle concentration per km for the region."[135]

National land-use plans and population distribution strategies have been developed and initiated in Bahrain, Qatar, and Saudi Arabia. A systematic inter-linkage has been established between urbanization problems, agricultural development, coastal zone management and environmental protection. It is increasingly evident that formulation of these national plans is based on intensive surveys, assessments and GIS (Global Information Systems) tools.[136]

In Bahrain, in order to protect the date palms and to maintain their cultivation, the Amiri Decree No. 29/83 was issued. Similarly, landfill areas, which are landscaped are to be monitored and protected from the urban encroachment. Therefore, zoning of agricultural areas is now under progress in collaboration with the Ministry of Housing, Environment and Municipalities. Agricultural zoning aims to protect these areas from urban encroachment.[137] However, the implications of rapid urban growth include increasing unemployment, environmental degradation, lack of urban services, overburdening of existing infrastructure and lack of access to land, finance and adequate shelter. Managing the urban environment sustainably will, therefore, become one of the major challenges for the future.

v. Deforestation

Forests contribute to environmental stability and are used as economic resources. In addition, it performs multiple roles, such as preventing soil degradation and erosion and limiting the greenhouse gases which contribute to global warming. According to experts, forests serve as natural habitats to almost two-thirds of all Earth's species, therefore, acting as a stronghold to safeguard biodiversity.

On an economic level, forests may be used as a direct source of energy or raw materials.[138]

Throughout history, the fate of the world's forests strongly reflected the pattern and intensity of land-use by societies. Demand for agricultural land, timber, and other forest products, as well as technological change in agriculture made significant impact on the mode and rate of transformation of forested areas. Society's special interest in deforestation, as compared to other land-use/land-cover change issues, may be partly attributable to the stark nature of the transition from forest area to cleared land. Deforestation occurs relatively quickly, in contrast to some other transitions (e.g., from crop land to pasture, or from productive land to degraded land).[139]

Despite the importance of forests, reports continue to indicate huge forest losses. Almost half of the planet's original forests were destroyed, mostly during the last three decades. During the 1990s, the total loss of existing natural forests was 16.1 million hectares per year, of which 15.2 million hectares occurred in the tropics.[140]

Deforestation leads to soil erosion especially in tropical areas where soils tend to be thin and nutrient-poor. Deforestation is also linked to habitat loss, which is a leading cause of species endangerment and biodiversity loss, particularly in humid tropical forests. Deforestation affects the hydrological cycle through changes in evapotranspiration and runoff. It contributes to greenhouse gas emissions that bring about climate change.[141]

Table 2.15: Forests, Woodlands and Desertified Areas in the GCC Countries

Sl. No.	*Country*	*Forests and woodlands*		*Desertified area (% in 1994)*
		% of total 1989-1991	*% of change 1991 over 1989*	
1.	Bahrain	0.0	0.0	100
2.	Kuwait	0.1	0.0	100
3.	Oman	0.0	0.0	89
4.	Qatar	0.0	0.0	100
5.	Saudi Arabia	0.7	19.9	92.4
6.	U.A.E.	0.0	0.0	100

Source: ESCWA, no. 24, p. 26.

Extensive land clearing for human settlements and agriculture, grazing by goats, sheep and other animals for thousands of years, illicit felling, burning for charcoal production, fires and inappropriate agricultural practices virtually exterminated the natural forests, including much of the former forests of pistachio, oak, juniper and cedar trees that were found in the north of the region.[142]

"Deterioration of forests in the Arab Region took several forms, namely, reduction of their areas, drop in the productivity of existing forests and loss of reproduction capabilities. Accurate estimates of forest areas in the region are not available or not complete."[143] Forests and woodlands of West Asia occupy only 3.66 million ha or 1 per cent of the region's land area and account for less than 0.1 per cent of the world's total forested area.[144] The majority of forest cover (62 per cent) is in the Arabian Peninsula with the remainder scattered in the mountains and hills of northern Iraq, Jordan, Lebanon, Syria and the Occupied Palestinian Territories.

Mangrove forests in UAE were rapidly depleted by overcutting to feed camels and other livestock, but there have recently been intensive conservation and rehabilitation efforts. On the other hand, the forests in the Dhofar mountains of south-western Oman were damaged by overgrazing, uncontrolled tourism and rapid development of rural communities.[145] The search for new agricultural land also led to the clearing of forest areas on sloping terrain, causing severe soil erosion in the mountainous watersheds of Oman. Road construction, quarrying and mining, and the construction of dams and irrigation canals further reduced forest areas and destroyed forest habitats in several countries in the region.[146]

Substantial afforestation and reforestation programmes needs to be launched to increase forest areas. Forest reserves were declared in Saudi Arabia through legislation. Work on sand dune fixation, green belts, roadside plantations and urban forests needs to be intensified.

vi. Industrialization

Due to mainly industrialization, the GCC countries have historically witnessed a number of positive gains in the socio-economic indicators, from life expectancy expansion to per capita income increase, to education and training progress. However, during the same period, impacts on natural resources depletion and environmental degradation rose dramatically as the scope and intensity of industrial and urban activities increased in an unprecedented scale.[147]

Industrialization involved a number of national plans to achieve goals of import substitution, adding value to local primary products, creating jobs, and finding new opportunities for accelerating exports. Throughout its history, West Asia was dependent on agriculture for its prosperity. Only in the second half of the 20th century the Petroleum Industry fundamentally altered the economic system. "From 1945 onward, and with increasing speed, the majority of the Gulf Arab States were transformed from a collection of small towns reliant on fishing, herding and trade to some of the world's leading exporters of oil with high per capita incomes, an unusual level of welfare services, and the beginnings of a modern petrochemical industry."[148]

Following the sharp increase in global oil prices in the 1970s and early 1980s, the GCC countries experienced "a swift acceleration in their economic development"[149] and recycled the windfall oil gains through a generous welfare system and massive public investment programmes. Governments in the GCC countries heavily invested in;

- Large infrastructure projects (housing, roads, airport, ports, telecommunications, sewage and power plants),
- Public services, (basic health and education),
- Heavy industries (cement, iron and steel, fertilizers, chemicals, petrochemicals), and medium industries (textiles), and
- Agriculture and land reclamation projects.

These heavily government-subsidized development activities, while being instrumental in the transformation of simple and mostly nomadic societies into modern communities, have discouraged conservation and increased inefficiency in resource allocation.[150]

The ratio of public expenditure to GDP, consequently, displayed a constant rising trend during this period in all the GCC countries except Oman, averaging 42 per cent in the 1970s and 46.7 per cent in the 1980s. Conversely, the ratio of revenue to GDP, which enjoyed an initial increase to an average of 50 per cent in the 1970s due to the two major oil price corrections, showed a descending trend due mainly to the changing composition of GDP with an increase in the share of the comparatively lightly taxed non-oil component of GDP.[151]

Under these kinds of circumstances, oil exporting Gulf countries decided to initiate the industrialisation process. The main objectives of their industrial planning were to reduce dependence on the single source of income from the export of oil and natural gas and to diversify the economic resources in order to establish a self-sustained economy. This move was in a complete contrast to most of the developing countries' industrialisation strategy.

There was a total lack of natural and human resources. The other prerequisite for industrialisation such as infrastructure, road, transport network, communication also were not adequately available. But in other developing countries in a relative sense the problem was only of finance. In other words, GCC countries lacked all the prerequisites for industrialisation except finance. The governments in the region ignored these tremendous obstacles on the road to a mature industrial economy.[152]

The countries started to undertake large-scale infrastructure developmental activities in the process of achieving industrialisation.[153] Large investments were made in infrastructure development. For example in Saudi Arabia from 1972 to 1975, 41 per cent of the total budget was allocated to infrastructure. During 1975 to 1980 it was increased to 49.3 per cent.

Table 2.16: The Sectoral Distribution of Expenditures (Saudi Arabia)

Year	*Human Development Value (SR billions)*	*Human Development Percentage*	*Economic Resources Percentage*	*Infrastructure Percentage*
1970-1975	10.5	30.9	27.7	41.1
1975-1980	78.6	22.6	28.0	49.3
1980-1985	176.2	28.2	30.7	41.1
1985-1990	177.0	50.7	20.4	28.9
1990-1995	218.3	66.6	10.6	22.8
1996	40.9	66.4	10.0	23.6
1998	65.3	68.5	–	–

Source: Rayed Krimly, "The Political Economy of Adjusted Priorities: Declining Oil Revenues and Saudi Fiscal Policies", *The Middle East Journal*, vol. 53, no. 2, 1999, p. 265.

Due to the massive oil revenue all the required raw material technology and manpower, were imported on a large scale. "Ports lying on the Arabian Gulf have witnessed basic changes in order to cope with the needs of the region."[154] "New Ports have been built at Aqaba, Dammam and Jeddah, Hudayda, Kuwait, Latakia, Tel Aviv.

etc., while the older ports have been enlarged."[155] In Saudi Arabia between 1970-1980 around "2000 villages (were) electrified, 15,000 kilometres paved roads were built, 700,000 telephones were installed and 30,000 housing units were constructed."[156] These developments severely affected the environment in the region.

The positive economic and social outcome of industrialization processes have been accompanied by serious environmental deterioration, as well as growing threats to health from occupational hazards.

> "In the GCC countries, industrial growth concentrated on the processing of raw materials into industrial products especially in the chemical industries. Not only are these processes resource intensive; but they also produce disproportionately large amounts of hazardous and toxic wastes, since a wide range of pollutants is associated with these industries."[157]

The GCC countries realized the potential of some of their solid wastes and have adopted recycling programmes and other strategies to make use of these wastes. Newer and larger industries are much more equipped to deal with industrial wastes and pollution with "end-of-pipe" procedures and technologies. Cleaner production applications are still relatively alien in these countries.

In these countries spontaneous settlements lack essential services and are at increased risks from industrial environmental problems and accidents. Few industrial establishments were created and scattered around residential areas in major Arab cities without sound planning or proper zoning considerations.

Conclusion

The GCC countries witnessed major socio-economic transformation and demographic change including substantial agricultural and industrial development, since oil was discovered at the beginning of the 20th century. These unprecedented levels of socio-economic transformation coupled with limited natural resources created a number of major environmental issues.

The scarcity of water and land resources is the most pressing. Deterioration of the marine and coastal environment, loss of biodiversity, increasing industrial pollution and poor management of hazardous wastes also threaten the socio-economic development of this region. Desertification has been a serious problem over the past decade, and the region's rangelands—important for food security—are deteriorating. Most land is either desertified or vulnerable to desertification. Fertile agricultural land around major cities was lost to urbanisation, industrial establishments and transportation infrastructure. Similarly, the deterioration of rangeland and farm productivity is forcing farmers to abandon agricultural land and migrate to cities, increasing pressure on services and infrastructure. For instance, Manama, grew from 3.3 km^2 in 1951 to 24.4 km^2 in 2000; 53 per cent of this increase came at the expenses of fertile agricultural lands, while remaining 47 per cent was accomplished through the reclamation of control areas.

Domestic and industrial water requirements of the GCC countries are satisfied through desalination and a limited amount of groundwater from both shallow and deep aquifers. However agricultural requirements of these countries are met through abstraction of water from shallow alluvial aquifers located in the coastal strips and inland basins. Improper management of irrigation and drainage leads to the salinisation of the productive soil. Groundwater resources in the GCC countries are in a critical condition because the volumes withdrawn far exceed natural recharge rates.

Efforts need to be made to rationalise optimum use of limited natural resources including water. Public awareness campaign and incentives to use modern technologies will address the issues of over-exploitation of natural resources.

References

1. Bahrain, Kuwait, Oman, Qatar, Saudi Arabia and the United Arab Emirates (U.A.E.).
2. The rentier State is the one in which the government relies for the lion's share of its revenue (certainly over 50 per cent, in the Gulf Monarchies usually over 75 per cent) on direct transfers from international economy, in the form of oil revenues, investment income, foreign aid, or other kinds of foreign direct payments.
3. Giacomo Luciani, 'Resources, revenues, and authoritarianism in the Arab world: beyond the rentier state?', in Brynen, Rex, *et al.*, (eds.), *Political Liberalization and Democratization in the Arab World* (London: Lynne Rienner Publishers, 1995), p. 211.

4. Ehteshami, Anoushiravan., "Reform from Above: the Politics of Participation in the Oil Monarchies," *International Affairs* (Blackwell Publishers, Oxford), vol. 79, 2003, p. 57.
5. UNCCD Secretariat, *The Third National Report for the Kingdom of Saudi Arabia about the Implementation of the United Nations Convention to Combat Desertification (UNCCD): Executive Summary*, (Bonn, 2006), p. 2.
6. UNCCD Secretariat, *Summary of the Second United Arab Emirates National Report to the UNCCD* (Bonn, 2002), p. 1.
7. World Bank, *A Water Sector Assessment Report on the Countries of the Cooperation Council of the Arab States of the Gulf*, (Washington D.C.: World Bank, 2005), p. 3.
8. Beaumont, Peter, *Drylands: Environmental Management and Development* (London: Routledge, 1993), p. 336.
9. Fasano, Ugo and Zubair Iqbal, "GCC Countries: From Oil Dependence to Diversification", International Monetary Fund Working Paper, (Washington, D.C.: IMF, 2003), p. 3.
10. Faruqi, Atiq Ahmad and Afrazul Hasan, "Oil Development in the Gulf", *Political Science Review*, vol. 22, no. 4, 1983, p. 372.
11. Ehteshami, n. 4, pp. 58-59.
12. World Bank, n. 7, p. i.
13. Winckler, Onn, *Arab Political Economy* (Brighton: Sussex Academic Press, 2005), p. 69.
14. El-Sherbini, A.A., "Recent Trends in Agricultural Development in the Middle East" in Kedourie, Elie and Sylvia G. Haim, eds. *Economic History of the Middle East* (London: Frank Cass, 1988), p. 97.
15. Kamrava, Mehran, *The Modern Middle: A Political History since the First World War,* (London: University of California Press, 2005), p. 371.
16. United Nations Environment Programme (UNEP), *Global Environmental Outlook 1997* (Nairobi: UNEP, 1997), p. 107.
17. UNEP, *Global Environmental Outlook 2000* (Nairobi: UNEP, 2000), p. 161
18. Gulf Research Centre (GRC), *Green Gulf Report* (Dubai: GRC, 2007), p. 6.
19. UNEP, n. 17, p. 169.
20. Hamid Mohtadi, "Environmentally Sustainable Development in the Middle East and North Africa" in Nemat Shafik, ed., *Prospects For Middle Eastern North African Economies: From Boom to Bust and Back?* (Houndmills: Macmillan, 1998), p. 265.
21. Sherbinin, Alex de., *A CIESIN Thematic Guide to Land-use and Land-cover Change,* (New York: Centre for International Earth Science Information Network (CIESIN), Columbia University, 2002), p. 22.
22. UNEP, n. 16, p. 106.
23. Nasr, M., "Assessing Desertification and Water Harvesting in the Middle East and North Africa: Policy Implications", Policy Paper

no. 10, Centre for Development Research, Bonn University, Germany, 1999, pp. 14-15.

24. ESCWA, *Survey of Economic and Social Development in the ESCWA Region 1998-1999*, (New York, 1999), p. 127.
25. Nasr, n. 23, p. 16.
26. Dregne, H.E., "Land Degradation in the Drylands", *Arid Land Research and Management*, vol. 16, 2002, pp. 124-125.
27. GRC, n. 18, p. 10.
28. *Ibid.*, p. 14.
29. Regional Office for West Asia/United Nations Environment Programme, *State of Environment in the Arab Region: A Progress Report*, (Manama: ROWA/UNEP, 2003, p. 15.
30. Nasr, n. 23, p. 16.
31. *Ibid.*, p. 15
32. Nasr, n. 23, p. 8.
33. *Ibid.*
34. Ali Abahussain, Asma, *et al.*, "Desertification in the Arab Region: Analysis of Current Status and Trends", *Journal of Arid Environments*, (Amsterdam), vol. 51, 2002, p. 523.
35. Amin, Ammar A., "The Extent of Desertification on Saudi Arabia", *Environmental Geology*, vol. 46, 2004, p. 27.
36. Ministry of Regional Municipalities, Environment and Water Resources, Government of Oman, *National Action Programme to Combat Desertification in the Sultanate of Oman*, (Muscat, 2005), p. 66.
37. Arab Centre for the Studies of Arid Zones and Dry Lands (ACSAD), *Inventory Study and Regional Database on Sustainable Vegetation Cover Management in West Asia (TN2)*, Prepared for the Sub-Regional Action Programme (SRAP) to Combat Desertification and Drought in West Asia, (Damascus: ACSAD, 2003), p. 69.
38. Katyal, Jagdish C. and Paul L.G. Vlek, "Desertification—Concept, Causes and Amelioration", Discussion Papers on Development Policy, Centre for Development Research, Bonn, October 2000, p. 28.
39. ROWA/UNEP, *Integrated Natural Resource Management for Combating Desertification in West Asia: UNCCD/SRAP Pilot Projects in Jordan, Lebanon, Syria and Yemen 2003-2006, Final Report*, (Manama: ROWA, 2006, p. 2.
40. GRC, n. 18, p. 15.
41. Katyal, n. 38, p. 29.
42. UNCCD Secretariat, *The National Report of the State of Qatar on the UNCCD Implementation*, (Bonn, 2000), p. 6.
43. International Centre for Agricultural Research in the Dry Areas and Arab Centre for the Study of Arid Zones and Dry Lands,(ICARDA) *Integrated Natural Resource Management for Combating Desertification in West Asia, Pilot Projects Proposal*, Prepared for the Sub-Regional Action

Programme (SRAP) for West Asia of the UN Convention to Combat Desertification (UNCCD), (Manama: ROWA/UNEP, 2003), p. 19.
44. *Ibid.*
45. Nasr, n. 23, p. 17.
46. Salinisation is the main desertification problem in irrigated agriculture. Salinisation involves a number of interrelated processes occurring in the soil, for example waterlogging, increasing salt content, and alkalinisation, in which some nutrients can no longer be absorbed due to the increasing *p*H-value of the soil. This problem is caused by the overuse of water through unsuitable irrigation techniques, accompanied by inefficient drainage systems. See Nasr, n. 23, p. 9.
47. GRC, n. 18, p. 15.
48. ACSAD, n. 37, p. 69.
49. *Ibid.*
50. Katyal, n. 38, p. 31.
51. ICARDA, n. 43, p. 26.
52. GRC, n. 18, p. 15.
53. Nasr, n. 23, p. 16.
54. Chasek, Pamela, "The Convention to Combat Desertification: Lessons Learned for Sustainable Development", *Journal of Environment and Development*, vol. 6, no. 2, 1997, p. 151.
55. Sherbinin, n. 21, p. 30.
56. Mohammad Al-Attar, "Role of Biosaline Agriculture in Managing Freshwater Shortages and Improving Water Security", (Dubai: International Centre for Biosaline Agriculture (ICBA), 2002), p. 5.
57. Milton-Edwards, Beverley, *Contemporary Politics of the Middle East* (Cambridge: Polity Press, 2006), p. 89.
58. UNEP, n. 17, pp. 159-160.
59. *Ibid.*, p. 160.
60. Bazza, Mohamed, "Policies for Water Management and Food Security under Water-scarcity Conditions: The Case of GCC Countries", Paper presented at the *7th* Gulf Water Conference, Kuwait, 19-23 November, 2005. p. 2. This paper is available online at *http://www.fao.org/world/Regional/rne/morelinks/Publications/English/Policiesfor Waterand FoodSecurityintheGCCCountries.pdf*, accessed on 7 th May, 2008.
61. UNEP, *Global Environmental Outlook 2003* (Nairobi: UNEP, 2003), p. 85.
62. UNCCD Secretariat, n. 42, p. 8.
63. Bazza, n. 60, p. 3.
64. Ministry of Works and Agriculture (MWA), Government of Bahrain, *National Report on the Implementation of the United Nations Convention to Combat Desertification* (Manama, April 2000), p. 13.
65. UNCCD Secretariat, n. 42, p. 6.
66. ACSAD, n. 37, p. 34.
67. World Bank, n. 7, p. 21.

68. *Ibid.*, p. 18.
69. UNCCD Secretariat, n. 42, p. 5.
70. Harris, R., "Remote sensing of agriculture change in Oman", *International Journal of Remote Sensing*, vol. 24, no. 23, 2003, p. 4837.
71. Mohammad Al-Attar, n. 56, p. 5.
72. MRMEWR, n. 36, p. 35.
73. *Ibid.*, p. 45.
74. UNEP, n. 17, p. 42.
75. Beaumont, n. 8, p. 349.
76. Bazza, n. 60, p. 4.
77. *Ibid.*, p. 3.
78. World Bank, n. 7, p. 20.
79. ACSAD, n. 37, p. 73.
80. "Kingdom to End Wheat Growing", *Arab News*, 9th January, 2008, [Online: web] Accessed on 23th June, 2008 URL:http://www.arabnews.com/?page=6&section=0&article =105447&d =9&m=1&y=2008.
81. UNCCD Secretariat, *Report of the Conference of Parties,* [Online: web] Accessed on 23th June, 2008 URL: http://www.unccd.int/cop/officialdocs/cop4/pdf/3add1(a)eng.pdf, p. 3.
82. MRMEWR, n. 36, p. 45.
83. UNCCD Secretariat, n. 42, p. 12.
84. Al-Weshah, Radwan, "The Role of UNESCO in Sustainable Water Resources Management in the Arab World", *Desalination*, vol. 152, 2002, p. 11.
85. MRMEWR, n. 36, p. 65.
86. ACSAD, n. 37, p. 53.
87. World Bank, n. 7, p. 11.
88. Dawoud, Mohamed A. "The Role of Desalination in Augmentation of Water Supply in GCC Countries," *Desalination,* vol. 186, 2005, p. 187.
89. Ali Abahussain, n. 34, p. 529.
90. UNEP, n. 61, p. 173.
91. ACSAD, n. 37, p. 37.
92. *Ibid.*, p. 92.
93. Bazza, n. 60, p. 8.
94. Bertrand Charrier, "Water, Conflict Resolution and Environmental Sustainability in the Middle East", *Arid Lands News Letters,* no. 44, 1998, p. 3.
95. Bazza, n. 60, p. 8.
96. Desalination is the process of removing dissolved salts from water. The two leading desalination technologies are thermal and membrane technologies. A thermal process involves the heating of saline water to produce water vapour that is, in turn, condensed to form fresh water. On the other hand the Membrane processes rely on permeable

membranes to separate salts from water. Membrane processes can either be pressure-driven (reverse osmosis) which is now the most commonly used method, or it could be voltage-driven (electro-dialysis).

97. Masahiro Murakami, *Managing Water for Peace in the Middle East: Alternative Strategies* (Tokyo: United Nations University Press, 1995), p. 114.
98. The desalination process primarily used in the GCC countries is Multi-Stage-Flash (MSF) distillation. This is an established technology and is combined with the co-generation of electricity which greatly improves the economics of desalination. It also exhibits significance and becomes critical for large scale production. An alternative technology is Multiple-Effect-Distillation (MED), which is more energy efficient even for smaller desalination plants than MSF. However, MSF is the most widely used technology in the GCC countries, which has a useful life of about 25 years that can be nearly doubled through proper maintenance and refurbishing of plants.
99. Beltrán, J. Martínez and S. Koo-Oshima eds., *Water Desalination for Agricultural Applications* (Rome: FAO, 2006), p. 14.
100. World Bank, n. 7, p. 11.
101. Beltrán, n. 99, p. 7.
102. Dawoud, n. 88, p. 187
103. World Bank, n. 7, p. 10.
104. MWA, n. 64, p. 6.
105. ROWA/UNEP, n. 29, p. 13.
106. Ali Abahussain, n. 34, p. 529.
107. UNEP, *Report on Millennium Ecosystem Assessment* (UNEP: Nairobi, 2006), p. 176.
108. Blaikie, P. and Brookfield H., *Land Degradation and Society,* (London: Routledge,1987), p. 45.
109. *Ibid.*, p. 47.
110. ESCWA, n. 24, p. 173.
111. *Ibid.*, p. 151.
112. Leighton, Michelle, "Desertification and Migration" in Johnson, P.M., *et al.*, (eds.), *Governing Global Desertification: Linking Environmental Degradation, Poverty and Participation* (Aldershot: Ashgate Publishing, 2006), p. 49.
113. Raju, K.V., "Urbanization in Asia—Issues and Challenges", *Monthly Public Opinion Surveys* (New Delhi), vol. 41. no. 8, 1996, p. 37.
114. UNEP, *One Planet, Many People: the Atlas of Our Changing Environment* (Nairobi: UNEP, 2005), p. 230.
115. UNEP, n. 107, p. 176.
116. UNEP, n. 114, p. 231.
117. Sherbinin, n. 21, p. 50.
118. *Ibid.*
119. Ali Abahussain, n. 34, p. 531.

120. UNEP, n. 114, p. 28.
121. United Nations Development Programme (UNDP), *The Arab Human Development Report 2002,*(New York: UNDP, 2002), p. 45.
122. UNEP, *Green Cities: Plan for the Future*, Annual Report, 2005,(Nairobi: UNEP, 2005), p. 17.
123. ESCWA, n. 24, p. 173.
124. Beaumont, n. 8, p. 334.
125. World Bank, *World Development Indicators 2001,* (Washington D.C.: World Bank, 2001), p. 29.
126. ESCWA, n. 24, p. 193.
127. ESCWA, *Proceedings of the Expert Group Meeting on Assessment of Economic and Social Developments in the ESCWA Region During the last 25 years and Priorities for the Next Decade 2000-2009*, (E/ESCWA/ED/1999/22), (New York: United Nations, 1999), p. 117.
128. ESCWA, *Youth in the Urban Environment in the ESCWA Region*, (E/ESCWA/HS/1997/7), (New York: United Nations, 1998), p. 2.
129. GRC, n. 18, p. 4.
130. *Ibid.*, p. 5.
131. *Ibid.*, p. 12.
132. ESCWA, *World Summit on Sustainable Development Assessment for the ESCWA Region*, (United Nations, New York, 2002), pp. 28-29.
133. *Ibid.*, p. 29.
134. UNEP/ROWA, n. 29, pp. 19-20.
135. ESCWA, n. 132, p. 26.
136. UNEP/ROWA, n. 29, p. 4.
137. MWA, n. 64, p. 19.
138. Global Forest Watch. "Frequently Asked Questions" [Online: web] Accessed on 23th June, 2008 URL:http://www.globalforestwatch.org/english/faqs.html.
139. Sherbinin, n. 21, p. 9.
140. Food and Agriculture Organization (FAO), *Global Forest Resources Assessment 2000*, (Rome: FAO, 2001), p. 12.
141. Sherbinin, n. 21, pp. 9-10.
142. UNEP, n. 17, p. 161.
143. Ali Abahussain, n. 34, p. 538.
144. FAO, n. 140, p. 12.
145. UNEP, n. 17, p. 162.
146. *Ibid.*
147. UNEP/ROWA, n. 29, p. 7.
148. Owen, Roger and Sevket Pamuk, *A History of Middle East Economies in the Twentieth Century,* (London: I.B. Tauris Publication, 1988), p. 202.
149. Mahmoud H. Fouad, "Petrodollars and Economic Development in the Middle East", *The Middle East Journal* (Washington, D.C.), vol. 32, no. 3, 1978, p. 307.
150. Al-Deen, Anwar Shaikh and Osama El-Kholy, *Industry and Sustainable*

Development in the Arab Region, (Manama: Arabian Gulf University, 2001), p. 4.

151. Al-Faris, A.F., "Public Expenditure and Economic Growth in the Gulf Cooperation Council Countries", *Applied Economics*, (London), vol. 34, 2002, p. 1187.
152. Knauerhase, Ramon "The Oil Producing Middle East States", *Current History*, (Philadelphia) vol. 76, no. 443, 1979, p. 10.
153. Presly, John R., *A Guide to the Saudi Arabian Economy* (Hong Kong: Macmillan, 1984), p. 53.
154. "Remarkable Expansion in Arab Ports". *The Arab Economist,* vol. 10, no. 108, September 1978, pp. 9-10.
155. Issawi, Charles, "Growth and Structural Change in the Middle East", *The Middle East Journal,* vol. 25, no. 3, 1971, p. 315.
156. Ibrahim, Saad Eddin, *New Arab Social Order: A Study of the Social Impact of Oil Wealth* (Boulder: West View Press, 1982), p. 105.
157. Al-Deen, n. 150, p. 7.

III

Environmental Administration in the GCC Countries

Public Administration represents the authority system for government in action, and is expected to carry out politically determined objectives, goals and values. Therefore, the most critical attribute of public administration is its place in the political system and the paramount influence it has on the implementation of sustainable development policies and programmes at the national level. "Environmental issues have an intrinsically transnational or global dimension, in which the actions of one party will affect the welfare of other interested parties."[1] In other words, environmental problems experienced at any given political level frequently have their origins at locations other than where their impact is most acutely felt.[2] Therefore, "(u)ndoubtedly, there is a growing global consensus that the environmental harm caused by some is a threat to all."[3]

This ramifying and ever changing character of environmental problems and the inability of governments solely by their own efforts to fully protect their environment and natural resources made environmental policy a subject for inter-governmental and international action.[4] No crisis in history has so clearly demonstrated the interdependence of nation states as the environmental crisis. The pressures wielded by the forces of economic globalization and technological change are transforming the global environment as never before.[5] Now "(n)o exit option remains for the nation state: the modern complex ecological interdependence binds all nations, which creates a new dependence of individual nation states—even the largest, most powerful ones—on the community of all other nations."[6]

> It is one of the ironies of history that the principle of national sovereignty and equality received its triumphal confirmation in the Charter of the United Nations at the time when the introduction of atomic weapons, the development of communications, the rapid industrialization and the awakening consciousness of the environmental risk made it unmistakable clear that all of humanity is interdependent and that the old concept of sovereignty is inadequate.[7]

Nevertheless, it is at the national level where the principal tasks of environmental protection must be performed.[8] However, "(g)lobalization and its consequences for the states and governments have serious implications for modern government and public administration in the twenty-first century."[9] The roles and responsibilities of the administrative system increased manifold. Similarly, the issues under its control became diverse, complex and highly inter-connected.

"In fact, the evidence indicates that Arab political systems lag behind the profound changes their societies are undergoing, instead of directing them into fruitful policies to manage the transition. Incumbent regimes have not developed clear, consistent national objectives with worthy strategies to achieve them."[10] Significantly in the GCC countries the rapid socio-economic changes "produced serious environmental management problems. State environmental authorities are generally young, inadequately staffed and short of the expertise needed not only to address current issues but also a substantial backlog of environmental problems, both in depleting natural resources and in polluting the environment."[11]

This chapter examines the role of the State in environmental protection and sustainable development. It analyses the administrative system in the GCC countries with an emphasis on its expansion, functions and reforms. It also traces the evolution of environmental administration in the GCC countries. The relationships of GCC countries' environmental management system with regional and international environmental institutional arrangements are also studied in this chapter.

I. State and Environmental Problems

Historically, States did not easily accept environmental responsibility.[12]

"As globalization continues apace, environmental problems have become increasingly complex, in some cases threatening the sustainability of human livelihoods in both rich and poor countries."[13] Humanity in the twenty-first century faces a new generation of environmental challenges. These differ significantly from past environmental problems. These new environmental issues share several common features. They are global in scope, transcending national boundaries and affecting all, or substantial portions of, the world's population and natural resources. Their long-term consequences are irreversible and far-reaching. The growing complexity of environmental problems makes it more difficult to get an overview of a specific problem in all its dimensions—ecological, economic, sociological and political.[14]

To effectively address "the integrated and interdependent nature of the new challenges and issues (which) contrasts sharply with the kind of institutions that exists today,"[15] an unprecedented level of international coordination and collaboration involving governments, inter-governmental bodies, the private sector and civil society is urgently required. Significantly, the complex nature of environmental problems are characterised by considerable degree of scientific uncertainties concerning their causes, impacts, feedbacks, and the interrelationships among complex natural and social parameters.

However "(u)ntil this point in history the nations of the world have lacked considered, comprehensive policies for managing the environment... Although changes have been taking place for a long time, they seem to have reached a threshold recently that has made public aware of them."[16] Similarly "the organization and procedures that the administrative state has developed for environmental protections often prove themselves to be dramatically ineffective."[17] The policy measures initiated by the governments were "conventional, involving modest reforms to the established procedures and structures of an administrative arrangement."[18] At the international level also "it was increasingly apparent that the existing network of global institutions centred on the United Nations was inadequate for the urgent task of taking remedial action to counter global process of environmental change."[19] Critical threats to the earth's habitability demand that human kind rise to the challenge of creating a new and more effective system of international environmental governance.[20]

Effective management of environmental issues is one of the most difficult areas of public action, demanding inputs of scientific and technical knowledge and of skills in the organization, planning, and coordination of complex programmes that are nowhere common attributes of government.[21] This led to an increasing concern for reorganization of State machineries and institutions, which have the responsibility to determine, guide and ensure sustainable development. In this regard "it has become clear, however, that earnest and bold departures from the past will have to be taken nationally and internationally if significant progress is to be made."[22]

"A growing appreciation of the complexity and interrelated character of environmental problems led first to a proliferation of administrative rules and programmes."[23] Accordingly there was a remarkable extension of the governmental role in environmental management during the last three decades of the twentieth century.[24]

> "All over the globe governments have been implementing actions, institutions, legal frameworks and public policies dealing with environmental protection. Problems related to the environment constitute a daily preoccupation of government in all parts of the world. Public administration at all levels has adapted itself to these new sets of priorities by creating new institutions and regulations."[25]

"In response to increased industrialization and populations, and the accompanying pollution, as well as better scientific information about the global and transboundary nature of environmental problems, nations have signed an increasing number of multilateral agreements to address an array of these problems. While the development of agreements in itself is a noteworthy accomplishment, their effectiveness in correcting problems depends on implementation by the parties."[26] In other words, it is effective implementation by States at the national level which will ensure success of global treaties.

Standing at the intersection between domestic, international, and global pressures, the State is the preeminent institution with requisite political authority and steering capacity to tackle ecological problems through multilateral environmental agreements and regulations of natural resources management.[27] In this regard States enjoy certain comparative advantages in Global Environmental Governance (GEG). They are well-established actors, equipped with the necessary tools to participate both in international environmental law-making and in its implementation. States have the capacity to negotiate global environmental agreements and adopt required measures to implement the same under its jurisdiction and territorial control. International efforts, regional or global, occur only with national participation or consent. The effectiveness of the United Nations and of its specialized agencies and affiliated organizations depends upon the support and the cooperation of national governments.[28] Therefore, the participation of States in international environmental governance is an asset that cannot be easily left aside.

Today, international environmental regimes led to new types of normative development, blurring the distinction between legally binding and non-legally binding norms, public and private standard setting, and international and domestic law.[29] Accordingly, States have to find their place within a complex environmental governance structure, which is based on a multitude of international environmental agreements, integrates a broad variety of actors, and extends across multiple and differing layers of governance, depending on the environmental problem at hand.

Despite the increasing importance of other actors in the international environmental process, states remain the dominant players in both the development and implementation of international environmental law. The ever expanding international organizations, under the umbrella of globalization and advancement of information and communication technologies can be a suitable example to be cited. These international organizations, lack the authority and capacity to implement international norms directly, and hence the role of State administrative arrangements is essential and critical.

Most of the substantive content of international environmental law—whether in the form of treaties or softer instruments such as codes of conduct or guidelines—are developed through a process of inter-State negotiation, even if other actors may play significant roles in that process. And implementation of these norms depends primarily on national action: enactment of international standards into domestic law, establishment of domestic permitting procedures, monitoring and reporting on regulated activities, punishment of violations, and judicial application.[30] It may be argued that States are a necessary intermediate level for the implementation of international environmental standards. Only States have sufficient legislative means at hand and it can provide the indispensable administrative infrastructure.[31]

This growing role of the State in GEG is due to the fact that new forms of governance provide the State much broader thematic scope to intervene and many more instruments to influence the behaviour of other actors under its territorial jurisdictions. While it is true that some traditional mechanisms were weakened due to globalization and the emergence of non-State actors in the global scene, the overall assessment of the role of the State in international environmental law is positive and proactive. Therefore, the emerging legal and institutional arrangement to address environmental problems is "not confronted with a paradigm shift but is experiencing a transformation of the role of the state that may—if properly used—be much to the benefit of international environmental law as a whole."[32]

At the national level, administrative institutional arrangements shape the process through which policy decisions are formulated and implemented. "Many institutions influence environmental policy choice and their implementation. Business and industry, federal and provincial government agencies, political parties, legislatures, judiciary, media and international organizations all play important roles. The variations in their responsibilities and in the rules governing their interactions have significant influence on environmental policy in each nation."[33]

Finally, it is the administrative system which translates the will of State. It plays the dynamic role of coordinating diverse actors in formulating and implementing the environmental policies and decisions. Therefore, a critical analysis of the nature and character of administrative arrangements is essential to determine the role of the State in ensuring sustainable development.

II. Administrative System in the GCC Countries

The State is the principal means by which the society is guided towards socio-economic developments. Bureaucracy translates the will of the State through planning and implementation of essential and far reaching socio-economic programmes. In the GCC countries, as elsewhere, it is the administrative system which is the main vehicle for the delivering of services, for social control and for the discharge of social justice. These governments cannot achieve its predetermined developmental objectives without an effective and efficient administrative institutional mechanism. "The role of Arab bureaucracies has been pivotal in the conceptualisation, design, formalization, implementation of developmental activities. The increasing state power underscores the strategic position of the bureaucracy in almost every Arab country."[34]

Historically the overall model of governance in the GCC countries is State-led, State-centred, and State-regulated. The rental State which emerged out of natural sources of wealth controlled by the State, "together with a political structure which took the form of traditional monarchies dominated by one family gave rise to public governance that minimises the role and participation of its civil society, magnifies the role of the state in the area of social welfare and distribution of rent."[35]

During the second half of the 20th century, the GCC countries "pursued a path of development through comprehensive central plans that incorporated policies, projects, and programmes formulated by the national governments. These development plans also required the creation of numerous organizational structures to implement proposed policies and objectives."[36] In the economic sphere the expansion of the State's role in the GCC countries was most remarkable "regardless of the size, political-institutional history, wealth or socio-political doctrine."[37] During 1970s and 1980s the public sector in these countries went through a wave of exponential growth in all sectors. Public investment and unregulated expenditure were the main source. As a result, the size of the public sector, public budget and public employment were on a growth path over more than three decades.

"An inflated public sector, an over regulated economy along with a system of bureaucratic administration relying on centralized command and control with little public accountability became a hindrance to growth and development and a source of its stagnation."[38] Large governments also permitted the State elites to monitor, and control their citizens to a greater extent than it was in the past, particularly through the expansion of their coercive apparatus—the military, the police, and the intelligence services.

i. Expansion of the Administrative System in the GCC Countries

The growth of government in the Gulf Monarchies did not actually begin with the oil boom of the 1970s. For example, Kuwait established a centralized Planning Board in 1962 and adopted its first Five Year Plan in 1967. Similarly, in Saudi Arabia, then Crown Prince Faysal's 1962 ten point reform programme led to administrative growth as the government sought to make good in its promise to foster educational, economic and infrastructure development. Four major Ministries were created in the 1960s.[39]

Before oil, government in the Arabian Peninsula was a very limited thing. These countries "did not have even the simplest type of (modern) administrative, economic and social organization or institution."[40] The traditional model of administration known in the oil Monarchies till the middle of the twentieth century was represented by the tribal style, the Clan convention and the Sheikhdom system. Basically "the State consisted of some ruling family members and a few trusted policy advisers. British colonialism brought a measure of bureaucratisation to the smaller States, particularly in the area of customs collection and the military."[41] Before independence in 1971, it was hard to speak of government in the bureaucratic sense in Qatar, the United Arab Emirates or Oman, outside of British advisers and British organized military and police units. According to Gause, "even at the turn of the twentieth century, you could assemble the entire 'civil service' of these States in one large reception room, and still have space left for the British advisers."[42]

However, the oil boom of 1973 spurred the growth of government in all six States. This large scale expansion of administrative arrangements "resulted from several factors: (1) unanticipated growth in some social and economic indicators (e.g. increase in the population including school age children; urbanization; imports; consumption; etc.), (2) increase in State revenues and expenditures, and (3) increased need of regulatory activities."[43] Much of this steady but uncontrolled growth in bureaucracy occurred spontaneously, in response to crises situations with little or no organizational planning.[44]

Mobilist regimes of the GCC countries generated unmet demands on an unprecedented scale. "If the bureaucracy does not provide adequate services the populace will be resentful and political system possibly destabilized by alienation rooted in economic shortage and dislocation, thus undermining ambitious long range-plans for modernization."[45] Accordingly new waves of government agencies and institutions were established which were structurally identical to those in the advanced countries. By the end of the 1980s these States built up large, if not bloated, administrative apparatus.

In Saudi Arabia seven Ministries were created in the 1970s. Bahrain implemented a new administrative structure, replacing twenty-one separate departments which grew up during the 1950s and 1960s with the thirteen member cabinet. In 1975 four new Ministries were created in Bahrain. The entire Federal structure of the UAE was developed after independence in 1971, along with the expansion in the bureaucracies of each of the seven Emirates themselves. A formal Council of Ministers was established in Oman only in 1971, but rapidly expanded since then to include eighteen formal Ministries and a number of independent development organizations reporting directly to the Sultan.[46]

In Saudi Arabia "(c)ivil service employees, who numbered not more than a few hundred in 1950, increased to about 37,000 in 1962-63 to 85,000 in 1970-71 and to over 245,000 in 1979-80. The ratio of public employees to the total population in the early 1980s was approximately 3.5 to 4 per cent, which is admittedly not excessive, but government civil servants represented 10 per cent of the total labour force and 13 per cent if one counts non-career personnel."[47] The size of the civil services in Kuwait more than doubled between 1966 and 1976 and then increased another 25 per cent by 1983. Between 1971 and 1986, the size of the civil service in Qatar almost tripled.[48]

Similarly in Kuwait the "numbers of government employees grew rapidly from 22,073 in 1966 to 113,274 in 1976, to 145,451 in 1980. According to official figures, government employees represented 12.5 per cent of the population and about 34 per cent of the total labour force of Kuwait in 1975."[49]

Clearly, the sudden wealth contributed to the rapid expansion of government agencies and to the growth of the labour force in the public and the private sectors.

ii. Functions of the Administrative System in GCC Countries

Public administration is embedded in its social environment and an integral part of it. Administration is a cultural and social product which reflects the values of society as a whole.[50] Similarly, the administrative system in GCC countries is not an exception and the same cannot be separated from the compelling political contexts. Enormous powers in the hands of Kings, Presidents, and Prime Ministers are uniformity centralized, excessive and mostly unchecked.

"Historically, the royal families used the apparatus of the state to present themselves as the 'natural' outgrowth of tribal forces in society, the true representatives of the *essence* of their nation. By doing so, they nullified any potential claims to rulership that other tribal chieftains or local notables might have had, thus eliminating an important source of possible opposition or, for that matter, societal independence. With varying degrees of success, they also sought to cultivate additional legitimacy on religious grounds, presenting themselves as the embodiment of religious piety and righteousness."[51]

The bureaucratic system acts as the regime's servant rather than as a source of independent professional decision-making.[52] The bureaucracy is necessarily subordinate to the political leadership in matters considered crucial to regime enhancement, legitimacy, and survival.[53] Tribal, religious, ethnic or regional interest cannot substitute for public interest as legitimizing foundations of political actions. At the same time, political leaders in these countries grew mistrustful of opposition and regularly increased concentration of powers in their hands, augmenting regime authoritarianism and further weakening public participation in governing. "As in Europe, the monarchies of the Middle East created centralized and repressive states to achieve tremendous social, political, and economic transformations in a short period of time."[54] Although the GCC countries "suffered substantial and deep economic and political reverses since the global recession of the early 1980s, they have managed to retain enough powers to (i) hold onto the reins of power and not be overwhelmed by societal pressures; (ii) manipulate enough social and cultural values to retain just enough popular legitimacy."[55]

Societal culture also lends support to the centralized, authoritarian character of the GCC States, with strong organizational cultures embedded within a regional culture based on tradition, religious values and community.[56]

> ...the major Arab cultural characteristics are derived from the influence of Islam, the Arabic legacy and the Bedouin way of life. In particular, there is a high degree of collectivism within 'in-groups' (tribe or extended family) and high individualism with 'out-groups' (non-kin and guest workers). In addition, tribal loyalty; pride in tradition; dependence on relatives and friends; emphasis on consultation with in-groups but authoritarianism with out-groups; *wasta* or the use of networks or personal connections and high uncertainty avoidance are important features of Arab culture that are expressed in organizational settings.[57]

In reaction, bureaucracies substituted "routine work, self-serving behaviour, and survival techniques to risk-taking management. Such bureaucratic behaviour has been a major obstacle to numerous campaigns for administrative reform, generally decreed by the political leaders. Thus, avoidance of responsibility, apathy, or inaction became among the survival technique frequently employed by bureaucrats."[58] The weak capacity for innovation coupled with clerkism in administration hampers effective implementation of development goals.[59]

Administrative system in the GCC countries "although simple until recently, is being steadily inflated due to an unclear vision of future objectives and the abundance of financial resources. It is suffering from structural and behavioural defects of both external and internal origin."[60] Bureaucratic dysfunctions are rampant in the midst of the GCC countries' political systems with excessive powers and unrestrained habits of intervention in every aspect of society. "During the past four decades public administration has been saddled with socio-economic development that has not served the cause of equity and social justice in the society."[61] The "list of bureaucratic deficiencies incorporates adjectives such as lethargic, apathetic, arrogant, corrupt, insensitive to the masses, non-innovative, venal and incompetent."[62]

Jreisat highlights "an alarming deterioration of developmental efforts in the Arab states since 1975. Several indicators confirm this trend: negative economic growth, high unemployment, hyper inflation, low investment in human development, and huge public debts."[63] Such a deplorable economic performance is clearly illustrative of fundamental defects in policy making and policy implementation.

The major problems before the GCC countries are "that their governments have found themselves obliged to act in several fields and expand their own activities and tasks. In addition, they have dominated the economy by establishing public institutions and firms. These agencies often fail to perform even their traditional tasks satisfactorily, and to be under an obligation to perform new development tasks, in addition to the traditional means lowering the standard of performance even further."[64]

These countries also lack adequate skilled manpower to cope with the emerging challenges. Almost in all the GCC countries a "large percentage of personnel in government agencies are labourers and servants. This category sometimes reaches 50 per cent of the total of government personnel. It is obvious that such a large percentage reflects the social security role of job provision in the public sectors. In the case of Kuwait, in spite of its precedence in education, the illiterate and those with only reading and writing skills still represent a large percentage of the total government personnel. The illiterates in Qatar constitute more than half the total government personnel, and a substantial percentage of the mixed sector. The situation in other states in no different."[65]

Oil revenues allowed these States to build large bureaucratic systems to provide important services, like health, and education directly to citizens. Bureaucrats in these countries have "the potential for developing their own centre of power, social relationships, and political ideals and goals. An unintended ramification is a potential loss of control over the population by the rulers as this control is increasingly mediated by possibly disloyal bureaucracy."[66]

Similarly, it was the same oil wealth which permitted the governments to create an infrastructure of control, limiting the political space available for their citizens to discuss issues and organize politically. Development decisions and plans "like most policy-making, have been top-down and communicated by decree or edict."[67] While citing the example of Saudi bureaucracy, Kiren Aziz Chaudhry says:

> Oil boom created new channels through which resources circulated within the bureaucracy, rendering extractive and regulatory agencies obsolete and reorienting bureaus towards distributive branches of government. Exogenous resources changed the institutional shape, organization, and capacities of the Saudi bureaucracy, severing earlier links between taxation and organizational change. The extractive and regulatory branches of the bureaucracy were replaced with dozens of distributive agencies that managed the economy through the deployment of oil revenues.[68]

Instead of effectively managing the transition, muddled political processes failed "to provide meaningful institutionalized participation. Incumbent regimes have not developed clear, consistent national objectives with worthy strategies to achieve them."[69] In the GCC countries "although national development is undermined by the poor performance of the bureaucracy, any reforms that affect the power relationships of the dominant elite are unlikely to be entertained."[70] Accordingly any "political/administrative change in the Arab World is not tolerated if it tampers with the extraordinary powers and privileges of the ruling group or dynasty."[71]

In total contrast with the emerging global trend of democratic decentralization, "(t)hese Gulf Monarchies have not learned the lessons of sharing responsibility and control with citizens, local authorities, or the private sector. Nor have these systems even begun to effectively employ modern notions of accountability in managing the State."[72] Luciani was arguing most emphatically that the "rentier nature of the state is a strong factor in discouraging democratization in all countries that have access to oil rent, and I would be surprised if any of the rentier states were to democratize."[73]

Likewise the task of the local agency is "no longer that of the previous traditional symbol or representative of the central authority or, at its best, a local agency offering limited services in its field of specialization. It is now that of an active agency in the dynamic development"[74] process of a nation. However, in the GCC countries the "local authorities have not been activated to share in the responsibilities of developing their community mainly because of dominance by the Central Governments."[75]

> In the GCC countries, "...effective public sector management is increasingly seen as more than just modernizing state institutions, (but) it is *also about fostering dynamic partnerships with civil society* and the private sector in order to improve the quality of service delivery, enhance social responsibilities and *ensure the broad participation of citizens in decision-making.*"[76] (Emphasis added)

In these countries "even where an emergent civil society is said to exist, it is rather elitist in nature, since large masses of the people are either marginalized within civil society—for example organized labour—or excluded from it—for, the urban and rural poor."[77]

iii. Reforms

> "Reforming public administration is a central and urgent task for Arab countries; it lies at the core of the wider agenda of institutional reform. The goals of reform include raising productivity and efficiency in public services and administration, establishing merit as the basis for recruitment; transparency and equity in the system of remuneration and incentives; reforming tax systems to promote equity and

> efficiency; exercising appropriate degree of regulation and measures; and improving access to information and markets..."[78]

Among other things, bureaucracy needs "to respond adequately to the challenges of socio-economic development. Further in order to reduce the gap between the bureaucracy and the citizenry, Arab political leaders need to create conditions for citizen involvement in the administration of their society. These are minimum conditions for administrative capacitation in the Arab world."[79]

However, lack of adjustment or adaptation in the political governance provided no strong impetus for reforming and improving public sector institutions and for enhancing the role of civil society in development. As a result, the inflated and inefficient public sector institutions functioned within weak public accountability. The public bureaucracy as the main instrument for development policy implementation became a major source of distortion, waste, and corruption, thus hindering rather than facilitating and accelerating growth and development.[80]

"Lacking the capacity to perform their duties and suffering their own constant shortcomings, contemporary Arab bureaucracies appeared in acute need of fundamental reforms"[81] and reorganization. "Despite the apparent vibrancy of ... international trends, especially when promulgated by institutions such as the UN (United Nations), the Gulf states appear to be highly resistant to administrative modernization."[82] Overall, the existing governance system in "the Gulf region appears to have produced an environment of rigidity and resistance to administrative reform."[83]

The transition from centralized, hierarchical patterns of organizations and management to more participatory modes of decision making is more than an organizational issue. It requires a different kind of socialization in the society and the commitment of forces inside and outside the organization to new inclusionary visions and values.[84] The experiences across the world "indicate that a chief obstacle to development is not insufficient finance, as it is widely believed, but lack of administrative potentials capable of successful running and coordination of projects as well as realising the desired objective."[85]

Poor performance and the "limited rationality in Arab bureaucracy means that administrative reform is hindered by a range of factors such as: overstaffing, low pay and productivity, a shortage of professional managers, excessive centralized decision-making, corruption, lack of participation, outmoded systems, expansion, laxity and avoidance of responsibilities."[86] One of the critical development factors in the GCC countries is "the shortage of able and appropriately educated and trained management manpower resources. A considerable amount of effort and resources, both financial and human, have been expended over the past several decades to develop, improve, and enhance the management capabilities of the civil services of the various Arab states."[87]

However, the specialized development organizations established in the past "to provide technical assistance, training, and research for individual countries for all Arab States are torn by internal feuds, bursts of poor leadership, and lack of resources. The task of generating administrative knowledge and providing technical assistance is still left to foreign consultants, institutions, and publications. Arab developmental institutions simply have not developed sufficiently from within to be able to shoulder the responsibilities thrust upon them."[88]

The outcome of these administrative reform measures in the GCC countries are "not commensurate with the extensive investments in institutions and programmes designated to build needed administrative capacities. So far, advanced academic educations as well as practical training in modern management have made only a small difference in building institutional capacities, solving chronic managerial problems, or responding to pressing managerial needs."[89]

> Research in this area is further exacerbated by the lack of official documentation publicly available concerning reform efforts. This is in line with major Arab cultural characteristics and practices, where the management culture is 'based on talking, not writing'. As a consequence, there is a lack of recorded information about policy decisions. Any information tends to be unreliable and restricted as most decisions are based on the personal preferences of the most senior leaders. For instance, the promotion of quality management in Bahrain's health service was the consequence of a Prime Ministerial order in the form of a personal communication to senior officials. Furthermore, most official publications lack detail on implementation, and have the aim

> of raising public expectation; 'the emphasis is objective—rather than procedure-oriented.'[90]

Attaching high priority to administrative reforms is a "necessary precondition to bringing about change. Nevertheless, rhetoric alone has achieved little and a more direct understanding of what education and training can do to help improve public administration in the regions and, more specifically, what kinds of management and administrative problems can be effectively addressed through educational programmes is needed."[91]

The present time might be characterised as a period of imbalance and transition, rapid changes in population, economy and environment, an increasing gap between the rich and the poor and increasing disequilibria between growth and the capacity of the environment to sustain it.[92] Equally, "(t)he narrowness of the economic base of the oil-producing countries in the peninsula has serious implications for the future, given the extreme shortage of water, the scarcity of arable land, and the primitiveness of the skills, institutions, and forms of organization essential to industrial development."[93] To face such a mounting challenge with limited natural resources and achieve objectives of sustainable development, an efficient environmental administrative mechanism is crucial in the GCC countries.

III. Environment Administration in the GCC Countries

The earth's finite natural resources are under tremendous pressure today. The unprecedented level of human activities are taking their toll and governments across the globe are fast realizing the need to stem this tide, introduce corrective policies and programmes and pursue a path of sustainable development in utilizing the available natural resources.

> The complex character of environmental problems and the multidisciplinary inputs necessary to cope with them make the administration of environmental affairs especially susceptible to 'weak-link' hazards. Because environmental issues characteristically cut across functional and jurisdictional boundaries, their management characteristically requires coordinated action in numbers of different agencies

> and jurisdictions. Inadequacy or failure at any point in a multi-sectored effort may reduce or destroy the effectiveness of the entire effort.[94]

The evolving framework of international environmental law and the development of national administrative arrangements provide a sound basis for addressing the major environmental problems of the twenty-first century and creating a sustainable future. The National Governments are ultimately responsible for taking legal and related measures to address environmental threats and achieve sustainable development.[95] It must be underpinned by a more coherent and coordinated approach among international environmental instruments.

Globalization played a crucial role in shifting the "focus from government to governance. Command-and-control strategies are losing favour while market-based mechanisms, voluntary initiatives, and partnerships with non-governmental organizations have gained wider acceptance. However, the shift to discussions of governance does not imply a reduction in the role of government. Governments remain central actors in environmental policy. They ensure the delivery of environmental protection to citizens, and help create the rules, norms, and many organizations that ensure environmental protection."[96]

Increasingly, environmental problems are too complex to be resolved through fixed international rules or straightforward exercises of State sovereignty. However, it has to be addressed through collaborative arrangements that pool and recombine the resources and competencies of a variety of State and non-State actors. These actors include the various organs of governments, multilateral institutions and the independent scientific community.[97]

In order to achieve these objectives the environmental administrative arrangements in the State needs to work with a wide range of actors. Environmental awareness is slowly but surely growing in the GCC countries as well, the proof of which lies in the measures initiated and implemented by these governments to protect and conserve the regions natural resources. The environmental administrative systems of the GCC countries are also actively working with institutions at the regional and international level.

All the GCC countries have environmental institutional mechanism in place. These arrangements were restructured in the recent past. The newly established or restructured arrangements were given higher political standing. At present two countries have Ministers for Environment in their cabinets, namely Oman (Ministry of Regional Municipalities and Environment) and Bahrain (Ministry of Housing, Municipalities and Environment).[98] Among the GCC countries, Oman was the first to establish a Ministry for Environment and Water in 1984. This Ministry, along with the Council for Conservation of the Environment and Prevention of Pollution were then merged into a new Ministry of Regional Municipalities and Environment in 1991. Other GCC countries also created environmental institutions, although not necessarily at Cabinet levels. Environmental Protection Councils were replaced by Environmental Authorities at the General Directorate level in Bahrain and Kuwait. UAE enacted a Federal law in 1993 creating the Federal Environment Agency, which is the first country-wide institution with legal powers to protect and conserve the environment.[99]

Saudi Arabia set up the Meteorology and Environmental Protection Administration (MEPA) by Royal Decree in 1981. MEPA is now the central authority responsible for environmental affairs at the national level. Saudi Arabia also formed environmental units in other relevant Ministries, namely in the Ministry of Agriculture and Water, the Ministry of Petroleum and Mineral Resources, the Ministry of Municipalities and Rural Affairs, the Ministry of Industry and Electricity, and the Ministry of Health. Some of the GCC countries also established separate institutions to deal with specific environmental issues (for example, the national committees and commissions for wildlife conservation and development in Saudi Arabia, Bahrain, Oman and Kuwait).[100]

Despite the plethora of new institutions, however, programmes, laws, and institutions were often established haphazardly and are generally sectoral in nature focusing on specific sectors such as agriculture, water, fisheries, mineral resources, development, human settlements, industry, transport, and tourism. Recent recognition of the complex nature of many environmental concerns led to developing cross-cutting policy institutions. These commonly take the form of Inter-Ministerial or Interdepartmental Committees, and national environmental strategies developed in cooperation with sectoral departments.[101]

However, governments are now reformulating their environmental laws and regulations, and also establishing cross-cutting approaches to deal with the real complexity of natural resource management. Environmental Impact Assessment (EIA) is receiving more attention and its use is spreading. Environmental considerations are slowly becoming part of the planning process.[102] Therefore the main challenge facing most decision-makers in these countries is

> "policy integration, namely how to effectively formulate, integrate and implement multi-sectoral sustainable development policies. This requires coordination and consultation between government institutions, as well as complementary and coherence between policy instruments being implemented by different Ministries. These difficulties are exacerbated by the centralized, yet compartmentalized nature of governance."[103]

Key environmental issues for policy action of the GCC countries are the development of environmentally-sound water resource management, land-use planning, combating various forms of land degradation and desertification, management of hazardous and toxic wastes, integrated management of the marine and coastal environment, biodiversity conservation, and the management of urban air quality.[104]

Absence of a framework of national laws and regulations, policy guidelines and institutional arrangements that effectively support sustainable development remains a serious gap. Environmental institutions of these countries "suffer from shortages of qualified manpower, inadequate funding and uneasy relations with other government institutions whose cooperation is essential in dealing with environmental issues. This has resulted in delays and failures to implement policies and enforce laws."[105] Similarly, these GCC countries are "relatively closed to effective public debate about environmental problems, their governments are prone to the kind of distortions (such as subsidies and corruption) that make efficient resource management more difficult, and their industries are actively engaged in environmental innovation."[106]

Despite improvements in environmental governance in the GCC countries, "a significant gap remains regarding the ability of newly-established institutional frameworks to manage effectively the sustainable development process."[107] The proliferation of Multilateral Environmental Agreements (MEAs) over the past quarter century presented a new set of challenges and opportunities for policy-makers in these countries.

i. Evolution of Environmental Institutions in the GCC Countries

The influences of globalization trends, innovations in information and communication technologies and easy movement of goods and services had a significant impact on the practice of governance and public administration in the GCC countries. These forces not only stimulated new opportunities but also presented many challenges requiring fundamental changes in the overall approach to the process of governance. Governments in the GCC countries responded positively to the requirements of global environmental governance.

There is a significant increase in the environmental commitments of the GCC countries over the years. This is manifested in the formulation of national environmental strategies and related plans of action, the ratification of multilateral and regional environmental agreements, conventions, treaties and protocols and the enactment of a number of laws and regulations in support of these environmental policies and directives. These environmental obligations were translated into the establishment of new environmental organizations and research institutions. Moreover, since the 1990s, these institutional arrangements underwent the processes of restructuring and strengthening to respond to the emerging complex environmental threats.[108]

The command-and-control approach, through legislation, is still the main environmental management tool in almost all the GCC countries. Governments introduced a number of other approaches in environmental management including technical assistance, advisory services, training, tax exemptions, cheap credit and fiscal incentives and disincentives. A number of national laws and decrees dealing with environmental protections were adopted within the past two decades.[109] These include legislations to address desertification, scarcity of freshwater, pollution, management of hazardous and toxic wastes, and conservation of biodiversity.

Environmental conceptual frameworks developed at the regional and international level influenced the structure of institutions responsible for environmental management and sustainable development in the GCC countries. Most significantly, these countries showed commitments and readiness to restructure the environmental institutions in order to respond more effectively to changing needs and priorities. Environmental institutional mechanisms in these countries generally experienced three periods of restructuring, each responding to changes in the conceptual framework regarding environmental management. Table 3.1 illustrates the transformation of the primary national environmental institutions in the GCC countries over the past three decades.

A. Shift from the Municipalities to the State (1960s-1980s)

"Under the Ottoman Empire and the subsequent French and British protectorates in the Arab region, while the management of natural resources remained centralized due to their economic contributions and resulting revenue streams, environmental management was largely the responsibility of municipalities."[110] The shift towards national level responsibility for environmental protection and natural resource management emerged following the United Nations Conference on the Human Environment (Stockholm Conference), 1972. The Conference called upon the National Governments to ensure the establishment of appropriate national institutions and "(entrust them) with the task of planning, managing or controlling the environmental resources of States with a view to enhancing environmental quality and sustainability." [111] This sets the stage for the creation of national level environmental institutions and enactment of legislations in the GCC countries.[112]

Initially the GCC countries chose to establish Environmental Committees and Councils instead of functional Ministries. Environmental Protection Councils were often cross-sectoral in nature and addressed issues ranging from water quality to the preservation of wildlife. However, these Councils operated mostly at academic and technical levels and rarely at a political level. Moreover, Ministries of Health tended to be the dominant players in Inter-Ministerial Councils and Committees until the 1990s.[113]

Given the initial perspective of environment as a purely public health concern, environmental responsibilities were at first carried out by environmental health departments in Ministries of Health to cover issues such as water quality, air quality, noise pollution, radioactive waste and pesticide residue in food and occupational health. However, growing demand for environmental services and infrastructure called for a centralized environmental management.

Table 3.1: Evolution of Environmental Institutions in the GCC Countries

	1972-1992			1992-2000			2000-2002		
	Institution	*Date*	*Status*	*Institution*	*Date*	*Status*	*Institution*	*Date*	*Status*
Bahrain	Environmental Protection Committee	1980	Dissolved	Ministry of Housing, Municipalities and (includes Environmental Affairs Agency)	1995	Functional	Ministry of Municipality Affairs and Environmental Affairs	…	Restructured
				National Committee for the Protection of Wildlife	2000			2002	Functional
Kuwait	Environmental Protection Council	1980	Dissolved	Environmental Public Authority	1995	Functional	Unchanged		Functional
				Supreme Council of EPA	1995	Functional	Unchanged		Functional
Oman	Ministry of Environment	Early 1980s	Expanded	Ministry of Regional Municipalities and Environment	1991	Expanded	Ministry of Regional Municipalities, Environment and Water Resources	2001	Functional
	Ministry of Regional Municipalities	1985	Expanded						
Qatar	Environment Protection Committee	1981	Dissolved	Environment Department, Ministry of Municipal Affairs and Agriculture	1995	Dissolved	Supreme Council for the Environment and Natural Reserves	2000	Functional

(*Contd.*)

	1972-1992			1992-2000			2000-2002		
	Institution	*Date*	*Status*	*Institution*	*Date*	*Status*	*Institution*	*Date*	*Status*
Saudi Arabia	Meteorological and Environment Protection Administration (Ministry of Defence and Aviation)	1980	Functional	Unchanged		Renamed	Presidency of Meteorology and Environment (Ministry of Defence and Aviation)	2002	Functional
	National Commission for Wildlife Conservation and Development,	1985	Functional	Unchanged			Unchanged		...
	Ministry Foreign Affairs Ministerial Committee on Environment	1990	Functional	Unchanged			Unchanged		...
							National Preparatory Committee (WSSD)		Functional
UAE	Higher Environmental Council	1975	Dissolved 1993	Federal Environmental Authority	1993	Functional	Unchanged		Functional
	Higher Environment Committee	1975	Reconstituted in 1981	Unchanged			Unchanged		

Source: Compiled from ESCWA, *Governance for Sustainable Development in the Arab Region: Institutions and Instruments for Moving beyond an Environmental Management Culture* (New York: ESCWA, 2003), pp. 13-16.

Consequently, the environmental problems were increasingly managed from the top-down according to national development priorities.

During this phase the management of natural resources remained outside the environmental framework. The main focus was to manage mostly the consumption aspects and not the conservation of natural resources, particularly in the fields of petroleum, fisheries, agriculture and land use planning.

B. Strengthening Environmental Institutions (1990s)

The declaration of Rio Summit, 1992, and the adoption of the GCC Framework on Environment played a significant role in the restructuring of environmental governance in the GCC countries. The Rio Summit asked the governments "to effectively integrate environment and development in the policies and practices of each country, (since) it is essential to develop and implement integrated, enforceable and effective laws and regulations that are based upon sound social, ecological, economic and scientific principles."[114]

The new conceptual framework expanded the scope of environment management. As such, issues traditionally under the purview of Ministries in the areas of social and economic affairs began to fall within the mandate of environmental institutions. Inter-sectoral issues that caught the national attention include irrigation and water quality and quantity, solid waste management, health, urban planning and zoning, environmental impact assessments and project clearance.

This increased the scope of issues addressed by environmental institutions and agencies and subsequently expanded their responsibilities and administrative burdens.[115] Accordingly the GCC countries strengthened their environmental arrangements to enable them to handle their new responsibilities.

The stand-alone Ministers or Joint Ministries responsible for the environment were established in Bahrain (1995), Oman (1991) and Qatar (1995).[116] Additionally, new or restructured environmental agencies or authorities were established in Kuwait (1995), and UAE (1993).[117]

However, despite these institutional transformations, the new environmental governance remained inadequate to address the expanded scope of environmental issues from a multi-sectoral perspective.

C. Rethinking Institutional Arrangements (Early 2000s)

Preparations for the World Summit on Sustainable Development, Johannesburg stimulated renewed thinking with regard to institutional frameworks for sustainable development. Few changes occurred at a national level since 1997. For example, Saudi Arabia established environmental sections in some Ministries to facilitate work with environmental agencies. Oman also expanded the scope of the Ministry of Regional Municipalities and Environment to include the important issue of management of water resources.[118]

ii. Guiding Principles for Environmental Administration

Besides national legislations and laws, there are a number of regional and international declarations and conventions which govern the environmental administration in the GCC countries. Among them, there are two which need specific mention. These are the GCC Framework Agreement on Environment, 1997 and the Gulf Green Initiatives, 2007. The GCC Framework agreement governed the environmental affairs of the GCC countries for a period of more than ten years. It provided the direction for sustainable use of limited natural resource in these countries. The Gulf Green Initiative, 2007 is a comprehensive document, which intends to unify all legislations and rules related with environmental issues in the GCC countries. This is certainly going to guide the environmental governance of these oil monarchies in the years to come.

A. The GCC Framework Agreement on Environment (GCCFAE), 1997

The rapid socio-economic transformation during the last few decades in GCC States created excessive strain on its limited natural resources. These are considered a clear threat to the fragile environment of the region. To facilitate a sustainable economic growth, there should be a balancing means between economic development and environmental sources.

As a result of such direct connection between development and environment stability, the need for specific rules and regulations to guarantee both development and environmental elements was felt in the GCC countries. Within this framework, the Supreme Council of the GCC, during its sixth session held in Muscat (Oman), in 1985 agreed to initiate a number of measures to ensure sustainable development. The GCC States adopted a strategic framework 'General Policies and Principles for Environment protection'.[119] The Council called for setting up a comprehensive system for the protection of the environment, incorporating the basic rules for the protection of the environment.

In accordance with this decision, the GCC Secretariat General, in collaboration with Member States, prepared draft rules, regulations and procedures for the protection of the environment in GCC countries. The GCC Ministers responsible for Environmental Affairs, in their fourth meeting convened on 20th April, 1994 in Abu Dhabi, agreed to adopt these rules and regulations as "General Regulations of Environment in the GCC States." The Supreme Council of the GCC in its 16th Session held in Muscat in December 1995 authorized the Ministerial Council to adopt these regulations after the completion of review on legal and institutional arrangements at the national levels. Subsequently the Ministerial Council adopted them at their sixtieth Session held in September 1996.[120] These regulations came into force in 1997.

B. The Gulf Green Initiative, 2007

The GCC countries are in the process of unifying all regulations, laws, and legislations that deal with various aspects of natural resource management.[121] The need for a comprehensive approach was felt across the GCC countries in the recent years. For example, in February 2008 the *Shura* Council of Bahrain discussed elaborately on this topic. According to Dr. Bahiya Jawad Al Jishi, Council Member, "Bahrain never needed such a law. Now, however, the contexts have changed-environment is being given a major thrust. In view of the prevailing conditions, a law encompassing air, water, sea, land, soil, micro-organisms, flora and fauna, reefs and even roads and their environment will be considered."[122] Secondly, during the last decade the GCC countries adopted a number of regional and international conventions which always call for comprehensive response to cope with environmental threats.

In this background, the GCC Summit held at Doha in December 2007 launched the Gulf Green Initiative (GGI).[123] The Green Initiative, which is comprehensive in nature, includes the setting up of a pioneer environment agency tasked with protecting the Gulf environment and to draft sustainable development strategies for the Gulf region that would take into consideration the environmental and health impact of development plans. The first step would be to harmonize the GCC countries' environmental laws with the provisions of international agencies to address the pressing environmental issues plaguing the present. After establishing a common legal framework, a set of collective plans addressing the issues of air, earth and water pollution, radioactivity, chemical pollution, water depletion, etc. will be formulated under the GGI.

It will also define the course of action, such as sustainable production and consumption, protection of natural resources, environmental awareness and waste recycling. The GGI is considered to be a holistic approach to the issue of environmental protection, which cannot be disengaged from sustainable economic and social development strategies.[124] The GCC countries should initiate all possible measures to implement the GGI. The proposed Arab Regional Centre for Environmental Law (ARCEL) in Kuwait[125] and the Regional Centre for Environmental Disasters and Crises[126] will supplement the efforts to achieve GGI.

iii. Environmental Decision-Making and Implementation

Governance is a challenging prerequisite to achieving sustainable development. It includes strengthening the institutional and legal frameworks, nurturing equitable participation in decision-making and promoting effective participation of the civil society and the private sector in the decision-making process.[127] The contemporary global and regional conventions embody international commitments, which shape national actions in translating these commitments. More broadly, these Conventions, by defining both general and detailed objectives, provide a framework for focusing policy development, programme implementation and data collection and analysis.

The complexity of international instruments requires integrated approaches to policy formulation and implementation at both the national and international levels. This cuts across the traditional institutional boundaries in addressing the interrelated environmental issues and their global consequences. Therefore, while formulating policies and programmes related with environment, the authorities need to take into account the commitments agreed under the regional and international conventions. The lack of effective coordination among these institutions widens the gap between the adoption of international environmental instruments and their effective implementation.

Table 3.2: Environmental Institutions and Agencies in GCC Countries

Sl. No.	Country	Policy Institutions	Executive Agency
1.	Bahrain	National Committee on Environment and Wildlife	Public Commission for the Protection of Marine Resources, Environment and Wildlife
2.	Kuwait	Environment Public Authority	Environment Public Authority
3.	Oman	Council of Ministers	Ministry of Municipalities, Environment and Water Resources
4.	Qatar	Council of Ministers (Permanent Commission for Environmental Protection)	Supreme Council for the Environment and Natural Reserves
5.	Saudi Arabia	Ministerial Committee on Environment	Presidency of Meteorology and Environment, National Commission for Wildlife Conservation and Development,
6.	UAE	Federal National Council	Ministry of Environment and Water

Source: GRC, Green Gulf Report (Dubai: GRC, 2006), p. 7.

In Oman, Qatar and UAE, the environmental policy decisions are taken by the Cabinet of their respective countries. On the other hand, in Bahrain and Saudi Arabia an Inter-Ministerial mechanism is available to formulate environmental policies. However, in Kuwait it is the Environment Public Authority, a stand alone Ministry, which decides policies on environmental issues. On the implementation aspects, Kuwait, Oman and UAE, the environment Ministries of their respective countries execute the environmental decisions. However, Bahrain, Qatar and Saudi Arabia have a separate agency to implement the environmental policies and programmes. In a rare example of public governance, in Kuwait the same agency involves in environmental policy making as well as its implementation.

C. Issues in Implementation

In the GCC countries, the newly created environmental institutions face overwhelming tasks and responsibilities. They often suffer from a serious lack of human, technical and financial resources. One notable weakness is in implementation of legislation and enforcement of standards. As a result, the full and effective enforcement of environmental legislation and sanctions for non-compliance remains an elusive goal in these countries. Other important reasons for poor performance are the fragmentation and duplication of responsibilities, lack of people's participation and non-availability of adequate date for policy formulation and implementation.

A number of obstacles to coordination emerge at the national level. They may be horizontal in nature, surfacing across government Ministries and agencies (e.g. between National Focal Points for negotiation and policy implementation, or between the Environment Ministry or agency and Development Planning Authorities). Institutional constraints may also arise on the vertical dimension, across different levels of governmental administration.

Lack of coordination between many government entities is mostly visible in all the GCC countries in administration, regulation and development of water resources.[128] UNEP's report on *State of Environment in the Arab Region* highlights that in GCC countries, "water governance remains fragmented among Ministries, which generate conflicts of interest, lack of standardization of specifications and criteria, dispersal of information and excess expenditure. In view of the need to improve coordination, several Arab countries have established coordination mechanisms for institutional frameworks in the water sector that are responsible for formulating water policies and elaborating plans and strategies (e.g. Bahrain, UAE). Decentralization of water management is also emerging in some instances, complemented by the establishment and maintenance of water databanks at the governorate or local level."[129] The World Bank also reports lack of coordination among environmental authorities.

> In the GCC countries, the responsibility for the administration, regulation, and development of water supplies is rather fragmented between many government entities while Oman and recently Saudi Arabia have embarked on institutional reforms for integrated water resources management.

> Fragmented institutional arrangements frequently result in conflicting policies, political competition between agencies, and lack of a comprehensive and coordinated policy for the allocation, management and use of water supplies.[130]

Saudi Arabia took commendable initiatives to bring effective coordination among its agencies for the sustainable use of limited water resources. Earlier in Saudi Arabia, three Ministries were involved with water resource management and development, namely the Ministry of Planning, Ministry of Agriculture and Water Resources and Ministry of Municipalities. To consolidate the government efforts in the water sector, in 2003 Saudi Arabia announced the establishment of the Ministry of Water and Electricity, bringing together two vital aspects of its economy under one Ministerial roof.[131]

However, more capacity building is needed to train local and national officials in analytical and management tools, as well as in collecting the necessary data to prepare and implement plans. Indeed, while the legal and institutional framework is gradually being strengthened in terms of land-use planning, however, implementation and enforcement still lag behind. The formulation of databases and efforts to narrow the digital gap through information support systems could help to overcome these constraints.[132]

Mastering modern tools of analysis can provide the policy-maker with an accurate estimate of the damage incurred by environmental problems. "Such tools include the calculation of externalities and the amendment of GNP (Gross National Product) statistics to show resources lost, environmental damage and the discounted value of investment over time. These tools are available and are becoming better and easier to apply. They can be of considerable...(importance) to the Arab decision-maker, helping her/him in making rational and confident decisions on environmental matters."[133]

Designing frameworks for linking across subjects and sectors, over various spatial scales, regions and themes, to give a more integrated perspective, is becoming essential to achieve effective coordination. Governments could support university and other networks for environmental and development education. Existing national and regional networks, which promote scientific research on sustainable development, should be strengthened, and new partnerships created with the business and other independent sectors for technology, know-how, and knowledge exchange.

These arrangements will provide valuable inputs to environmental policy-making and its implementation, since

> (t)here is a general lack of reliable, up-to-date information and data on the state of the environment. This relates to the lack of standardization of data formats and consistent environmental monitoring, data collection and reporting. Reports are often located in different public and private organizations, between which there is little or no cooperation. This results in gaps and duplication of data, and limited utilization of the information. This, in turn, hinders policy development, planning, implementation and follow-up.[134]

For example, "(t)here have been efforts to assess and combat desertification in the past two to three decades in the GCC countries. However, there is still shortage of information regarding the magnitude of the different causes of desertification, their extent and impact."[135] Therefore, the governments in cooperation with international and regional organizations should strengthen or establish Centres of Excellence in interdisciplinary research and education in environmental and developmental sciences. Such centres may be encouraged for promoting cooperative research and information sharing and dissemination at the national and regional levels.

If the GCC countries are "to be successful in promoting a balance between development and environment and quality of life, they must bring environmental issues into their strategic plans and implementation of their policies. This is no easy task, for in many Middle Eastern countries, serious environmental policies are non-existent; when they exist they are not systematically formulated. Quite often, the problem is compounded by a lack of awareness and a lack of human and financial resources."[136] Implementation of environmental action plans and education of citizens and their leaders on environmental issues can constitute significant steps in addressing environmental issues in these countries.[137]

IV. Cooperation with Regional Organization for Environmental Protection

Besides the national-level, several regional environmental institutions and councils were created to address these global issues at a regional level.[138] Regional and sub-regional organizations are essential players for the efficient and effective implementation of global agreements at the national level. These regional organizational set up can coordinate and assist in the translation of global commitments into national action plans through information sharing, education and training schemes, and capacity building in member States. Finally, regional agencies can also monitor implementation of global treaties and make an assessment of the effectiveness.

Traditionally these regional institutions were involved in the areas of peace, security and economic development. The significance of regional arrangements in maintaining international peace and security is well recognized by the UN in its Charter 8. However, regional environmental cooperation is relatively new and can be traced to the 1970s. Recognition of the transnational character of environmental problems and the close interconnection between the environment and socio-economic development led to the proliferation of regional institutional arrangements in the field of environment.[139]

Regional institutions provide a high level forum to map the regional environmental agenda, articulate regional goals and build relevant regional norms and standards to promote sustainable development. They facilitate in providing regional inputs during the negotiation of global conventions and their subsequent implementations. They can play a larger role in integrating global programmes into existing regional policy issues in the light of the prevailing conditions in their respective regions. Equally they can provide a number of services that are critical to the success of global and regional initiatives as well as national action plans. These include capacity building and strengthening of institutional frameworks through the development of regional database and information sharing arrangements as well as preparing regional training programmes. They can also act as interface among the regional networks of governments, knowledge communities, NGOs, etc.

The major environmental issues in the West Asian region include climate change, land and soil degradation, forest degradation and deforestation, freshwater scarcity as well as quality, pollution of coastal and marine areas, loss of habitats and species, growth of unplanned settlements and mounting solid waste, and increasing drought.[140] "As in many countries, the region also faces challenges associated with moving from a sector-based approach to environmental management to a dynamic multi-sectoral approach, which is needed to tackle complex sustainable development issues such as trade and environment."[141]

In the Arab region, regional institutions emerged over the past three decades that reflected changes in the conceptual framework regarding environment and development. For example, the 1960s and 1970s were characterised by the establishment of regional economic and social organizations. In the 1970s and 1980s, several regional environmental institutions and councils were set up, including the Council of Arab Ministers Responsible for the Environment (CAMRE), by the Arab League in 1987. CAMRE provided the first political forum for addressing environmental matters in the region.[142] CAMRE is mainly concerned with environmental policy issues at the regional levels.

During the 1990s, two institutions focusing on the environment and development were established, namely, the Centre for Environment and Development in the Arab Region and Europe (CEDARE), which was created as a non-governmental think tank and Joint Committee on Environment and Development in the Arab Region (JCEDAR), which was established under the auspices of the Arab League as an Inter-Ministerial Advisory Committee to CAMRE with regional institutions serving as advisors, including ESCWA and the United Nations Environment Programme (UNEP). [143]

The membership of JCEDAR is both governmental and non-governmental and includes representatives of national environmental agencies, NGOs, private sector associations and regional organizations. However, the success of these institutions in advancing regional sustainable development policies is constrained by the difficulty of coordinating a number of Ministries at the national level. The Joint Secretariat is also responsible for coordinating regional follow-up to the WSSD.[144]

At the Sub-regional level, the heads of States of the GCC member countries approved environmental principles in 1985 to protect the natural resources from degradation and exploitation. The GCC Secretariat now includes a regional Directorate of Man and Environment that organizes regional surveys, assessments, education, and training and information exchange at national, sub-regional and regional levels.[145]

Regionally binding agreements also led to the establishment of regional organizations to coordinate implementation efforts. Two such important organizations need special mention. These are the Regional

Organizations for the Protection of the Marine Environment (ROPME) and the Regional Organization for the Conservation of the Environment of the Red Sea and Gulf of Aden (PERSGA).

The Regional Organization for the Protection of the Marine Environment (ROPME), with a head office in Kuwait, was established in 1979 by the parties to the Kuwait Regional Sea Convention to serve as its Secretariat (under the supervision of UNEP). It has a network of collaborating Focal Points in all eight member countries. A Marine Emergency Mutual Aid Centre was established in Bahrain in 1982 to assist ROPME in matters related to information, capacity building, reporting and cooperation with other organizations. A major survey on critical marine habitats, initiated by ROPME and carried out by the member States, identified all sensitive marine habitats in the region.[146]

The national action plans were developed by all eight signatories to the Kuwait Regional Convention and its protocols. However, no new national institutions were established to implement the conventions dealing with the marine environment, the responsibility of which lay with the national institutions responsible for managing coastal areas or marine resources. Similarly, no new national laws were enacted in relation to these two conventions, the protection of the marine and coastal zone being covered by existing national laws.

Changes in perspectives and concepts regarding sustainable development in the Arab region are best observed in the declarations issued following regional forums. The scope of the topics included in regional sustainable development declarations evolved and expanded over the past decade.

Table 3.3: Regional Economic and Social Development Institutions (1960s-1970s)

Sl. No.	*Regional Economic and Social Development Institutions (1960s-1970s)*	*Year*
1.	Arab League Council of Arab Health Ministers	1970
2.	Arab Planning Institute (API)	1972
3.	Islamic Development Bank (IDB) (established 1973, opened 1975)	1973
4.	Arab Fund for Economic and Social Development (AFESD) (established 1968, opened 1974)	1974
5.	Economic Commission for Western Asia (became ESCWA in 1985)	1973

Source: ESCWA, n. 110, p. 19.

In the Arab region "(w)hile the orientation of topics still centres on institution building, capacity building, natural resource management, international cooperation, technology transfer and financing, more attention is being placed on economic issues (trade liberalization), international issues (multilateral environmental agreements, debt and financing) and participatory approaches to sustainable development (women, youth) in recent declarations."[147]

i. Regional Specialized Agencies

A number of technical organizations are working with environmental issues at the regional level. These include the Arab Centre for Studies of Arid Zone and Dry Lands (ACSAD), the Centre for Environment and Development for the Arab Region and Europe (CEDARE), and other Arab specialized organizations. Almost all provide technical assistance and respond to capacity building needs. The followings are the few important institutions working on environmental issues.

Table 3.4: Regional Environmental Institutions (1970s-1990s)

Sl. No.	*Regional Environmental Institutions (1970s-1990s)*	*Year*
1.	Arab Centre for the Studies of Arid Zones and Dry Lands (ACSAD)	1971
2.	Mediterranean Action Plan (MAP)	1675
3.	International Centre for Agricultural Research in the Dry Areas (ICARDA)	1977
4.	Regional Organization for the Protection of the Marine Environment (ROPME)	1978
5.	Bahrain Centre for Studies and Research	1984
6.	Economic and Social Commission for Western Asia (ESCWA)	1985
7.	Council of Arab Ministers Responsible for the Environment (CAMRE)	1987
8.	Middle East Desalination Research Centre (MEDRC)	1996
9.	Centre for the Affairs of Man and the Environment (CAME)	1996
10.	Regional Organization for the Conservation of the Environment of the Red Sea and Gulf of Aden (PERSGA)	1996

Source: ESCWA, n. 110, p. 19.

A. Centre for Environment and Development in the Arab Region and Europe (CEDARE)

The CEDARE was established in 1992 as an international inter-governmental Organization with diplomatic status. This was in response to the convention adopted by the Council of Arab Ministers Responsible for the Environment (CAMRE), in 1991 and upon the initiative of the Arab Republic of Egypt, the United Nations Development Programme (UNDP) and the Arab Fund for Economic and Social Development (AFESD.

The important functions of CEDARE related with land management include:

- Conducting regional studies and projects with emphasis on sustainable development of the available resource base.
- Capacity building of national institutions/personnel working in the fields of land degradation, conservation and combating desertification, through provision of training, workshops and special programmes.
- Providing demand driven technical assistance.
- Networking among national, regional and international institutions.
- Coordination of programmes and activities with the regional and international organizations.[148]

B. Arab Centre for the Studies of Arid Zones and Dry Lands **(ACSAD)**

ACSAD was established in Damascus, Syria in 1968. ACSAD is a specialized Arab organisation working within the framework of the League of Arab States with the objective of unifying the Arab efforts which aim to develop the scientific agricultural research in the arid and semi-arid areas, helping in the exchange of information and experiences and making use of the scientific progress and the modern agricultural techniques in order to increase the agricultural production.[149]

C. Arab Organization for Agriculture Development (AOAD)

The AOAD was established in 1970, upon the desire of the Arab countries. Realizing the vital role of agriculture within the region's economy, the Arab countries recognized the need for coordination between their different policies in agriculture, natural and human resources as well as economic development, in order to achieve the ultimate goal of fully integrated Arab economies. Due to the abundance of Sudan's natural resources, in particular in agriculture, Khartoum was selected to host the organization's headquarters.[150]

D. International Centre for Agricultural Research in the Dry Areas (ICARDA)

Established in 1977, ICARDA is one of the 15 centres strategically located all over the world and supported by the Consultative Group on International Agricultural Research (CGIAR). With its main research station and offices based in Aleppo, Syria, ICARDA works through a network of partnerships with national, regional and international institutions. The geographic mandate of ICARDA covers the countries of Central and West Asia and North Africa (CWANA), as well as developing countries with subtropical and temperate dry areas. These are collectively referred as to "dry areas", which account for an estimated one-third of the world's land. ICARDA also has a major interest in improving agricultural productivity in the highlands. In the WANA region alone, highlands constitute about 40 per cent of the total land area and contribute nearly 30 per cent of the region's agricultural production.[151]

Besides, many UN organizations and their regional offices operate in the region to effectively address environmental issues. They facilitate funds for technical assistance and support environmental management programmes, environmental policies and institutional capacity building. Important UN agencies include the United Nations Environment Programme Regional Office for West Asia (UNEP/ROWA), the Economic and Social Commission for West Asia (ESCWA), World Health Organization's Regional Centre for Environmental Health Activities. There is also the Mediterranean European Technical Assistance Programme, a regional partnership of the European Commission, the European Investment Bank, the World Bank, UNDP, and countries of the region that mobilize grant funds for technical assistance, to strengthen environmental management and establish environmentally sound policies.

Table 3.5: Regional Sustainable Development Institutions (1990s-2000s)

Sl. No.	*Regional Sustainable Development Institutions (1990s-2000s)*	*Year*
1.	Centre for Environment and Development in the Arab Region and Europe (CEDARE) (Proposed for establishment by CAMRE in 1992, opened in 1993)	1992
2.	Joint Committee for Environment and Development for the Arab Region (JCEDAR)	1993
3.	United Nations University, International Network on Water, Environment and Health (UNU/INWEH)	1996
4.	A Joint Secretariat to prepare for WSSD and follow up on the Arab Initiative (technical secretariat of CAMRE, UNEP/ROWA and ESCWA)	2001

Source: ESCWA, no. 110, p. 17.

Nevertheless, regional coordination was possible in several areas. Regional preparations for the World Summit for Sustainable Development were coordinated by the Joint Secretariat composed of the CAMRE Technical Secretariat, ESCWA and UNEP/ROWA. This led to the adoption of the Sustainable Development Initiative in the Arab Region in July 2002, which was subsequently presented as a regional contribution to the WSSD. The Joint Secretariat is also responsible for coordinating regional follow-up to the WSSD.[152]

Although considerable achievements was observed in developing regionally integrated efforts to combat desertification, this approach were not systematically fostered. Consequently, affected regions often found themselves competing for attention on the international policy agenda. As cooperation and exchange is strengthened on regional and sub-regional levels, efforts are also needed to foster inter-regional policy coordination."[153]

> "Good intentions are not enough to achieve effective and advanced environmental action; neither can we expect miracles from an Arab Council of Ministers (Responsible for Environment) which lacks funds and experts."[154]

Therefore, improving the performance of CAMRE is "a matter of urgency. The Council needs to be able to examine relevant environmental matters in a rigorous, efficient way and to provide decision-makers with optimum but realistic options for addressing regional and international environmental issues. It needs to function

Table 3.6: Regional Declarations on Sustainable Development (1986-2002)

Sl. No.	*Declaration or Initiative*	*Year*
1.	Arab Declaration on Environment and Development	1986
2.	Arab Statement on Environment and Development and the Future Outlook	1991
3.	Regional Action Programme for Sustainable Development	1992
4.	Declaration of the First International Symposium on the Environment From an Islamic Perspective	2000
5.	Abu Dhabi Declaration on Perspectives of Arab Environmental Action	2001
6.	Oman Declaration on Environment and Sustainable Development	2001
7.	Arab Declaration to the World Summit on Sustainable Development	2002
8.	Joint Ministerial Declaration on Sustainable Development by the African Ministerial Council on the Environment (AMCEN) and CAMRE	2002
9.	Arab Initiative for Sustainable Development	2002

Source: ESCWA, no. 110, p. 6.

efficiently, tend to joint environmental resources, settle potential disputes among Arab countries over the shared use of these resources, enhance Arab cooperation and defend Arab interests at international forums."[155]

The Arab specialized research institutes and organizations also fail to make an impressive presence at various international conferences and technical meetings. Najib Saab summarises it excellently.[156] The lack of general data and information at a national level is echoed at the regional level. Although some regional organisations initiated action for information management and networking, the dissemination and accessibility to data banks remains insufficient and there needs to be improved co-ordination among relevant organizations.[157]

The existing mechanism includes the Arab Environmental Information Network, initiated by CAMRE and JCEDAR, with technical support from CEDARE and UNEP/ROWA. Other initiatives include the ACSAD's arid zones and drylands information network, ROPME's database development, and UNDP's Sustainable Development Networking Programmes. Regional technical organizations also have inadequate information management and networking. In recent years, these institutions initiated efforts to strengthen cooperation with other regional and international organizations. For example, ACSAD published, jointly with UNESCO, the hydrogeological map of the Arab region and the adjacent areas. It is also preparing a water resources database, including an integrated data base management system that stores and retrieves data related to the assessment of water resources in the region.[158]

At present, various plans exist for the creation of a Worldwide Web (www) site to facilitate information dissemination in the region. Each country is expected to provide information for the site, which could be a basis for sharing information and experience. The centre for monitoring and administering the Web site could also be the information centre for standardized data collection and analysis of all environmental data for the West Asia region. Reports and studies could be produced and distributed in hard copy as well as through the Website.

The level of response and compliance for regional MEAs is generally higher than for global MEAs.[159] Although all the GCC countries are fulfilling their commitments as signatories, it is difficult to assess the impacts of regional MEAs on the protection of the environment. These largely depend on the agreement itself, the level of economic development of the country and the barriers to implementation in each sub-region and between and within countries. Limited access to adequate information also makes evaluation of the impact of the MEAs difficult. In many cases, it is too early to identify impacts as countries are still at the stage of building up institutional and technical capacities and barely started implementation.[160]

V. Implementation of Multilateral Environmental Agreements (MEAs)

Environmental problems do not respect national boundaries. The nature of transboundary environmental problems changed over the years. First, the nature and scope of these problems increased manifold. Secondly, these new category of global environmental issues affect everyone and can only be effectively managed on the basis of cooperation among the governments. Third the increasing scale of many regional or local environmental problems has far reaching consequences with international repercussions.

As indications of widespread ecological deterioration became acknowledged in the 1960s, voices were quickly raised for expanding UN activities into the environmental field. In 1970, UN Secretary-General U. Thant remarked that "never in the twenty-five year history of the United Nations has there been a problem of more relevance to all nations than the present environment crisis," and added that "the time has come for the United Nations, in the spirit and letter of the Charter, to be a centre for harmonizing the actions of nations in solving the problems of the human environment."[161]

The development of international environmental law after the Stockholm Conference in 1972 cannot be grasped without taking into consideration the role of international institutions.[162] The international agencies involved in global environmental governance are a heterogeneous set of actors. Their legal status, competences, and tasks vary considerably. They are linked to each other through cooperative arrangements, which concern a multitude of different issues.[163] "While international organizations played an important role in shaping international environmental policies and protocols, they have little authority over implementation, monitoring or enforcement of these policies and protocols. Such authority resides largely with nation-states."[164]

The GCC countries are active participants in international conventions dealing with the preservation of the environment and the conservation of limited natural resources.[165] These countries ratified or acceded to 64 international and regional environmental conventions and agreements. "The level of participation by the countries in West Asia in international agreements and conventions related to the environmental issues is rather sporadic."[166] Overall, the GCC countries concentrated their efforts on developing institutions or expanding the mandates of existing institutions to implement MEAs. The focus is on priority studies, the preparation of strategies and the development of action plans and programmes, with little progress in implementation at the field level.

While ratification is at a fairly high level, compliance is limited, mainly due to lack of funding. Awareness campaigns did not target decision-makers, stakeholders or the national figures who are the key to succcssful public participation. In addition, few pressure groups were formed to influence the business sectors.[167]

Even though some countries are in the process of formulating by-laws relating to specific conventions, most rely on existing legal

Table 3.7: Status of the GCC Countries' Participation in MEAs

Country	*Cities*	*UNFCCC*	*Kyoto Protocol*	*UNCBD*	*UNCCD*	*POPs*
Bahrain	...	1994^	2006**	1996^	1997*	2002#
Kuwait	2002^	1994*	2005**	2002^	1997^	2001#
Oman	...	1995^	2005**	1995^	1996*	2005^
Qatar	2001*	1996*	2005**	1996^	1999*	2004*
Saudi Arabia	1996*	1994*	2005**	2001*	1997*	2002#
UAE	1990*	1995*	2005**	2000^	1998*	2002^

Signatory, ^ Ratified, * Accession, ** Entry into force
UNFCCC: United Nations Framework Convention on Climate Change
UNCBD: United Nations Convention on Biological Diversity
UNCCD: United Nations Convention to Combat Desertification
CITES: Convention on International Trade in Endangered Species of Wild Fauna and Flora
POPs: (Stockholm Convention on) Persistent Organic Pollutants

Source: GRC, *Green Gulf Report*, (Dubai: GRC, 2006), p. 9.

instruments for dealing with all major environmental issues. Economic instruments to improve the implementation of MEAs are still not well formulated. Policy instruments such as incentives, taxes and charges, pricing strategies and other indirect measures are, however, starting to be applied to some MEAs.

The Montreal Protocol received most attention, because international interest is high and funding, capacity building and systems for monitoring and reporting were available. Laws and decrees are issued in Bahrain and Kuwait to regulate the import, export and use of ozone-depleting substances and encourage the use of alternatives. Saudi Arabia is developing comprehensive by-laws to implement this convention. Special commissions or ozone units were established within existing institutions, including ozone units in Bahrain, Kuwait and Saudi Arabia.[168]

There were pilot projects to implement the Convention on Biological Diversity (CBD) in the GCC countries. National committees were set up to conduct national studies and formulate strategies and action plans. Most countries prepared national studies on biodiversity and a number of protected sites were declared. Studies were completed in Oman and are under way in other GCC States. Saudi Arabia's sixth development plan (1995-2000) included a number of measures to develop and preserve biodiversity on a large scale. The League of Arab States called for a meeting of Arab Experts on

Biodiversity in 1995. In addition, the Arab League Education, Scientific and Cultural Organization (ALESCO) adopted a comprehensive programme to encourage Arab States to participate fully in CBD activities. Capacity building among officials is needed to formulate national strategies and action plans for biodiversity. In a joint effort to promote the implementation of the CBD, the Global Environmental Facility and its implementing agencies are providing technical assistance.[169]

Kuwait, Oman, Qatar and Saudi Arabia prepared National Biodiversity Strategy and Action Plans (NBSAPs). These plans spell out the strategic goals and action plans based on Islamic principles to conserve biodiversity.[170] Saudi Arabia enacted legislation on Endangered Wildlife Species and their Products. The National Commission for Wildlife Conservation and Development acts as the nodal agency in Saudi Arabia to implement the CBD. It is assisted by two prominent research institutes, namely the King Khalid Wildlife Research Centre and the National Wildlife Centre. At present Kuwait does not have an effective nodal agency to deal with biodiversity issues.[171]

Measures taken by the GCC countries under the UN Convention to Combat Desertification (UNCCD) are discussed in the fifth and sixth chapters.

With the exception of the Montreal Protocol, the monitoring of compliance with other MEAs is not well developed or enforced. In all cases, lack of resources is a major obstacle and capacity building is urgently required. All the GCC countries that signed the UNFCCC are preparing their national plans with technical and financial support from United Nations agencies in capacity building. Some of the GCC countries prepared first drafts of their Green House Gas (GHG) inventories.

Public awareness about MEAs varies. The Montreal Protocol, CBD, UNCCD and UNFCCC received considerable attention. The mass media played a major role in enhancing public awareness by drawing attention to the seriousness of the environmental issues involved. Television and radio programmes on land degradation and desertification, loss of biodiversity and marine pollution are broadcast regularly in all countries. These issues have also been covered at national and international events (such as biodiversity day, ozone day, world environment day and Arabian environment day). Newspapers and magazines in some countries allocate special pages for environmental affairs.[172] Although it is too early to assess the impact of the conventions, public awareness is growing and positive attitudes towards most MEAs are developing rapidly.

"The relatively low level of representation in many international conventions and the priority given to their implementation is partly due to the shortcomings of domestic legislation. It is also due to the large amount of professional and administrative expertise and resources needed to implement the complicated legal and administrative requirements of conventions."[173]

In fact international events including conferences and meetings provide effective forums to articulate the region's environmental problems. However, the level of participation and preparation for such important gatherings are found to be lacking in these countries. One best example was the Global Ministerial Environment Forum recently held in 2001, which was poorly represented by the Arab Ministers in general and GCC countries in particular.[174]

In several cases, organizations for environmental cooperation have not yet been fully and satisfactorily developed. There are still gaps between the planning and the implementation stages. Insufficient capacity in terms of technical, personnel and financial resources are among the major obstacles for the GCC countries to implement environmental governance programmes and plans.

Conclusion

Standing at the intersection between national, international, and global pressures, the State is the preeminent institution with requisite political authority and steering capacity to address ecological problems through multilateral environmental agreements and domestic regulations of natural resources management. The centralised and authoritarian character of GCC countries administrative arrangements find it difficult to cope with the emerging challenges. The environmental institutions are newly established and are in the process of consolidation. To confront the underlying causes of environmental degradation, the governments need to integrate environmental considerations into the mainstream of decision-making.

Natural renouncement policies must be dynamic and adaptive to the changing dynamics of global environmental governance. In the GCC countries the government institutions must search for innovative approaches and ideas that enhance their ability to adapt and respond to the dynamic environment. Similarly, these countries must adopt new technologies that save time and energy, promote productivity in the work place, implement public policy with high standards, and service broad public interest and promote public trust in government and administration.

Management of environmental issues is one of the most difficult areas of public action, demanding inputs of scientific and technical knowledge and of skills in the organization, planning, and coordination of complex programmes that are nowhere common attributes of government. There is a need to strengthen information exchange by enhancing technologies and capacities necessary to promote environment and development education and public awareness.

Since the civil society plays an important role in bringing emerging environmental issues to the attention of policy makers, raising public awareness and promoting innovative ideas and approaches, the governments need to encourage active participation of civil society in both plan formulation and implementation.

References

1. Seong-lin Na and Hyun Song Shinf, "International Environmental Agreements under Uncertainty", *Oxford Economic Papers*, vol. 50, 1998, p. 173.
2. Caldwell, Lynton K. "Management of Resources and the Environment: A Problem in Administrative Coordination," *International Review of Administrative Sciences*, vol. 38, 1972, p. 115.
3. United Nations Environment Programme (UNEP), *Annual Report 2000*, (Nairobi: UNEP, 2000), p. 4.
4. Caldwell, n. 2, p. 115.
5. UNEP, n. 3, p. 1. Many environmental problems—such as addressing climate change and reducing emissions of greenhouse gases, the protection of the ozone layer and of biodiversity—"are global, in the sense that they cannot be tackled effectively in isolation by any country and that they require international coordination of environmental policies."(Ecchia, Giulio and Marco Mariotti, "Coalition Formation in International Environmental Agreements and the Role of Institutions", University of Bologna, Bologna, Italy, 1997, p. 1).
6. Biermann, Frank and Klaus Dingwerth, "Global Environmental Change and the Nation State", *Global Environmental Politics*, vol. 4, no. 1, 2004, p. 6. "...obligation of States not only to manage their

natural wealth and resources in such a way as to avoid significant harm to (the 'sovereign' territory of) other States, but also to manage their natural wealth and resources properly for the sake of their own people, including future generations." (Schrijver, Nico, *Sovereignty over Natural Resources*, (Cambridge: Cambridge University Press, 1997), p. 234.

7. Åström, Sverker, "Global Consensus or Global Catastrophe?" *Ambio*, vol. 1, no. 1,1972, p. 4.
8. Caldwell, n. 2, p. 115.
9. Farazmand, Ali., "Globalisation and Governance: A Theoretical Analysis" in Farazmand, Ali, ed., *Sound Governance: Policy and Administrative Innovations* (Westport: Praeger/Greenwood, 2004), p. 46.
10. Jreisat, Jamil, "Managing National Development in the Arab States", *Arab Studies Quarterly,* (Association of Arab-American University Graduates, New York), vol. 14, no. 2/3, 1992, p. 7.
11. UNEP, *Global Environmental Outlook 2000* (Nairobi: UNEP, 2000), p. 159.
12. Marauhn, Thilo, "The Changing Role of State" in Bodansky, Daniel, *et al.*, (eds.), *The Oxford Handbook of International Environmental Law* (Oxford: Oxford University Press, 2007), p. 729.
13. Paehlke, Robert and Douglas Torgerson, eds., *Managing Leviathan: Environmental Politics and the Administrative State* (Ontario: Broadview Press, 2005), p. 271.
14. Ryding, Sven-Olof, *Environmental Management Handbook*, (Amsterdam: IOS Press, 1998), p. 5.
15. Vogler, John and Andrew Jordan, "Governance and Environment" in Berkhout, Frans, *et al.*, eds, *Negotiating Environmental Change: New Perspectives from Social Science,* (Cheltenham, JK: Edward Elger, 2003), p. 310.
16. Caldwell, Lynton Keith, *Environment Policy: From the Twentieth to Twenty-First Century* (London: Duke University, 1996), p. 54.
17. Torgerson, Douglas and Robert Paehlke, "Environmental Administration: Revisiting the Agenda of Inquiry and Practice" in Paehlke, n. 13, p. 7.
18. Paehlke, n. 13, p. 46.
19. Vogler, n. 16, p. 137.
20. Young, Oran R., *International Governance: Protecting the Environment in a Stateless Society*, (Ithaca, New York: Cornell University Press, 1994), p. 140.
21. Caldwell, no. 2, p. 119. "Devising ways to sustain the earth's ability to support diverse life, including a reasonable quality of life for humans, involves making tough decisions under uncertainty, complexity, and substantial biophysical constraints as well as conflicting human values and interests."(Dietz, Thomas, *et al.*, "The Struggle to Govern the Commons", *Science*, vol. 302, 2003), p. 1907.

22. Caldwell, n. 16, p. 54.
23. Meadowcroft, James., "From Welfare State to Ecostate" in Barry, John and Robyn Eckersley, eds., *The State and the Global Ecological Crisis*, (Cambridge: MIT Press, 2005), p. 19.
24. *Ibid.*, p. 3.
25. Pagaza, Ignacio Pichardo, "Environmental Protection and Public Administration in Latin America", *International Review of Administrative Sciences*, vol. 72, no. 1, 2006, p. 144.
26. Leonard, Barry, ed., *International Environment: International Agreements Are Not Well Monitored,* Report to Congressional Requesters, (Darby (U.S.A.): Diane Publishing Company, 1992), p. 8.
27. Barry, and Eckersley, n. 23, p. ix. "It is only the state that presently has the power and legitimacy to regulate the actions of disparate actors who, in their pursuit of individual gain, might otherwise destroy shared environmental resources." (Raustiala, Kal, "States, NGOs and International Environmental Institutions", *International Studies Quarterly*, vol. 41, 1997, p. 736).
28. Caldwell, n. 2, p. 118.
29. Bodansky, Daniel, *et al.*, "International Environmental Law: Mapping the Field" in Bodansky, n. 12, p. 24.
30. *Ibid.*, p. 17.
31. Marauhn, n. 12, p. 746.
32. *Ibid.*, p. 747.
33. Desai, Uday, "Institutions and Environmental Policy in Developed Countries" in Desai, Uday, ed., *Environmental Politics and Policy in Industrial Countries*, (London: MIT Press, 2002), pp. 7-8.
34. Jreisat, n. 10, p. 10.
35. Ashour, Ahmed Sakr, "Development-Driven Public Governance Reform in the Arab Countries", Conceptual Paper (Draft), 2005, [Online: web] Accessed on 23rd June, 2008 URL: http://www.arabgov-initiative.org/publications/egov/admin-reform-e.pdf, p. 9.
36. Jreisat, Jamil E., "Bureaucratization of Arab World: Incomplete Influence" in Farazmand, Ali ed., *Handbook of Comparative and Development Public Administration"* (New York: Marcel, Dekker, 2001), p. 1007.
37. Ayubi, Nazih N., *Over-Stating the Arab State: Politics and Society in the Middle East,* (London: I.B. Tauris, 1995), p. 290.
38. Ashour, n. 35, p. 9.
39. Gause, F. Gregory, *Oil Monarchies: Domestic and Security Challenges in the Arab Gulf States*,(New York: Council on Foreign Relations, 1994), p. 62.
40. Ansari, Shahid Jamal, *Political Modernization in the Gulf,* (New Delhi: Northern Book Centre, 1998), p. 146.
41. Gause, no. 39, p. 62.
42. *Ibid.*

43. Abu-Laban, Baha, *et al.*, "Introduction: Development and the Arab World" in Abu-Laban, Baha, *et al.*, eds, *The Arab World: Dynamics of Development,* (Leiden, the Netherlands: E.J. Brill, 1986), p. 6.
44. *Ibid.*
45. Merriam, John G., "Bureaucrats as Agents of Development in the Middle East", in Farazmand, n. 36, p. 565.
46. Gause, n. 39, p. 62.
47. Ayubi, Nazih, "Arab Bureaucracies: Expanding Size, Changing Roles" in Luciani, Giacomo (ed.) *The Arab State* (London: Routledge, 1990), p. 132.
48. Gause, n. 39, p. 62.
49. Ayubi, n. 47, p. 132. Onn Winckler points out that "(t)he Gulf rulers have been careful to distribute the oil wealth in politically useful ways and have ensured that the economic benefit reach the entire citizenry, including the lower strata. This distribution policy has been implemented via two major mechanisms: first and foremost, through giving governmental employment to almost the entire national workforce. In so doing, however, they afford nationals the luxury of being selective regarding their employment decisions... the second mechanism was the provision of large-scale social services to the indigenous populations, either free of charge or heavily subsidized." (Winckler, Onn, "The Demographic Dilemma of the Arab World: the Employment Aspect", *Journal of Contemporary History*, vol. 37, no. 4, 2002, p. 629).
50. Gerald E. Caiden, *Administraive Reform* (Chicago: Aldine Publishing Company, 1969), p. 11. Yusif A. Sayigh argues that "(u)nderstandably, the public administration of the various units in the Peninsula is still backward, again except for Kuwait, which has taken large strides towards modernization, the former Aden Colony, and lastly Saudi Arabia."(Sayigh, Yusif A., "Problems and Prospects of Development in the Arabian Peninsula", *International Journal of Middle East Studies*, vol. 2, no. 1, 1971, p. 46).
51. Kamrava, Mehran and Mora, Frank, "Civil Society and Democratisation in Comparative Perspective: Latin America and the Middle East", *Third World Quarterly*, (London), vol. 19, no. 5, 1998, p. 907. "All six (GCC) states remain monarchies with dirigiste governments; patriarchical rulers lead them, and extensive ruling families occupy the upper echelons of the regimes, forming a distinct caste above the people. Powerful governments have been built up to control and direct many aspects of the lives of the citizenry..." (Peterson, J.E., "The Arab Gulf States: Further Steps towards Political Participation,", GRC Gulf papers series, Gulf Research Centre, Dubai, 2006, p. 7).
52. Jreisat, n. 36, p. 1012.
53. Merriam, n. 45, p. 566.

54. Lucas, Russell, "Monarchical Authoritarianism: Survival and Political Liberalization in a Middle Eastern Regime Type", *International Journal of Middle East Studies*, (Cambridge), vol. 36, no. 1, 2004, p. 106.
55. Kamrava, n. 51, p. 910.
56. Common, Richard, "Administrative Change in the Gulf: Modernization in Bahrain and Oman", *International Review of Administrative Sciences*, vol. 74, no. 2, 2008, p. 183.
57. *Ibid.*
58. Jreisat, n. 36, p. 1014.
59. Clerkism is a behavioural trait evidenced in administrator's preoccupation with small and routine matters to the detrimental of overall policies of the organisational and in isolation from environmental reality.
60. Ansari, n. 40, p. 143.
61. Jreisat, Jamil E., "The Predicament of Administrative Reform in the Arab States" in Farazmand, Ali, *Administrative Reform in Developing Nations,* (London: Praeger, 2002), p. 168.
62. Jreisat, n. 36, p. 1008. "The defects of public administration are composite; they include a low level of education and of specialization, particularism, and the weakness of administrative tradition. Even in Kuwait, the country with the largest reservoir of skills to draw upon, the civil service suffers from serious shortcomings. The welfare philosophy of the state has resulted in the accumulation of a huge civil service-a total of over 75,000 in a population of 468,000. A fraction of this number, well chosen from among the total, could handle the task of administration more efficiently, and of course, at lower cost." (Sayigh, Yusif A., "Problems and Prospects of Development in the Arabian Peninsula", *International Journal of Middle East Studies,* vol. 2, no. 1, 1971, p. 46).
63. Jreisat, Jamil E., *Politics without Process: Administering Development in the Arab World,* (London: Lynne Rienner Publishers, 1997), p. 67.
64. Ansari, n. 40, pp. 137-38.
65. *Ibid.*, p. 152.
66. Crystal, Jill, "Coalitions in Oil Monarchies: Kuwait and Qatar", *Comparative Politics*, vol. 21, no. 4, 1989, p. 438.
67. Jreisat, n. 63, p. 67.
68. Kiren Aziz Chaudhry, *The Price of Wealth: Economies and Institutions in the Middle East* (Ithaca, NY: Cornell University Press, 1997), p. 141.
69. Jreisat, n. 36, p. 1014.
70. Common, n. 61, pp. 182-83.
71. Jreisat, n. 10, p. 8.
72. Jreisat, n. 36, p. 1014. According to Lewis W. Snider, the fundamental problem confronting the ruling establishments in the GCC countries is that "rulers' efforts to manage the effects of rapid political and social change is one of creating new political institutions to accommodate

pressures for broader participation in political life without establishing a political alternative to their own rule." (Snider, Lewis W., "Comparing the Strength of Nations: The Arab Gulf States and Political Change," *Comparative Politics,* vol. 20, no. 4, 1988, p. 461).

73. Giacomo Luciani, 'The Oil rent, the Fiscal Crisis of the State and Democratization', in Ghassan Salame, ed., *Democracy without Democrats: the Renewal of Politics in the Muslim World* (London: I.B. Tauris, 1994), p. 152.
74. Al-Awaji, Ibrahim, "Bureaucracy and Development in Saudi Arabia: the Case of Local Administration" in Jabbra, Joseph G., *Bureaucracy and Development in the Arab World*, (New York: E.J. Brill, 1989), p. 57.
75. Jreisat, n. 36, p. 1014.
76. Sarrouh E., "The UNDP Role in Public Administration Reforms in the Arab Region", paper prepared for The Expert Consultative Meeting on Public Administration and Public Accounting Developments, With Stress on Electronic Tools., UNESCWA in collaboration with UNDP and DPDAM, July, Beirut, Lebanon, 2003, p. 6.
77. Kamal al-Sayyid, Mustapha, "The Concept of Civil Society and the Arab World" in Brynen, Rex, *et al.*, eds, *Political Liberalization and Democratization in the Arab World,* (London: Lynne Rienner Publishers, 1995), p. 144.
78. Sarrouh E., n. 76, p. 10.
79. Abu-Laban, n. 43, p. 6.
80. Ashour, n. 35, p. 9.
81. Jreisat, n. 61, p. 168.
82. Common, n. 56, p. 180.
83. *Ibid.*, p. 184.
84. Jreisat, n. 63, p. 61.
85. United Nations, *A Handbook of Public Administration* (New York: UN, 1961), p. 209.
86. Common, n. 56, p. 181.
87. Roy, Delwin A. "Management Education and Training in the Arab World: A Review of Issues and Problems", *International Review of Administrative Sciences,* vol. 43, 1977, p. 221.
88. Jreisat, n. 36, p. 1014.
89. *Ibid.*
90. Common, n. 56, p. 179.
91. Roy, n. 87, p. 223.
92. Ryding, n. 14, p. 13.
93. Sayigh, Yusif A., "Problems and Prospects of Development in the Arabian Peninsula", *International Journal of Middle East Studies*, vol. 2, no. 1, 1971, p. 50.
94. Caldwell, no. 2, p. 115.
95. UNEP, *Annual Report 2001*, (Nairobi: UNEP, 2001), p. 12.
96. Sathaye, J., *et al.*, "Sustainable Development and Mitigation", in Metz,

B. *et al.* (eds.), *Climate Change 2007: Mitigation*, Contribution of Working Group III to the Fourth Assessment Report of the Intergovernmental Panel on Climate Change (Cambridge: Cambridge University Press, 2007), p. 708.

97. Karkkainen, Bradley C. "Post-Sovereign Environmental Governance: The Collaborative Problem-Solving Model" in Biermann, Frank, *et al.*, (eds.), *Global Environmental Change and the Nation State*, (Potsdam, Germany: Potsdam Institute for Climate Impact Research, 2002), p. 206.
98. UNEP, *Global Environmental Outlook 1997,* (Nairobi: UNEP, 1997), p. 201.
99. *Ibid.*
100. *Ibid.*, p. 202
101. *Ibid.*
102. UNEP, n. 11, p. 312.
103. Economic and Social Commission for West Asia (ESCWA), *World Summit on Sustainable Development Assessment for the ESCWA Region*, United Nations, New York, 2002, p. 57.
104. *Ibid.*
105. *Ibid.*, p. 310.
106. Esty, Daniel C., *et al.*, "Environmental Sustainability in the Arab World" [Online: web] Accessed on 20th June, 2008 URL:http:// www.yemenembassy.org/economic/Reports/WEF/Pages_236_248 _Environment.pdf.
107. Arab Governance, p. 1.
108. Betsill, Michele M. and H. Bulkeley, "Transnational Networks and Global Environmental Governance: The Cities for Climate Protection Programme", *International Studies Quarterly*, vol. 48, 2004, p. 481.
109. UNEP, n. 4, p. 318.
110. ESCWA, *Governance for Sustainable Development in the Arab Region: Institutions and Instruments for Moving beyond an Environmental Management Culture* (New York: ESCWA, 2003), p. 12.
111. Ayubi, Nazih N., "Policy Developments and Administrative Changes in the Arab World", in Dwivedi, O.P. and Hederson, Keaith M., eds., *Public Administration in World Perspective,* (Ames: Iowa State University Press, 1990), p. 63.
112. *Ibid.*
113. ESCWA, n. 110, p. 17.
114. UNEP, *Training Manual on International Environmental Law*, (Nairobi: UNEP, 2006), p. 17.
115. ESCWA, n. 110, p. 17.
116. *Ibid.*
117. *Ibid.*
118. *Ibid.*, p. 18.
119. Gulf Research Centre (GRC), *Green Gulf Report* (Dubai: GRC, 2007), p. 6.

120. Gulf Cooperation Council, [Online: web] Accessed on 23rd June, 2008 URL: http://www.gcc-sg.org/cooperation.html.
121. GRC, n. 119, p. 7.
122. Arrackal, Alexander M., "Environment to hold the Stage: Shura discusses Comprehensive Bill today", *The Bahrain Tribune,* 4th February, 2008, [Online: web] Accessed on 23rd June, 2008 URL: http://www.bahraintribune.com/ArticleDetail.asp.
123. Bibbo, Barbara, "GCC Plans for Green Development", *Gulf News* (Dubai), 29th December, 2007[Online: web] Accessed on 23rd June, 2008 URL: http://archive.gulfnews.com/articles/07/12/29/10177981.html.
124. *Ibid.*
125. Regional Office for West Asia (ROWA)/United Nations Environment Programme, *State of Environment in the Arab Region: A Progress Report*, (Manama, ROWA/UNEP, 2003), p. 30.
126. "GCC Environment Centre agreed," *Khaleej Times*, 26th May, 2005, [Online: web] Accessed on 23rd June, 2008URL:http://www.khaleejtimes.com/DisplayArticleNew.asp?section=theuae&xfile=data/theuae/2005/may/theuae_may738.xml
127. ROWA, n. 125, p. 29.
128. GRC, n. 119, p. 56.
129. ROWA, n. 125, p. 10.
130. World Bank, *A Water Sector Assessment Report on the Countries of the Cooperation Council of the Arab States of the Gulf* (Washington, D.C.: World Bank, 2005), p. 28.
131. ROWA, n. 125, p. 13.
132. *Ibid.*, p. 5.
133. United Nations Development Programme (UNDP), *The Arab Human Development Report 2002,*(New York: UNDP, 2002), p. 47.
134. UNEP, n. 11, p. 323.
135. GRC, n. 119, p. 26.
136. Jabbra, Joseph G and Nancy W Jabbra, "Governmental Response to Environmental Challenges in the Middle East" in Jebbra, Joseph and O.P. Dwivedi, eds, *Governmental Response to Environmental Challenges in Global Perspective,* (Oxford: OIS Press, 1998), p. 132.
137. *Ibid.*
138. GRC, n. 119, p. 6.
139. Alagappa, Muthiah., "Environmental Governance: the Potential of Regional Organisations" in Chase, Pamela S., ed., *The Global Environment in the Twenty-First Century: Prospects for International Cooperation* (New Delhi: Mana Publication, 2004), p. 225.
140. UNEP, *The State of Environment 1972-2002*, (Nairobi: UNEP, 2002), p. 299.
141. Makdisi, Karim and Carol Chouchani Cherfane, *Southern Agenda on Trade and Environment Phase II: Arab Region,* Resource Paper,

International Institute for Sustainable Development (Winnipeg (Canada), 2000, p. 19.
142. ESCWA, n. 110, p. 18.
143. *Ibid.*
144. Makdisi, n. 141, p. 20.
145. UNEP, n. 98, p. 206.
146. UNEP, n. 11, p. 315.
147. Makdisi, n. 141, p. 20.
148. Centre for Environment and Development in the Arab Region and Europe (CEDARE), [Online: web] Accessed on 23rd June, 2008 URL: http://land.cedare.int/.
149. Arab Centre for the Studies of Arid Zones and Dry Lands (ACSAD), [Online: web] Accessed on 23rd June, 2008 URL: http://www.acsad.org/aboutACSAD.htm.
150. Arab Organisation for Agriculture Development (AOAD), [Online: web] Accessed on 23rd June, 2008 URL: http://www.aoad.org/about_en.htm.
151. International Centre for Agricultural Research in the Dry Areas (ICARDA), [Online: web] Accessed on 23rd June, 2008 URL: http://www.icarda.cgiar.org/AboutICARDA.htm.
152. Makdisi, n. 141, p. 20.
153. Adeel, Zafar, "Overcoming One of the Greatest Environmental Challenges of Our Times: Re-thinking Policies to Cope with Desertification", A Policy Brief based on the Joint International Conference on Desertification and the International Policy Imperative Algiers, Algeria, 17-19th December, 2006, p. 16.
154. Saab, Najib "Arab Environment Institutions in Coma", *Mectat,* March 2001, [Online: web] Accessed on 23rd June, 2008 URL:http://www.mectat.com.lb/contents/page36.htm.
155. UNDP, n. 133, p. 49.
156. At the Global Ministerial Environment Forum (2001) held in Nairobi the most conspicuous absence was that of the specialized agencies related to the environment within the Arab League, while there was a huge turnout of similar agencies affiliated to other regional groups. Desertification, water resources and genetically-modified foods were prominent concerns on the agenda. The Arab Centre for the Studies of Arid Zones and Dry Lands (ACSAD), and the Arab Organization for Agricultural Development both were absent The meeting discussed industry and clean production measures, while the Arab Organization for Industrial Development was also absent. The Arab League's Education, Culture and Science Organization (ALECSO) was also absent, missing the chance to have input not only on scientific and educational matters, but cultural topics such as the environmental perspective for dialogue between civilizations. *This conspicuous Arab absence from a meeting that will decide future issues is pitiful it is pathetic to*

observe the Arab delegates' resigned attitude during such international meetings, as if they were powerless to contribute to any change.(Emphasis added) (For further reference Saab, Najib, "Arab Environment Institutions in Coma", *Mectat,* March 2001, [Online: web]
Accessed on 23rd June, 2008 URL: http://www.mectat.com.lb/contents/page36.htm, accessed on 28th June, 2008.

157. UNEP, n. 98, p. 207.
158. *Ibid.*, p. 208
159. UNEP, n. 11, p. 315.
160. *Ibid.*
161. Conor, Robin and Stephen Dovers, *Institutional Change for Sustainable Development* (Cheltenham, U.K.: Edwar Elgar Pub., 2004), p. 98.
162. Bodansky, n. 29, p. 18.
163. Hey, Ellen., "International Institutions", in Bodansky, no. 5, p. 750.
164. Desai, n. 33, p. 18.
165. GRC, n. 119, p. 17.
166. UNEP, n. 98, p. 208.
167. UNEP, n. 11, p. 313.
168. *Ibid.*
169. *Ibid.*, pp. 313-314.
170. GRC, n. 119, p. 24.
171. *Ibid.*
172. Jordan, Andrew. *et al.*, (eds.), *New Instruments of Environmental Governance: National Experiences and Prospects* (London: Francass, 2003), p. 76.
173. UNEP, n. 98, p. 208.
174. The Global Ministerial Environment Forum held in Nairobi in 2001 was yet another chance that the Arab countries missed in order to catch up with the environmental challenges of the new millennium. At the top of the agenda of this forum, which was attended by 90 Ministers, was the discussion of an environmental plan of action for the World Summit on Sustainable Development in South Africa in 2002. They came as individuals and regional groups, bringing with them programmes and a clear conception of what their countries are expecting from the second Earth Summit. The spectrum covered the developed and developing countries. So what level of presence did Arabs have in this turning point for humanity? There were four Arab Ministers, while other Arab representation was rather low-key. Lebanon was absent, in spite of the elaborate environment plan pledged in the government's policy statement. Whilst many delegations from poor countries included experts in specialised fields of environmental and international law, the Arab delegations were signified by administrative personnel.
    Even though the Arab League was represented by the secretariat of the Council of Arab Ministers Responsible for the Environment

(CAMRE), the event deserved a stronger political presence at the level of the secretary-general of the league. The meeting discussed a series of plans presented by countries and regional groups, the most significant of which came from Canada, Germany, Britain, the European Union and groups of Northern European countries and Asia; no Arab plans were presented to express a clear opinion on the agenda at hand. One of the Arab delegates, defending his general statement, said that his Ministry was not informed of the contents of the agenda (even though the agenda had been posted on the internet months in advance!). For further details see: Saab, Najib, "Arab Environment Institutions in Coma", *Mectat,* March 2001, [Online: web] Accessed on 23rd June, 2008 URL: http://www.mectat.com.lb/contents/page36.htm, accessed on 28th June, 2008.

IV

United Nations Convention on Desertification

Global environmental issues did not really play a significant role on the international political stage until the early 1970s, as far as the United Nations (UN) and other formal negotiation settings are concerned. The consciousness of the necessity for a sustainable use of natural resources was basically, if at all, limited to national initiatives. In 1945 when the United Nations was created, the protection of environment was not an issue of global concern.[1] The UN Charter made no provision for ecological security. "Paradoxically, it is a subsidiary organ of the Economic and Social Council (ECOSOC) (of the UN), the Economic Commission for Europe, that has taken responsibility for certain questions with environmental implications. Thus, in 1956 its Transport Committee turned its attention to the question of the pollution of continental navigable waterways. Afterwards, the coal and energy committees concerned themselves with air pollution caused by coke works and power stations."[2]

Thus even though the new organization was given a significantly broader mission than that of the League of Nations, especially on economic, social and humanitarian matters,[3] the framers of the UN Charter never anticipated that environmental issues would accelerate in such a large scale and complexity.

No major international organization whose primary mission was broadly environmental, in contrast to the economic realm, in which three powerful Bretton Woods institutions—the World Bank, the International Monetary Fund, and the General Agreement on Tariffs and Trade (GATT)—shaped the development of an increasingly intergraded global economy. The existing forms of international environmental governance were rudimentary and highly fragmented across many largely independent international institutions and agencies, for whom environmental issues were secondary to their central objectives in sectors such as transport, labour, weather, health, energy and science.[4]

"Despite the absence of a specific mandate and competence over environmental matters, the very broad nature of the purposes of the UN, as expressed in Article 1 of the Charter, allowed it to develop its environmental functions within the context of its economic, social and humanitarian responsibilities."[5] Accordingly once "environmental threats did erupt on the global scene, many UN agencies and programmes responded from their area of competence. In turn, ecological concerns altered policies, programmes, and structures within the UN system."[6]

Beginning in the late 1960 and early 1970s, the UN specialized agencies "gradually developed more intentional, comprehensive, and coordinated responses to environmental problems, spurred by new scientific understandings of the earth as a total system and by increasing public awareness of global environmental threats. Legal instruments like convention, treaty, legislation, and protocol for addressing environmental issues multiplied both within and between countries."[7] Among them the United Nations Convention to Combat Desertification (UNCCD) is an example of an international regime that was set up by the initiative of the developing countries despite the unwillingness of the industrialized countries.[8] This convention made a significant contribution to take the decades-old issue of combating desertification beyond Africa and turning it into a global policy area.[9] "For a number of reasons, UNCCD is thus often regarded more as a developmental treaty than an environmental one."[10]

This chapter examines the efforts of the international community to protect global environment especially since Stockholm Conference. It studies the emergence of Multilateral Environmental Agreements (MEAs) as a mechanism to address environmental problems within the framework of global environmental governance. It also explores the evolution of UNCCD with special emphasis on the outcome of the Nairobi Conference 1977, the Rio Earth Summit 1992 and the deliberations of the Intergovernmental Negotiation Committee on Desertification (INCD). It finally analyses the structure of UNCCD including its administrative and financial aspects.

I. Stockholm Conference (1972)

Threats to the earth's flora and fauna, water system, and atmosphere are well recognized by scientists and conservationists for more than century, but only in the past few decades that nations began to address these issues on a global scale. Environmental concerns gained attention in the developed world in the 1960s through what contemporaries call "a crescendo of public concern."[11] Although environmental conditions were superior to what they were a generation earlier, the recent global threats of toxic chemicals, atomic radiation, and massive destruction of natural ecosystems exemplified a more complex reality where human impact took on a new significance.[12]

The United Nations convened the Stockholm Conference on the Human Environment in 1972, which was the first in a series of UN mega-conferences including the 1992 Rio Conference on Environment and Development (Earth Summit) and the 2002 Johannesburg World Summit on Sustainable Development.

The UN General Assembly in 1968 "recommended to the Secretary-General the collection of data on the condition of the environment in all regions of the world and suggested protective measures."[13] Accordingly in 1969 U Thant, the then UN Secretary General presented a report entitled *Man and His Environment*[14] and "stressed that a common global foe confronted all humanity, requiring a new planetary politics and concerted global action."[15] In response to this report, the UN General Assembly requested the United Nations Educational, Scientific, and Cultural Organization (UNESCO) to organize regional symposia (held between 1969 and 1971 in Asia, America, the West Asia, and Europe), and prepare a World Conference on the environment. The Conference was preceded by a report, in 10 languages, written by more than 100 scholars, entitled, *Only One World.*[16]

However, it really was the culmination of an intense preparatory process going back to Resolution 1346 (XLV) of the UN Economic and Social Council on 30th July, 1968. Based on an ECOSOC resolution and discussions in the UN General Assembly, UN member countries on December 3, 1968 decided unanimously to hold a 'UN Conference on the Human Environment.' This resolution has been described as a "conceptual milestone in the history of the relationship between humans and their environment."[17] The conference "was not given formal decision-making powers, and decisions on all outcomes of the conference had to be formally taken by the UN General Assembly during its fall session after the conference."[18]

The Stockholm 'watershed' or 'paradigm shift' so initiated must be seen in the context of several concurrent discourses. These were: first, a global rise in environmental risks, highlighted by a series of eco-disasters starting with the 1967 *Torrey Canyon case* (oil pollution in the North Sea) and the 1971 *Minamata cases* (river pollution by organo-mercury in Japan). Secondly, a growing public awareness of the 'world eco-crisis', alerted by media attention, and by seminal publications such as Rachel Carson's 1962 *Silent Spring*, Max Nicholson's 1969 *Environmental Revolution*, and the Club of Rome's 1972 *Limits to Growth*—readily espoused by the civic protest movements of the late 1960s and early 1970s and finally, innovative examples of national legislations enacted in response to the environmental challenge, including Japan's 1967 Kogai Act, Sweden's 1969 Miljoskyddslag, and the 1970 United States National Environmental Policy Act.[19]

However, Maria Ivanova, an eminent expert on Global Environmental Governance, traces the convening of Stockholm Conference in a different perspective. According to her it was basically an initiative of small group of diplomats at the UN to address environmental problems.[20]

The Stockholm Conference was called "to serve as a practical means to encourage and provide guidelines for action by governments and international organisations designed to protect and improve the human environment and to remedy and prevent its impairment, by means of international cooperation, bearing in mind the particular importance of enabling developing counties to forestall occurrence of such problems."[21] Basically the Conference was aimed at creating a foundation for comprehensive consideration within the United Nations of the problems of the human environment and to focus the attention of government and public opinion in various countries on the importance of the problem.[22]

This decision of UN is considered to be the single most turning point in the history of Global Environmental Governance. Because when the Conference was convened there was "a rather vague concept of the need for the protection of the environment, at least at the level of international law and politics. The Conference gave concrete expression to environmental concern and created momentum for further concerted international action. The work of the Conference provided, in effect, the basis of all subsequent developments."[23] Significantly, it "marked the beginning of organized international efforts to devise a comprehensive agenda to safeguard the environment while also promising economic development."[24] This conference was originally intended to be a technical and scientific meeting. However, it was expanded in the planning process to cover broader policy issues.

Delegates from 113 States and over 400 international agencies attended the Conference and discussed wide range of topics and issues concerning environmental problems.[25] Notably the former Soviet Union and most of its allies did not attend the Conference.[26] Western countries, led by the United States insisted that the Stockholm Conference would only be open to members of the UN or any of its specialized agencies (according to the so-called "Vienna formula"). This meant that East Germany would be excluded from the Stockholm Conference, as it was neither an UN member nor a member of any UN specialized agency. In contrast, West Germany, as a member of UNESCO and WHO, could attend the conference. Members of the East Bloc argued that that the environment was a global issue that transcended State borders, and that all countries should be part of the conference, including East Germany. In December 1971, however, the UN General Assembly decided in a 104-9 vote that the Stockholm Conference would be open only to members of the UN or any of its specialized agencies.[27]

"Although no binding treaties were adopted at Stockholm,"[28] the United Nations Environment Programme (UNEP)[29] was established, creating a permanent forum for monitoring global environmental trends, convening international meetings and conferences, and negotiating international agreements. UNEP is considered "as the environmental conscience of the United Nations system."[30]

Nairobi, capital of Kenya was chosen as the headquarters of UNEP. It significantly became the first one among the developing countries to host a UN agency.[31] The Nairobi proposal largely was based on the aspiration of developing countries to have the headquarters of a major UN organization in a developing country, rather than a strong belief in the importance of UNEP. The General Assembly decided that UNEP should be located in Nairobi. The decision was passed with 93 states in favour, 30 abstentions (most industrialized countries), and one opposed (United States).[32] The placement of UNEP in Nairobi was "not just a symbolic act; it was a strategic necessity without which the developing countries might never have accepted the creation of an environmental organ."[33]

This Conference was "without doubt the landmark event in the international environmentalism. It was the first occasion on which the political, social and economic problems of the global environment were discussed at an intergovernmental forum with a view to actually taking corrective action."[34] Similarly, the Conference "helped the environment from a protest movement to an established international policy agenda item."[35] This Conference "advanced the notion that environmental issues must be addressed at the international and global levels."[36] The Stockholm Conference, a watershed in international relations, "legitimised environmental policy as a universal concern among nations and so opened a place for environmental issues on many national agendas where previously they had been unrecognized."[37]

It "provided a sense of direction to the environmental policy."[38] Many States "defined the environment as a new area of governmental activity"[39] and "established environmental Ministries or environmental protection agencies ...(which) grew from 10 in 1970 to 100 by 1982.... In addition, NGOs and citizen action groups in many countries were encouraged and energised by Stockholm and increased their efforts locally and nationally."[40] The Conference also provided new global contacts and important opportunities for networking and information-sharing arrangements between scientific, educational, NGO and citizen action groups.

Recognizing the socio-economic impact on environment, the Stockholm Conference produced a seminal paper-known as the Founex Report[41] on the problems of environment and poverty.[42] An important part of the preparatory efforts to find common ground between the global North and global South was a panel of 27 experts that gathered in a small mountain village called Founex in Switzerland, from June 4-12, 1971. The Founex panel tried to develop a conceptual platform to bridge the gap between developing and industrialized countries in their attitudes towards environment and development.[43] The Founex Report also "emphasized that developing countries do indeed have environmental problems, but they differ from those of industrialized countries, and that they, in fact, result from the lack of industrial development and from the process of industrialization itself."[44]

This pioneering report, which advocated the differential

responsibility[45] among nations towards environmental protection "stressed the need to find a synthesis between environmental demands and the need for economic development of the poor nations in the world. While developing nations should make the protection of human environment (as) part of their development planning, the Western States should guarantee (that) their concern for environmental problems would not be at the expenses of economic progress in the lesser developed world."[46] Maurice Strong, chairman of the Stockholm Conference rightly, called the Founex Report, as a "major contribution to the preparations for the Conference and a historic turning point in the development-environment dialogue."[47]

> Southern position at Stockholm, so forcefully articulated in the Founex Report, has remained consistent and unchanged in the last three decades. The point that needs to be added here is that the Southern position at Stockholm—which was essentially a position of contestation, questioning the very legitimacy of the global environmental agenda as it was then conceived—not only had a deep impact on the 1972 Stockholm Conference but has had a lasting impact on the global environmental discourse since then, including at Rio in 1992 and Johannesburg in 2002.[48]

The Founex discussions and findings were followed up by a series of regional meetings held in Bangkok, Addis Ababa, Mexico City and Beirut between August and October 1971, where regional experts and environmental administrators sought to build a common ground across regions.[49]

According to Adil Najam, developing countries came to Stockholm "quite reluctantly and after much cajoling by the Conference Secretary General, Maurice Strong. They questioned the need for such a conference and viewed it not just as a distraction but as a threat to their interests; indeed, at one point before Stockholm there was the real fear that the developing countries might decide not to show up for the conference."[50] This was because in 1972 the governments of the developing countries were

> "deeply suspicious of the motives of those who sought a new concern for the human environment and its scarce resources, (and) had in mind a long history among the developed

> countries of exploitation abroad combined with protectionism at home. *They were readily convinced of the need for care of a threatened environment, but they were wholly unconvinced by the motives of those who urged such care upon them.*"[51] (Emphasis added)

This was clearly reflected when the then India's Prime Minister Indira Gandhi while addressing the Stockholm Conference, held industrialized countries responsible for many of the problems plaguing developing countries:

> "Many of the advanced countries of today have reached their present affluence by their domination over other races and countries, the exploitation of their own masses and own natural resources. They got a head start through sheer ruthlessness, undisturbed by feelings of compassion or by abstract theories of freedom, equality, or justice."[52]

Even though in the 1950s and 1960s, a host of international agencies such as UNESCO, Food and Agriculture Organization (FAO), World Meteorological Organization (WMO), and International Union on Conservation of Nature (IUCN), "conducted research and collected a wealth of information on environmental constrains in arid zones (still) desertification attracted little attention"[53] at the Stockholm Conference.

Since then, despite ebbs and flows in international concern about the environment, there was a remarkable growth, overall, in the number and range of international instruments and institutions addressing environmental problems.[54] Similarly, despite its limitations, the Stockholm Conference provided the international institutional arrangements for collectively addressing environmental problems. In other words, it laid the foundation for global environmental governance. The Stockholm Conference can rightly be "regarded as the beginning of a period in which international environmental problems were no longer perceived as technical problems only, but also as socio-economic problems."[55]

II. Multilateral Environmental Agreements (MEAs)

An important part of the global environmental governance architecture is multilateral environmental agreements (MEAs).[56] In seeking long-lasting solutions to the complex environmental problems, treaties and conventions have proved an important mechanism by which States make promises to each other to administer natural resources and manage the global environment.[57] The development of Multilateral Environmental Agreements (MEAs)[58] over the last decades has been remarkable. "There are now more than 500 international treaties and other agreements related to the environment, of which 323 are regional and 302 date from the period between 1972 and the early 2000s."[59] The emergence of regional integration bodies concerned with the environment in regions such as Europe and Central America has contributed to this increasing trend of regional conventions and treaties.[60]

This rapid proliferation of MEAs reflects more than just an emerging realization of the scope of environmental decline and its consequences. It also stems from the significant increase in the total number of nations after the independence movement of the 1950s and 1960s in Asian, African and Latin American countries. As the number of nations and national boundaries increased, the occurrences of transboundary effects were clearly witnessed. Consequently the need for MEAs to address these common problems became more apparent.[61]

Similarly, each nation is both a creator and a victim of pollution. Thus it becomes impossible for nations to protect their own environment without regional or international collaboration. Many developing countries are seriously placed in disadvantaged position due to their limited planning and administrative structure and resource constraints. Often their ability to plan effectively is also thwarted by poverty, low level of public awareness, and lack of public participation. The absence of effective legislative and administrative procedures for incorporating ecological data into decision making process constitutes another hindrance to effective natural resource management in these countries.[62]

The Stockholm Conference in 1972 "launched a global effort to protect, preserve and enhance the environment. International environmental accord-treaties and agreements were central components of this effort."[63] These global environmental instruments are collectively known as Multilateral Environmental Agreements (MEAs). These are "the legal framework for international environmental governance. They are the official expressions of the collective will of national governments to protect the environment and steward the Earth."[64] The doctrine of State sovereignty prescribes that "the state holds a monopoly on legitimacy to enter international negotiations on environmental regulations. In turn, this doctrine is institutionalized in international law and the Constitution of the United Nations systems. In consequence, it is not surprising that international environmental agreements between states are seen as the principal form of international environmental cooperation."[65]

The MEA is a broad term that relates to any of a number of legally binding international instruments through which national governments commit to achieving specific environmental goals. These agreements may take different forms, such as convention, treaty, agreement, charter, final act, pact, accord, covenant, protocol, etc."[66] However, it is widely considered that the convention[67] is "the main form of multilateral legal instrument used to address global environmental problems."[68] MEAs in many cases were developed through the United Nations specialized agencies or programmes.

Most MEAs create a series of institutional structures to administer the agreement, such as secretariats and technical and scientific committees, and invest the power to alter and amend the treaty in a Conference of the Parties (COPs), which acts by consensus in almost all cases. As a result MEAs not only embody commitments among States, they also create organisations that guide future cooperation. Moreover, the secretariats of these MEA-based regimes are either linked to the United Nations or administrated by its agencies or programmes.[69]

Although these MEAs are the primary mechanism of global environmental governance but they are not new. The first bilateral treaties on hunting and fishing were forged in the 18th century, and the first multi-country treaty focused on endangered species was signed in 1900—a treaty between the European colonial powers to conserve a number of African wildlife species.[70] Similarly the 1916 Convention for the protection of migratory birds in the United States and Canada and the treaty for the preservation and protection of fur seals are other early examples of international cooperation.[71] The number, range, complexity and political significance of international environmental agreements increased enormously on a bilateral, regional and global basis since the early 1970s.[72]

"While most countries initially confined their attention to specific environmental problems inside their borders, they are now focusing on transnational issues such as biodiversity, the depletion of ozone layer, and global warming."[73] Accordingly the nature of environmental treaties changed over the decades since 1972. Conventions negotiated in the 1970s and early 1980s were usually limited to single issues "which characterized the formative years of international environmental cooperation."[74] By the mid-1980s and early 1990s, attention shifted to broader treaties that provided the comprehensive framework for action on overarching topics.

The Earth Summit held in Rio in 1992 provided the inspiration and became the launching event for MEAs of comprehensive and integrated nature.[75] The Summit also crystallized the concept of sustainable development[76] proposed by the Brundtland Commission.[77]

Today international cooperation to address the complex environmental issues is at the core of every MEA which would not exist if nations do not come together and agree to adopt international law that governs a particular environmental issue or resource. Although actions at the national level are vital for the implementation and enforcement of MEAs, these agreements provide mechanism for nations to share experiences, approaches and policies for effective implementation.

However, the resource constraints of developing countries limit their active and larger participation during the negotiation processes.[78] These constraints make implementing environmental commitments all the more challenging. In fact, given the multitude of meetings taking place annually, developing countries are often used to send representatives from missions or embassies located in or closest to the country where meeting is taking place. As a result, developing countries, particularly the least developing countries, often are unable to draw upon the combination of diplomatic skills, as well as substantive and technical expertise that would help them during the negotiations.[79]

The principle of common but differentiated obligations and responsibilities "to a large extent determines the complex nature of the many global MEAs and the institutional structure related to them."[80] The differentiation between "developed and developing states has had consequences for the further content of the regime based on an MEA. It constitutes the basis for the financial mechanisms connected to MEAs."[81]

Despite the emergence of non-State actors, and the transfer of some responsibilities to the global, regional, and local level institutions, governments continue to be the nodal points and still control major resources for implementing environmental policies. Most countries have a basic organizational framework for environmental policies, such as environmental legislations, Ministries and specialized agencies to monitor and enforce environmental standards. However, administrative responses to complex environmental problems were ambivalent. The measures initiated by the governments were "conventional, involving modest reforms to the established procedures and structures of an administrative arrangement."[82]

The institutional capacities to cope with the challenging tasks of achieving a cleaner environment and the integration of environment and development are often either lacking or inadequate in many developing countries. Further, the legislative and institutional mechanisms for the implementation of global and regional environment conventions are too often non-existent or inadequate. Full and effective participation in treaty making process is also hampered by inadequate information and perhaps also by inadequate consultation among relevant national institutions and interest groups.[83]

However, inadequacy and ineffectiveness of existing national environmental law is a major hindrance to effective environmental management for sustainable development.[84] Because of these limitations, governments especially in developing countries, which often lack effective national policy instruments to cope with these problems, are forced to look to international agreements and co-operation frameworks.[85] The overwhelming majority of MEAs do not have scientifically or technically based indicators for appraising the performance of the MEA in improving the quality and sustainability of the environment.[86] The UNCCD through its Committee on Science and Technology (CST) continues to work on the development of benchmarks and indicators.[87]

III. Towards a UN Convention on Desertification

i. UN Conference on Desertification (Nairobi), 1977

In 1977, the United Nations' Conference on Desertification was held in Nairobi, Kenya. It was aimed at examining the causes and consequences of desertification, to assess its overall incidence, and to generate commitments from donors and countries affected by desertification to tackle these problems. The UN requested "the

Secretary-General, in cooperation with the competent bodies of the United Nations concerned, particularly the United Nations Environment Progamme, to convene an ad hoc interagency task force to assist the secretariat of the Conference."[88]

The task of this *ad hoc* inter-agency included: to prepare a world map of areas affected and areas likely to be affected by the process of desertification, to assess all available data and information on desertification and its consequences on the development process of the countries affected by desertification and to prepare an effective, comprehensive and coordinated action programme against desertification, including the building up of the indigenous and autonomous science and technology capacity in the areas concerned.[89]

The UN also asked the United Nations Development Programme (UNDP) and the UNEP "to provide financial and technical assistance for undertaking the collection of data and information, analyses and studies on all aspects of the problem of desertification and on that basis, as part of the preparatory process for the Conference and in consultation with the Governments, concerned, to sponsor, in co-operation with the regional commissions, technical meetings at the regional and sub-regional levels as appropriate."[90]

Accordingly the Conference was preceded by four regional intergovernmental conferences and a number of technical experts meetings. Four scholarly reviews were commissioned to examine the relationship of desertification to climate, ecological change, technology and society. Besides these, a number of studies funded by the UN Development Programme analyzed not at the global scene but at the actual processes of desertification in developing countries. They critically examined the processes of desertification in different ecological and socio-economic circumstances, and looked at the efficacy of remedial action. Yet another group of scientists considered the feasibility of transnational attempts to fight desertification. Global and regional desertification maps were prepared. Based on all these, an overview was prepared, which served as the main document for conference delegates.[91]

In contrast with the popular expectation, the Nairobi Conference "did not produce any tangible results."[92] After extensive consultations and debates, the conference adopted Plan of Action to combat desertification. The UNEP was entrusted with the task of following up and coordinating the implementation of the PACD.[93] UNEP established a Desertification Branch, an Inter-agency Working Group and a Consultative Group on Desertification Control (CGDC). In 1978 the Desertification Control/Programme Activity Centre was set up in the newly established UNEP to follow up on the commitments made, and to provide technical support to countries undertaking plans of action to combat desertification.[94] Inter-agency co-ordination was also addressed through the UN Administrative Committee on Co-ordination (ACC). The UNEP Governing Council reported annually to the UN General Assembly on progress achieved in implementing the PACD including reporting on the Sudano-Sahel region.[95]

In 1984 an assessment was undertaken to review the progress made in combating desertification. This was done by sending out a questionnaire to all nations, requesting information on changes in the incidence of land suffering or at risk from desertification. The report showed a very large increase in areas affected by desertification and substantial parts were at risk. However, this was attributed to changes in definition of desertification which included the dry sub-humid zone, and adding in not only land suffering, but also land thought to be at risk from desertification.[96] In 1984 the UN General Assembly noted "with great concern that, during the seven years since the United Nations Conference on Desertification in 1977, desertification has continued to spread and intensify in developing countries, particularly in Africa."[97]

In order to expedite the process it decided "to expand the role of the Consultative Group for Desertification Control, which (was) financed from voluntary contributions to include explicitly responsibility for advising the Executive Director"[98] of UNEP. The expanded areas included: to examine the progress and effectiveness of activities implemented under the Plan of Action by identifying constraints and possible solutions to problems, taking account of relevant evaluations and case studies, to enhance the programme priorities of the UNEP related to desertification and to suggest measures required to improve implementation of the Plan of Action on a regional and worldwide basis.[99]

To give further impetus to the process of combating desertification, the UN again urged governments in the countries "prone to or suffering from desertification to give priority to the establishment of national programmes to combat desertification and to consider setting up appropriate national machinery or assigning responsibility to existing national machinery, where appropriate to that end."[100]

The Action Plan called for a yearly investment of $5-8 billion over 20 years for full implementation.[101] The UN General Assembly established a Special Account for anti-desertification project finance, despite opposition from certain donor nations. However, this was not destined to be successful.[102] By December 1988 a total of $166,886 had been paid into the account. [103] The UNEP itself spent $20 million on desertification between 1974 and 1983, but over all only $7 billion was spent between 1978 and 1983 ($17 million per year or 0.2 per cent of that needed). The donor community did not contribute and only the developing countries expressed support.[104]

However, UNEP made substantial efforts to implement the PoA. Sixty-one training courses, seminars and workshops were sponsored by UNEP worldwide. It has provided additional anti-desertification training for 1873 professional and basic training for over 1600 people. Furthermore 5000 people were trained.[105]

The PACD envisaged both transnational projects (for example a transnational green belt in North Africa) and action by national governments. It was not a success. A major reason for this was that the investment in the form of aid from donor nations did not materialize. UNEP estimated in 1980 that about US $90 billion would be required to finance a programme to meet the demands of the core of the PACD over twenty years. This would have rehabilitated all desertified irrigated land, 70 per cent of rain-fed cropland and 50 per cent of range lands.[106] Similarly the national planning to combat desertification was also faltered. By 1984 only two countries (Sudan and Afghanistan) had drawn up anti-desertification plans, although there were nine others in draft.[107]

In 1990 an external review was undertaken on the implementation of PoA and the extent to which UNEP fulfilled its mandate. The report observed that despite the plethora of plans, activities and organizations to combat desertification at national, regional and international levels, the efforts to combat desertification met with limited success. This was due to lack of political will, lack of funds, lack of people's participation, lack of coordination, destructive land tenure policies, war, misdirected research priorities, failure to include desertification control activities in national development plans and failure of governments to make desertification a priority.[108]

It concluded that the principles contained in the Plan of Action remained valid, but that a number of shortcomings within the Plan hindered its implementation.[109] While acknowledging the validity of the PoA, the report recommended "slight revisions that should give greater emphasis to socio-economic factors associated with desertification."[110] This was in fact the turning point towards the need for a comprehensive approach to address desertification. UNEP undertook another review in 1992 for the Earth Summit. This time GPS monitoring systems and satellites were used to analyze the desertification. It became impressively evident that desertification worsened rapidly. Based on this UNEP published a World Atlas of Desertification.

The PACD was a purely declarative paper not only without any legally binding status, but also without benchmarks, indicators or monitoring and evaluation scenarios. It proved to be least effective.[111] Despite the initial optimism, according to all assessments the Action Plan has largely failed.[112] Moreover, few countries ever showed deeper interest to commit themselves to support the implementation process of the PACD.[113] "Chronic inadequacy of funding, in the context of a monumental challenges has thwarted possible efforts"[114] in addressing the issue of desertification in a sustained a manner.

Despite numerous international efforts, in the early 1990s it was concluded that PACD was not working and the problem of land degradation was actually intensifying, rather than abating, globally.[115] However, the "Action Plan became the framework for national and international action for the next 15 years under the general guidance of UNEP"[116] to address desertification. In other words, the "non-binding PACD not only served as the precursor to the legally binding (UN)CCD but laid down the foundation of the latter's substance and architecture."[117] Also the period between Stockholm and Rio "witnessed several trials (with financing mechanism), national surveys, field experiments for combating mobile sands, experiments with tree planting including agro-forestry in drylands, experiments with mobilizing popular support and participation including involvement of societal organizations, etc."[118] This institutional interest and the persistence of Sahelian and African drought through the 1970s and 1980s kept desertification on the international agenda.[119]

ii. Earth Summit (Rio Summit), 1992

The number and severity of environmental problems with global implications increased significantly over recent years. The new scientific data on environmental problems have led to an increase in awareness and concern about the present condition of the earth's ecosystem. "In the 1980s, it was increasingly apparent that the existing network of global institutions centred on the United Nations (UN) was inadequate for the urgent task of taking remedial action to counter global process of environmental change"[120] including desertification.

The World Commission on Environment and Development rightly said "(t)he integrated and interdependent nature of new challenges and issues contrasts sharply with the nature of institutions that exist today. These institutions tend to be independent, fragmented and working to relatively narrow mandates with closed decision processes... the real world of interlocked economic and ecological systems will not change; the policies and institutions concern must change."[121]

Against this background the UN convened a Conference on Environment and Development (UNCED) (also known as the Earth Summit) in June 1992 in Rio de Janeiro, Brazil in June 1992, which provided a platform for addressing a number of major global environmental concerns such as climate change, biodiversity, deforestation, etc. The Rio Summit also highlighted the problem of desertification. The Earth Summit "marked an unprecedented endorsement of an environmental agenda for the twenty-first century, Agenda 21. This agenda represents a global consensus and political commitment to sustainable development at the highest level of governments."[122] At the Rio Summit, "it became clear that if the developed countries of the world wanted the environment to be secured for the future generations, then they would have to radically assist the South in choosing a different road to development than the one they had currently been travelling on."[123]

Equally the Rio Summit is "regarded as incomparable and the most important event to date in global environmental politics. The conference represented a watershed due to (its) comprehensive calls for linking environmental and development issues... Expectations of the representatives from the 180 participating countries ran high, and the concept of sustainable development, which had become a sort of slogan, introduced a new quality in international cooperation."[124]

On their part the Non-Governmental Organizations (NGOs) were actively involved in the Rio conference in a number of ways. In fact UNCED is "associated with the beginning of the participatory turn of global environmental governance."[125] A number of NGOs with "specific expertise took part in working groups on various issues that were convened by the secretariat to provide input into the process of developing draft documents. At the preparatory committee meetings and at the conference itself, many groups participated actively in the negotiations by lobbying delegates directly to make changes to the negotiating texts."[126] Some even served as members of official delegations at these events. Other NGOs made their influence felt outside the official proceedings by interpreting events for international media or by organizing parallel gatherings.[127] "Reference should also be made to the 'alternative treaties'[128] prepared at Rio by the International NGO Forum, in the context of the parallel independent sector 'Global Forum 92' which was attended by more than 8000 non-governmental groups and organizations."[129]

The UNCED is considered as a landmark event as far as the issue of desertification convention is concerned. During the 1977-92 period there has been disheartening slowness in effective action for combating desertification.[130] PACD, "which many felt had not given the desired results, mainly because of a lack of funding. For this reason, the African countries in particular looked the Rio process as an opportunity to make a new start on the subject (desertification)."[131] They saw "an opportune moment at the Earth Summit in Rio to push for a more binding international agreement which is more forceful in nature than the UNCOD Plan of Action."[132]

The UN General Assembly, through its Resolution 44/228 invited the UNCED "to accord high priority to desertification control and consider all means necessary, including financial, scientific and technological resources, to halt and reverse the process of desertification with a view to preserving the ecological balance of the planet,"[133] and invited UNEP to provide a report on the progress of the implementation of the PACD. More significantly, on the insistence of African members of the G77, desertification was afforded a very special place of prominence in this resolution. In fact, in specifically calling upon UNCED to accord high priority to desertification control, UN resolution gave much more importance to desertification than, for example, issues like climate change, biodiversity and deforestation.[134]

The UN elected the outstanding Singaporian diplomat and scholar Tommy Koh to chair the Preparatory Committee (Prepcom) of the UNCED. The Preparatory Committee for the Rio Summit was "organized into three plenary Working Groups. It was decided that Working Group I, dealing with Agenda 21 chapters on atmosphere, land management and biological diversity, would be chaired by representative from OECD group. The post was initially flagged for the Netherlands, but when their candidate had to abstain, a Swede seemed a logical choice....since (Sweden) had initially proposed the holding of the Rio Conference, 20 years after the Stockholm Conference on human environment, in 1972."[135] Ambassador Bo Kjellen of Sweden became the Chairman of the Working Group I, which dealt with the issue of desertification.

In contrary to the UN mandate, the UNCED preparatory process paid little attention to desertification. Since the UN Resolution did not mention about Convention, it just invited the UNCED to 'accord high priority', therefore desertification was given little attention during the first three sessions of the UNCED Preparatory Committee (PrepCom). At PrepCom I, decision 1/15 (Soil Loss, Desertification and Drought) invited UNEP to report on the implementation of the PACD and requested the UNCED Secretariat to consult with the specialized agencies dealing with the implementation of the PACD and report on the results achieved, the control measures applied and the need for further international cooperation to combat desertification. They also requested that the Secretariat prepare a study on the ways and means of expanding reforestation activities to combat land degradation and desertification. At PrepCom II, the UNCED Secretariat presented a document on the protection and management of land resources. The governments requested the Secretariat to elaborate on these proposals at PrepCom III.[136]

At PrepCom III the UNCED Secretariat presented a "Report of the Secretary-General of UNCED on Combating Desertification and Drought" that contained a review of the issues, a report on current work in the area by the various UN agencies and a discussion of progress made on the implementation of measures to address desertification. Annexes to this document included a UNEP progress report, a review of drought monitoring and research activities and reports on reforestation activities to combat desertification, and alternative and sustainable systems of production and livelihoods in marginal lands.

Working Group-I did not address desertification until the third week of the session and discussion was cut short due to lack of time and unavailability of relevant documents in all working languages. There was criticism, especially on the part of the developing countries, of the proposed programme areas for Agenda 21. In decision WG.I/L.29, the governments requested the Secretariat to present a revised set of proposals for PrepCom IV and, at the insistence of the

African Group, it was later decided that Working Group-I would put the issue of desertification at the top of its agenda for PrepCom IV,[137] to be held just a couple of months before the Rio Conference.

Meanwhile to learn more about the problem of desertification, Bo Kjellen, Chairman of the Working Group-I, undertook a trip to the region of West Africa in early 1992. In the words of Kjellen,

> "(t)his visit to the drylands of Mauritania and Mali was a real eye-opener for me and convinced me of the need for using the Rio process to promote more efficient action by the international community on the problems of drought and desertification. It was also during the trip that we learnt that African Ministers....had called for regional convention on drought and desertification. Our small delegation felt that this could offer a real opportunity for the Rio Conference, provided a convention could be worked out in a way that would lead to real improvements in the situation."[138]

This visit had profound impact on Bo Kjellen and at the closing session of INCD what he said is a clear reflection of this impact.

> "...I cannot cease to remember the image I had of the sandstorm in Mauritania: women and men in a struggle for life. At one of our former sessions I emphasized that we should give to these women, to these men, the necessary instruments. Now the instruments are there. The action can begin. It is not diplomacy, drafting texts and phrases, that counts any more. The reality will judge and tell us if this convention will be successful."[139]

In 1991 the focus of the preparatory session changed when the African Ministers for Environment formally called for adoption of a convention to combat desertification. In December 1991 more than 40 Ministers of Environment from African States met in Abidjan, Cote d'Ivoire for a regional preparatory meeting for UNCED and adopted the African Common Position on Environment and Development accompanied by the Abidjan Declaration. Among other things, this document strongly called for a convention to combat desertification as one of the concrete outcomes to be included in Agenda 21."[140]

This spirited call for convention from the African countries "reflected their sense of frustration with the emphasis and direction taken by the debate, with its focus largely on climate change and biodiversity—both issues of much greater interest and importance to the richer nations. They felt that their priority concerns regarding poverty, drought and food insecurity were not received the attention (as) they deserved."[141] The African countries "felt that their problems were not given sufficient attention, neither by the government of industrialized countries nor by the Non-Government organization (NGO) community, which began to yield considerable influence in the Rio process."[142] The African intention was "clearly to put the drylands problems on an equal footing with these other conventions."[143] The "OECD countries promised, as a consequence, to start negotiations for a desertification convention as a means of keeping African governments engaged in the Rio process."[144]

At the last PrepCom meeting before Rio in March 1992, the African Group made a consolidated proposal on desertification and drought, a text which became the Chapter 12 of *Agenda 21*. The questions of a convention remained controversial however. Within the developing countries also there was disagreement on the nature of convention on desertification. The African proposal for a convention to combat desertification "got rather lukewarm reception from the rest of the G77 when the entire Group met in Kuala Lumpur in early 1992 and failed to endorse the African call in its communiqué. Although the issue had not yet become an open dispute within the G77, the seeds of dissent had been sown."[145] Representatives of the other parts of the developing world "underlined that they had problems of the same nature, and that a convention had to be global."[146] "The Group of 77 ... modified the original African proposal—which had called for a regional convention on Africa—into a global convention."[147]

The draft, which later became Chapter 12 of *Agenda 21* was tabled at PrepCom IV as the first substantive item of business for Working Group I. The African Group presented a series of amendments, including a new programme area, "Encourage and Promote Popular Participation and Environmental Education Focusing on Desertification Control," to this document and the revised text became the basis for negotiation. By the end of the session, the PrepCom had adopted almost the entire *Agenda 21* chapter on combating desertification. However, they were unable to reach consensus on two paragraphs that dealt with a future binding convention on desertification.

Desertification was added to the global agenda at the UNCED because of African persistence and the unexpected support from US for the African position. At UNCED in Rio de Janeiro, Ambassador Tommy Koh of Singapore, Chair of the Main Committee, took personal responsibility for holding informal consultations on the issue of adopting a convention to combat desertification. These consultations were facilitated when the US delegation announced that it changed its position and could now support the idea of a convention. "This support came, it is believed, in response to the environmental criticism, the US received for failing the Biodiversity Convention and for dragging its feet in the preparations for Climate Change Convention."[148] Adger, W. Neil, *et al.*, argues that the "concession of US support for a desertification convention can also be interpreted as part of a trade-off between North and South—the EU and the US expected the African States to be supportive regarding the remaining issues in the Rio declaration. Thus...the desertification crisis rhetoric is directly tied to the political and managerial outcomes."[149]

However, when compromise text was brought to the Main Committee, the European Community (EC) announced it could not accept a global convention to combat desertification. "They felt that desertification was not a global problem of the same kind as, for example, climate. It was certainly a problem of global significance, but that would not necessarily warrant a global arrangement."[150] Only France, with its special historical ties with Africa, expressed support for the idea of a global convention. Most industrialised countries and even the World Bank argued that the primary problems were with the structure and macroeconomic policies of African Governments.[151] Intense negotiations followed between the Africans and the Europeans as well as within the EC.[152] Finally, the EC announced that it would accept the wording proposed by the Chair that would request the UN General Assembly to establish an Inter-governmental Negotiating Committee (INC) to elaborate a convention to combat desertification. Since the beginning the industrialized countries opposed the Convention because "they were not willing to undertake any financial responsibility for arresting the process of desertification."[153]

Finally, Chapter 12 of Agenda 21 included the provisions for a convention and fulfilled at least in principle the long standing demand of African nations and other developing countries. UNCED requested "the General Assembly at its forty-seventh session to establish, under the aegis of the General Assembly, an inter-governmental negotiating committee for the elaboration of an international convention to combat desertification, in those countries experiencing serious drought and/or desertification, particularly in Africa, with a view to finalizing such a convention by June 1994."[154] However, by requesting the UN to establish an Inter-governmental Committee to negotiate a Convention, the UNCED in fact shifted the battleground from Rio to New York.

iii. Intergovernmental Negotiation Committee on Desertification (INCD)

While the idea of a convention to combat desertification was discussed during the UNCED preparatory process, it was in Rio where language was adopted requesting the UN General Assembly (GA) to establish an inter-governmental negotiating committee for the purpose of negotiating the convention. However, the Rio Summit, which concluded on 14th June, 1992, left a series of specific recommendations[155] to be considered by the UN General Assembly at its 47th Session. The deliberations on UNCED follow-up were the responsibility of the Second Committee of the UNGA, which dealt with economic and social issues. To save time, the Second Committee agreed that all negotiations on UNCED-related issues would take place in a special open-ended *ad hoc* working group of the Second Committee under the Chairmanship of Malaysian Ambassador Razali Ismail.[156]

In early October 1992, the African Group began consultations on a draft resolution presented by Algeria, Mauritania and Tunisia. By 28th October, 1992, the African economic experts' group, chaired by Benin, agreed on a draft resolution. The draft was procedural in nature, since the African Group chose to leave the more complicated details regarding the terms of reference until after the establishment of the Inter-governmental Negotiation Committee on Desertification. The draft resolution was then approved by the African Group at the Ambassadorial level on 30th October, 1992 and forwarded to the Group of 77 as a "non-paper". The draft resolution called for "an INC to prepare an International Convention "to combat desertification in those countries experiencing serious drought and/or desertification, particularly in Africa" by 1994."

This non-paper presented by the African Group was slightly modified within the G-77, which made changes to the title and several paragraphs in order to bring the language used in conformity with the exact wording found in Chapter 10, paragraph 40 of *Agenda 21*. The draft resolution was formally introduced by Pakistan on behalf of the G-77 member States to the Razali Group on 7th November, 1992.[157] After Razali Committee submitted its report, Algeria, on behalf of the G-77 and China, introduced the draft resolution on the Convention to Combat Desertification in the Second Committee on 15th November, 1992.[158]

Based on the recommendations of the Second Committee and the Razali Group, the UN decided "to establish, under its auspices, an Inter-governmental Negotiating Committee for the elaboration of an international convention to combat desertification in those countries experiencing serious drought and/or desertification, particularly in Africa, taking into account proposals that may be submitted by States participating in the negotiating process, with a view to finalizing such a convention by June 1994."[159] It also welcomed the candidature of Ambassador Bo Kjellen (Sweden) for the Chairmanship of the Committee.

The UN requested "the Secretary-General to establish at Geneva as soon as possible an *ad hoc* secretariat of appropriate size and calibre, drawing, *inter alia*, on staff resources of the United Nations system, in order to ensure that the *ad hoc* secretariat embodies the requisite technical expertise to assist the Inter-governmental Negotiating Committee in the fulfilment of its mandate."[160] Responsibility for administering the negotiation was delegated to this *ad hoc* secretariat, "answerable directly to the General Assembly, not to the UNEP. This was a reflection of the growing disillusion of developing countries with UNEP, because they perceived it to be increasingly biased towards Northern environmental concerns. Stripping UNEP of a leading role in environmental negotiations and giving overall control to the UN General Assembly theoretically gives greater powers to developing countries, because they are in the majority, and places greater emphasis on development."[161] The Resolution requested "the head of the *ad hoc* secretariat to make available to the Inter-governmental Negotiating Committee, at the first substantive session, the most relevant and recent information available, in conformity with its mandate."[162]

The UN also decided "to establish a multidisciplinary panel of experts to assist the *ad hoc* secretariat and, under its authority, to provide the necessary expertise in the scientific, technical, legal and other related fields, making full use of the resources and expertise within and available to Governments and/or organizations of the United Nations system dealing with drought and desertification."[163]

Importantly the panel included not only scientific and technical experts but social scientists as well. "There were 15 on the panel, representing all regions of the world. The panel was scheduled to meet roughly six weeks before each meeting session."[164]

During the CCD negotiations (unlike in previous eras) science was not considered the primary resource for understanding causes and consequences of desertification and devising its solutions. Therefore, this panel "played a minor role in Convention negotiations."[165] Similarly, "(u)nlike participants in the 1977 (Nairobi) Conference, INCD delegates did not identify a single category, such as land use, as responsible for desertification. They pointed instead to complex interactions among ecological, social and political factors."[166]

At the organizational session of the INCD in January 1993, delegates elected Bo Kjellén as Chair of the Committee. The first session of the INCD was held in Nairobi from 24th May-3rd June, 1993. The first week of the session focused on the sharing of technical information and assessments on various aspects of drought and desertification. The second week focused on the structure and elements to be contained in the Convention.

Delegates also exchanged ideas about the CCD and its objectives. The second session of the INCD met in Geneva from 13-24th September, 1993. The Committee considered the compilation text of the CCD prepared by the Secretariat and agreed on the future programme of work of the Committee, including the elaboration of regional instruments for Africa, Asia and Latin America. The third session of the INCD was held at UN Headquarters in New York from 17-28th January, 1994. At this session the two working groups focused on the draft negotiating text of the Convention that was prepared by the Secretariat. Progress was made in shaping the Convention and in identifying the areas of convergence and divergence. The INCD also discussed the elements to be contained in the regional instrument for Africa.[167]

The fourth session of the INCD was held in Geneva from 21-31st March, 1994. The two working groups continued negotiating the Draft Convention text. Delegates also formally considered the Regional Implementation Annex for Africa for the first time. The Asian and Latin American regional groups produced their own draft regional implementation instruments. Although these annexes were not discussed in detail, the initial reaction was positive.

Table 4.1: Time Table of the UNCCD's Evolution

Sl. No.	*Pre-negotiation Phase (1989-1992)*	*Negotiation Phase (1993-94)*	*Interim Phase (1995-1997)*
1.	UN General Assembly (Res. 44/228), December 1989	Organizational Session, New York, January 1993	INCD-6 New York, January 1995
2.	Meeting of African Environmental Ministers, Abidjan, November 1991	INCD-1 Nairobi, June 93	INCD-7 Nairobi, August 1995
3.	UNCED Pre Com-IV, New York, March 1992	INCD-2 Geneva, September 1993	INCD-8 Geneva, February 1996
4.	UNCED, Rio de Janeiro, June 1992	INCD-3 New York, January 1994	INCD-9 New York, September 1996
5.	UN General Assembly, December 1992	INCD-4 Geneva, March 1994	INCD-10 New York, January 1997
6.	—	INCD-5 Paris, June 1994	UN General Assembly, special session, New York, June 1997
7.	—	—	INCD-10 (resumed) Geneva, August 1997
8.	UNGA decision to negotiate a Convention on Desertification, 22nd December 1992	CCD adopted, 17th June, 1994	CCD came into force, 26th December 1996

Source: Najam, Adil, "Dynamics of the Southern Collective: Developing Countries in Desertification Negotiations". *Global Environmental Politics* (Massachusetts Institute of Technology), vol. 4, no. 3, 2004, p. 132.

The fifth session of the INCD was held in Paris from 6-17th June, 1994. During this session, delegates worked through long nights to reach agreement on the remaining bracketed text in the Convention and to finalize the four regional implementation annexes for Africa, Asia, Latin America and the Caribbean, and the Northern Mediterranean. The Convention was adopted on 17th June, 1994 and opened for signature at UNESCO Headquarters in Paris.[168]

> "This (legally) binding instrument under international law came into being primarily at the instigation of the African countries, which see the UNCCD as 'their' convention."[169]

Along with the UNCCD, the Resolutions that recommended urgent action for Africa and interim arrangements for the period between adoption of the UNCCD and its entry into force was also adopted.[170] The United States is "a signatory but has not ratified the convention."[171] "The 50th ratification of the convention was announced by Chad in September 1996, leading to the treaty entering into force in December 1996."[172]

After the UNCCD was adopted, the UN decided to extend the term of INCD beyond its five sessions which was originally mandated. This was made due to the following reasons:

(a) To prepare for the first session of the Conference of the Parties to the Convention, as specified in the Convention;
(b) To facilitate the implementation of the provisions of Committee resolution 5/1 on urgent action for Africa, through the exchange of information and the review of progress made thereon;
(c) To initiate measures relating to the identification of an organization to house the global mechanism to promote actions leading to the mobilization and channelling of substantial financial resources, including its operational modalities;
(d) To elaborate the rules of procedure of the Conference of the Parties; and
(e) To consider other relevant issues, including measures to ensure the implementation of the Convention and its regional annexes.[173]

The interim period of two to three years was due to the time taken for national governments to ratify the convention by passing legislation through their national Parliaments. A minimum of fifty such ratifications is needed for the ICD to enter into force. The first COP will be held six months after the fiftieth ratification of the Convention is notified to the UN.

During the interim period, it was planned to hold several meetings bringing together representatives of national governments and international agencies. It is unclear what agenda such meetings will follow, given that the negotiations of the ICD were completed in June 1994. The first of these interim meetings was held in January 1995 in New York, the second in August 1995 in Nairobi, and the next is scheduled for early 1996. Although United Nations General Assembly Resolution 47/188 called for only five sessions of INCD, the 49th General Assembly extended the INCD's mandate during the interim period before the convention's entry into force.[174]

IV. UN Convention on Desertification

The history of desertification as a global policy issue predates the history of the desertification convention. "Although the Great Sahelian Drought (1968-1973) was devastating large parts of Africa at that very time, desertification as an issue was not on the international environmental policy radar at the 1972 United Nations Conference on the Human Environment (UNCHE) at Stockholm."[175]

Still the Stockholm Conference is considered as a milestone in global environmental governance. For the first time it raised the environmental issues to the highest level of international politics. In 1974, the United Nations called for global action on desertification with the passage of Resolution 3337 (XXIX) recommending a Conference on Desertification (UNCOD) in 1977. It took another 15 years, however, for an internationally sanctioned plan of action to be developed in the form of the UN Convention to Combat Desertification (UNCCD), one of the three "Rio Conventions" (so-named because they were created at the 1992 UN Conference on Environment and Development held at Rio).[176]

The UNCCD is "the newest link in the evolving international system for environmental governance. In linking a serious environmental concern with development issues, this convention can be viewed as an important step towards building a multilateral framework for sustainable development."[177] The UNCCD has successfully "raised the profile of desertification issues at the national and regional levels, and has boosted support for those at the national level who have responsibility for implementing it."[178] This Convention recognizes desertification "primarily (as) a problem of sustainable development, poverty and human well-being, and environmental preservation. Social, and economic issues, including food security, migrations and political instability are closely linked to land degradation."[179] The UNCCD is "more strongly based on upon socio-economic criteria than the Convention on Biological Diversity."[180] Therefore, it is "a much more comprehensive treaty than earlier efforts"[181] to combat desertification. Similarly "the perceived failure of the plan of action to combat desertification contributed significantly to the distinctive character of the convention,"[182] since desertification in the beginning was treated "as a stand-alone problem best addressed through technical interventions."[183]

The Desertification Convention created important political conditions by defining basic requirements for combating desertification. Among others, these are increasing efficiency through bilateral and multilateral cooperation, exchange of data and mutual information between donors, public participation of the population, strengthening support through transfer of research and technology, taking local conditions into consideration and providing for active participation of affected countries.

The UNCCD is unique in a number of ways. First, by its geographical focus on drylands, the Convention brought attention to some of the most vulnerable ecosystems and people in the world. Second, it is the only international instrument that emphasizes on sustainable land management, an issue traditionally addressed within the strict scope of national policies and programmes. And third, this is the only global treaty that focuses on developing countries, specifically in Africa, and on improving living conditions for rural populations, who represent an important proportion of the world's poor.[184] In the words of Bo Kjellen, INCD Chair, UNCCD is "a robust Convention that is coherent, legally consistent, innovative and balanced between the perception of desertification as a global problem and the obvious need for specific recognition of regional differences."[185]

Desertification impacts the economic growth of not only the affected region, but also the countries as a whole, their social and economic development. Desertification and drought affect sustainable development through their interrelationships with important social problems such as poverty, poor health and nutrition, lack of food security, and those arising from these such as migration, social conflicts and unrest.

Therefore, UNCCD recognizes: the *physical, biological and socio-economic aspects of desertification*. The core of the CCD is the development of national and subregional/regional action programmes by national governments in cooperation with donors, local populations and Non-Governmental Organizations (NGOs).

The Convention includes a number of innovations in the field of international law, in particular the notion of "demand-oriented technology transfer", i.e. countries concerned define by themselves, in the context of national action programmes, what the best way to combat desertification is for their specific situation, and the bottom-up approach, i.e. the involvement of the local population in the development and implementation of such national action plans.

An important sign of the UNCCD's commitment to the bottom-up approach was the COP-1 invitation for NGOs to organize a plenary dialogue with delegates on building partnerships for the UNCCD. Conference of Parties' first meeting (COP-1) delegates adopted a decision calling for plenary meetings at future COPs to be devoted to similar NGO dialogues.

The Convention itself contains one Preamble and 38 Articles divided into six parts: Part I: Introduction (Articles 1 to 3); Part II: General Provisions (Articles 4 to 8); Part III: Action Programmes, Scientific and Technical Cooperation and Supporting Measures (Articles 9 to 21); Part IV: Institutions (Articles 22 to 25); Part V: Procedures (Articles 26 to 32); and Part VI: Final Provisions (Articles 33 to 38). Regional implementation annexure are considered to be an integral part of the convention and have same legal standing as the rest of the convention (Article 29 of the Convention).[186]

i. Objectives

The important objective of the Convention as stated in Article 2 is "to combat desertification and mitigate the effects of drought in countries experiencing serious drought and/or desertification, particularly in Africa, through effective action at all levels, supported by international cooperation and partnership arrangements, in the framework of an integrated approach which is consistent with Agenda 21, with a view to contributing to the achievement of sustainable development in affected areas."[187]

In order to achieve these objectives, the Convention specifies the following four principles. These are (i) participation of populations and local communities, (ii) improved cooperation and coordination at sub-regional, regional and international levels, (iii) cooperation among all levels of government, communities, NGOs and land-holders, and (iv) full consideration taken of the special needs and circumstances of affected developing countries Parties, particularly the least-developed among them (Article 3).

Besides these principles the convention creates three kinds of obligations. These are general obligations applicable to all members. There are some specific obligations for the developing and developed countries.

General obligations of all Parties include to:

- adopt integrated approaches addressing the physical, biological and socio-economic aspects of desertification and drought;
- give due attention to international trade, marketing arrangements and debt issues;
- promote cooperation among affected country Parties for environmental protection and the conservation of land and water; and
- promote the use of existing bilateral and multilateral financial mechanisms that mobilize and channel substantial financial resources to affected developing country Parties in combating desertification and mitigating the effects of drought.

In recognition with the diversity of socio-economic development and natural resources of various regions, the UNCCD provided regional annexes to facilitate its implementation. In an innovative example of a global treaty combining general principles and obligations with region specific guidelines and measures, the UNCCD originally established four regional implementation annex[188] for Africa, Asia, Latin America and the Carribbean, and the North Mediterranean. For the Central and Eastern Europe region[189], in the fourth session of the Conference of the Parties (COPs-4) in 2000 a fifth annex was adopted[190] and which came into force on 6th September, 2001.[191]

These Annexes, an integral part of UNCCD "which provide guidelines for implementation constitute an integral part of the convention. All the annexes contain, *inter alia*, detailed rules concerning commitments and obligations of the parties, national, sub-regional and regional programmes, financial issues, technical assistance and transfer of technology."[192] The African Annex is "the most detailed and contains provisions for financial mechanisms and resources, co-ordination, partnership and follow-up arrangements."[193]

ii. Administrative Structure of UNCCD

For the purpose of facilitating implementation, MEAs adopted after

1972 generally have the following institutional elements: a Conference of the Parties (CoP), a secretariat, advisory bodies, a clearing-house mechanism and a financial mechanism. Other important measure to ensure the effectiveness of MEAs is the provision for reporting requirements aimed at verifying and monitoring the implementation of the Convention.[194] Subsidiary bodies are generally advisory in nature. Several conventions and protocols have subsidiary scientific and technical bodies that provide advice and recommendations to their respective CoPs on the scientific and technical aspects of the implementation.

The administrative arrangements established by many MEAs represent a new form of international cooperation. This institutional set up "provides the backbone to the agreement and ensures that the legal mechanism is implemented by the states parties to it. There are variations among different MEAs as regards the institutional structures laid down on the basis of requirement of the specific environmental issue." [195] The administrative mechanism of MEAs is hierarchic, with the CoPs being the supreme body. This formation means that the subsidiary bodies and the secretariat must follow the decisions and instructions adopted by the CoPs. The organization hosting the secretariat has no power to instruct either the CoP or its subsidiary bodies.[196]

Like other MEAs, the UNCCD sets up an elaborate institutional structure to guide and support its implementation. These are CoPs, Secretariat, two subsidiary bodies—Committee to Review the Implementation of the Convention and Committee on Science and Technology and Global Mechanism as a financial arrangement.[197]

A. Conference of Parties (CoPs)

It is the Conference of Parties[198] (CoPs), which reflects the political will of the contracting States. The CoPs is "the governing body of a Convention that meets periodically and advances the implementation of the Convention. This includes defining work programmes and evaluating how countries are meeting goals related to the Convention."[199] It cannot only interpret the authority of the convention but also give effect to the in-built law-making process. Formal amendments to the convention or adoption of separate protocol to the convention require acceptance and/or ratification of the parties. All subsidiary bodies of MEAs function under the supervision of the CoPs.

Thus the institutional mechanism laid down under a MEA revolves under the CoP and is designed to realize the objectives of the agreement as well as to help it keep pace with the changing requirements of global environmental governance. There are some other subsidiary bodies which cater to various aspects of the MEA's objectives.[200] Treaty parties may have several reasons for choosing the CoPs model rather than traditional IGOs.[201]

The followings are the important mandates of CoPs to UNCCD:

1. Regularly review the implementation of the Convention.
2. Promote and facilitate the exchange of information on measures adopted by the parties and determine the shape of the time table for transmitting the information to be submitted by the parties and review the reports and making recommendation on them.
3. Establish the subsidiary bodies and provide guidance to them.
4. Approve the programme and budget for its activities.[202]

Table 4.2: Meetings of Conference of Parties (CoPs)

Sl. No.	Conference of Parties	Venue	Date
1.	CoP-1	Rome (Italy)	29 September-11 October 1997
2.	CoP-2	Dakar (Senegal)	30 November-11 December 1998
3.	CoP-3	Recife (Brazil)	15-26 November 1999
4.	CoP-4	Bonn (Germany)	11-22 December 2000
5.	CoP-5	Geneva (Switzerland)	1-12 October 2001
6.	CoP-6	Havana (Cuba)	25 August-5 September 2003
7.	CoP-7	Nairobi (Kenya)	17-28 October 2005
8.	CoP-8	Madrid (Spain)	3-14 September 2007
9.	CoP-(E-S)-1*	New York, USA	26 November 2007
10.	CoP-9	Buenos Aires, Argentina	21 September-2 October 2009

* Extraordinary Session

Source: http://www.unccd.int/cop/officialdocs/menu.php, accessed on 2nd April, 2010.

The "CoP also maintains a roster of independent experts with expertise and experience in the relevant fields that may be called upon by the CoP to provide advice on specific issues."[203] Post-negotiation, CoPs were held annually from 1997 to 2001 (Rome, Dakar, Recife, Bonn and Geneva). It was decided that subsequent CoPs would be held biennially, interchanging with sessions of the Committee for the Review of the Implementation of the Convention (CRIC). The first meeting of CRIC was held in Rome in 2002, while the sixth meeting of the CoP was held in Havana in 2003.[204]

B. Secretariat

The Secretariat of a Convention[205] is responsible for the daily operations. It performs vital functions within an MEA. It is the only visible and permanent institutional form, which services both the contracting states as well as maintains contacts with the outside world. It is a servicing arm subject to the control and supervision of the CoP. The nature of functions assigned to a Secretariat of an MEA may vary in view of the special character of each such convention.[206]

While the scope and mandate of MEA secretariats can vary, from a functional point of view they can broadly be divided into two categories: (a) secretariats that prepare and service the meetings of the CoPs and their subsidiary bodies and coordinate with other international organizations (UNFCCC, the Montreal Protocol, CBD, the Ramsar Convention, etc.); and (b) secretariats that, while carrying out the functions of the first category, are also involved in implementing programmes or projects at the regional and country levels (the Basel Convention, the UNCCD, Regional Seas Conventions and Action Plans, etc.).[207]

The functions of the secretariat are generally spelled out in the MEA. Typical functions include conducting studies, preparing draft decisions for the CoPs and subsidiary bodies, providing technical assistance to the parties, and receiving and circulating reports on the implementation of commitments. The secretariat may also serve as the conduit for cooperation with other MEAs and relevant international organizations and bodies, including financial institutions.[208] In 1999, a permanent Secretariat of the UNCCD was established in Bonn, Germany.

The issue on physical location of UNCCD was addressed during a meeting where the three countries (Canada, Germany and Spain) bidding to host the Permanent Secretariat made presentations on their offers.[209] During the first week of INCD-10, an informal group comprised the three governments involved, members from the main Bureau and the Chairs of the two Working Groups agreed on the selection procedure used at CoP-1 for the Biodiversity and Climate

Change Conventions and decided to consult further on the modalities for follow-up and the details of the procedures to be followed at CoP-1.[210]

During the resumed session the Contact Group recommended that an informal and confidential poll be conducted during a plenary meeting. Only accredited delegates of Parties will participate and their votes will be counted in the presence of the three countries offering to host the permanent secretariat and the Executive Secretary. If one city obtains an absolute majority of valid preferences it shall be proposed as the consensus decision. If no city obtains such a majority, a second round of "eliciting preferences" shall be carried out.[211] Delegates to CoP-1 on 3rd October, 1997, at the plenary session took a consensus decision after the first round of voting for the location of the Permanent Secretariat. Bonn received an absolute majority. Now it hosts the Permanent Secretariat.[212] As per the commitments, Germany provides substantial contribution towards smooth functioning of Secretariat.[213]

The important functions of the Secretariat include:

1. To provide services to the CoPs by arranging meetings, preparing documents, coordinating with other relevant bodies, compiling and transmitting information and facilitating consultations.
2. To provide assistance to affected developing countries in the compilation and communication of information that is required by the Convention particularly in Africa.[214]

The UNCCD Secretariat follows what could be described as an advocacy approach. Its work strives to support particular affected countries, occasionally even against the apparent interests of powerful developed countries. [215] Notwithstanding the limited bargaining power of the developing countries and the low priority given by developed countries on desertification, considerable achievements were made in the institutionalization of the UNCCD as well as in furthering its implementation in affected regions. These achievements can be partially attributed to the activities of the Secretariat, and notably so its strong leadership.[216] Rather than confining itself to 'doing its job' the Secretariat installed itself as a vocal advocate of affected country parties that actively challenged the constraints it faced by way of problem structure.[217]

C. Committee on Science and Technology (CST)

Many environmental regimes provide for a scientific commission or other technical committee, comprised experts. In most cases, they include members designated by governments or by the CoP, although they generally function independently.[218] Modern communications, satellite imagery, and genetic engineering are only a few examples of modern tools that can help in combating desertification. Better weather forecasts and alerts can help to maintain or increase the land's productivity while improving food security and local living conditions. New plant and animal varieties can be resistant to pests, diseases, and other dryland stresses. Photovoltaic cells and wind energy may reduce the consumption of scarce fuelwood.

For all these reasons, the UNCCD mandates to promoting technological cooperation. It calls for the promotion and financing of the transfer, acquisition, adaptation, and development of technologies that help to combat desertification or cope with its effects. These technologies should also be environmentally sound, economically viable, and socially acceptable.[219]

To facilitate the processes the Convention establishes under article 24 a Committee on Science and Technology as a subsidiary body to the Conference of the Parties. The CST provides the CoP with information and advice on scientific and technological matters relating to combating desertification. It is a "multidisciplinary committee open to all parties, composed of government representatives competent in the relevant fields of expertise"[220] from countries that ratified the Convention.

The Bureau of the CST is responsible for following up on the work of the Convention in-between CoP sessions, e.g. The committee surveys the existing networks institutions, agencies and bodies. The CST sets up and maintains a roster of independent experts and draws on it to form *ad hoc* panels to give it information and advice on specific issues. The roster shall be based on nomination received in writing from the Parties, taking into accour t the need for multidisciplinary approach and broad geographical representation. These experts shall have scientific backgrounds and field experience. The Committee on Science and Technology elects its own Bureau.[221]

D. Committee for the Review of the Implementation of the Convention (CRIC)

The CRIC finds no mention in the UNCCD. The Convention provides the power to review its implementation of the Convention with CoPs. However, due to increasing volume of work and paucity of time, the need for a separate specialized institution was felt.

The Conference of the Parties (CoP), by its decision 1/CoP.5, established the CRIC to assist the CoP in regularly reviewing the implementation of the Convention, in the light of experience gained at the national, sub-regional, regional and international levels, and to facilitate the exchange of information on measures adopted by the Parties, pursuant to Article 26 of the Convention, in order to draw conclusions. The CRIC was asked to propose to the CoP concrete recommendations on further steps in the implementation of the Convention.[222]

However, the CRIC was established not without controversies. Discussion of the approach to review implementation of UNCCD was prompted by draft decision submitted by the G-77 and China on the last day of the resumed INCD-10 Session in August 1997. It called for creation of a committee to review the implementation of the Convention (CRIC). Discussions on draft "started at CoP-1 and were conducted through open-ended informal consultations.

The OECD countries questioned whether the Convention provided for such a committee and argued that it is premature and can only be considered, at the earliest, by CoP-3. Further, the cost of such a committee could be as high as that of the CoP. Given that the CoP will be meeting each year until CoP-3, the need for an intersessional meeting to review implementation was unnecessary. The OECD even "questioned whether the proposed approach to review implementation was the most appropriate, adding that the responsibility to review implementation was vested in the CoP."[223] However, the developing countries argued that the Convention does not rule out the possibility of establishing a committee. In fact, Articles 22 (a) and (c), 26 and 27 (of UNCCD) provided for the CoP to establish institutions it deems necessary to enable it fulfil its mandate. Setting up a committee is delegating, not abdicating, responsibility. Finally, it was decided to transmit the proposal to CoP-3 if discussion was still considered premature.[224]

However, the matter came up for discussion at the CoP-2. It was agreed at the meeting "that additional time was needed to consider establishing a mechanism to assist in the regular review of implementation of the Convention. It invited Parties to make submissions regarding this issue to the Secretariat by 30th April, 1999 for compilation and consideration by CoP-3. The Secretariat was asked to include decision 10/CoP.1, which calls on CoP-3 to consider whether to establish a mechanism to assist in regularly reviewing implementation, in the CoP-3 agenda.[225]

On 26th November, 1999, the Plenary Session of CoP-3 adopted a Resolution on additional procedures or institutional mechanisms to assist the CoP in regularly reviewing the implementation of the Convention. The decision stated "that an *ad hoc* working group (AHWG) should be established at CoP-4 to review and analyze reports submitted at CoP-3 and 4."[226] It recalled that reports by governments, together with advice and information provided by the CST and the Global Mechanism, would be the basis for the review of the implementation of the Convention at CoP-4. It again invited the "Parties and other interested institutions and organizations to submit written proposals on the need to establish a committee to review the implementation of the Convention no later than 30th April, 2000, to be compiled by the Secretariat to facilitate consideration, and take a decision at its fourth and, if necessary, at its fifth session."[227] A total of 10 submissions were received from March to July 2000. Saudi Arabia was also among the one who submitted the proposal. Saudi Arabia argued that "the formation of a committee or body to supervise and control the implementation of the United Nations Convention is too early, since on national, regional and sub-regional level the implementation has not really started."[228]

On 20th December, 2000, Nigeria, for the G-77/China, took the initiative to convene and chair a Contact Group to discuss how to regularly review CCD implementation. It discussed the necessity of a committee for the review of implementation of the Convention (CRIC) and prepared a draft decision. The CoP-4 adopted the draft decision on the review of implementation of the Convention. According to this decision "the AHWG should fulfil its mandate and draw up conclusions and recommendations for further steps in implementation; and further proposals by Parties based on the experience and review of the AHWG on recommendations for review and implementation, including on the establishment of a CRIC, be submitted through the Secretariat for consideration at CoP-5."[229]

Based on the recommendations of the AHWG, the CoP-5 decided to establish a CRIC as a subsidiary body of the CoP to regularly review CCD implementation. It also adopted terms and references for CRIC which covers mandate and functions, composition, frequency of sessions and organization of the work, nature of the review and methodology and the review process.[230] It was also decided to review the working of the CRIC at the CoP-7 on the basis of lessons learned. The CoP-5 invited the "Parties to submit written proposals to the Secretariat by January 2002, criteria against which the review will be undertaken and, with others, to contribute financially to the organization of regional meetings." The Secretariat was also asked to prepare a preliminary analysis of the reports along thematic lines for submission to the CoP and the Executive Secretary to facilitate the preparation of regional inputs for the review process.[231]

The CRIC performs important functions in measuring progress in implementing the UNCCD and in serving as a platform to share best practices. However, it has not met all expectations due to the absence of an effective measurement framework with clear reporting guidelines and due to difficulties in organizing its work in a manner conducive to learning. Substantial and interactive discussions at CRIC sessions must be facilitated.[232]

iii. Financial Mechanisms of the Convention

A financial mechanism is important not only to support implementation efforts of the governments under a MEA. The realization over the years that some implementing measures can be costly and hence difficult for developing country parties to undertake resulted in parties including provisions of a financial mechanism within MEAs.[233]

The UNCCD did not make any provision for establishing a separate fund to finance desertification related projects unlike the Climate Change, Biodiversity and Ozone Protection Conventions."[234] On the other hand it established a brokering institute called 'Global Mechanism'. Therefore, the "desertification convention has not until now benefited from access to any specific financial mechanism."[235] This in fact "slowed progress in its implementation."[236]

During the negotiation of UNCCD, the G-77 and China claimed that the Convention "would be pointless unless it was backed by new resources and insisted on a new, independent, specialized fund capable of mobilizing resources. They (even) pointed to UNGA resolution 44/288 (establishment of UNCED) and chapters 12 (combating desertification) and 33 (financial resources and mechanism) of agenda 21, where commitments had been made for mobilization of new and additional financial resources."[237]

The industrialized countries, on the other hand feared that establishing new institutions would only add to an increasing international bureaucracy. The "OECD countries ...strongly opposed to establishing a financial mechanism of the same type as that of the United Nations Framework Convention on Climate Change (UNFCCC)."[238] They wanted to rationalize and strengthen existing resources before committing to provide new and additional ones. They specifically emphasized the need for an institution to coordinate the available national, bilateral and multilateral funding mechanism. They also noted that special funds were not always served effectively, and pointed out the discouraging examples of the Special Account created for implementing the PoA of Nairobi Conference.[239] "(I)n Paris in 1994, the G77 was not ready to accept the (existing) Global Environmental Facility (GEF) as such a mechanism."[240]

The deadlock on a funding mechanism was broken only after the United States proposed a Global Mechanism (GM) under the authority of the Conference of the Parties (CoPs), to be housed within an existing international organization. The purpose of Global Mechanism is to improve monitoring and assessment of existing aid flows and increase co-ordination among donors. Developing countries were dissatisfied because the GM would not increase development assistance to South. They had to accept the compromise as the only one acceptable to the donor countries. Therefore, Global Mechanism was a political compromise. GM acts as a coordinator and facilitator of funding and not an independent fund itself. Question of the globality of desertification is connected to the issue of funding mechanism: donors opposed the definition of desertification as a global problem, because they did not want to open the Global Environmental Facility window. Lack of a proper funding mechanism has hampered the relations cf industrialized and develop'ng countries throughout the negotiations.[241]

A. Global Mechanism (GM)

The UNCCD's broad approach to desertification requires a multi-source, multichannel approach to financing. However, the UNCCD achieved "no multilateral financial mechanism, but the *Global Mechanism (GM)*, which is understood as a broker or clearing house body, and also acts as consultancy and training providing entity."[242]

Under Article 21(4) of UNCCD,[243] the mandate of Global Mechanism is to promote actions leading to the mobilization and channelling of substantial financial resources to affected developing country Parties. It is not a central fund, duplicating existing funding sources and mechanisms, but rather a brokering institution which helps to rationalize the allocation of resources and mobilize additional financial resources, where necessary.

This mechanism was not conceived to raise or administer funds. Instead, the GM encourages and assists donors, recipients, development banks, NGOs, and others to mobilize funds and to channel them to where they are most needed. This process involves drawing on the classical funding instruments of bilateral and multilateral development cooperation agencies as well as GEF resources and other sources of funds.[244] The GM is under the authority of the CoP, which periodically reviews its policies, operational modalities and activities.

The CoPs-1 selected the International Fund for Agricultural Development (IFAD) to house the GM. The GM acts as a hub for a dynamic network of partners, committed to focusing their energies, resources and knowledge on combating desertification. In addition, COP-6 in 2003 accepted the *Global Environment Facility* (GEF) as a financial mechanism of the UNCCD. This decision corresponds to the establishment of land degradation as a new GEF focal area, operationalized through the Operational Programme on Sustainable Land Management.

There is evidence that the GEF's position at the centre of more than one MEA helped it avoid funding projects in one focal area that could have undermined the objectives of another focal area.[245] Since the "UNCCD offers an appropriate frame for democratic and participative action to combat desertification....much needs to be done to strengthen relations between donors and affected countries and among national actors to ensure concerted and effective"[246] mobilization of adequate financial resources to combat desertification.

B. Global Environment Facility (GEF)

The Global Environment Facility (GEF) was specifically designed to facilitate integrated responses for major environmental challenges. It acts as a financial mechanism to the Convention on Biological Diversity and the United Nations Framework Convention on Climate Change and as an interim mechanism to the Stockholm Convention and the Desertification Convention.

The GEF was established in "pursuant to an initiative by France[247], supported by Germany and World Bank ... to mobilize (new and) additional funding for basic issues of environmental concern"[248] in four focal areas: climate change, biological diversity, international waters and ozone layer depletion. The World Bank came under intense criticism in the 1980 since "(f)rom an environmental policy perspective in particular, the World Bank's lending policy has been criticized for not requiring any investigation of the environmental impacts of funded projects." [249] The "creation of GEF was one part of the World Bank's general strategy of 'greening."[250] "Well-known examples of the World Bank's poor performance in this respect are for instance the Polonoroeste regional development programme (North-eastern Brazil Integration Development Programme) or the coal-fired power project in Singrauli, India, which is currently the world's largest single source of CO_2 emissions."[251]

> "In the face of mounting criticism that it (World Bank) lends money for projects that destroy forests, farmlands, watersheds, and other natural systems, the bank sharply changed its policy in May 1987 in order to protect the environment in developing countries. It moved the environmental concerns from the periphery to the centre of the bank's development policies by creating a top-level environment department with 100 full-time staff members, which is to take the lead in integrating environmental considerations into all of the bank's lending policies."[252]

Following decision at the second GEF Assembly held in Beijing in October 2002, "the GEF Instrument was amended to include two new focal areas in land degradation and persistent organic pollutants."[253]

The roots of the present day institutional structure of GEF lie in

March 1990 Paris meeting convened by the World Bank, where 17 donor countries[254] expressed their interest in setting up a ' facility' to fund global environmental projects. At the two subsequent meetings in July and September in 1990, seven developing countries including Brazil, China, India and Mexico, joined the deliberations. It gave the mandate to the World Bank to develop a framework for the proposed GEF.[255] As a result, the (GEF) took shape as a global environmental funding institution.[256] Under a pilot phase, intended to examine its workability, several key details were worked out, especially concerning operational modalities, organizational arrangements and governance, size of the facility and funding modalities. Its governance was entrusted to three entities—UNDP, UNEP and the World Bank—but it was housed within the World Bank.[257]

The Pilot Phase ran from 1991 to mid-1994. Toward the end of the Pilot Phase, an independent evaluation of the GEF concluded that the GEF should be replenished for another three year period. In 1994, the *Instrument for the Establishment of the Restructured Global Environment Facility* was adopted, describing the governance, operational, financial and administrative oversight procedures for the GEF.[258]

Since 1991, GEF has distributed over $6.2 billion in grants and generated over $20 billion in co-financing from other sources to support over 1,800 projects that produce global environmental benefits in 140 developing countries and countries with economies in transition.[259]

Table 4.3: Projects Implemented through Global Environmental Facility

Sl. No.	*Scale*	*No. of Projects*	*Funds ($ US)*
1.	National	41	221.976
2.	Regional	16	95.04
3.	Global	8	47.297
	Total	65	346.313

Source: McDonagh, John and Yuelai Lu, "Success Stories in Reversing Land Degradation and the Role of UNCCD", Technical Paper 2 produced for UK Department for International Development (DFID), (University of East Anglia: Overseas Development Group,2007), p. 8.

The Fund is administered by the GEF secretariat, while projects are developed and undertaken by the three Implementing Agencies (IAs) and seven Executing Agencies[260] in collaboration with the recipient countries. Recipient countries propose projects to the Implementing and Executing Agencies.

The GEF does not disburse funds directly but through its implementing agencies and executing agencies. Each of the implementing agencies has a particular strength and focus. For example UNEP supports technical and scientific inputs. The UNDP focuses on capacity building to improve the livelihoods of the poor while encouraging economic growth and the World Bank promotes larger scale investments. Donor countries also provide funding to these institutions directly to carry out their mandates.[261]

Table 4.4: Operational Programmes of Global Environmental Facility

Sl. No.	*OP*	*Subjects*
		Biodiversity
1.	OP-1	Arid and Semi-Arid Zone Ecosystems
2.	OP-2	Coastal, Marine, and Freshwater Ecosystems
3.	OP-3	Forest Ecosystems
4.	OP-4	Mountain Ecosystems
5.	OP-13	Conservation and Sustainable Use of Biological Diversity Important to Agriculture
		Climate Change
6.	OP-5	Removing Barriers to Energy Efficiency and Energy Conservation
7.	OP-6	Promoting the Adoption of Renewable Energy by Removing Barriers and Reducing Greenhouse Gas Emission
8.	OP-7	Reducing the Long-term Costs of Low Greenhouse Gas Emitting Energy Technologies
9.	OP-11	Promoting Environmentally Sustainable Transport
		Water
10.	OP-8	Waterbody-based Operational Programme
11.	OP-9	Integrated Land and Water Multiple Focal Area Operational Programme
12.	OP-10	Contaminant-Based Operational Programme
		Multi Focal Area
13.	OP-12	Integrated Ecosystem Management
		Persistent Organic Pollutants
14	OP-14	Operational Programme on Persistent Organic Pollutants
		Land Degradation
15.	OP-15	Operational Programme on Sustainable Land Management

Source: Compiled from UNEP, *A Guide to the Global Environmental Facility for NGOs* (Nairobi: UNEP, 2005), pp. 25-66.

Before land degradation was included one of its focal points, the GEF provided grants and concessional funds to developing countries to finance incremental costs for programmes, projects, and activities related with desertification under the focal areas of climate change, biodiversity, ozone depletion, and international waters.[262] In August and September 2002, at the World Summit on Sustainable Development (WSSD) taking place in Johannesburg, South Africa, governments called on the Global Environment Facility (GEF) to become a financial mechanism of the UNCCD. Subsequently, in October 2002 the Second Assembly of the GEF convened in Beijing, China, and adopted a decision to designate land degradation as its fifth focal area,[263] and to establish the GEF as a financial mechanism of the UNCCD.[264]

Accordingly, "the GEF was established as a financial mechanism of the UNCCD (OP-15). This has greatly strengthened the ability of developing countries to source funds for moving forward with implementing the Convention. The GEF funded projects focus on a number of areas including integrating sustainable land management into national development priorities and fostering partnerships with land users and other stakeholders working at all levels."[265]

V. UNCCD Relationship with other Rio Conventions

Numerous multilateral environmental agreements have been signed and ratified in recent years addressing specific aspects of sustainable land management, environmental degradation and resource depletion. Among these, three Rio Conventions (CBD, UNCCD and UNFCCC) have a lot of common objectives and needs constructive coordination and synergies.[266]

> Each of the three (Rio) global environmental conventions deals with the interrelationships between humans, animals, plants, soil, air and water. The environmental issues are themselves intertwined: climate change is a major threat to conservation of biodiversity and is likely to exacerbate desertification and drought in some regions; deforestation reduces biodiversity, reduces carbon stocks in biomass and soil thereby exacerbating climate change, and can lead to desertification; desertification further contributes to climate change through increase in land-

> surface albedo; dryland salinity, a symptom of desertification, threatens biodiversity.[267]

In order to avoid duplication, overlaps or contradictory developments, coordination of individual processes under global environmental and sustainability policy is necessary. There is an obvious need for arrangements to facilitate constructive cooperation between different MEAs in order to comprehensively address the global environmental problems.[268]

> The large number of MEAs can result in institutional coordination challenges as different authorities and institutions assume responsibility for implementing different but related MEAs. Similarly, it is interesting to note that coordination problems at the national level can sometimes cause coordination problems at the international level, as the process of international consensus building often builds upon national approaches and institutions.[269]

Accordingly the UNCCD itself seeks to co-ordinate its activities with other instruments of environmental governance.[270] Article 8 of the UNCCD mandates the governments to "encourage the coordination of activities carried out under this Convention ... (with) other relevant international agreements, particularly the United Nations Framework Convention on Climate Change and the Convention on Biological Diversity, in order to derive maximum benefit from activities under each agreement while avoiding duplication of effort."[271] The Convention also directs the parties to undertake "joint programmes, particularly in the fields of research, training, systematic observation and information collection and exchange, to the extent that such activities may contribute to achieving the objectives of the agreements concerned."[272]

A Joint Liaison Group (JLG) was thus established in 2001 between the secretariats of the three Rio conventions. The JLG collects and shares information on the work programmes and operations of each convention.[273] Accordingly, the UNCCD developed a work programme with the CBD and is working with UNFCCC to develop joint objectives. A memorandum of cooperation was signed on 5th December,1998 between its Secretariat and the Ramsar Convention Bureau.[274] The UNCCD has collaborated on multiple initiatives, including with UNEP on the land degradation assessment for drylands and the millennium ecosystem Assessment. Other arrangements for cooperation with the UNDP, the UNESCO, and WMO are also established. Since desertification is closely linked with global climate change and loss of biodiversity, synergies among these three conventions will ensure sustainable management.

Interlinkages between key global environmental issues and policy responses emerging from UN-based, global conventions are a complex and multifaceted topic. It can be examined through a variety of analytical lenses including: institutional (between MEA governing mechanisms, between national focal points); cross-cutting scientific issues (research, capacity building, technology transfer, etc.); and governance (between local, regional, and national actors and partners).[275]

However,

> "the problem is that each of the different environmental conventions... (is) rather territorial and act in parallel, rather than in unison. Each of their CoPs... (has) their own agenda. Five different parallel processes create complexities, because then, instead of achieving synergy, we may end up getting entropy."[276]

Similarly "(a)t the secretariat and administrative level, each convention has its own Constitution, set of priorities and procedures and is at its own stage of evolution and progress, making it difficult to focus sufficiently on the important synergies and interdependencies between sustainable development, poverty reduction, desertification, climate change and biodiversity."[277]

"From the initial experiences gained from interaction with both CBD and UNCCD focal points, practitioners and others, it appears that the understanding of scope, similarities, synergies and differences between the issues underlying each agreement... are not very clear to practitioners. The primary concern is that there would be a level of redundancy and duplication of mandates."[278] More work has to be done to enhance understanding and appreciation of the inter-linkages and interdependencies between desertification, climate change and biodiversity. Such process should complement the ongoing discussion and action on developing synergies between the three Rio Convention Secretariats and through the support provided by the Joint Liaison Group.[279]

Conclusion

Threats to the earth's flora and fauna, water system, and atmosphere are well recognized by scientists and conservationists for more than century, but only in the past few decades that nations, the UN specialized agencies gradually developed more intentional, comprehensive, and coordinated responses to environmental problems. The Stockholm Conference in 1972 launched a global effort to protect, preserve and enhance the environment. International environmental accord-treaties and agreements were central components of this effort.

The UNCCD is the newest link in the evolving international system for environmental governance. In linking a serious environmental concern with development issues, this convention can be viewed as an important step towards building a multilateral framework for sustainable development. The UNCCD is more strongly based on upon socio-economic criteria than the Convention on Biological Diversity. Therefore, it is a much more comprehensive treaty than earlier efforts to combat desertification.

Like other MEAs, the UNCCD sets up an elaborate institutional structure to guide and support its implementation. These are CoPs, Secretariat, two subsidiary bodies—Committee to Review the Implementation of the Convention and Committee on Science and Technology and Global Mechanism as a financial arrangement. These institutional arrangements are in the processes of evolution and consolidation.

Despite its various limitations, the convention achieved remarkable success in highlighting the global threat of desertification. It made best efforts in coordinating the wide range of actors. The convention played key role in directing the financial and technical resources from developed countries to desertification affected developing countries.

References

1. Rechkemmer, Andreas, *Global Environmental Governance: the United Nations Convention to Combat Desertification,* (Berlin: Wissenschaftszentrum Berlin für Sozialforschung (WZB), 2004), p. 31.
2. Momtaz, Djamchid, "The United Nations and the Protection of the

Environment: from Stockholm to Rio de Janeiro, *Political Geography*, vol. 15, no. 3/4, 1996, p. 261.

3. Soroos, Marvin S., "Global Institutions and the Environment: An Evolutionary Perspective", in Vig, Norman J., and Regina S. Axelrod, eds., *The Global Environment: Institutions, Law and Policy* (London: Earthscan, 1999), p. 29.
4. *Ibid.*, p. 30.
5. Fitzpatrick, Donald, "The United Nations General Assembly and the Security Council", in Werksman, Jacob, ed., *Greening International Institutions*, (London: Earthscan, 1996), p. 3.
6. Mische, Patricia M. *et al.*, "Ecological Security and the United Nations System", in Alger, Chadwick F., *The Future of the United Nations System: Potential for the Twenty-First Century*, (Tokyo: United Nations University Press, 1998), p. 315.
7. *Ibid.*, p. 320.
8. Jokela, Minna, "European Union as a Global Policy Actor: The Case of Desertification" in Biermann, Frank, Rainer Brohm and Klaus Dingwerth, eds., *Global Environmental Change and the Nation State*, (Potsdam, Germany: Potsdam Institute for Climate Impact Research, 2002), p. 309.
9. German Advisory Council on Global Change, *World in Transition: Fighting Poverty through Environmental Policy*, (London: Earthscan, 2005), p. 131.
10. Rechkemmer, n. 1, p. 70.
11. Caldwell, Lynton Keith, *Environment Policy: From the Twentieth to Twenty-First Century* (London: Duke University, 1996), p. 35.
12. Ivanova, Maria, "Designing the United Nations Environment Programme: A Story of Compromise and Confrontation," *International Environmental Agreements: Politics, Economics and Law*, vol. 7, no. 3, 2007, p. 4.
13. Mische, n. 6, p. 323.
14. Andersson, Magnus, *Change and Continuity in Poland's Environmental Policy*, (London: Kluwer Academic Publishers,1999), p. 49.
15. Mische, n. 6, p. 323.
16. *Ibid.*
17. Caldwell, n. 11, p. 58
18. Selin, Henrik and Björn-Ola Linnér, "The Quest for Global Sustainability: International Efforts on Linking Environment and Development," Working Paper No. 5, Centre for International Development, Harvard University, 2005, p. 20.
19. Sand, Peter H., "The Evolution of International Environmental Law" in Bodansky, Daniel *et al.*, (eds.), *The Oxford Handbook of International Environmental Law*, (Oxford: Oxford University Press, 2007), p. 34.
20. In 1967, Inga Thorsson, Swedish diplomat at the United Nations, set out to derail the United Nations plan to convene the fourth

International Conference on the Peaceful Use of Atomic Energy. A strong and dedicated supporter of disarmament, she called for the cancellation of the expensive UN Conference on Nuclear Energy as it mostly benefited the North's nuclear industry. Under her influence, and under the leadership of Sverker Astrom, then Sweden's Permanent Representative at the United Nations, the Swedish delegation decided, without instructions from Swedish Government, to challenge the UN Atomic Energy Conference proposal when it was presented at the General Assembly.

On 13th December, 1967, the Swedish representatives proposed an alternative plan to the General Assembly by calling the UN to focus the interest of member countries on the extremely diverse and complex problems related to the human environment. After extensive consultations with other delegations in 1968, the Swedish delegation in New York, led by Astrom, convinced the Swedish Government to start a formal initiative. The UN supported the convening of the first UN Conference on the Human Environment in 1972 and accepted the proposal of Sweden to host the conference in its capital city, Stockholm. For the first time, environmental issues commanded attention at such a high level of international politics. According to Maria, surprisingly the UN Secretariat, however, possessed neither the scientific nor the administrative capacities to deal with what came to be known as "the Swedish matter." For detail, refer Ivanova, Maria "Designing the United Nations Environment Programme: A Story of Compromise and Confrontation," *International Environmental Agreements: Politics, Economics and Law,* vol. 7, no. 3, 2007. Henrik Selin and Björn-Ola Linnér provides further the details on this. According to them, "Sweden proposed to the UN Secretary-General U Thant on May 20, 1968 that the UN Economic and Social Council (ECOSOC) should include the issue of a global environmental conference on the agenda of its summer session. In addition, the Swedish UN mission sent an "explanatory memorandum" to U Thant outlining why the UN should organize such a conference. The memorandum called attention to ecological issues. It stated that "problems of human environment" should be understood both as human influence on the natural environment... and the influence of natural surroundings on human health and living conditions... The memorandum recognized existing efforts by the WHO, FAO and UNESCO to address some of these issues, but it was argued that it was time to give them more prominence within the UN system" (Selin, n. 18, pp. 19-20).

21. Timagenis, G.R.J., *International Control of Marine Pollution* (New York: Ocean Pub., 1980), p. 84.
22. McCormick, John. *Reclaiming Paradise: The Global Environmental Movement,* (Bloomington: Indiana University Press, 1989), p. 88.
23. Timagenis, n. 21, p. 83.

24. Vig, Norman J., "Introduction: Governing the International Environment", in Vig, n. 3, p. 1.
25. Mark, Allan Gray, "The United Nations Environment Programme: An Assessment" *Journal Environmental Law*, vol. 20, no. 2, 1990, p. 293.
26. All the Eastern European countries except Romania did boycott the Conference in solidarity with East Germany. East Germany was not allowed to participate because it was not a member of the UN or one of its specialised agencies as per the UN protocol called the "Vienna Formula", which specifies the criteria to be followed to send invitations. East Germany, North Korea, North Vietnam and, for sometime, China did not qualify. Since West Germany was a member of World Health Organization (WHO) and United Nations Educational, Scientific Cultural Organization (UNESCO), it was allowed to participate in the Stockholm Conference. All Eastern European countries did, however, take part in the two year preparatory process for the Conference and the Soviet Embassy in Stockholm was briefed daily on the discussions during the two-weeks of the Conference. Also see United Nations Environment Programme (UNEP), *Global Environmental Outlook-3,* (Nairobi, 2002), p. 4.
27. Rowland, Wade *The Plot to Save the World.* (Toronto and Vancouver: Clarke, Irwin and Company Limited, 1973), p. 41.
28. Vig, n. 24, p. 1.
29. The UNEP institutionalizes the conceptual framework of the Stockholm declaration that the environment is the common concern of mankind. In accordance with the Conference's recommendations, the UN General Assembly, in Resolution 2997 of 15th December, 1972, established four pillars as the basis of the new environment programme to address global environmental crises. These are the Governing Council, the Environment Co-ordination Board (ECP), a small secretariat and the Environment Fund. UNEP became the first major UN environmental institution. For further see, Desai, Bharat H., "Revitalizing International Environmental Institutions: The UN Task Force Report and Beyond", *Indian Journal of International Law*, New Delhi, vol. 40, no. 3, 2000, p. 456.
30. UNEP, *Annual Report 2000*, (Nairobi: UNEP, 2000), p. 3. UNEP was established to be catalytic and performed remarkably well with fairly scarce resources. "But things have changed dramatically in the last 30 years with the spread of environmental consciousness and the proliferation of Multilateral Environmental Agreements (MEAs). UNEP is now under-funded, over-loaded and remote. It is relatively obsolete, eclipsed in resources and prestige by other international institutions that have taken on new environmental responsibilities, such as the World Bank, the EU for Europe, and even, to the dismay of many environmentalists, the WTO." (Haas, Peter M., "Addressing the

Global Governance Deficit," *Global Environmental Politics*, vol. 4, no. 4, 2004, pp. 2-3).

31. To host UNEP's headquarter there were proposals for Geneva, New York, London, Malta, Vienna, Monaco, New Delhi, Mexico City, Cairo, and Nairobi. It was widely believed that Geneva would be chosen due to the proximity to many of the international agencies, availability of good communications, and low set-up and operational costs. The UN Secretary-General interestingly prepared estimates of the cost of the new institutional arrangements for Geneva only. However, a vast surprise was in store for everybody. Developing countries for long wanted an international agency to be located in the Third World and saw the creation of UNEP as their golden opportunity. Nairobi was in the run as the future home for United Nations Industrial Development Organization (UNIDO) in 1966 but lost to Vienna in a secret ballot vote. On 3rd November, 1972, Kenya introduced draft Resolution sponsored by the African Group on the location of the new secretariat.

    The Resolution raised two points: more equitable geographical distribution of United Nations agencies and the location of the new Environment Secretariat in Nairobi. The first issue was based on a matter of principle. Since the UN was a global body, it was unfair that its specialized agencies should be confined to North America or Western Europe. The second was a specific proposal for the new environment secretariat to be located in Nairobi. Manifestly excluding all other candidate cities, the proposal violated the consensus reached in Stockholm and came as a surprise to many. Nairobi was one of four developing country capitals competing to be the host for this new UN agency. New Delhi, Mexico City and Cairo were also in the running but finally agreed to pull out and reluctantly supported the Third World solidarity in favour of Nairobi. Finally, this outnumbered developed countries by far, leading to a decisive vote in favour of Nairobi. For detail, refer Ivanova, Maria "Designing the United Nations Environment Programme: A Story of Compromise and Confrontation," *International Environmental Agreements: Politics, Economics and Law*, vol. 7, no. 3, 2007.
32. Selin, n. 18, p. 33.
33. Najam, Adil, "The Case Against a New International Environmental Organisation", *Global Governance*, vol. 9, 2003, p. 374.
34. McCormick, n. 22, p. 88.
35. Desai, Uday, "Institutions and Environmental Policy in Developed Countries" in Desai, Uday, ed., *Environmental Politics and Policy in Industrial Countries*, (London: MIT Press, 2002), p. 7.
36. Untawale, Mukund G., "Global Environmental Degradation and International Organizations", *International Political Science Review*, vol. 11, no. 3, 1990, p. 372.

37. Caldwell, n. 11, p. 48.
38. Untawale, n. 36, p. 375. Stockholm Conference is widely considered the "cocoon from which the chrystalis of international environmental law emerged as a legal subject in its own rights", (Kelly, Michael J., "Overcoming obstacles to the Effective Implementation of International Environmental Agreements", *Georgetown International Environmental Review*, vol. 9, 1997, p. 450).
39. Vogler, John and Andrew Jordan, "Governance and Environment" in Berkhout, Frans, *et al.*, eds., *Negotiating Environmental Change: New Perspectives from Social Science* (Cheltenham, JK: Edward Elgar, 2003), p. 138. Governments "for the first time set up environmental Ministries, starting with the first environmental Ministry that was established in 1971 by the United Kingdom, ending in 1995 when there were 103 environmental Ministries in total.... domestic institutional change was often supplementled with an intensified domestic enactment of environmental legislation and controls." Burkina-Faso was the first African country to establish Environment Ministry in 1974 (Selin, no. 18, p. 55). "While a number of these national measures might well have been taken anyway in the more industrialized countries, most of what was done in the developing countries clearly is attributable to the (Stockholm) Conference and to the special assistance which was provided to many of them during the preparatory period", (Strong, Maurice, "One Year after Stockholm: An Ecological Approach to Management", *Foreign Affairs*, vol. 51, no. 4, 1973, pp. 694-95).
40. Mische, n. 6, pp. 325-326.
41. Concern for environmental issues arose first in the Western Industrialized States. Many developing nations originally saw environmental pollution as chiefly a concern and consequences of production and consumption pattern in the West. In an effort to emphasise the importance of environmental issues to both developed and developing nations, the Netherlands was the main initiator of the symposium on environment and development that was convened by the UN Secretary-General at Founex, near Geneva, in 1971. It resulted in a report on development and environment, the Founex Report which was one of the basic documents submitted to the Stockholm Conference. (For details refer: Baehr, Peter, "The Netherlands and the United Nations: the Future lies in the Past" in Alger, Chadwick F. *et al.*, (eds.), *The United Nations System: the Policies of Member States,* (Tokyo: United Nations University Press, 1995). Adil Najam describes this thirty pages long Founex Report as "one of the most authentic enunciations of the South's collective interests on issues of environment and development." (Najam, Adil, "The View from the South: Developing Countries in Global Environmental Politics" in Regina S. *et al.*, (eds.), *Global Environmental Policy: Institutions, Law and Policy*, (Washington D.C.: CQ Press, 2004), p. 231.

42. Campbell, Tim, "Urban Development in the Third World: Environmental Dilemmas and the Urban Poor" in Leonard, H. Jefferey *et al.*, (eds.), *Environment and the Poor: Development Strategies for Common Agenda,*(Oxford: Transaction Book,1989), p. 187. According to Andresen, "(d)uring the preparations for the Stockholm Conference, developing countries voiced their concern about the one-sided understanding of environmental problems as pollution problems related to industrialization. They lobbied for an understanding that would also encompass the negative consequences of both poverty and prosperity for the environment. Ultimately, that understanding found its way into the so-called Founex Report and the Stockholm Declaration."(Andresen, Steinar and Ellen Hey, "The Effectiveness and Legitimacy of International Environmental Institutions," *International Environmental Agreements*, vol. 5, 2005, pp. 214-15).
43. Campbell, Tim E.J. "The Political Meaning of Stockholm: Third World Participation in the Environment Conference Process", *Stanford Journal of International Studies*, vol. 8, 1973, pp. 139-141.
44. Bassow, Whitman, "The Third World: Changing Attitudes Toward Environmental Protection", *The ANNALS of the American Academy of Political and Social Science*, vol. 444, no. 112, 1979, p. 114.
45. The principle of common but differentiated responsibilities entails that developed states, given their historic and present contribution to environmental problems and their economic wealth and technical capabilities, should take the lead in implementing measures that protect the environment. (Andrese, Steinar n and Ellen Hey, "The Effectiveness and Legitimacy of International Environmental Institutions", *International Environmental Agreements*, vol. 5, 2005, p. 216). This principle would hold that developed countries bear a special burden of responsibility in reducing unsustainable problems of consumptions and providing assistance, by way of the transfer of technical and financial resources to developing countries to meet global sustainable development goals (Segger, Marie-Claire Cordonier, "Significant Developments in Sustainable Development Law and Governance: A Proposal", *Natural Research Forum,* vol. 28, 2004, p. 63). French Duncan argues that "(i)n view of their main historical and current responsibility for global environmental degradation and their capability to address this common concern, developed countries shall provide adequate, new and additional financial resources and environmentally sound technologies on preferential and concessional terms to developing countries to enable them to achieve sustainable development." (French, Duncan, "Developing States and International Environmental Law: The Importance of Differentiated Responsibilities," *International and Comparative Law Quarterly*, vol. 49, 2000, p. 36).
46. Baehr, Peter, "The Netherlands and the United Nations: the Future lies in the Past" in Alger, Chadwick F. *et al.*, (eds.), *The United Nations*

System: the Policies of Member States, (Tokyo: United Nations University Press, 1995), p. 301.

47. Bassow, n. 44, p. 114.
48. Najam, Adil, "Developing Countries and Global Environmental Governance: From Contestation to Participation to Engagement," *International Environmental Agreements: Law, Politics and Economics* (Springer Link), vol. 5, 2005, p. 309.
49. Selin, n. 18, p. 22.
50. Najam, n. 48, pp. 307-308.
51. Brookfield, H.C., "Development and the Environment: Politics, Production and Pollution", *Pacific Affairs*, vol. 53, no. 4, Winter,1980-1981, p. 663.
52. As quoted in Selin, n. 18, p. 27.
53. Corell, Elisabeth, "Drylands Degradation: Africa's Main Environmental Challenge" in Chaytor, Beatrice and Kevin R. Gray, eds., *International Environmental Law and Policy in Africa* (London: Kluwer Academic Publishers, 2003), p. 6.
54. Bodansky, Daniel, *et al.*, "International Environmental Law: Mapping the Field" in Bodansky, n. 19, p. 3.
55. Andresen, Steinar and Ellen Hey, "The Effectiveness and Legitimacy of International Environmental Institutions", *International Environmental Agreements*, vol. 5, 2005, p. 215.
56. Jones, Tom, "Policy Coherence, Global Environmental Governance, and Poverty Reduction", *International Environmental Agreements: Politics, Law and Economics,* vol. 2, 2002, p. 395.
57. Roberts J. Timmons *et al.*, "Who Ratifies Environmental Treaties and Why? Institutionalism, Structuralism and Participation by 192 Nations in 22 Treaties", *Global Environmental Politics*, vol. 4, no. 3, August 2004, p. 22.
58. MEAs are typically brief and formal documents that describe the problem being addressed, the commitments of the governments involved, and the institutional mechanism to be created. They are commonly cast in the form of binding international treaties, though some are non-binding statements of principles or aspirations. Basically these MEAs are evolutionary documents, intended to initiate a long-lasting cooperation to address the global environmental problems.
59. UNEP, *Global Environmental Outlook 4* (Nairobi: UNEP, 2007), p. 379. Nico Schrijver points out that the "unprecedented rise in the number of these treaties (from an average of 1 per year before 1970 to 5 per year since then), as well as that of the signatories, exemplifies the increasing willingness of States to accept international obligations to conserve nature and natural resources, both at an international level and within their boundaries." (Schrijver, Nico, *Sovereignty over Natural Resources*, (Cambridge: Cambridge University Press,1997), p. 221).

60. UNEP, *International Environmental Governance: Multilateral Environmental Agreements (MEAs),* (Nairobi: UNEP, 2001), pp. 8-9.
61. Barrett, S., *Environment and Statecraft: the Strategy of Environmental Treaty-Making,* (New York: Oxford University Press, 2002), p. 136. "The common denominator among agreements concluded prior to the 1970s is that they were designed to remedy environmental problems after a significant amount of damage had been done....A shift giving rise to a new approach took place after 1972, such that environmental treaties negotiated subsequently were preventive in nature." (Kelly, Michael J., "Overcoming obstacles to the Effective Implementation of International Environmental Agreements", *Georgetown International Environmental Review*, vol. 9, 1997, pp. 449-50).
62. Boon, Emmanuel K., "Environmental Planning" in Nath, Bhaskar, ed., *Environmental Management in Practice: Instruments for Environmental Management* (London: Routledge, 1998), p. 72.
63. Jacobson, Harold and Edith Brown Weiss, "Compliance with International Environmental Accords: Achievements and Strategies" in Rolen, Mats, *et al.*, (eds.), *International Governance on Environmental Issues*, (London: Kluwer Academic Publishers, 1997), p. 78.
64. United Nations Development Programme (UNDP) *et al., World Resources 2002-04, Decisions for Earth: Balance, Voice and Power,* (Washington, D.C.: World Resource Institute, 2003), p. 145.
65. Kutting, Gabriela, *Environment, Society and International Relations* (London: Routledge, 2000), p. 3.
66. UNEP, *Manual on Compliance with and Enforcement of Multilateral Environmental Agreements* (Nairobi: UNEP, 2006), p. 51.
67. The term Convention has both a generic and a specific meaning. The generic term is synonymous with a treaty. With regard to convention as a specific term, in the last century it was regularly employed for bilateral agreements but now it is generally used for formal multilateral treaties. Usually, the instruments negotiated under the auspices of the United Nations are entitled conventions (e.g. the 1992 Convention on Biological Diversity, the 1982 United Nations Convention on the Law of the Sea and the 1996 UNCCD).
68. Kamieniecki, Sheldom, "Emerging Forces in Global Environmental Politics" in Kamieniecki, Sheldom (ed.), *Environmental Politics in the International Arena: Movements, Organizations and Parties,* (Albany: State University of New York Press, 1993), p. 9. "By and large,...(MEAs) have grown from bilateral local regimes to multilateral global regimes. Over time, the design of these agreements has evolved not in a linear fashion, as would be expected, but rather in a multifaceted way." (Kelly, Michael J., "Overcoming obstacles to the Effective Implementation of International Environmental Agreements", *Georgetown International Environmental Review*, vol. 9, 1997, p. 452).
69. Hey, Ellen, "International Institutions," in Bodansky, n. 19, p. 753.

70. Sand, "Environment: Nature Conservation" in Managing P. Simmons and C. Oudraat, eds., *Global Issues: Lessons Learned,* (Washington, DC: Carnegie Endowment for International Peace, 2001), p. 3.
71. Cramer, Phillip F., *Rethinking Environmental Protection: A Natural Approach to Nature* (Lanham (USA): Lexington Books, 2000), p. 70.
72. Kelsey, Elin, "Implications of the Nation-State System on Public Involvement in Environmental Problem-Solving" in Biermann, n. 8, p. 117.
73. Kamieniecki, n. 68, p. 3.
74. Kutting, n. 65, pp. 3-4.
75. UNDP, n. 64, p. 148.
76. The idea of sustainable development is linked to a long term, more integrated vision of managing natural resources and sharing environmental burdens and to a greater appreciation of connection between the environment, on the one hand, and development, distributive justice, democracy, and participation on the other.
77. On 19th December, 1983, the General Assembly created the World Commission on Environment and Development consisting of independent persons and charged with reviewing environmental and developmental issues in the context of a long-term strategy for the year 2000. The report was submitted to the General Assembly on 20th March, 1987, known as the Brundtland Report after the Commission's President.
78. Over the last decade, the great increase in negotiations related to the new or existing MEAs caused a serious problem of MEA proliferation and attendant pathologies of 'negotiation fatigue', particularly amongst developing country delegates. This placed an immense burden on most developing countries, which simply do not have adequate resources to keep up with the frantic pace of increasingly complex negotiations processes. Moreover, the frenzy to complete negotiation as quickly as possible left behind a legacy of less-than-perfect agreements or satisfying enough or resulted in too little attention being paid to questions of implementation. It makes sense to pause and make sense of how these various MEAs fit together. For further see Najam, Adil, "The Case Against GEO, WEO, or Whatever-else-EO", in Esty, Daniel *et al.*, *Global Environmental Institutions: Perspectives on Reform* (London: Royal Institute of International Affairs, 2002), p. 39. Also see, Najam, Adil, "The Case Against a New International Environmental Organisation", *Global Governance,* vol. 9, 2003, p. 378.
79. At the Inter-governmental level, Ministries of Foreign Affairs traditionally oversaw all diplomatic encounters, including multilateral environmental negotiations. This practice changed in industrialized countries and some developing ones with the involvement of other functional Ministries equipped with the technical understanding of the issues. Most developing countries, however, lack the financial and

often the professional capacity to send large delegations to these negotiations.

80. Andresen, n. 55, p. 216. According to Steven Bernstein, "Global environmental norms, institutions and agreements, especially in the post-Rio Summit (1992) era, often entrench differential obligations and recognize differential capacities of developed and developing countries. They also frequently attempt to combine global concerns with local decision-making and accountability, where activities are focused", (Bernstein, Steven, "Legitimacy in Global Environmental Governance," *Journal of International Law and International Relations*, vol. 1, nos.1-2, 2005, p. 140).
81. Andresen, n. 55, p. 216.
82. Paehlke, Robert and Douglas Torgerson, eds., *Managing Leviathan: Environmental Politics and the Administrative State* (Ontario: Broadview Press, 2005), p. 46.
83. Kaniaru, Donald and Lal Kurukulasurya, "Capacity Building in Environmental Law" in Lin, Sun, ed., *UNEP's New Way Forward: Environmentul Law and Sustainable Development,* (Nairobi: UNEP, 1995), p. 173.
84. *Ibid.*, p. 172-73.
85. Zoeteman, Kees and Eric Harkink, "Collaboration of National Governments and Global Corporations in Environmental Management" in Wijen, Frank, *et al.*, (eds.), *A Handbook of Globalization and Environment Policy: National Government Intervening in a Global Arena*, (Cheltenham: Edward Elgar Publishing, 2005), p. 186.
86. UNEP, n. 60, p. 37.
87. *Ibid.*
88. UN, *UN General Assembly Resolution 3337*, adopted on 17th December, 1974.
89. *Ibid.*
90. *Ibid.*
91. UNEP, *The Plan of Action of the United Nations Conference on Desertification,* (Nairobi: UNEP, 1977), p. 2.
92. Momtaz, n. 2, p. 267.
93. UNEP, *Twenty Years since Stockholm* (Nairobi: UNEP, 1993), p. 96.
94. Toulmin, Camilla, "Combating Desertification: Encouraging Local Action within a Global Framework", in Helge Ole Bergesen and Georg Parmann, eds., *Green Globe Yearbook of International Co-operation on Environment and Development,* (Oxford: Oxford University Press, 1994), p. 83.
95. Kassas, M., "Desertification: A General Review", *Journal of Arid Environments*, vol. 30, 1995, p. 123.
96. *Ibid.*, p. 83.
97. UN, *UN General Assembly Resolution 168,* adopted on 17th December, 1984 at its 39th Session.

98. *Ibid.*
99. *Ibid.*
100. *Ibid.*
101. Glenn, E. *et al.*, "On Our Failure to Control Desertification: Implications for Global Change Issues, and a Research Agenda for the Future", *Environmental Science and Policy*, vol. 1, 1998, p. 71.
102. The UN General Assembly, in 1989 decided "to close the Special Account to finance the implementation of Plan of Action to Combat Desertification." (Resolution, 44/172, 19th December, 1989).
103. Kassas, M., n. 95, p. 123.
104. UNEP, n. 93, p. 96.
105. *Ibid*, p. 98.
106. Adams, William Mark, *Green Development: Environment and Sustainability in the Third World* (New York: Routledge, 2001), p. 209.
107. *Ibid.*, p. 210.
108. Darkoh, M.B.K., "The Nature, Causes and Consequences of Desertification in the Drylands of Africa", *Land Degradation and Development*, vol. 9, 1998, p. 16.
109. Toumlin, n. 94, p. 84.
110. Darkoh, n. 108, p. 16.
111. Rechkemmer, n. 1, p. 56. The Plan of Action was "ineffective and largely ignored, having little backing from either developed or developing countries, and even less from potential donors" (Gisladottir, G. and M. Stocking, "Land Degradation Control and Its Global Environmental Benefits", *Land Degradation and Development*, vol. 16, 2005, p. 104).
112. Glenn E., *et al.*, n. 101, p. 71.
113. Rechkemmer, n. 1, p. 56.
114. Untawale, n. 36, p. 380.
115. Reynolds, James F., "Desertification" in Levin, Simon Asher, ed., *Encyclopedia of Biodiversity*, (London: Academic Press, 2001), p. 68.
116. Glenn, E., *et al.*, n. 101, p. 71.
117. Najam, Adil., "Dynamics of the Southern Collective: Developing Countries in Desertification Negotiations", *Global Environmental Politics*, (Massachusetts Institute of Technology), vol. 4, no. 3, 2004, p. 130.
118. Kassas, M., n. 95, p. 124.
119. Adams, n. 106, p. 177.
120. Vogler, n. 39, p. 137. At the first meeting of the preparatory committee for the Stockholm Conference, the then UN Secretary-General, U Thant, stated that "Mankind is also coming to the realization that a new dimension of time, reaching substantially into the future, must be added to its thinking, planning, and endeavours ... We must carefully weigh the effects of present behaviour on the future if we do not wish to be considered by later generations as having failed our foresight."

(Cordier, Andrew W. and Harrelson, Max, *Public Papers of the Secretaries-General of the United Nations, Volume VIII, U Thant 1968-1971*, (New York: Columbia University Press, 1977), p. 347.

121. Vogler, n. 39, p. 137.
122. World Bank, *New Opportunities for Development: The Desertification Convention*, (Washington D.C.: World Bank, 1998), p. 1. The official name of the Rio Earth Summit was also crafted, after some debate, to signify that 'environment and development' were complementary rather than contradictory categories. (Najam, Adil, "Unravelling of the Rio Bargain", *Politics and the Life Sciences*, vol. 21, no. 2, 2002, p. 46.
123. Batabyal, Amitrajeet, "On the Design of International Environmental Agreements for Identical and Heterogeneous Developing Countries", *Oxford Economic Papers*, vol. 52, 2000, p. 560. French, Duncan states that "(e)nvironmental protection will ultimately be self-defeating if it fails to take into account the socio-economic realities, particularly of countries in the South" (French, Duncan, "Developing States and International Environmental Law: The Importance of Differentiated Responsibilities," *International and Comparative Law Quarterly*, vol. 49, 2000, p. 42.
124. Rechkemmer, n. 1, p. 36.
125. Bäckstrand, Karin, "Democratizing Global Environmental Governance? Stakeholder Democracy after the World Summit on Sustainable Development", *European Journal of International Relations*, vol. 12, no. 4, 2006, p. 470.
126. French, Hilary, "The Role of Non-State Actors" in Werksman, n. 5, p. 254.
127. *Ibid.* According to Bernstein, the "Stockholm Conference originated the idea of a parallel NGO Forum, which attracted some 400 groups, and has since become a regular feature of such events. At Rio, 1420 accredited NGOs, about one-third from the South, participated in the official proceedings as a result of the Secretariat's unprecedented decision to relax accreditation rules to allow non-ECOSOC NGOs to participate (another 11,000 participated in the parallel Global Forum). Again, the relaxed rules became the norm for subsequent World Conferences." (Bernstein, Steven, "Legitimacy in Global Environmental Governance," *Journal of International Law and International Relations*, vol. 1, nos.1-2, 2005, pp. 148-49.)
128. The 'alternative treaties' were not intended as legally binding instruments, nor as a substitute for the important simultaneous input of NGOs to the official UNCED process and other ongoing efforts at international environmental policy making process. They served mainly as a focus of civic interaction between NGOs in the joint articulation of goals and action plans (Sand, Peter H. "International

Environmental Law after Rio", *European Journal of International Law*, vol. 4, no. 1, 1993, p. 385).

129. Sand, Peter H. "International Environmental Law after Rio", *European Journal of International Law*, vol. 4, no. 1, 1993, p. 385.
130. Kassas, M., n. 95, p. 124.
131. Kjellën, Bo., "The Saga of the Convention to Combat Desertification: the Rio/Johannesburg Process and the Global Responsibility for the Drylands", *Reciel*, vol. 12, no. 2, 2003, p. 127.
132. Jamal, Alia, "The United Nations Convention to Combat Desertification in those Countries Experiencing Serious Drought and/or Desertification, Particularly in Africa: Implementing Agenda 21", *Reciel*, vol. 6, no. 1.1997, p. 1.
133. UN, *The UN General Assembly Resolution 228*, adopted at 44th Session on 22nd December, 1989.
134. Najam, n. 117, p. 133.
135. Kjellën, n. 131, p. 127.
136. *Earth Negotiation Bulletin*, vol. 4, no. 1, http://www.iisd.ca/vol04/0401018e.html, accessed on 24th June, 2008.
137. *Ibid.*
138. Kjellën, n. 131, p. 128.
139. United Nations Non-Governmental Liaison Service, "The International Convention to Combat Desertification in Countries Experiencing Serious Drought and/or Desertification, Particularly in Africa", *The Sustainable Development Treaty Series,* vol. I, no. 1, 1994, p. 4.
140. Kjellen, Bo. "The Desertification Convention: Towards Creating a Multilateral Framework for Coping with Global Threats" in Rolen, Mats *et al.*, (eds.), *International Governance on Environmental Issues,* (London: Kluwer Academic Publishers, 1997), p. 71.
141. Toulmin, Camilla, "The Desertification Convention" in Dodds, Felix, ed., *The Way Forward: Beyond Agenda 21,* (London: Earthscan, 1997), p. 58.
142. Kjellën, n. 131, p. 127.
143. Kjellen, n. 140, p. 71.
144. Toulmin, n. 141, p. 58.
145. Najam, n. 117, p. 133.
146. Kjellën, n. 131, p. 128.
147. Kjellen, n. 140, p. 71.
148. Adger, W. Neil., *et al.*, "Advancing Political Ecology of Global Environmental Discourses", *Development and Change,*(Oxford), vol. 32, 2001, p. 690.
149. *Ibid.*
150. Kjellën, n. 131, p. 128.
151. Jokela, n. 8, p. 309.

152. Najam, Adil., "An Environmental Negotiation Strategy for the South" *International Environmental Affairs,* vol. 7, no. 3, 1995, p. 253.
153. UNEP, *The State of Environment, 1972-2002,* (Nairobi: UNEP, 2002), p. 18.
154. UNEP, *The United Nations Conference on Environment and Development: Agenda 21,* Chapter 12, paragraph 40, (Nairobi: UNEP, 1992). The Rio Summit raised the profile of the problem by catalyzing negotiations for a global Convention to Combat Desertification. The UNCCD was "especially favoured by developing countries who saw it as more closely aligned with their development priorities than its more environmentally-oriented sister Conventions on Biodiversity and Climate Change, also initiated at that (Earth) Summit."(Winslow, M. *et al.,* "Desertification, drought, poverty and agriculture: research lessons and opportunities", (Aleppo, Syria: Centre for Agricultural Research in the Dry Areas (ICARDA)), 2004, p. 5.
155. The various components of *Agenda 21* required further elaboration and/or decisions by the UN Assembly. These include: Convention to combat desertification, inter-governmental consideration of marine and coastal issues, sustainable development of small island states, patent protection and intellectual property rights, access to and transfer of environmentally-sound technology, etc. However, finally, it was decided that the "Razali Group would limit its negotiations during this UNGA session to five issues: (1) the endorsing resolution on the report of UNCED; (2) sustainable development of small island states; (3) desertification/drought; (4) straddling and highly migratory fish stocks; and (5) the creation of the Commission on Sustainable Development."
156. *Earth Negotiation Bulletin,* vol. 3, no. 2, 1992, http://www.iisd.ca/vol03/0302001e.html, accessed on 20th June, 2008.
157. *Ibid.*
158. Chasek, Pamela, "An Interim Report on the INC for the Elaboration of an International Convention to Combat Desertification", *Earth Negotiation Bulletin,* vol. 4, no. 56, 1994, p. 6.
159. UN, *UN General Assembly Resolution 188,* adopted its 47th Session on 22nd December, 1992.
160. *Ibid.*
161. Carr, Susan and Roger M Pande, "Does the Definition of Issue Matters: NGO Influence and the International Convention to Combat Desertification" in Potter, David, ed., *NGOs and Environmental Policies: Asia and Pacific* (London: Routledge, 1996), p. 150
162. *UN General Assembly Resolution 188,* n. 159.
163. *Ibid.*
164. Carr, n. 161, p. 150.
165. Martello, Marybeth Long, "Expert Advice and Desertification Policy:

Past Experience and Current Challenges," *Global Environmental Politics,* vol. 4, no. 3, 2004, p. 93.

166. *Ibid.*, p. 94.
167. Rechkemmer, n. 1, p. 145.
168. *Ibid.*, p. 58.
169. German Advisory Council on Global Change (GACGC), *New Structures for Global Environmental Policy,* (London: Earthscan, 2001), p. 75.
170. Johnson, P.M. *et al.*, (eds.), *Governing Global Desertification: Linking Environmental Degradation, Poverty and Participation* (Aldershot: Ashgate Publishing Limited, 2006), p. 257.
171. Boczeck, Boleslaw Adam, *International Law: A Dictionary* (Lanham, Maryland: Scarecrow Press, 2005), p. 214.
172. Toulmin, n. 141, p. 59.
173. UN, *UN General Assembly Resolution 234*, adopted by its 49th Session on 23nd December, 1994.
174. William G. Kepner, ed., *Desertification in the Mediterranean Region: A Security Issue,* (New York: Springer: 2005), p. 134.
175. Najam, n. 117, p. 130.
176. Sherbinin, Alex de., *A CIESIN Thematic Guide to Land-use and Land-cover Change,* (New York: Centre for International Earth Science Information Network (CIESIN), Columbia University, 2002), p. 22.
177. Kjellen, n. 140, p. 71.
178. Batterbury, S.P.J. *et al.*, "Responding to Desertification at the National Scale: Detection, Explanation, and Responses", in Reynolds, J.F., and D.M. Stafford Smith, eds., *Global Desertification: Do Humans Cause Deserts*? (Dahlem University Press, 2002), p. 379.
179. Onchere, Naftali Maddy, "The United Nations Convention to Combat Desertification in Eastern Africa" in Arnalds, Olafur and Steve Archer, eds., *Rangeland Desertification* (London: Springer, 1999), p. 198.
180. Wolfrum, Rudiger, and Nele Matz, *Conflicts in International Environmental Law* (London: Springer, 2003), p. 96.
181. Kemp, David D., *The Environment Dictionary,* (London: Routledge, 1998), p. 99.
182. Humphreys, David and Susan Carr, "Land Degradation and Sustainable Resource Management in an African Context" in Thomas, Alan *et al.*, eds., *Environmental Policies and NGO Influence: Land Degradation and Sustainable Resource Management in Sub-Saharan Africa* (London: Routledge, 2001), p. 33.
183. McDonagh, John and Yuelai Lu, "Success Stories in Reversing Land Degradation and the Role of UNCCD", Technical Paper 2 produced for UK Department for International Development (DFID), (University of East Anglia: Overseas Development Group, 2007), p. 5.
184. UNCCD Secretariat, *Situational Analysis of UNCCD*, (Bonn: UNCCD Secretariat, 2007), p. 2.

185. Chasek, Pamela, "An Interim Report on the INC for the Elaboration of an International Convention to Combat Desertification", *Earth Negotiation Bulletin,* vol. 4, no. 56, 1994, p. 3.
186. UNCCD Secretariat, "The United Nations Convention to Combat Desertification" [Online: web] Accessed on 23rd June, 2008 URL: http://www.unccd.int/convention/text/convention.php.
187. *Ibid.*
188. Shine, Clare and Cyrille de Klemm, *Wetlands, Water and the Law* (Bonn: International Union for Conservation of Nature, 1999), p. 36.
189. Russia and the Central and Eastern European countries had "for various reasons, kept a certain distance from the Convention and it soon became clear that one way to secure their interest was to give them the opportunity to have a regional implementation annex of their own. After a number of consultations, ...fifth annex was adopted and the Convention has now almost universal membership" (Kjellën, n. 131, p. 131).
190. Martello, n. 165, p. 87.
191. UNCCD Secretariat, "Fact Sheet," [Online: web] Accessed on 23rd June, 2008 URL:http://www.unccd.int/publicinfo/factsheets/showFS.php?number=15.
192. Boczeck, n. 171, p. 215.
193. UNEP, *Compliance Mechanisms under Selected Multilateral Environmental Agreements,* (Nairobi: UNEP, 2006), p. 21.
194. UNEP, *Training Manual on International Environmental Law,* (Nairobi: UNEP, 2006), p. 41. "... the institutional arrangements of MEAs have become increasingly perceived as crucial to their effectiveness.... the lack of proper institutions makes it very difficult to develop, update, and adapt MEAs to changing circumstances, which is necessary for two main reasons: first, knowledge of the environmental issues with which MEAs deal is constantly expanding. Second, when an MEA is initially concluded, the parties may reach only limited political agreements on how to tackle the environmental problem at issue; but over time consensus on taking stricter measures may gradually emerge."(Churchill, Robin R and Geir Ulfstein, "Autonomous Institutional Arrangements in Multilateral Environmental Agreements: A Little-Noticed Phenomenon in International Law", *The American Journal of International Law,* vol. 94, no. 4, 2000, p. 628).
195. Desai, Bharat H., "International Environmental Institutions: An Overview" in Dolzer, Rudolf and Joseph Thesing, eds., *Protecting Our Environment,* (Sankt Augustin: Konard-Adenauer-Stiftung, 2000), p. 258.
196. Ulfstein, Geir, "Treaty Bodies" in Bodansky, n. 19, p. 881.
197. Boczeck, n. 171, p. 215.
198. The first environmental treaty to use the term Conference of the Parties was the Convention on Trade in Endangered Species of Wild Fauna

and Flora (CITES), 1973. Although a few MEAs used an existing Inter-Governmental Organizations, or established a new IGO, more recently, COPs become the preferred institutional machinery for cooperation under MEAs. They were established, for example, by global treaties addressing climate change, ozone depletion, and biodiversity as well as by regional agreements addressing acid rain in Europe and hazardous wastes in Africa. For details refer Ulfstein, n. 196, p. 878. The World Heritage Convention is structured differently in the sense that instead of a CoPs it has a General Assembly of States Parties to the Convention, which meets during the UNESCO's General Conference.

199. Martin-Mehers, Gillian., *et al.*, eds., *Achieving Environmental Objectives* (Cambridge (UK):IUCN (World Conservation Union), 2004), p. 121. "...all the conventions negotiated after CITES under the auspices of UNEP "contain the CoP as their institutional arrangements. It is not surprising that having devised an institutional model for CITES that worked, UNEP utilized it in the later MEAs." (Churchill, Robin R. and Geir Ulfstein, "Autonomous Institutional Arrangements in Multilateral Environmental Agreements: A Little-Noticed Phenomenon in International Law", *The American Journal of International Law*, vol. 94, no. 4, 2000, p. 630). "Some CoPs allow non-party states, Non-Governmental Organizations (NGOs), and other non-parties to observe and sometimes participate in discussions and negotiations. However, the voting members of the CoP are representatives of the states parties and have one vote per state." (Wiersema, Annecoos, "The New International Law-Makers? Conferences of the Parties to Multilateral Environmental Agreements", *Michigan Journal of International Law*, vol. 31, no. 231, 2009, p. 235).

200. Desai, n. 195, p. 260. "...the supremacy of the CoP means that the international organization hosting the secretariat may exercise only the powers flowing from this particular function, and has no power to instruct the CoP or its subsidiary bodies. Thus, the UN General Assembly and Secretariat have no right to instruct these bodies even though the United Nations hosts several MEA secretariats.... the Conference of Parties (CoPs) to the convention has an independent legal character and is not a subsidiary of the General Assembly or of any other body." (Churchill, Robin R and Geir Ulfstein, "Autonomous Institutional Arrangements in Multilateral Environmental Agreements: A Little-Noticed Phenomenon in International Law", *The American Journal of International Law*, vol. 94, no. 4, 2000, p. 634).

201. First, using an existing IGO may have the disadvantage of including States that are not parties to the relevant MEA. Second, the establishment of a new IGO may be perceived as more costly and bureaucratic. Third, CoPs offer greater flexibility since they do not

have a permanent seat but may instead convene meetings in different countries and in different parts of the world, also see Ulfstein, n. 196, p. 878.

202. World Bank, *Desertification: Implementing the Convention, a World Bank View,* (Washington, D.C.: World Bank, 1994), p. 23.
203. Corell, n. 53, p. 13.
204. Najam, n. 117, p. 131.
205. Of the 41 core MEAs, UNEP provides the secretariats for 22 MEAs which include 12 of the 18 global MEAs and 10 of the 22 regional MEAs. Among the MEAs which benefit the secretariat services of UNEP include 7 of the 17 regional seas conventions and action plans. These secretariats are under the institutional and administrative structure of the UNEP secretariat and their staffs are employed as UNEP staff members (UNEP, *International Environmental Governance: Multilateral Environmental Agreements (MEAs),* (Nairobi: UNEP, 2001), pp. 23-24). "Secretariats (of COPs) are the organizational glue that holds the actors and parts of a treaty system together. The interdependence and inter-sectoral nature of global environmental systems requires the involvement of a range of actors. Stakeholders in international environmental agreements, unlike those in arms-control and trade treaties, are rarely limited to nation states." Sandford, Rosemary, "International Environmental Treaty Secretariats: Stage-Hands or Actors?", in Helge Ole Bergesen and Georg Parmann, (eds.), *Green Globe Yearbook of International Co-operation on Environment and Development 1994,* (Oxford: Oxford University Press, 1994), p. 17.
206. Desai, n. 195, p. 258.
207. UNEP, n. 60, p. 4.
208. Ulfstein, n. 196, p. 880.
209. In a well-attended session, Spain's Minister for Environment made the first presentation, which was followed by a film on Spain and the host city, Murcia. The Spain Minister enumerated several cultural, social, economic and infrastructural benefits of the city, and noted ongoing desertification research in the region. Further Spain promised to "provide 1100 square metres of office space indefinitely,.... US$1 million every year in technical assistance to the Secretariat and nearly US$8 million for desertification projects in developing countries. Canada's offer was presented by the Mayor of the bidding city, Montreal. The Mayor noted the low cost of living and the presence of other international organizations as among the advantages. Canada's total offer amounted to approximately US$5.2 million. On the other hand Germany's Director General for Development Cooperation offered the city of Bonn as host, and stressed: the city's relatively low cost of living by European standards; its proximity to cities in other continents; and the need for UNCCD to have similar working conditions as the Climate Change Convention. Among many other

commitments, Germany will provide: approximately US$1.3 million annually, without a time limit, for the Secretariat and Secretariat events for the UNCCD, in addition to their assessed contributions; rent-free office space without a time limit; and relocation costs and German language courses for the Secretariat staff.

210. Chasek, Pamela, "A Summary Report on the Tenth Session of the INC for the Convention to Combat Desertification", *Earth Negotiation Bulletin*, vol. 4, no. 105, 1997, p. 4.

211. Corell, Elisabeth "A Summary Report on the Resumed Tenth Session of the INC for the Convention to Combat Desertification", *Earth Negotiation Bulletin*, vol. 4, no. 106, 1997, p. 3.

212. Corell, Elisabeth, "Summary of the First Conference of the Parties to the Convention to Combat Desertification", *Earth Negotiation Bulletin*, vol. 4, no. 116, 1997, pp. 3-4.,
Germany noted the significance of Bonn's election on Germany's national holiday celebrating its unification, a historical event that shaped a new world order.

213. The UNCCD is financed by regular contributions from countries that are Parties to the Convention, and by voluntary donations. In addition to the regular contributions, Germany, as host country of the UNCCD Secretariat, employs a staff of 43 and makes a voluntary contribution of around € 511,300 annually towards the core budget of the Secretariat. Besides, Germany contributes a further € 511,300 annually to help fund Conferences organized by the Secretariat.

214. UNCCD Secretariat, "Secretariat" [Online: web] Accessed on 23rd June, 2008 URL:http://www.unccd.int/secretariat/menu.php.

215. Bauer, Steffen, Per-Olof Busch and Bernd Siebenhüner, *Administering International Governance: What Role for Treaty Secretariats?*, Global Governance Working Paper No. 29, (Amsterdam: Vrije Universiteit, Global Governance Project, 2006), p. 29.

216. Diallo began to enter the United Nations as the Director of the United Nations Sudano-Sahelian Office from 1979-1983. After leaving the U.N., Diallo became the Foreign Minister of Upper Volta (now Burkina Faso) under Captain Thomas Sankara from 1983-84. From 1988-89, Diallo served as the Ambassador to China, India and Japan. Thereafter, Diallo returned to the United Nations as the Special Representative of the Secretary-General for the Conference on Environment and Development from 1990-1992 and Executive Secretary of the United Nations Convention to Combat Desertification since 1996.

217. Bauer, n. 215, p. 18.

218. UNEP, n. 194, p. 12.

219. UNCCD Secretariat, "Fact Sheet," [Online: web] Accessed on 23rd June, 2008 URL:http://www.unccd.int/publicinfo/factsheets/showFS.php?number=7.

220. Corell, n. 53, p. 12.

221. Martello, n. 165, p. 86.
222. UNCCD Secretariat, "Frequently Asked Questions," [Online: web] Accessed on 23rd June, 2008 URL: http://www.unccd.int/knowledge/faq.php#answer8.
223. Corell, Elisabeth, "Summary of the First Conference of the Parties to the Convention to Combat Desertification: 29 September-10th October, 1997", *Earth Negotiations Bulletin*, vol. 4, no. 116, 13th October, 1997, p. 6.
224. *Ibid.*
225. Bai, Changbo, "Summary of the Second Conference of the Parties to the Convention to Combat Desertification: 30th November-11th December, 1998", *Earth Negotiations Bulletin,* vol. 4, no. 127,1998, p. 6.
226. Churie, Angela, "Summary of the Third Conference of the Parties to the Convention to Combat Desertification: 15-26th November, 1999", *Earth Negotiations Bulletin,* vol. 4, no. 138, 1999, p. 6.
227. *Ibid.*
228. "The reasons for this are several obstacles and different problems, for example that a lot of countries concerned did not prepare their national strategies and programmes for the implementation of the mentioned agreement. On the other hand, the international institution, which is responsible for the financing of the implementation of the agreement, is still in the stage of foundation. For these reasons the Ministry for Agriculture and Water of the Kingdom of Saudi Arabia suggests to wait with the formation of a committee or a body to monitor and supervise the implementation of the Convention of the United Nations". Also see UNCCD Secretariat, *Implementation of the Convention consideration of additional procedures or institutional mechanisms to assist the Conference of the Parties in regularly reviewing the implementation of the convention* (Bonn: UNCCD Secretariat, 2000), p. 16.
229. Churie, Angela, "Summary of the Fourth Conference of the Parties to the Convention to Combat Desertification: 11-22th December, 2000", *Earth Negotiations Bulletin,* vol. 4, no. 149, 2000, p. 6.
230. Mandel, Jenny, "Summary of the Fifth Conference of the Parties to the Convention to Combat Desertification: 1-13th October, 2001", *Earth Negotiations Bulletin,* vol. 4, no. 160, 15 October 2001, p. 10.
231. *Ibid.*
232. UNCCD Secretariat, n. 184, p. 8.
233. UNEP, n. 194, p. 42.
234. Ayton-Shanker, Diana, ed., *A Global Agenda: Issues before the 57th General Assembly of the United Nations* (New York: Rowman and Littlefield Publishers, 2002), p. 170.
235. Cullet, Phillippe, *Differential Treatment in International Environmental Law* (Aldershot: Ashgate Publishers, 2005), p. 109.
236. Ayton-Shanker, n. 234, p. 170.
237. Corell, n. 53, p. 18. According to French Duncan, ".... the argument

of many developing States that as such assistance is contained within binding multilateral environmental agreements, it should not be treated as charitable. Consequently, the institutional structures created to manage such assistance should not be dominated by the donor countries, but rather more equitable representation between North and South."(French, Duncan, "Developing States and International Environmental Law: The Importance of Differentiated Responsibilities," *International and Comparative Law Quarterly*, vol. 49, 2000, p. 51).

238. Kjellën, n. 131, p. 130.
239. Corell, n. 53, p. 19.
240. Kjellën, n. 131, p. 130.
241. Jokela, n. 8, p. 309.
242. Rechkemmer, n. 1, p. 74. The Global Mechanism was "born out of a political process and as a last-minute compromise that failed to fully satisfy the different negotiating positions expressed by interested and regional groups." (Ortiz, Even Fontaine and Tadanori Inomata, *Assessment of the Global Mechanism of the United Nations Convention to Combat Desertification*, Report prepared by the Joint Inspection Unit, the United Nations, Geneva, 2009, p. 3).
243. Article 21(4) says "(i)n order to increase the effectiveness and efficiency of existing financial mechanisms, a Global Mechanism to promote actions leading to the mobilization and channelling of substantial financial resources, including for the transfer of technology, on a grant basis, and/or on concessional or other terms, to affected developing country Parties, is hereby established. This Global Mechanism shall function under the authority and guidance of the Conference of the Parties and be accountable to it." UNCCD Secretariat, n. 130.
244. http://www.unccd.int/cop/officialdocs/cop5/pdf/4eng.pdf., p. 10. accessed on 1st July, 2008.
245. Adams, n. 106, p. 48. During the negotiation process developing countries "sought to establish different MEA-based funds with universal participation, in which developed and developing states could equally participate in decision making, while developed states aimed at establishing a single fund within the World Bank in which the Bank and donors would have strong positions. In the end the restructured GEF was established as a single fund administered by the World Bank, with the Bank, UNEP and UNDP as implementing agencies. The double majority voting system used in the Council (of GEF) provides a more balanced participation for developed and developing states in decision making than was the case in the GEF pilot phase."(Andresen, n. 55, p. 213). In fact "Northern countries strenuously objected to the "one country, one vote" system of governance, favouring instead the Bretton Woods system of "one dollar, one vote" in which they dominate" (Horta, Korinna *et al.*, "The Global Environmental Facility:

First Ten Years-Growing Pains or Inherent Flaws?" (Washington, D.C.: Environmental Defense, 2002, p. 9). As evidence of its increased legitimacy, membership (of GEF) grew from twenty-nine countries in the pilot phase (1991-1994) to over 173 members by 2002. Where critics still maintain that actual practices have not lived up to the deliberative ideal, the GEF 'has adopted and implemented democratic procedures virtually unmatched in global politics.' (Bernstein, Steven, "Legitimacy in Global Environmental Governance," *Journal of International Law and International Relations,* vol. 1, nos.1-2, 2005, p. 150).

246. Adeel, Zafar, "Overcoming One of the Greatest Environmental Challenges of Our Times: Re-thinking Policies to Cope with Desertification", A Policy Brief based on the Joint International Conference on Desertification and the International Policy Imperative Algiers, Algeria, 17-19th December, 2006, p. 16.
247. The French proposal was for setting up of a facility to the order of SDR 1 billion, coupled with an offer to contribute 900 million Francs. At subsequent discussions between the Bank and potential donors, four global environmental areas of ozone layer, greenhouse gases, biological diversity and international waters were identified as priority concerns.
248. Caldwell, n. 11, p. 132. According to Korinna Horts, "(d)onor governments were adamantly opposed to establishing the GEF as a new organization. Instead, they chose the World Bank, the world's most influential development agency, to manage the GEF. While initially reluctant, the World Bank soon recognised the strategic importance of the proposed facility. The GEF represented an opportunity to help "green" the Bank's tarnished institutional image, reflect its donors interest in environment and to increase leverage over recipient by adding environmental grants and incentives to its loan portfolio". (Horta, Korinna *et al.*, "The Global Environmental Facility: First Ten-Year-Growing Pains or Inherent Flaws?" (Washington, D.C.: Environmental Defense, 2002), p. 8.)
249. GACGC, n. 169, p. 115.
250. Raustiala, Kal, "States, NGOs and International Environmental Institutions", *International Studies Quarterly*, vol. 41, 1997, p. 734.
251. GACGC, n. 169, p. 115.
252. Untawale, n. 36, p. 379.
253. UNEP, n. 194, p. 68.
254. These 17 donor countries were: Australia, Austria, Belgium, Canada, Denmark. Finland, France, Germany, Italy, Japan, Netherlands, Norway, Spain, Sweden, Switzerland, U.K., U.S., New Zealand joined at the second meeting.
255. The operation and structure of the GEF are defined by the Instrument for the Establishment of the Restructured Global Environment Facility

adopted in 1994 and amended in 2003 subsequent to agreements of the second GEF Assembly held in 2002.

256. Desai, n. 195, p. 251.
257. *Ibid.*, p. 252.
258. UNEP, *A Guide to the Global Environmental Facility for NGOs* (Nairobi: UNEP, 2005), p. 9.
259. UNEP, *Multilateral Environmental Agreement Negotiator's Handbook*, (Nairobi: UNEP, 2007), pp. 3-102 (refers to p. 102 of the third chapter).
260. The Implementing Agencies (IAs) are World Bank, UNDP and UNEP. The Executing Agencies are Food and Agriculture Organization (FAO), United Nations Industrial Development Organization (UNIDO), Asian Development Bank (ADB), Inter-American Development Bank (IDB), African Development Bank (AfDB), International Fund for Agricultural Development (IFAD) and the European Bank for Reconstruction and Development (EBRD).
261. UNEP, n. 259, pp. 5-6 (refers p. 6 of the chapter 5).
262. Biermann, F., 'Strengthening Green Global Governance in a Disparate World Society. Would a World Environment Organisation Benefit the South?', *International Environmental Agreements*, vol. 2, 2002, p. 310.
263. Rechkemmer, n. 1, p. 59.
264. A brief analysis of the relevant UN Resolutions shows that the decision to include desertification as a focal area of GEF was initiated long before the Johannesburg Summit which was held in 2002. For example the UN General Assembly Resolution, 555/204 welcomed "the decision of the Council of the Global Environment Facility, at its meeting held from 1st to 3rd November, 2000, to request the Chief Executive Officer to explore the best options for enhancing the support of the Facility in assisting affected countries, especially those in Africa, in implementing the (UNCCD) Convention, taking into account the third replenishment." Similarly in another Resolution passed in the subsequent year, the UN also welcomed "the decision taken by the Council of the Global Environment Facility at its May 2001 session to pursue the designation of land degradation, primarily desertification and deforestation, as a focal area of the Facility, as a means of enhancing its support for the successful implementation of the Convention."
265. McDonagh, n. 183, p. 8.
266. Cowie, Annette, *et al.*, "Potential synergies between existing Multilateral Environmental Agreements in the implementation of land use, land-use change and forestry activities", *Environmental Science and Policy*, vol. 10, 2007, p. 337.
267. *Ibid.*, p. 338.
268. Ulfstein, n. 196, p. 887.
269. UNEP, *Manual on Compliance with and Enforcement of Multilateral Environment Agreement* (Nairobi: UNEP, 2006), p. 269.

270. Johnson, Pierre Marc *et al.*, "The United Nations Convention to Combat Desertification in Global Sustainable Development Governance" in Johnson, n. 170, p. 4.
271. Article 8(1) of UNCCD, the text of the Convention is available at http://www.unccd.int/convention/text/convention.php, accessed on 24th June, 2008
272. *Ibid.*
273. Kimball, L.A., 'Institutional Linkages between the Convention on Biological Diversity and Other International Conventions', *Reciel,* vol. 6, no. 3, 1997, p. 240.
274. Shine, n. 188, p. 36.
275. Adeel, n. 246, p. 20.
276. Kalbermatten, Grégoire de "Reviewing the Options", in Federal Ministry for Economic Cooperation and Development, FMECD (Germany), *The Role of Governance in Combating Desertification*, (Berlin: GTZ Haus, 2007), p. 34.
277. Adeel, n. 246, p. 16.
278. Zeidler, Juliane and Kalemani Jo Mulongoy, "The Dry and Sub-humid Lands Programme of Work of the Convention of Biological Diversity: Connecting the CBD and UN Convention to Combat Desertification", *Receil,* vol. 12, no. 2, 2003, p. 172.
279. Adeel, n. 246, p. 4.

V

Implementation of UNCCD in the GCC Countries

National Governments play a central role in regulating many activities affecting ecosystems and the use of their services since "(e)nvironmental problems are deeply embedded in the socio-economic fabric of countries in all regions."[1] They represent sovereign nation-states at international negotiations and become parties to Multilateral Environmental Agreements (MEAs). The growing realization that environmental challenges need global responses led to an increasing number of MEAs. "These MEAs are a result of international action by governments to develop standards through treaties and conventions that come from influential international declarations, resolutions, and conference documents."[2]

Basically MEAs, at the international level, are "the means to identify and recommend specialized sectoral measures. They can set objectives, targets and standards that establish a threshold for management in particular locations and systems, but the details of application will have to be worked out in relation to the particular environmental conditions, social circumstances and economic activities in place."[3]

> "The process and required actions for implementation of MEAs normally depend upon the provisions of the treaty but in most cases the actions range from implementing national measures provided for in the environmental treaty such as adopting policies, developing and/or strengthening

national legislation and institutions, and/or taking up administrative action to implement MEAs."[4]

Implementation is what transforms an MEA from a legal document to a functioning regime. "Implementation is said to occur in three phases: first, by adopting national legal measures; second, by enforcing them; and third, by reporting on the implementation measures."[5] Implementation of MEAs at the national level is "the ultimate key, both to the efficacy of the GEG (Global Environmental Governance) system and to meaningful environmental improvements."[6] Therefore, it is typically a critical step towards compliance of a global treaty.[7]

However, implementation of MEAs at the national level often meets significant challenges, especially in countries with weak governance structures and poor institutional capacity.[8] Millennium Ecosystem Assessment shows that "the governance features of a country determine the quality of its treaty implementation, and effective implementation and compliance involve numerous other factors, including the characteristics of the treaty, the political will to support it, the human resources committed to monitoring and reporting, the financial resources allotted sanctions and enforcement, and country capacities. In addition, monitoring by civil society can encourage implementation."[9]

In the era of globalization, the winds of changes amended the context within which governments operate. Policy makers now find themselves working in international environments with multiple actors, consequently they have to take into consideration the global implications of their domestic policies.[10] Accordingly the national public administration must actively engage with policies and plans of international organizations.[11]

The emerging new patterns of interaction between government and society at various levels can be observed in areas such as social welfare, environmental protection and natural resource management, education and physical planning. This changing nature of collaboration and partnership are apparently aimed at discovering other ways of coping with complex global problems or of creating new possibilities for governing.[12] Therefore, the effectiveness of international agreements and the regime embodying them will depend on the extent to which national policy efforts and initiatives actually comply with the international obligations.[13] Because, "(t)here is no functional equivalent to National Governments as highly visible, legitimised and competent territorial actors and protectors."[14] "From legislation to regulation to enforcement, it is the actions taken by nations at the domestic level that ultimately count most for success at the global level."[15] However, the GCC countries "lag behind the rest of the world in the core domestic institutions that make basic environmental governance possible, and in their contributions to global processes of shared environmental management."[16]

In this background, this chapter analyses the various measures taken by the GCC countries to combat desertification including the implementation of Plan of Action of Nairobi Conference, 1977. It studies the initiatives undertaken by the GCC countries within the framework of United Nations Convention to Combat Desertification (UNCCD). It also surveys the implementation of West Asian Sub-regional Action Programme in the GCC countries. Besides this, it examines the role of GCC countries in executing UNCCD at the regional level.

I. Implementation of Plan of Action of the Nairobi Conference

The United Nations Conference on Desertification (UNCOD) held in Nairobi in 1977 "desertification as a major economic, social and environmental problem of concern to all countries. It adopted the UN Plan of Action to Combat Desertification (PoA or PACD), which consisted of basic guidelines and detailed recommendations. The plan of action aimed to contain the advance of desertification, and to make areas vulnerable to desertification more stable and productive."[17] The UN General Assembly subsequently approved the report of the UNCOD and called upon the governments to consider, on a priority basis, the recommendations for national action and establish a national authority to coordinate and implement national anti-desertification action programmes.[18]

The governments in the GCC countries showed lack of interest in implementing the PoA. It was the UN specialized agencies and progammes that made substantial efforts to implement the PoA. In the West Asian region, the UN Economic and Social Commission for West Asia (ESCWA) made tremendous efforts to implement the recommendations of the Nairobi Conference.

The United Nations requested its regional commissions "to undertake intensified and sustained action in support of national efforts to combat desertification, to assist governments, at their request in the implementation of the plan of action to combat desertification and convene as appropriate, in cooperation with interested Governments and regional organizations, intergovernmental regional meetings, technical workshops and seminars to consider the immediate implementation of the recommendations."[19] As a follow-up to the UNCOD, the ESCWA considered the issue of desertification at its sixth session in 1979 and adopted Resolution 71(VI) on combating desertification in the region, which emphasized the need to identify and implement a set of action-oriented, problem-solving activities. Accordingly an Expert Meeting on Management,

Conservation and Development of Agricultural Resources held in Damascus in 1981 in cooperation with the Food and Agriculture Organization (FAO) and the Arab Centre for the Study of Arid Zones and Dry Lands (ACSAD). This meeting proposed a set of concrete recommendations to protect natural resources in this region, which formed the basis of ESCWA work in the area of desertification control.[20]

Since the convening of Nairobi Conference, the Agriculture Division of the ESCWA served as a Focal Point for the activities related with combating desertification in this region. It mostly focused its attention in undertaking studies and research on the assessment and integrated development of areas prone to desertification, preparing national action plans to combat desertification, formulating specific desertification control projects, and conducting training programmes in resource conservation and management.[21] These activities were undertaken by ESCWA either unilaterally or multilaterally in cooperation with concerned governments and other United Nations specialized agencies or regional and international organizations.[22]

i. National Action Programmes under PoA

The most important component of PoA was the formulation and implementation of National Action programme by the governments. "Although these national plans differ markedly in their details owing to the different socio-economic conditions in each member country, as well as resources potential, land-use practices and policies and other major factors influencing the phenomenon of desertification, the plans are in conformity with regard to the principal topics addressed."[23]

Table 5.1: Measures taken by the GCC Countries to address Desertification

Sl. No.	*Country*	*Measures initiated to address desertification*
1.	Bahrain	Issuing suitable legislations
		Improving farming and irrigation practices
		Surveys of the natural resources
		Drawing up a national plan
2.	Kuwait	Protection from the sand dunes
		Increasing afforestation
		Making surveys and evaluations of the range plant resources
		Establishing protected areas
		Issuing legislations
3.	Oman	Efforts to develop the agricultural production
		Improve and protect the water resources
		Enhance the productive efficiency of the lands
		Rehabilitate the rangeland areas and
		Implement programmes for rangeland and afforestation
4.	Qatar	Establishment of protected areas
		Expanding the growing of date palm
		Fixing sand dunes and
		Drawing up national programme for combating desertification
5.	Saudi Arabia	Making plant surveys
		Afforestation
		Fixing the sand dunes
		Developing the water sector
		Establishing scientific centres
		Supporting the research programmes
		Issuing regulations to protect natural resources
6.	U.A.E.	Afforestation
		Establishment of green belts to provide protection from soil wind erosion conservation of the rangelands
		Development of the farms
		Conservation of the water resources
		Adoption of sound environmental management policies on the agricultural lands

Source: Compiled from UNEP/ROWA, *State of Desertification in the Arab World*, Manama: UNEP/ROWA, 2004, pp. 9-17.

By 1993, only three GCC countries prepared their national Action programmes. These were Bahrain, Oman and UAE. (Table 5.2)

II. Implementation of UNCCD at the National Level

Threats to the environment appear to be distributed throughout the world regardless of the political, economic, or social systems of

Table 5.2: The GCC Countnries National Action Programmes Under UNCOD

Sl. No.	*Country*	*Status*	*Year of Submission*
1.	Bahrain	Prepared	1991
2.	Kuwait	Not available	—
3.	Oman	Prepared	1992
4.	Qatar	Not available	—
5.	Saudi Arabia	Not available	—
6.	U.A.E.	Prepared	1993

Source: ESCWA, n. 20.

particular countries. Therefore, the governments, "should, in a spirit of international solidarity and partnership, improve cooperation and coordination at sub-regional, regional and international levels, and better focus financial, human, organizational and technical resources where they are needed."[24]

The UNCCD also mandates the governments to "develop, in a spirit of partnership, cooperation among all levels of government, communities, non-governmental organizations and landholders to establish a better understanding of the nature and value of land and scarce water resources in affected areas and to work towards their sustainable use."[25] Accordingly the GCC countries initiated a number of measures to implement the UNCCD at three levels—national, sub-regional and regional.

"Due to the severity of desertification experienced in the sub-region, all countries had undertaken measures to address the problem prior to the entry into force of the Convention in 1994. It was amply expressed in the reports that environmental strategies and programmes related to desertification are integrated into overall development strategies of Governments at a fairly early stage."[26] However as a signatory to an international convention, every government has the obligations to take certain measures to implement the global treaty. Under UNCCD, the GCC countries implemented the Convention at the national level through establishing Focal Points and National Coordination Committees, enacting legislations, creating administrative arrangements and formulating National Action Programmes.

i. Signing and Ratification

A State is bound by an agreement when it becomes a Party to that (in certain instances, non-State actors, such as the European Community and other regional economic organisations, can also become Party to a regional or international agreement). It can do so by ratifying, accepting, approving, or acceding to the convention.

> "The fundamental principle of international law is *pacta sunt servanda* ("agreements must be observed"). States generally are only bound by those agreements to which they agree to be bound. A State may become Party to an MEA for many reasons: because it is in the State's best interest, because the State wants to be a responsible international actor, because it wants to access financial or technical resources, because other States encourage it, etc."[27]

Ratification is a process through which national legislature approves the signing of a global treaty. Such process implies not only an expression of interest as indicated by the signature, but the transformation of the treaty's principles and obligations into national law.[28] In other words, through ratification of the conventions, contracting parties (governments) agree in principle to apply the listed obligations and in some cases to transpose them into national legislation. In so doing they agree to protect the environment as specified in the convention texts.[29]

The instrument of ratification must be deposited with the Depositary which, in the case of the UNCCD, is the Secretary-General of the United Nations. The country will become a Party of the Convention by the completion of a period of 90 days after the deposit of the instrument of ratification. All the GCC countries signed the Convention and subsequently ratified the same. Table 5.3 shows the details.

Only Kuwait signed the UNCCD when it was opened for signature, i.e. before the convention came into force. All the other GCC countries became Party to the Convention after it came into force in 1996. The available data does not suggest the specific reasons for the delay in signing the convention by majority of the GCC countries. The possible causes might be two. First one is administrative procedures that could have caused delay. Secondly, the UNCCD does not include hyper arid zones while defining land degradation.

Table 5.3: The UNCCD and the GCC Countries

Sl. No.	*Country*	*Date of Signing*	*Date of Ratification*	*Date of Accession***	*Date of Entry into Force*
1.	Bahrain	—	—	14.07.1997	12.10.1997
2.	Kuwait	22.9.1995	27. 6.1997	—	25.09.1997
3.	Oman	—	—	23.07.1996	26.12.1996
4.	Qatar	—	—	15.09.1999	14.12.1999
5.	Saudi Arabia	—	—	25.06.1997	23.09.1997
6.	U.A.E.	—	—	21.10.1998	19.01.1999

** *Accession* is the means by which a State can become a Party to an agreement when it did not sign the treaty within the established period; and accession usually occurs after the agreement enters into force.

Source: UNCCD Secretariat, "Regional Profile-Asia" [Online: web] Accessed on 28th March, 2010 URL: http://www.unccd.int/regional/asia/menu.php.

This is discussed in the first chapter in detail. Since this region mostly consists of hyper arid zones, these countries might have delayed in signing the UNCCD. These observations need further verification and investigations.

ii. Creation of Focal Points

Domestically, the task of coordinating the implementation of environmental commitments specified in a MEA is facilitated by the designation of National Focal Points (NFPs) or lead agencies, which would usually be the most competent Ministry or department related to a particular agreement.[30] A representative from each country serves as the Focal Point for the Convention to liaise with the Convention Secretariat and to assist in inter-sessional work. National Focal Point "may be responsible to report information from the Convention Secretariat to governmental bodies and report back to the Conference of Parties (CoPs) on national implementation efforts."[31]

Parties to a MEA often designate one or more Focal Points responsible for a MEA. There are two types of Focal Points: political and technical. The political Focal Point is usually responsible for the international processes, such as negotiating MEAs and participating in the CoPs. Most States designate their Ministry of Foreign Affairs or a similar body as the political Focal Point. The technical Focal Point often bears the responsibility for implementing the MEA at the national level.[32]

Most governments generally designate the Chief Officer of the nation's Environment Agency as their technical Focal Point. In some cases the other government management and scientific authorities may also serve as Focal Points for specific purposes under particular MEA. In the GCC countries the Focal Points are mostly technical. Data on political Focal Points in the GCC countries are not available. Except in Bahrain where there are two persons acting as Focal Points for the UNCCD, all the other GCC countries have one person as a Focal Point. See Table 5.4.

Table 5.4: The UNCCD Focal Points in the GCC Countries

Sl. No.	*Country*	*Focal Points*
1.	Bahrain	1. Under-Secretary for Agriculture Ministry of Municipalities Affairs and Agriculture 2. Director of Agricultural Engineering Ministry of Municipalities Affairs and Agriculture
2.	Kuwait	Chairman and Director General Environment Public Authority
3.	Oman	Director of Coordination and Follow-up Ministry of Regional Municipalities, Environment and Water Resources
4.	Qatar	Member Supreme Council for the Environment and Natural Reserves
5.	Saudi Arabia	Director General Range and Forestry Department Ministry of Agriculture
6.	U.A.E.	Director General Federal Environmental Agency

Source: UNCCD Secretariat, "Focal Points", [Online: web] Accessed on 25th March, 2010 URL: http://www.unccd.int/focalpoints/focalpoints.php.

The growing number of agreements to which states are becoming parties significantly increased the number of Focal Points and these are often spread across Government Ministries. This dispersion creates administrative and coordination challenges for most governments, particularly for the developing countries which lack the necessary capacity—both institutional and individual—to respond to and comply with environmental treaty obligations.

The Joint Inspection Unit (JIU) of UN also noted that UNCCD Focal Points are often located in weak Ministries and appointed at a junior level. Moreover, many developing country Parties' Focal Points lack the financial and human capacities to effectively participate in CoPs and associated Convention processes. This led to unequal participation among Parties and to a disconnect between COP decisions and implementation at the national level.[33] In order to discharge their functions effectively, the national institutions responsible for implementation of and reporting on MEAs need to be given high status in the government organization with a clear mandate.[34]

To ensure active involvement "further support in the form of information and training programmes should be made available to the National Focal Points (NFPs), including training for negotiation, integrative programme planning and awareness of resource mobilization opportunities in relation to the programming cycles of bilateral and multilateral development partners. Information should also be provided to UNCCD focal points and stakeholders, including NGO representatives, in order to familiarize them with the GEF tools and modalities."[35]

iii. Setting up National Coordination Bodies (NCBs)

It is important to underline the closed-loop relationship between the national implementation process and the follow-up of inter-governmental negotiations, each contributing significantly to the dynamics of the other. Managing these dual processes requires a mixture of knowledge, skills, legal competence and administrative coordination.

Environmental protection and natural resources management entail new responsibilities for most governments and require the bringing together of functions not previously related. Coordination, therefore, becomes one of the principal problems and tasks of environmental administration.[36]

Similarly, the UNCCD is a comprehensive global treaty touching upon every aspect of the sustainable development process. Therefore effective implementation of this convention mainly depends on constructive cooperation of all concerned stakeholders. In this regard the role of National Coordination Bodies[37] is crucial. The GCC countries nominated particular Ministries as NCBs (see Table 5.5).

These Ministries are expected to set up a National Coordination Committee comprising various Ministries, research institutes and civil society representatives. This committee will coordinate all the activities related with UNCCD implementation including the formulation of National Action Programmes.

Table 5.5: National Coordination Bodies (NCBs) in the GCC Countries

Sl. No.	*Country*	*National Coordination Bodies (NCBs) for UNCCD*
1.	Bahrain	Ministry of Municipalities Affairs and Agriculture
2.	Kuwait	Environment Public Authority
3.	Oman	Ministry of Regional Municipalities, Environment and Water Resources
4.	Qatar	Supreme Council for the Environment and Natural Reserves
5.	Saudi Arabia	Ministry of Agriculture and Water
6.	United Arab Emirates	Ministry of Environment

Source: GRC, *Green Gulf Report* (Dubai: GRC, 2006), p. 17.

Accordingly in Bahrain the "Ministry of Works and Agriculture—the responsible authority for combating desertification…is prepared to form a National Committee from the relevant organizations for combating desertification and to help organizing their activities. The Ministry will work on this subject to put it in action."[38]

The Environment Public Authority (EPA) in Kuwait "established the National Committee to combat Desertification which was assigned to study the Convention, follow-up all subjects related to it, evaluate Desertification activities, prepare national action programmes and a strategy according to the Convention's articles and the Asian Annex."[39]

In Oman "a committee to follow up the implementation was established by Ministerial Decisions in 2002. The committee has undertaken several activities on rehabilitation of degraded lands. These activities were used in the sustainable management of natural resources and helping to reduce the number of animals to 1970s' level."[40]

In 1997, Saudi Arabia "established a National Committee. The Committee consists of representatives from all Government ministries and agencies pertinent to desertification and renewable natural resources and was mandated to prepare the Kingdom's national action programme to combat desertification. The members of this committee include: The Ministries of Agriculture and Water, Interior, Finance and National Economy, Higher Education, Planning, Municipality and Rural Affairs, Communication and Ministry of Information. Specialized institutions such as King Abdulaziz City for Science and Technology, General Council for Meteorology and Environmental protection, National Commission for Wildlife Conservation and Development and Prince Sultan Centre for Environment, Water and Desert Research (King Saud University) are also members of the national committee."[41]

In UAE the Federal Environmental Agency (FEA) established the National Committee for the Follow-up of the UNCCD on 17th June, 2001. The committee consists of 25 members representing 17 bodies working in the fields related to the UNCCD.[42]

There is no such committee in Qatar. According to its report to UNCCD Secretariat "the national coordination activity of desertification is still in its very infant stage. It has no financial autonomy, separate human resources and logistic or independent entity organization. Even though, most activities could successfully be carried through the very powerful cooperation and harmonic element existing within the Ministry and with other bodies such as the university and its research centres..."[43]

National Coordination Committees on MEA "represent one type of mechanism that facilitates multi-stakeholder involvement in decision-making. The extent and nature of multi-stakeholder participation in NCs depends largely on the decision-making culture of the country, the nature of the party's treaty obligations, and the technical needs and capacity of the focal points and lead agencies to meet their commitments."[44] Even though all the GCC countries, except Qatar established National Coordination Committees, the composition shows a lack of people's participation, especially NGOs. Only a few research institutes are included in these committees. Lack of people's participation in the UNCCD related activities is in contrast with the very spirit of UNCCD principles and objectives.

iv. Submission of National Reports

"MEAs can require that Parties monitor, report, and verify environmental compliance data. Reporting, monitoring, and verification measures can assist States in tracking their compliance under the respective MEAs."[45] Under Article 26(1) of UNCCD "(e)ach Party shall communicate to the Conference of the Parties for consideration at its ordinary sessions, through the Permanent Secretariat, reports on the measures which it has taken for the implementation of the Convention. The Conference of the Parties shall determine the time table for submission and the format of such reports."[46] The affected parties shall provide a description of the strategies established, and other relevant information. On the other hand the developed country Parties need to report on steps taken to assist in the preparation and implementation of action programmes.[47] In addition to this, any group of affected country Parties may make a joint communication on measures taken at the sub-regional and/or regional levels within the framework of UNCCD.

Reporting is the basis for an effective assessment of the implementation of the Convention and for taking informed decisions on how to achieve the ultimate goals. Reports are the backbone of the review of the implementation of the Convention. It facilitates experience-sharing and provides Parties with additional information on how better to tackle desertification. National reports are critical because they provide the specific information to show that each country is meeting its obligation under UNCCD.[48]

Among the GCC countries, there was no reporting from Bahrain and Oman since 2000. Only Saudi Arabia and UAE submitted all the reports. Secondly, "Parties are required to communicate their reports in one of the official languages of the CoP. Parties are also encouraged to submit their reports, or at least their summary, in English in order to disseminate them widely."[49] However Bahrain (2000), Kuwait (2002 & 2004), Saudi Arabia (2000) and UAE (2006) submitted their reports in Arabic without summary in English (Table 5.6). This affects the wider circulation of the details of the status of desertification related activities in the GCC countries.

Since reporting is a key strategy to encourage compliance with the provisions of an international instrument, it requires robust guidelines, performance indicators, adequate capacity and financing. However, reporting guidelines adopted under the UNCCD are not robust enough to promote implementation and improve compliance. Moreover, as noted in the JIU report, UNCCD reporting is under-funded compared to its Rio sister conventions.[50]

Similarly most MEAs "require parties to report at regular intervals on the measures they have taken to implement the agreement. In recent years, there has been a growing recognition that the reporting burden

Table 5.6: The GCC Countries' National Reports under the UNCCD

Sl. No	*Country*	*1st Reporting (CoP 3/4) 2000*	*2nd Reporting (CRIC-1) 2002*	*3rd Reporting (CRIC-5) 2006*
1.	Bahrain	Submitted Report: Arabic No Summary	—	—
2.	Kuwait	Submitted Report: Arabic No Summary	Submitted Report: Arabic No Summary	—
3.	Oman	Submitted Report: English No Summary	—	—
4.	Qatar	Submitted Report: English No Summary	Submitted Report: English No Summary	—
5.	Saudi Arabia	Submitted Report: Arabic No Summary	Submitted Report: Arabic Summary: English and Arabic	Submitted Report: Arabic Summary: English
6.	U.A.E.	Submitted Report: Arabic Summary: English	Submitted Report: Arabic Summary: English and Arabic	Submitted Report: Arabic No Summary

Source: UNCCD Secretariat, "Reports of the Asian Countries" [Online: web] Accessed on 22nd March, 2010 URL: http://www.unccd.int/cop/reports/asia/asia.php.

has increased."[51] Similarly "as governments accede to more agreements, they are confronted with a multitude of reports to prepare. The reporting formats are often complex, and many questions are similar to those for other conventions, which often leads to duplication of work between the focal points of different conventions."[52] In order to ensure that reports are uniform and comparable, it is recommendable to prescribe detailed, standardized international reporting formats.[53] Attempts need to be made to streamline the reporting process which, hitherto, has not been successful because different MEAs require different types of information.[54]

v. Formulation of National Action Programmes

The fight against desertification requires a multi-layered approach, integrating the environmental aspect into a broader socio-economic framework. The UNCCD stands at the helm of this process. Its main tool is National Action Programmes (NAPs) to combat desertification, which evaluates the nature and intensity of the problem in each country and identify the necessary action to be taken.[55] A central element within the text of UNCCD is "the commitment by the affected countries to devise national action programmes to combat desertification, which are intended to map out a set of priorities to include policy change, training needs, economic incentives, drought preparedness and clarification of tenure rules."[56]

Under Article 10 (1) of UNCCD the "purpose of national action programmes is to identify the factors contributing to desertification and practical measures necessary to combat desertification."[57] Therefore, the NAPs are at the heart of the Convention and constitute the conceptual and legal framework for implementing it at the national and local levels.[58] Since the issue of desertification is very closely linked to the development process itself, the UNCCD mandates the government to formulate comprehensive policies for sustainable development at national, sub-regional and regional levels.[59] Through NAPs, the UNCCD

> "provides a much broader framework, because it has the potential to serve as the starting point for developing comprehensive sustainability policies for the countries concerned and for developing democratic structures. Its special value lies in this function as a catalyst of comprehensive social development."[60]

Table 5.7: The GCC Countries' National Action Programme under the UNCCD

Sl. No.	*Country*	*Status*	*Year of Submission*
1.	Bahrain	Under preparation	—
2.	Kuwait	Under preparation	—
3.	Oman	Submitted	2005
4.	Qatar	Under preparation	—
5.	Saudi Arabia	Submitted	2005
6.	U.A.E.	Submitted	2003

Source: UNCCD Secretariat, "National Action Programmes of the Asian Countries" [Online: web] Accessed on 20th March, 2010 URL: http://www.unccd.int/actionprogrammes/asia/asia.php.

Accordingly these national level Action programmes are supplemented by Sub-regional and Regional Action Programmes. Activities in the NAPs can be divided into general and specific categories. The general actions include promoting awareness about underlying causes of desertification and providing the enabling institutional and legal framework for addressing desertification. The specific actions are the establishment of early warning systems, strengthening of drought preparedness, establishing food security, establishing alternative livelihoods, and developing sustainable irrigation schemes.[61]

Most importantly, NAP preparation should be preceded by a survey of the state of the environment in the affected areas to assess the causes and consequences of desertification in specific areas and to determine priority areas for action [Article 4.1 (c), Asia Annex of UNCCD], and should take into account the assessments based upon systematic observations referred to in Article 16 of UNCCD and evaluations referred to in Article 4.1 (f), Asia Annex of UNCCD.[62]

The NAPs are also expected to spell out its linkages with resource-users, grassroots level organisations working at community level, policy and decision makers at various levels, programmes of co-operation with other governments, international organisations and donor agencies, synergies amongst the various Rio Conventions and recommend a plan of action for addressing the problems of desertification in the dryland regions of the country.[63] "It is important for national governments to insure that other groups (especially scientists and civil society organizations) are involved in the dialogue leading to National Action Plan formulation."[64] Significantly these NAPs are "the prerequisite for the involvement of the donor states, i.e. financial and technical assistance will be *"country-driven"*, as opposed to being predetermined by the developed countries."[65]

Among the GCC countries, Oman, Saudi Arabia and UAE completed the preparation of their NAPs and submitted them to the UNCCD Secretariat. During this authour's meeting with Experts at Arabian Gulf University, Manama, it was learned that the NAP of Bahrain was finalized and submitted to the government for final approval. The preparation of NAPs in other GCC countries is at the various stages. The reason for the delay is considered to be as follows:

> Due to the severity of desertification experienced in the sub-region, all countries had undertaken measures to alleviate

> the problem *prior to the entry into force of the Convention in 1994*. It was amply expressed in the reports that environmental strategies and programmes related to desertification are integrated into overall development strategies of Governments at a fairly early stage. Perhaps because countries of this Asian sub-region are so used to dealing with an arid environment, *it might have been difficult at first to identify additional efforts that could have been undertaken under the UNCCD.* Due to these circumstances the preparation/review of National Action Programmes under the UNCCD was generally delayed in West Asia. This situation was compounded by still another aspect. Given the fact that some countries faced and still face an acute lack of financial resources, the implementation of a comprehensive NAP structure had to be postponed.[66] (Emphasis added)

vi. Establishment of Administrative Institutions

The process for implementation of MEAs normally depend upon the provisions of the treaty but in most cases the actions range from adopting policies, developing and strengthening national legislation and institutions to implement MEAs.[67] The rapid and profound changes initiated by the socio-economic development process produced serious environmental management problems in the GCC countries. "State environmental authorities are generally young, inadequately staffed and short of the expertise needed not only to address current issues but also a substantial backlog of environmental problems, both in depleting natural resources and in polluting the environment."[68] This situation is beginning to change.

Environmental issues are gradually coming to the forefront of national concerns. There are also encouraging signs of an emerging awareness among the public of the need to protect the natural resources. The past few decades witnessed the emergence of environmental NGOs that are beginning to promote popular support for national efforts and initiatives to protect the environment. The industries also started to take its environmental responsibilities more seriously.[69]

In the GCC countries, government established or designated the national institutions or organisations for formulating and implementing desertification related programmes under the UNCCD.

They generally involve in different types of activities related to monitoring of vegetation cover degradation and rehabilitation of degraded lands.

A. Bahrain

Joint Ministries existed in Bahrain. These provided Ministers with joint responsibility over an Environmental Directorate and one or two related sectors. The aim of linking national and local environmental issues resulted in the combination of municipalities and environmental affairs under one Ministry.[70] "Independent environmental authorities or commissions that are independent but linked to an environmental Minister or to the Council of Ministers, which exist in Bahrain. The board of directors tends to be led by a Minister from a line Ministry exclusively or jointly responsible for environment matters. However, there are no legal ties between the Minister and the environmental agency."[71]

The national institutions involved to combat desertification include the Ministries of Housing and Agriculture, Municipalities and Environment, the Institute of Wild Life Production, University of Bahrain, Arabian Gulf University, and Non-Governmental Organisations such as Technology Association, Association of Youth and Environment.[72] Besides these, the Bahrain Centre for Studies and Research and the Water Science and Technology Associations are also playing important role in implementing desertification related programmes.[73]

B. Kuwait

Inter-Ministerial Environmental Council led by the Deputy Prime Minister with an Environmental Authority exists in Kuwait. This model gives the chairmanship of the Environmental Council to a high-level politician who promotes those environmental agendas that he or she supports. This gives the Environmental Authority some means to work outside inter-Ministerial politics.[74]

In Kuwait, a number of institutions at the national level involve directly or indirectly in activities related to desertification. The Kuwait Institute of Scientific Research undertakes research activities. The Environment Public Authority (EPA) focuses on implementation of desertification related programmes. Kuwait University, Public

Authority for Applied Education and Training (PAAET) and EPA engage in training. PAAET also involves in formulating policies and plans under UNCCD.[75] "A database was established for each authority involved in Combat of Desertification, and they will be connected among a complete information network in the future."[76]

C. Oman

The important national institution concerned with desertification in Oman is the Ministry of Regional Municipalities, Environment and Water Resources, which has prime responsibility for desertification control and carries out planning and research activities in the field of desertification monitoring and control.[77]

Other institutions related with the implementation of the UNCCD in Oman include "Ministry of Agriculture and Fisheries, the Ministry of National Economy, the Ministry of Communication and Transportation, the Ministry of Information and the Sultan Qaboos University are all involved in one way or another in desertification control. The role of each one in desertification control, however, is not always spelled out in their establishment decrees or order."[78] Besides, there are other national level institutions in Oman that carry out activities related to combating desertification. These are the Council for the Conservation of the Environment and Prevention of Pollution, the Office of the Adviser for Conservation of the Environment and the Planning Committee for Development and Environment in the Governorate of Zufar.[79]

Oman established several meteorological stations covering different regions of the country. The development of a network for agro meteorological data collection and processing is also considered. In 1991, Oman completed the preparation of a National Resources Master Plan to strengthen the institutional and legal framework to provide effective management of water resources.[80]

D. Qatar

Environmental Directorates in line Ministries previously existed in Qatar. In Qatar, during the 1990s, environmental matters were brought under the mandate of the Ministry of Municipal Affairs and Agriculture until the establishment of an Environmental Council in 2000.[81] Inter-Ministerial Environmental Council with environmental secretariat exists in Qatar. This Environmental Council is an inter-Ministerial body with technical secretariats that take action on specific decisions endorsed by the Council. [82]

The Department of Agriculture and Water Research and the Department of Agricultural Development are the important institutions involved in desertification related activities. Prior to joining the UNCCD, "the Head of the Soil Research Section of the Department of Agricultural and Water Research was assigned to coordinate and liaise all activities relevant to desertification at all local, regional and international levels."[83]

University of Qatar engages in teaching and research related with issues of desertification and land degradation. It also provides consultation to the government on policies and programmes related with desertification.[84] "An information centre had been formulated which started and still (is) in process of acquiring all informations necessary for agricultural development in some sorts of databases."[85]

E. Saudi Arabia

Environmental Directorates in line Ministries exist in Saudi Arabia. Typically, an Environmental Directorate is an agency or Department within a Ministry. In Saudi Arabia, meteorological responsibilities of the environmental agency are under the purview of the Ministry of Defence and Aviation. [86] The prominent national institutions concerned with desertification in Saudi Arabia are the Ministry of Agriculture and the Prince Sultan Centre for Environmental, Water and Desert Studies in King Saudi University. The first one involves different activities related to desertification such as research, implementation, planning and training. The second one undertakes researches on important areas related with desertification. The research areas include desertification monitoring, desert natural resources and their development and the use of modern technologies.

Besides these institutions there are a number of other national organisations concerned with desertification such as the National Authority for Wild Life Protection and Development, the Saudi National Remote Sensing Centre in the city of King Abdul Aziz for Sciences and Technology, Centre of Rangeland Development in Al Jouf, natural resources and environment research institutions in Saudi Universities.[87]

Recently Saudi Arabia established a number of institutions and committees crucial for conservation of renewable natural resources and the environment. These include the Ministry for Water, the Supreme Tourism Authority, the Saudi Agency for Geologic Survey, the Supreme Council for Investment and the National Committee for the preparation of concrete action programme for preparedness to natural disasters.[88]

F. United Arab Emirates (UAE)

Inter-Ministerial Environmental Council with Environmental Secretariat exists in the United Arab Emirates. In the United Arab Emirates, the Council of the Federal Environmental Agency is heavily dependent upon the support of the environmental agencies in that country to implement programmes. [89] A number of institutions are involved in protecting the environment, combating desertification[90] and the rehabilitation of the degraded lands and the vegetations cover in UAE.

These are the Federal Agency for Environment, the Ministry of Agriculture and Fishery, the Ministry of Transportation, Forest Management in Al Ain, the Faculty of Agricultural Science at the University of UAE and many other institutes in each Emirate.[91] Besides these, UAE established the National Facility which consists of the main Centre for Metrological Predictions, Centre for Metrological Communication, Centre of Measuring Metrology Methods, Workshop for Meteorological Systems Maintenance and General Library for Meteorology.[92]

vii. Enactment of Legislations

A significant part of national level enforcement of a State's obligations under multilateral environmental agreements is the incorporation of international law into national law.[93] Under Article 5 (e) of UNCCD, governments of the desertification affected countries must "provide an enabling environment by strengthening, as appropriate, relevant existing legislation and, where they do not exist, enacting new laws and establishing long-term policies and action programmes."[94]

> "It is also important to ensure that there is adequate coordination of different sectors or Government Ministries handling environmental issues in the planning and

> management of various environmental resources and national legislation can streamline this coordination, by a link with other players, e.g. NGOs and Civil Society."[95]

The GCC countries passed numerous laws dealing with the environment. In Kuwait, as early as 1964, the first law was passed to protect navigable water from oil pollution. Articles 15, 16, and 21 of the Constitution of Kuwait were subsequently amended in 1976 and in 1980 to incorporate environmental protection principles and to establish mechanisms to enforce the implementation of environmental laws.[96] "Despite the often fragmented nature of organisational responsibilities for the environment, legislation in the region has been fairly cross-sectoral and all-encompassing since the 1980s. These laws, sometimes known as framework laws, facilitate to restructure the fragmented approaches to environmental management."[97]

With respect to legislation on combating desertification, the GCC countries in their report to the UNCCD Secretariat claimed that

> "...appropriate laws relating to natural resources and land management are in place. The majority of these laws and legislative frameworks (which dealt with land tenure and land use, agriculture and grazing, forestry, water use and conservation, environmental protection, environmental management, environmental impact assessments, mining and mineral resources, zoning, urban development, etc.) were enacted prior to the entry into force of the Convention. They are in the process of reviewing their current legislative frameworks with a view to making them more consistent with the current situation. Many Parties have identified gaps in their present legislation and acknowledge the need for revision to strengthen its force."[98]

The followings are the country specific legislations related with desertification.

A. Bahrain

In Bahrain there are eleven legislations concerned with environment, wildlife, fisheries, veterinary medicine, palm trees production, environmental standard and groundwater.[99] In Bahrain the "laws, in the face of alarming water and land situation, have been formulated and made more stringent in 1997 to control and to monitor the abstraction and use of water for agriculture and landscape, beside domestic and industrial uses."[100] Besides, "the Amiri Decrees in respect of organizing date palm protection and land drainage system are effective to protect the state infrastructure to combat the menace of shrinking agricultural land."[101]

B. Kuwait

Kuwait makes efforts to combat desertification in a number of ways including enacting appropriate environmental legislations. The important legislations are rangeland law, camping control in rangelands, agriculture protection and quarrying exploration control.[102] In Kuwait "(t)hrough analysis of available information, data and the past laws and decisions, it was noticed that there is a need to improve and reformulate laws and decisions by determining standards and environmental stipulations to protect and promote the environment and natural resources."[103] Accordingly some important legislations were enacted recently including constructing natural reserves law and Environmental Impact Assessment law.[104]

C. Oman

The Arab Centre for the Studies of Arid Zones and Dry Lands (ACSAD) carried out a detailed survey on the existing administrative and legislative mechanism available in Oman to Combat Desertification in the GCC countries. However, this report did not include any legislative frameworks which exist in Oman to address the issues related with desertification. On the other hand the Oman national action programme to Combat Desertification proposes a project to be completed within a year with the following objectives:[105]

- Revise relevant existing laws and legislation
- Identify gaps in existing legislation
- Compare the existing legislation with the obligations under the environmental conventions
- Identify the necessary steps to ensure the domestication of the Conventions
- Prepare a comprehensive legislative framework
- Revise laws accordingly

Even in the report submitted to the UNCCD Secretariat Oman did not give specific legislations related with desertification. On the other hand it simply says that "Oman has realized the importance of the conservation of the environment, natural resources and their optimum utilization for the benefit of the present and future generations in a sustainable manner through the following:

- Formulation of environmental legislation;
- Provision of administrative and technical bodies to ensure enforcement of the laws..."[106]

D. Qatar

There are about 82 legislations in Qatar which are related to different environmental activities such water resources, well drilling, use of waste water, control of grazing afforestation, urbanization over agricultural land, etc. Violation of these legislations is common in Qatar.[107]

E. Saudi Arabia

Through its efforts to Combat Desertification, Saudi Arabia enacted a number of legislations such as: rangeland and forest legislation which deals with the protection of range and forest lands. Land legislation regulates land allocation and exploitation. Legislation on water resources conservation rationalises the use of water resources. Saudi Arabia promulgated some other legislations related to the protected areas and environmental protection. Keeping in view of emerging challenges, Saudi Arabia is in the process of reviewing and updating some of the legislations.[108] The updated legislation for forest and range and the strategy and the national forest programme was approved.[109]

F. UAE

UAE enacted a number of laws to protect the environment and the natural resources. These legislations are the Federal Law on Environmental Protection and Development (FLED)(24/1999), the Federal Law on the Establishment of the Department of Water Resources (21/1981), the Federal Law on Regulating the Hunting of Birds and Wild Animals (9/1983). Besides these some other important federal laws were also passed to regulate the handling of the production and importation of seedlings, fertilizers, pesticides, and seeds.[110]

viii. Making provisions for People's Participation

A progressive environmental policy is less meaningful if it is not accepted and carried out on a broader scale including all sections of society.[111] The implementation of MEAs at the national level always remains a multi-actor and multi level process.[112] While implementing MEAs, increasing importance is placed on public participation and voluntary agreements as well as horizontally rather than hierarchically structured process of policy development and enforcement.[113] This is because

> "...the scientific and technical knowledge of NGOs and the private sector in many instances surpasses the capacity available within national governments, MEA secretariats and inter-governmental and regional organizations. While some NGOs may specialize along sector-specific lines, many undertake broader projects and activities that serve the objectives of multiple conventions, and are also effective in addressing important crosscutting concerns such as awareness raising and capacity building."[114]

The underlying assumption is that participation and representation by non-state actors in the implementation of MEAs strengthen the democratic basis of environmental governance.[115] The "(i)nclusion of the so-called marginalized groups, such as women, indigenous people and youth, has been perceived as particularly critical to the achievement of sustainable development."[116]

Public participation brings legitimacy, credibility, and effectiveness to the policy making process and its implementation. A common challenge to ensuring participation in environmental decision-making is that not all affected stakeholders are equally well positioned to express their views. For some people, there are still barriers of distance, time, language, literacy, and connectivity that might prevent effective participation. To involve meaningfully, people need access to information: about the environment, the decisions made and their environmental implications, and the decision-making process itself. A recent survey shows that citizens, by and large, feel that governments do not provide them with as much environmental information, or opportunity to participate in environmental decision-making, as they would like.[117]

In the era of globalization, civil society found new and effective modes of expression of popular sentiments and concerns. Civil society plays an important role in bringing emerging environmental issues to the attention of policy-makers, raising public awareness, promoting innovative ideas and approaches in environmental decision-making at different levels. According to Beverley "Civil society, the amalgamation of non-governmental and autonomous social organisation such as trade unions, women's groups, professional associations, trade guilds, religious groups, chambers of commerce and voluntary associations associated with issues. are perceived as a prerequisite of democracy and democratic life in any society and its relations to the state."[118]

Within the civil society it is the NGOs which dominate the public policy spheres. The old two-way relationships between governments and the public were radically changed with the emergence of large numbers of NGOs. For example, some environmental NGOs employ scientists who play important roles in bridging scientific communities to assess environmental problems, educating the public, and influencing the political process.[119] The rapid development and multiplication of NGOs in the last few years resulted in growing awareness of environmental issues and the increasing social participation in environmental protection initiatives. The number of NGOs with consultative status with the United Nations Economic and Social Councils (ECOSOC) increased steadily from about 200 in 1950 to almost 1000 in the early in 1990s and 1500 by 1995.[120]

These NGOs cover a wide variety of areas, including ecological promotion, conservation activities, environmental education and research, surveillance of polluting industries, promotion and diffusion of environmental education, advisory services, protection of animal and plant species in danger of extinction, and promotion of community participation. The heightened public awareness of global and local environmental issues in many countries drew attention to the inadequacies of the existing political, economic and regulatory structures.

Information technology and modern communication technologies facilitated cost-effective information sharing, enabling e-mail exchange among communities of practice, list servers among

Table 5.8: The UNCCD Accredited NGOs at the GCC Countries

Sl. No.	Country	Name of the NGO	Head Office
1.	Bahrain	Youth and Environment Society	Manama
2.	Kuwait	—	—
3.	Oman	—	—
4.	Qatar	—	—
5.	Saudi Arabia	Arab Urban Development Institute	Riyadh
6.	U.A.E.	Emirates Environmental Group	Dubai

Source: UNCCD Secretariat, "Non-Governmental Organisations" [Online: web] Accessed on 20th March, 2010 URL: http://www.unccd.int/ngo/accreditationDB/results.php.

environmental journalists, on-line debates, e-learning and discussion forums. The Internet is used to mobilise people quickly and in large numbers on specific issues.[121]

Civil society participation is a key to the achievement of the UNCCD objectives of transparency, monitoring and the sharing of best practices,

> "...the sectoral and technology-oriented approach taken during the early years of efforts to Combat Desertification... resulted in limited success and inadequate results. The sectoral approaches generally did not involve the local populations and disregarded their needs and perspectives. This presented major obstacles for addressing problems of land degradation and poverty."[122]

In the light of decision 18/CoP.3, the UNCCD Secretariat endeavoured to facilitate and encourage greater involvement of civil society at all levels of the UNCCD implementation process, particularly NGOs. However, the limited financial resources available to assist NGOs to make their contribution remain a major limiting factor to their full participation. Past experience shows that with a minimum of support to the NGO community it is possible to accomplish numerous relevant activities and provide momentum to the implementation process.[123]

Under the UNCCD, the participation of NGOs in desertification related activities in the GCC countries are analysed at two levels—national and international. The participation of NGOs at the national level is in the processes of formulating and implementing the desertification related programmes. The only forum available for this purpose is the national coordination committees. However, the composition of National Coordination Committees in the GCC countries, where they were established shows that there is no participation of civil society except few representatives from research and academic institutes. This affects the very spirit of the UNCCD which calls for people's participation in the formulation and implementation of desertification related programmes. The decentralized approach is at the core of the implementation of the convention.

Secondly, the number of NGOs accredited,[124] in the UNCCD Secretariat from the GCC countries are negligible. The accredited NGOs get the opportunity to influence the policies made at the COPs level and important subsidiaries of UNCCD. Due lack of support from the GCC countries, only three NGOs were able to get the status of accredited NGOs. This affects the civil society's role, from this region in providing inputs in the policy making processes of UNCCD.

Table 5.9: The UNCCD Accredited NGOs at the Global Level

Sl. No.	*Major Grouping of Nations*	*No. of NGOs Accredited by the UNCCD Secretariat*
1.	Africa	427
2.	Asia	131
3.	Central and Eastern Europe	17
4.	Northern Mediterranean	79
5.	Latin America and Caribbean	115
6.	Other countries	0
	Total	769

Source: UNCCD Secretariat, "Non-Governmental Organisations" [Online: web] Accessed on 20th March, 2010 URL: http://www.unccd.int/ngo/accreditationDB/results.php.

While acknowledging the important contributions, the *Arab Human Development Report 2002* calls for systematic and urgent engagement of NGOs in environmental protection.

> In some rare and laudable cases, NGOs have exhibited expertise and knowledge of environmental issues, adopted

> environmental issues of interest to the public, and defended them with conviction and determination. However, without a larger number of civil associations working to protect the environment in Arab countries, the effectiveness of the federation of these associations set up in the late twentieth century will remain limited unless efforts are made to strengthen such associations as a popular force in support of governments and professional organizations in their efforts to overcome environmental problems."[125]

The Abu Dhabi Declaration on Agricultural Development and Desertification Control (2002) also called for "enhancement of the role of non-governmental organizations in these fields."[126]

Civil society empowerment is advancing, which is expected to have a positive impact on the decision-making process, public participation, and effective engagement in environmental protection and sustainable use of natural resources.[127] However constructive support from the governments will go a long way in strengthening the role of the civil society in environmental protection.

III. Implementation of the UNCCD at the Sub-Regional Level

"Given that States within a particular geographic region or sub-region often share many of the same challenges and concerns when it comes to implementing a particular MEA, implementation action plans that are created by and for that particular region or sub-region can be extremely helpful."[128] One of the key instruments in the implementation of the UNCCD is National Action Programmes (NAPs). The Convention also promotes the development of Regional and Sub-regional Action Programmes to supplement the efforts at the national level.

Under Article 11 of UNCCD, governments "shall consult and cooperate to prepare, as appropriate, in accordance with relevant regional implementation annexes, sub-regional and/or regional action programmes to harmonize, complement and increase the efficiency of national programmes.... such cooperation may include agreed joint programmes for the sustainable management of transboundary natural resources, scientific and technical cooperation, and strengthening of relevant institutions."[129]

For this purpose, the West Asian countries adopted a Sub-

Regional Action Programme (SRAP) to Combat Desertification in the region and to strengthen cooperation in the sub-region. "The SRAP was developed in highly consultative manner involving key stakeholders from participating countries, UNCCD, the Global Mechanism and a number of international, regional and sub-regional institutions."[130]

i. Sub-Regional Action Programme for West Asia

The SRAP focuses on two strategic areas, common to all member countries of the sub-region. These provide for effective sub-regional cooperation in addressing desertification and in promoting experience and innovation sharing among the members. Water resources and their sustainable management, in strategic terms, are a key issue for the future development of the sub-region. Similarly, vegetative cover, particularly forests and rangelands, and its sustainable management are also an issue of concern in Combating Desertification in this region.[131] Therefore, the SRAP operates through two Thematic Networks (TNs). These are:

TN1: Sustainable Water Management
TN2: Sustainable Management of Vegetative Cover

The first formal meeting to prepare the SRAP was held in Damascus, in 1997.[132] The preliminary proposals for several networks were submitted separately by the Arab Centre for the Studies of Arid Zones and Dry Lands (ACSAD) the Arab Organization for Agriculture Development (AOAD), the Centre for Environment and Development in the Arab Region and Europe (CEDARE), and the International Centre for Agricultural Research in the Dry Areas (ICARDA).[133] The meeting endorsed three thematic networks to support the SRAP. These were information and monitoring, drought preparedness and strategic studies, research and training needs.[134] It was decided to convene an International Expert Group Meeting for the preparation of a SRAP. To facilitate the Expert Group meeting, it was also agreed to revise the respective Research Centres.[135]

The International Expert Group Meeting was held in Muscat on 14-16th September 1998.[136] The draft proposals for the programme networks presented by ACSAD, CEDARE, and ICARDA were reviewed by the Experts. The meeting invited "these institutions to

- restructure the proposals in the light of the comments made at the meeting so as to better reflect the complementarities between the proposals, highlight the role of national institutions in the networks, and integrate the views of sponsoring institutions and the governments party to the UNCCD."[137]

The Muscat meeting authorised Oman to forward the recommendations to the Global Mechanism (GM), with a view to soliciting GM support in the mobilisation of resources required to fund SRAP operations. In March 1999, the GM began implementing the recommendations of the Muscat meeting, through a series of consultations with Oman, the Islamic Development Bank (IsDB), ICARDA, ACSAD, and CEDARE.[138]

Table 5.10: Thematic Networks of West Asian SRAP

Sl. No.	*Thematic Networks*	*Areas*	*Institute responsible for Study*	*Participating Countries*
1.	Thematic Network 1	Water Resource and its Sustainable Management	International Centre for Agricultural Research in the Dry Areas (ICARDA)	Bahrain, Iran, Jordan, Kuwait, Lebanon, Oman, Qatar, Saudi Arabia, Syria, UAE, and Yemen
2.	Thematic Network 2	Vegetative Cover and its Sustainable Management	Arab Centre for the Studies of Arid Zones and Dry Lands (ACSAD)	Bahrain, Iran, Jordan, Kuwait, Lebanon, Oman, Qatar, Saudi Arabia, Syria UAE and Yemen

Source: Compiled from the ACSAD, no. 72, pp. 94-95.

There was general agreement that the SRAP required further development in terms of the roles and responsibilities of the various actors involved. As a result, the GM engaged two consultants to assist the GM in finalising the task assigned to it. The consultants visited all the SRAP member countries to seek the opinions of the UNCCD Focal Points, Senior Government Officials, NGOs, the regional and international centres, and other institutions concerned with the development of NAPs in order to incorporate the stakeholders' vision and conception of the SRAP.[139]

These consultations were jointly reviewed by the UNCCD, UNDP and the GM. This review enabled the three partners to develop the basis for the SRAP Framework. The GM further developed this framework, in direct response to the recommendations of the Muscat meeting and the views and comments expressed by the governments.[140]

A working meeting was convened by the GM from 24th to 26th October, 1999, at Cairo, Egypt, which discussed the reformulation of the SRAP based on the findings of two consultants. The main thrust of the reformulation was the redefinition of activities to be implemented by the SRAP and the orientation of the outcome of the Muscat meeting towards the establishment of a Regional Coordination Unit (RCU) charged with operations and logistics.[141] During the CoP-3 of the UNCCD held in Recife, Brazil, in November 1999, the GM and its partners convened a broad consultation meeting with the West Asian affected country Parties, donor agencies and the regional centres. The views and comments expressed in Recife were included in the final text of SRAP. On February 2000 at Dubai,[142] the SRAP was adopted unanimously. Regional Office for West Asia (ROWA) of UNEP was designated as SRAP Coordinator.[143]

Subsequently, the GM made available, through the SRAP Coordinator US$150,000 to support SRAP implementation in West Asia, including conducting Inventory Studies and preparing a Regional Database on Sustainable Water and Vegetation Cover Management, and preparing a proposal for pilot projects on integrated natural resource management in the region.[144] The Arab Centre for the Studies of Arid Zones and Dry Lands signed a memorandum of understanding with ROWA/UNEP on 21st August, 2001 for undertaking Inventory Study and Regional Database on Sustainable Vegetation Cover Management in West Asia (TN2). On the same day the International Centre for Agricultural Research in Dry Areas (ICARDA) also signed a MoU with ROWA/UNEP for Inventory Study and Regional Database on Sustainable Management of Water Resources and Drought Mitigation in West Asia. A pilot project proposal also was prepared by these two research centres together.

A. Priority Areas

In 2003, an inventory/regional database for each of the SRAP Thematic Networks was completed. Both databases were established in close cooperation with the national UNCCD Focal Points in West

Asia. These database projects were instrumental in the facilitation of linkages, exchange of information and sharing of existing knowledge among concerned stakeholder at the national and regional levels. The outcome of these projects led to the identification of three priority areas for intervention.[145]

These priority areas endorsed by the Focal Points of the West Asia member countries included:

(a) Mountainous areas in Iran, Lebanon, Oman and Yemen;
(b) Rangeland in Jordan, Saudi Arabia and Syria; and
(c) Coping with salinity problems: Bahrain, Kuwait, Qatar, UAE, etc.[146]

The project proposal identified potential pilot sites selected by each participating country under the three priority areas. The proposals were invited on the problems of land degradation found in each site and the activities to cope with those problems with respect to the conservation of biodiversity and the mitigation of the impacts of climate change and drought. The GCC countries' pilot sites proposals are complied and given below.

1. The Mountainous Areas

Mountainous areas in Lebanon, Yemen, Oman and Iran have a special importance with relation to agricultural production systems. Although the rainfall is often higher, due to their inaccessibility mountainous areas tend to be the most isolated and marginalized areas. The complex landscape of the mountainous areas consists of steep slopes, terraced croplands, sloping rangelands, and scattered patches of shrubs and trees. The degradation in mountainous areas includes severe soil erosion by water run-off on unprotected slopes, which in extreme cases can lead to loss of agricultural land and degradation of natural vegetation and depletion of biodiversity.[147]

2. Rangeland Improvement

About 85 per cent of the area of West Asia lies within the arid and semi-arid zones and is largely rangelands. Saudi Arabia has vast areas of rangelands.[148]

The annual average rainfall in these areas ranges between 100 and 250 mm and is highly variable both within and across seasons. Moreover, a significant portion of the limited rainfall is lost as runoff.

Table 5.11: Rangeland in Saudi Arabia

Sl. No.	*Status of Range Land*	*Area/ha*	*% of total Rangeland Area*
1.	Excellent	14000000	8.4
2.	Good	53000000	31
3.	Moderate	56000000	32.5
4.	Poor	48000000	28.1
	Total	171 000000	100

Source: ACSAD, n. 72, p. 54.

The people in these areas are vulnerable to the effects and risks of seasonal changes in the harsh climatic conditions. Frequent droughts coupled with mismanagement of resources, such as overgrazing accelerated the process of desertification.[149]

Degraded rangelands are more vulnerable to wind erosion leading to desertification. The loss of vegetation over large areas reduces the carbon absorption rate, ultimately contributing to global warming and climate change. In addition the expansion of land degradation occurring in the rangelands is affecting the adjacent productive croplands.

3. Coping with Salinity

Water scarcity is a major feature in the GCC countries. Increasing population and water demand resulted in water shortage. As fresh water resources are limited and are not able to meet the increasing demands, there is a huge potential for utilizing other sources. This includes saline groundwater, treated effluent water, and agricultural drainage water. Countries under water scarcity cannot afford to ignore the use of low quality water, not only to support restricted plant production and enhance environment protection but also to improve the soil and water productivity. There are, however, problems associated with the use of low-quality water. Most important are social and environmental issues.[150]

It should be a priority for the GCC countries to develop proper means for using this water safely and in an environment-friendly way. One of the recommended uses of treated sewage effluent is to support restricted agriculture with additional moisture to improve the vegetative cover and production in marginal areas. Saline and drainage waters can also be used in agricultural production without causing problems if suitable soils, appropriate plant species and management are properly considered. This source of marginal water, if properly utilized will contribute to combating desertification in areas where fresh water is extremely scarce.

B. Pilot Projects in the GCC countries

All the GCC countries except UAE[151] sent their pilot projects site with required details regarding the existing problems and the proposed activities. Of the five GCC countries, Oman's pilot project addresses the degradation of mountainous areas. The pilot project of Saudi Arabia deals with combating desertification in its rangelands. On the other hand the proposed projects in Bahrain, Kuwait and Qatar will focus on coping with salinity which threatens large scale arable lands in these countries. The GCC countries' selected pilot project site, identified problems and the recommended activities are given below.

1. Dhofar-Salalah Watershed (Oman)

Dhofar-Salalah Watershed is located in the south of Oman along the coast. Monsoon climate in summer that prevails in this region sometimes results in intensive rainfall.

Table 5.12: SRAP-Pilot Project in Oman: Dhofar-Salalah Watershed

Priority area/name of the pilot projects/country	*Problems identified in the pilot project site*	*Recommended activities to address the problems*
Mountainous Areas/Dhofar-Salalah Watershed/Oman	• soil erosion • heavy grazing of forest and rangeland by cattle, goats and camels • physical degradation of shallow soils (crusting and compaction), • lack of vegetative cover, • inefficient use of water • lack of proper agricultural practices.	• Rehabilitation • Establish nursery • Construct appropriate structure for soil and water conservation • Establish measures for controlling sheet and gully erosion in agricultural lands. • Protecting stream banks and wadi floor • Demonstrate improved technologies of water harvesting. • Install rainfall and runoff water measurements devices

Source: Compiled from ICARDA, n. 146, pp. 20-21.

Average annual rainfall varies from 200-300 mm. Heavy storms of 75 mm can occur. Altitude varies between 500-900 m above sea level. The watershed comprises undulating topography with dissecting medium to high hills. Slopes are steep in the deep wadi and more moderate downstream. Vegetation and trees are common but rapidly degrading. Almost all rangeland is heavily grazed. Cattle, camels and goats are the main types of animals.[152]

2. Al Emariah, Jouf, (Saudi Arabia)

The pilot area is located near Al-Emariah village, approximately 90 km to the North of Sakaka near Sakaka-Arar national highway between Al-Jouf and the northern border of Saudi Arabia. The entire area of about 1,000 ha, between two *wadis,* is rangeland, and is an important grazing area. The soil depths are medium. The *wadis* collect water mainly interflows resulting from showers. Vegetation and grazing trees were the main source of range, which degraded badly.[153]

Table 5.13: SRAP Pilot Project in Saudi Arabia: Al Emariah, Jouf

Sl. No.	*Priority area/ name of the Pilot projects/ country*	*Problems identified in the pilot project site*	*Recommended activities to address the problems*
1.	Rangeland Improvement/ Al Emariah, Jouf,/Saudi Arabia	• Wind erosion and sand encroachment • Inefficient use of available water and water erosion, • Overgrazing and poor vegetative cover, • Shrub uprooting for fuel weak soil structure.	• Establishment of nursery • Reseeding of native local species such as Atriplex, Salsola, etc. • Fixation of sand movement • Design and implement contour ridges, pits, on sloppy lands and micro-catchments on mild areas for shrub and herbs rehabilitation. • Introduce mechanized micro-catchment. • Construct suitable dikes and ridges • Implement sound range management and grazing options • design and implementation of suitable water harvesting techniques.

Source: Compiled from ICARDA, n. 146, pp. 25-26.

The wide area of rangelands in Saudi Arabia and its various vegetation cover is poor in general, because of its scattered vegetation cover especially in the mountains and hilly areas in the northern part, central region and in other rangeland areas which were degraded due to the intensive exploitation, and urban expansion at the expense of rangelands.

3. Bahrain: Al-Areen area (Bahrain)

Al-Areen area is divided into two equal parts of 400 hectares each. One part is open for the use of community, while the other part is protected. The protected area is provided with two surface reservoirs for flora and fauna. The unprotected area is heavily grazed and the dominant sandy soils are exposed to weathering. Groundwater of low quality is very shallow.[154]

Table 5.14: SRAP Pilot Project in Bahrain: Al-Areen Area

Sl. No.	*Priority area/name of the pilot projects/country*	*Problems identified in the pilot project site*	*Recommended activities to address the problems*
1.	Coping with Salinity/Al-Areen area/Bahrain	• Overgrazing • Sand encroachment • Mismanagement of low-quality water • Depletion of water • Salinity • Lack of drainage • Marginal-quality water • Degraded vegetation cover	• Design and implementation of irrigation and drainage systems with control accessories for the pilot area. • Establishing appropriate plantations of selected halophytes species and fodder crops, wood, and shade trees • Periodic sampling of soils, water and plants • Development of guidelines for irrigation with treated wastewater. • Sand fixation and improve soil quality. • Establishment of nurseries irrigated with treated sewage water

Source: Compiled from ICARDA, n. 146, p. 26.

4. Al Maklaa (Kuwait)

Desert sand largely dominates in Kuwait. There is minimal rainfall, very high temperatures and wind erosion prevails almost everywhere. The pilot area has been severely degraded by quarries that are a major source of sand for the construction industry. The vegetation is highly sparse in this area.[155]

Table 5.15: SRAP Pilot Project in Kuwait: Al Maklaa

Sl. No.	*Priority area/name of the pilot projects/country*	*Problems identified in the pilot project site*	*Recommended activities to address the problems*
1.	Coping with Salinity/ Al Maklaa/ Kuwait	• Sand encroachment brackish water mismanagement of low-quality water • Sparse vegetation cover • Wind erosion • Poor soil fertility.	• Design and implementation of appropriate irrigation systems with control accessories for the pilot area. • Establishing appropriate plantations of selected woody trees and shrubs. • Periodic sampling of soils, water and plants to monitor soil salinity • Development of guidelines for irrigation with saline water. • Test and verify different measures to help sand fixation and improve soil quality. • Establishment of on-site nurseries irrigated with brackish water for seedling supply within the project area

Source: Compiled from ICARDA, n. 146, p. 27.

5. Umal Ghab (Qatar)

Qatar suffers from high water scarcity problem. Rainfall is insignificant and evaporation is high. Sparse shrubs are common. Soils are shallow and gravel mixed. Small-scale irrigation farming in patches can be seen at places. Land degradation with the wind action increases desertification. Use of marginal-quality water to establish range shrubs could stabilize the land and halt the degradation. About 68 farms went out of production due to salinisation. The yield in state farms decreased by 30 per cent or about 1500 ha from irrigated soil degraded due to salinisation. The total area in Qatar affected by salanisation is about 113000 ha.[156]

Table 5.16: SRAP Pilot Project in Qatar: Umal Ghab

Sl. No.	*Priority area/name of the pilot projects/country*	*Problems identified in the pilot projects site*	*Recommended activities to address the problems*
1.	Coping with Salinity/ Umal Ghab/ Qatar	• Salinization, • Soil crusting • Wind erosion • Overgrazing • Wood cutting • Physical soil removal	• Developing on-site nurseries of salt tolerant plant species • Re-vegetation of degraded land with the use of marginal quality water. • Grazing management • Periodic sampling of soils, water and plants • Soil fertility improvement • Plantation of degra-ded area with native plant species

Source: Compiled from ICARDA, n. 146, p. 27.

The pilot area is located on El-Shahaniya road. The community in the nearby village is interested in participating in the project. Desert plants and sparse vegetation are the main land uses. Groundwater of limited quantity is available.[157]

C. Implementation of First Phase of Pilot Projects

The GM mobilized US$ 350,000 committed by the Organization of Petroleum Exporting Countries (OPEC) Fund for International Development to support the implementation of start-up demonstrative pilot projects on "Integrated Natural Resources

Management to Combat Desertification in West Asia" for mountainous and rangeland rehabilitation in four West Asian countries.

These funds, however, were not sufficient to support activities in all participating member countries. Therefore, it was agreed to implement the projects in phases as funds become available. Accordingly, criteria to start up activities were developed in consultation with ICARDA, ACSAD, and the GM. Four countries were finally selected to start pilot projects. These were Lebanon and Yemen for the mountainous areas and Syria and Jordan for rangeland rehabilitation. Furthermore, as the funds are insufficient to support activities beyond four years, this sub-project lays out the activities that will be conducted in the four sites over an initial period of four years within the context of the overall project. It was expected that during this time additional funds will be secured.[158]

These projects were implemented and coordinated by UNEP/ROWA and were executed by the Arab Centre for Studies in Arid and Drylands (ACSAD) for Syria and Yemen and the International Centre for Agricultural Research in Dry Areas (ICARDA) for Jordan and Lebanon.[159] The pilot projects were started in 2003 and completed in 2006.

The implementation report of these pilot projects which was made available in 2007 proposes the following recommendations.[160] These will be useful for the GCC countries that are likely to start the next phase of the SRAP pilot projects.

- Rainwater management proved to be instrumental for the success at pilot scale. More work on this shall be undertaken.
- The outcomes of the project were very promising. Therefore, workshops should be held in other West Asia countries to disseminate the obtained results from this project.
- More emphasis should be given to sustainable land management.
- The capacity-building of concerned technical staff on measures for land and vegetation rehabilitation and management is recommended.

- Water harvesting techniques from roof top proved to be excellent techniques to provide additional water resources and is therefore replicated.
- Sustainable information systems on natural resources to support decision-making on policy formulation and interventions to combat desertification is urgently needed.
- Optimal utilisation of traditional knowledge and enhancing local communities participation is essential for successful land rehabilitation interventions.
- Provision of economic incentives and other policies that can motivate resource users to improve resource management.
- For slightly and moderately degraded land, protection with minimal interventions can result in regeneration of vegetation cover within three years.
- The rehabilitation techniques for degraded terraces as well as rainwater harvesting techniques from buildings roofs were well perceived by local communities.
- Applied measures of rainwater harvesting and plant seedling were found to be successful in area with average annual rainfall ranging between 120 mm and140 mm.

ii. Sustainable Arid Land Management (SALAM) Project in the GCC Countries

In West Asia the GM is collaborating with International Fund Agriculture Development (IFAD) to constructively engage the GCC together with the neighbouring Arab States for promoting Sustainable Land Management (SLM) practices.[161]

The GM proposed to develop a multi-country programme that brings the GCC countries together with the neighbouring Arab States in a partnership for SLM practices to facilitate improved livelihoods and ecological services. This programme aimed at responding to the special requirement of the region with regard to the respective countries' different development trajectories and unique ecological context. Beyond the borders of the GCC countries, the region also includes countries with economies in transition that face challenging socio-economic, political and environmental hurdles.[162]

Table 5.17: Components of SALAM Projects

Sl. No.	*Components*		
	I	*II*	*III*
	Focus on GCC Countries	*Focus on the neighbouring Arab States of the GCC Countries*	*Focus on creating a Multi Forum*
1.	It is tailored to respond to the GCC Countries' specific requirements with regard to technical, knowledge and other needs related to pursuing SLM.	This is designed in response to the needs of the neighbouring Arab States with regard to access to technical and financial support for adoption of SLM.	This facilitates in establishing a multi-country forum for SLM bringing together the countries, development cooperation partners, research institutes and the private sector.

Source: Compiled from the Global Mechanism, n. 162.

In this context, the GM developed the SALAM project. It is considered as a complementary initiative for further strengthening the respective countries' initiatives to address desertification related issues. The programme is expected to be formulated and implemented with a participatory approach involving a wide range of national, regional and international stakeholders. SALAM consists of three components (Table 5.17).

The programme shall be implemented over a period of five years, focusing on sharing state-of-the-art-knowledge on SLM and pioneering innovative initiatives at national level. Similarly it seeks to enhance the enabling policy, legislative, institutional and incentive frameworks, as well as the approach to land-use planning, through establishing a cycle of expert thematic consultation forums within the region under the SALAM Partnership Platform (SPP).

Launching this programme during the International Year for Deserts and Desertification (IYDD), 2006 provided an appropriate context for strengthening the visibility and importance of dryland issues on regional and international environmental agendas. This was expected to give an opportunity to build the required collaborative efforts between the diverse Arab and international donors and institutions working on SLM.

However, the programme is still in the preparatory phase and is not launched yet. In an e-mail response to this author's request for details about the programme, Walid Nasr, Adviser, Asia and Pacific,

Global Mechanism of UNCCD mentioned that "(c)urrently we have no material related to its implementation. Actually, and as you may know, initiating such programmes in the GCC is difficult task and consumes lots of time."[163] Efforts should be made to speed up the process of formulating this innovative programme. Since the project covers neighbouring Arab States also, constructive cooperation should be promoted to implement the project.

IV. Implementation of UNCCD at the Regional Level

Under Article 11 of UNCCD, the countries affected by desertification "shall consult and cooperate to prepare, as appropriate, in accordance with relevant regional implementation annexes, sub-regional and/or regional action programmes to harmonize, complement and increase the efficiency of national programmes."[164] Accordingly the Regional Action Programmes along with the Sub-regional action programmes supplement the National Action Programmes. These are to be designed through consultations among the affected countries of each region (such as Africa) and sub-region (such as West Africa). In addition to boosting the efficiency of national programmes, SRAPs and RAPs can promote joint activities for the sustainable management of shared rivers and other cross-boundary ecosystems.

While formulating the Regional Action Programmes, "(e)lements for incorporation in action programmes shall be selected and adapted to the socio-economic, geographical and climatic factors applicable to affected country Parties or regions, as well as to their level of development."[165] Regional implementation annexes provide guidelines for the preparation of action programmes and their exact focus and content for particular sub-regions and regions. The Regional Implementation Annex for Africa and the Northern Mediterranean specify that their national action programmes must contain provisions for monitoring the implementation of the Convention.[166] With relations to the GCC countries, considering their geographical proximity, two Regional Action Programmes need to be analysed. These are the Asian Regional Action Programme and the Regional Action Programme for WANA.

i. Asian Regional Action Programme (ARAP)

Asia as the world's largest region in terms of land area and also human population has an eclectic portfolio of environmental challenges, reflecting the diversity of its sub-regions. Some of the key environmental issues facing the region include land and forest degradation, habitat loss, water scarcity and pollution, greenhouse gas emissions and climate change, waste management, and natural disasters such as floods, droughts and earthquakes.[167]

In Asia the regional activities were launched through Thematic Programme Networks (TPNs). Each network deals with one core aspect, which is either a cause or an effect of desertification, and aims at providing and promoting regional solutions through improved and innovative regional cooperation and exchange of information.[168]

Of significance to this formulation process were the two Regional Conferences whose decisions formed the basis for subsequent actions in this region. The first Regional Conference on the Implementation of the UNCCD in Asia held in New Delhi in 1996 and endorsed the concept of decentralised programme networks and the identification of cross cutting elements to be included in the programmes of each network. The second Regional Conference held in Beijing in 1997 adopted Thematic Programme Networks (TPNs) as an approach for the preparation of the ARAP.

The New Delhi Conference identified few key elements of cooperation amongst Asian members of the UNCCD. These include scientific cooperation and technological transfers, public participation and consensus building, education curricula promotion and awareness raising, capacity and institution building, regional cooperation and land degradation across different climatic sub-regions and research study on the enabling macro-policy framework.[169]

Following the Delhi Conference, a Ministerial meeting was held at Beijing in May 1997. This crucial meeting conceptualized a framework for the formulation of the ARAP and development of NAP. It identified six TPNs for co-operation amongst the affected Asian countries.[170]

In November 1998 an International Expert Group (IEG) meeting held in Bangkok to discuss the technical issues for the preparation of RAP for Asia. The meeting was attended by 65 experts and decision-makers representing Asian and donor countries as well as international organisations and NGOs. The meeting decided to formulate and implement the TPNs based on the existing knowledge and experience as well as for strengthening partnership among the desertification affected countries, donor countries and international and regional research institutions. Flexible modalities of cooperation were acknowledged as the guiding principle to develop TPNs. It was recommended that regional and international financing institutions lend their technical and financial support to the preparation and implementation of NAP.[171] The regional coordination unit of Asia was set up at the headquarters of the Economic and Social Commission for Asia and the Pacific (ESCAP) of the United Nations and started its operation on 1st September, 1999.[172]

The implementation of the NAPs was advanced by the promotion of regional cooperation and capacity-building at national and sub-regional levels through the six TPNs adopted at the Beijing Ministerial Conference. These are Desertification Monitoring and Assessment (hosted by China and launched in July 1999), Agro Forestry and Soil Conservation (hosted by India and launched in May 2000), Rangeland Management and Fixation of Shifting Sand Dunes (hosted by Iran and launched in May 2001), Water Resources Management for Arid-Land Agriculture (hosted by Syria and launched in July 2002), Strengthening Capacities for Drought Impact Mitigation and Combating Desertification (hosted by Mongolia and launched in July 2003), and Assistance for the Implementation of Integrated Local Area Development Programmes (hosted by Pakistan and launched in June 2004).

Table 5.18: Asian TPNs and GCC Countries Participation

Sl. No.	*TPN*	*Thematic Programme Networks (TPNs)*	*Host Country*	*GCC Members Participation*
1.	TPN1	Desertification Monitoring and Assessment	China	Saudi Arabia
2.	TPN2	Agro-forestry and Soil Conservation in Arid, Semi-arid and Dry Sub-humid areas	India	Saudi Arabia
3.	TPN3	Rangeland Management in Arid Areas including Sand-dune Fixation	Iran	Oman, Qatar and Saudi Arabia
4.	TPN4	Water Resources Management for Agriculture in Arid, Semi-arid and Dry, Sub-humid Areas	Syria	Qatar and Saudi Arabia
5.	TPN5	Strengthening Capacities for Drought Impact Mitigation and Combating Desertification	Mongolia	****
6.	TPN6	Assistance with the Implementation of Integrated Local Area Development Programme	Pakistan	****

Source: http://www.unccd.int/actionprogrammes/asia/asia.php#regional, accessed on 20 March 2010/June 2008.

Only Saudi Arabia participated in four TPNs.[173] Qatar was involved in two and Oman in one. The other GCC countries did not show interest to participate at the regional level. This reflects two things. Firstly, the majority of the GCC countries failed to fulfil the commitments under the UNCCD to cooperate at the regional level. Secondly, the GCC countries also failed to obtain the benefits they could have received if they participated in these programmes. In Asia, the initiatives taken at various levels (national, sub-regional and regional) resulted in large databases being set up, and the work of harmonizing the desertification monitoring/assessment procedures is very well advanced. Discussions are in progress to establish a frame of reference that can be used as a kind of control panel, so as to monitor progress on Combating Desertification.[174]

ii. Regional Programme for WANA

The GM in cooperation with West Asian and North African (WANA) region countries launched a Regional Programme for Promotion of Sustainable Development in Rainfed areas of WANA (Regional Programme for WANA). The GM also signed partnership with five funding agencies: the Arab Fund for Economic and Social Development (AFSED), OPEC Fund, Islamic Development Bank (IsDB), IFAD and World Bank to increase the flow of investments in dryland areas to address desertification.[175]

The GM was responsible for the preparation of both the Ministerial Meeting and the preceding technical preparatory meeting convened in Cairo on 13-14th May, 2001 under the patronage of the Deputy Prime Minister and hosted by the Government of Egypt. The meeting report and recommendations have been widely circulated among the countries, the donor agencies and the financing institutions.[176]

A Technical Preparatory Meeting was convened on 13th May, 2001 in Cairo to identify opportunities for sustainable investment in rainfed areas of WANA with the financial and technical support of a group of Multilateral Agencies including AFSED, IFAD, IsDB, OPEC Fund, World Bank and the GM. The outcome of the meeting was the drafting of a strategic policy framework to promote sustained partnerships between the participating countries of the WANA region and the group of multilateral and bilateral donor agencies.[177]

As a follow-up to the Cairo Preparatory Meeting, a Ministerial

Meeting with donor agencies was convened on 25th June, 2001 in Rabat to strengthen the commitment of participating countries, and multilateral and bilateral donors to implement the decisions taken at Cairo. Several high-ranking officials from the participating countries, including 16 Ministers reiterated their commitment to assign the UNCCD a high national priority.[178]

The meeting decided to develop a regional programme for the drylands of WANA. This was expected to build a foundation for regional cooperation and promote technical collaboration through sharing of local and global information and knowledge. The important objective was to strengthen national capacities to facilitate the design and implementation of national policy and institutional improvements as well as investment programmes. The programme is also expected to support the implementation of UN Conventions such as the Convention to Combat Desertification and promote synergies between the UNFCC, UNCBD and UNCCD. The GM was requested by participants to prepare a draft programme to be presented and discussed at a follow-up meeting.

Subsequent to the Rabat Ministerial Level Meeting, a follow-up meeting was held in Aleppo, Syria on 23rd March, 2002. The draft programme was presented and adopted at this meeting. The Regional Action Programme for WANA is centred on a core group of five clusters for addressing dryland development needs of WANA countries. These are development of an enabling environment conducive to investment in drylands, technological innovations, approaches to funding mechanisms, regional networking and knowledge sharing and capacity building of regional, sub-regional and national institutions.[179]

Project and programme proposals are to be developed in line with the objectives of the five clusters. The GM in close cooperation with ICARDA pursues a resource mobilization strategy for financing the Regional Programme for WANA targeting governments of the region, the Arab donor community and other interested institutions. The GM agreed to continue its role as focal point for the donor group. The participating countries of WANA regional programme are Algeria, Egypt, Iran, Jordan, Libya, Mauritania, Morocco, Oman, Sudan, Syria, Tunisia, Yemen, and the Palestinian Authority.

Despite having similar physical and natural features and closer geographical proximity, except Oman, none of the GCC countries showed interest to get involved in the WANA regional programme.

Although considerable achievements have been observed in developing regionally integrated efforts to combat desertification, this approach has not been systematically fostered.

> "The region (Economic and Social Commission for West Asia, ESCWA) lacks a comprehensive approach to combating desertification despite the numerous activities at the national level. Actions at the regional level are intended to promote information sharing, and enforcement of legislation to prevent industrial pollution. Regional coordination of National Action Plans and Programmes to Combat Desertification, however, is relatively limited. Consequently, a low percentage of these plans are successfully implemented, and there is a disconnect between scientists and policy-makers." [180]

Conclusion

National Governments play a central role in regulating many activities affecting ecosystems and the use of their services. They represent sovereign nation-states at international negotiations and become parties to Multilateral Environmental Agreements (MEAs). However, implementation of MEAs at the national level often meets significant challenges, especially in countries with weak governance structures and poor institutional capacity.

The GCC countries initiated a number of measures to implement the UNCCD at three levels—national, sub-regional and regional. At the national level these countries established the Focal Points and National Coordination Committees, enacted legislations, created administrative arrangements and formulated National Action Programmes.

At the Sub-Regional level, the GCC countries adopted a Sub-Regional Action Programme (SRAP) to Combat Desertification and to strengthen cooperation. The SRAP focuses on two strategic areas, common to all member countries of thc sub-region—water and vegetation. In 2003, an inventory/regional database for each of the SRAP Thematic Networks was completed. The outcome of these projects led to the identification of three priority areas for intervention. The pilot projects were selected by each participating country under the three priority areas.

However, funds were not sufficient to support activities in all participating member countries. Therefore, it was agreed to implement the projects in phases as funds become available. Accordingly, four countries were finally selected to start pilot projects. These were Lebanon and Yemen for the mountainous areas and Syria and Jordan for rangeland rehabilitation. Since the GCC countries were not included in the first phase, any assessment on the implementation of UNCCD under Sub-Regional framework would be premature.

At the regional except Saudi Arabia, other GCC countries showed poor response as far as Asian regional action programme is concerned. However, with respect to Regional Programme for WANA, Oman only actively involved. Lack of political will and inefficiency of administrative arrangements are the major reasons for poor implementation of UNCCD at various levels.

References

1. Yencken, David, "Governance for Sustainability", *Australian Journal of Public Administration*, vol. 61, no. 2, 2002, p. 79.
2. United Nations Environment Programme (UNEP), *Training Manual on International Environmental Law*, (Nairobi: UNEP, 2006), p. 39.
3. Steiner, Achim *et al.*, "Global Governance for the Environment and the Role of Multilateral Environmental Agreements in Conservation", *Oryx*, vol. 37, no. 2, 2003, p. 231.
4. UNEP, n. 2. p. 39.
5. UNEP, *Compliance Mechanisms under Selected Multilateral Environmental Agreements*, (Nairobi: UNEP, 2006), p. 21.
6. Najam, Adil *et al., Global Environmental Governance: A Reform Agenda*, (Winnipeg: International Institute for Sustainable Development, 2006), p. 5.
7. Kline, Karen and Kal Raustiala, "International Environmental Agreements and Remote Sensing Technologies", Background paper prepared for the Workshop on Remote Sensing and Environmental Treaties: Building More Effective Linkages, December 4-5, 2000, sponsored by the Socio-Economic Data and Applications Centre (SEDAC), Centre for International Earth Science Information Network, Columbia University, New York, p. 28.
8. Persson, Linn, *et al.*, "Multilateral Environmental Agreements on the Ground-Lessons from Supporting Implementation of the Montreal Protocol" Policy and Institutions Programme—Working Paper, Stockholm Environment Institute, Stockholm, 2007, p. 1.

9. UNEP, *Report on Millennium Ecosystem Assessment* (UNEP: Nairobi, 2006), p. 154.
10. Anderson, Jonathan F., "The Challenge of Globalisation to Public Administration Identity" in Farazmand, Ali and Pinkowski, eds, *Handbook of Globalisation, Governance and Public Administrations* (New York: CRC Press, 2006), p. 51.
11. Farrell, Mary, "Regional Integration, Regionalism and Pledge Administration: Bridging the Global-National Divide in Decision-Making and Policy Implementation" in Farazmand, no. 10, p. 208.
12. Kooiman, Jan, "Social-Political Governance: Introduction" in Kooiman, Jan, ed., *Modern Governance: New Government-Society Interactions*, (New Delhi: Sage Publications, 1993), p. 1.
13. Hans, Kenneth, "Implementing International Environmental Policies" in Blowers, Andrew and Pieter Glasberger, eds, *Environment Policy in an International Context*, (London: Arnold, 1996), p. 201.
14. Jänicke, Martin, "No Withering Away of the Nation State: Ten Theses on Environmental Policy", in Biermann, Frank, Rainer Brohm and Klaus Dingwerth, eds., *Global Environmental Change and the Nation State*, (Potsdam, Germany: Potsdam Institute for Climate Impact Research, 2002), p. 137.
15. United Nations Development Programme (UNDP), *et al.*, *World Resources 2002-04, Decisions for Earth: Balance, Voice and Power*, (Washington, D.C.: World Resource Institute, 2003), p. 138.
16. Esty, Daniel C., *et al.*, "Environmental Sustainability in the Arab World" [Online: web] Accessed on 20th June, 2008 URL:http://www.yemenembassy.org/economic/Reports/WEF/Page_236_248_Environment.pdf.
17. United Nations Non-Governmental Liaison Service, "The International Convention to Combat Desertification in Countries Experiencing Serious Drought and/or Desertification, Particularly in Africa", *The Sustainable Development Treaty Series*, vol. I, no. 1, 1994, p. 144.
18. UN, *UN General Assembly Resolution 172*, adopted its 32nd Session on 19th December, 1977.
19. *Ibid.*
20. Economic and Social Commission for West Asia (ESCWA), *The Role of ESCWA in Resources Conservation and Management and the Combat of Desertification*, [Online: web] Accessed on 23rd June, 2008 URL: http://www.fao.org/docrep/x5322e/x5322e00.HTM.
21. *Ibid.*
22. *Ibid.*
23. *Ibid.*
24. UNCCD Secretariat, "The United Nations Convention to Combat Desertification" [Online: web] Accessed on 23rd June, 2008 URL: http://www.unccd.int/convention/text/convention.php.

25. *Ibid.*, Article 3(c) of UNCCD. The effective implementation of UNCCD faces many "challenges arising due to the enormous variation in political, environmental, socio-economic, cultural and technological contexts in which the convention is being implemented; in selecting how, when and which groups should be involved…; and in determining how desertification should be conceptualized, interpreted and prioritized at the national policy level and by international funding and resource mobilization agencies." (Stringer, Lindsay C., *et al.*, "Implementing the UNCCD: Participatory challenges", *Natural Resources Forum*, vol. 31, 2007, p. 198).
26. UNCCD Secretariat, *Report of the Conference of Parties, Fourth Session, 2000*, [Online: web] Accessed on 23rd June, 2008 URL: http://www.unccd.int/cop/officialdocs/cop4/pdf/3add1(d)eng.pdf, p. 37.
27. UNEP, *Manual on Compliance with and Enforcement of Multilateral Environment Agreement* (Nairobi: UNEP, 2006), p. 54.
28. *Ibid.*, p. 175.
29. Boere, Gerard and Douglas Taylor., "Global and Regional Governmental Policy and Treaties as tools towards the mitigation of the effect of Climate Change on waterbirds", *Ibis* (British Ornithologists' Union), vol. 146 (suppl.1), 2004, p. 112.
30. Boyer, Brook, *et al., Synergies and Coordination among MEAs: Regional and National Approaches,* (United Nations University: Tokyo, 2002), p. 7.
31. Martin-Mehers, Gillian, *et al.*, eds., *Achieving Environmental Objectives,* (Cambridge (UK): IUCN (World Conservation Union), 2004), p. 121.
32. UNEP, n. 27, p. 179.
33. UNCCD Secretariat, *Situational Analysis of UNCCD*, (Bonn: UNCCD Secretariat, 2007), p. 8.
34. Persson, Linn, n. 8, p. 1.
35. UNCCD Secretariat, *Report of the Committee to Review the Implementation of Convention*, First Session, 2003, [Online: web] Accessed on 28th June, 2008.
URL: http://www.unccd.int/cop/officialdocs/cric1/pdf/10eng.pdf, p. 36.
36. Caldwell, Lynton K. "Management of Resources and the Environment: A Problem in Administrative Coordination," *International Review of Administrative Sciences*, (Sage Publications Ltd.), vol. 38, 1972, p. 116.
37. The National Coordinating Body (NCB) is the Government Ministry or Agency designated to coordinate the work of the UNCCD at the national level and the National Focal Point (NFP) is the contact person for the UNCCD within the NCB. For further details refer UNCCD Secretariat, *Regional Implementation Annex for Asia National Reports on the UNCCD Implementation: Help Guide*, (Bonn: UNCCD Secretariat, 1999).

38. Ministry of Works and Agriculture (MWA), Government of Bahrain, *National Report on the Implementation of the United Nations Convention to Combat Desertification* (Manama, April 2000), p. 21.
39. UNCCD Secretariat, n. 26, p. 42.
40. Ministry of Regional Municipalities, Environment and Water Resources, Government of Oman, *National Action Programme to Combat Desertification in the Sultanate of Oman*, (Muscat, 2005), p. 77.
41. UNCCD Secretariat, *Summary of the Second National Report of the Kingdom of Saudi Arabia on the Implementation of the United Nation's Convention to Combat Desertification* (Bonn, 2002), p. 3.
42. UNCCD Secretariat, *Summary of the Second United Arab Emirates National Report to the UNCCD* (Bonn, 2002), p. 4.
43. UNCCD Secretariat, *The National Report of the State of Qatar on the UNCCD Implementation*, (Bonn, 2000), p. 12.
44. Boyer, n. 30, p. 20.
45. UNEP, n. 27, p. 129. As argued by Kal Raustiala, "(t)he doctrine of sovereignty creates barriers to intrusions into domestic affairs. States are resistant to information gathering within their borders by other states or by international organizations. As a result, nearly every international environmental agreements, and many other international agreements as well rely on national self-reporting....(However)...states have routinely lied or distorted their information, and most commonly have simply failed to report it at all. This is often a result of a lack of capacity as much as a lack of good-faith effort; many states simply do not have the necessary tools, personnel, and resources to adequately gather the needed information." (Raustiala, Kal, "States, NGOs and International Environmental Institutions", *International Studies Quarterly*, vol. 41, 1997, p. 728.)
46. Article 26(1), no. 24.
47. UNCCD Secretariat, "Frequently Asked Questions," [Online: web] Accessed on 23rd June, 2008 URL: http://www.unccd.int/knowledge/faq.php#answer5.
48. UNEP, n. 9, p. 154.
49. UNCCD Secretariat, *Regional Implementation Annex for Asia National Reports on the UNCCD Implementation: Help Guide*, (Bonn: UNCCD Secretariat, 1999), p. 5.
50. UNCCD Secretariat, n. 33, p. 8.
51. UNEP, *Annual Report 2006*, (Nairobi: UNEP, 2006), p. 51.
52. *Ibid.*
53. German Advisory Council on Global Change (GACGC), *New Structures for Global Environmental Policy*, (London: Earthscan, 2001), p. 95.
54. UNEP, n. 2, p. 42.
55. Diallo, Hama Arba, "Seizing the Chance", *Our Planet* (the Magazine of the United Nations Environment Programme), vol. 17, no. 1, p. 10.

56. Toulmin, Camilla, "The Desertification Convention" in Dodds, Felix, ed., *The Way Forward: Beyond Agenda 21* (London: Earthscan, 1997), p. 58.
57. Article 10 of UNCCD, n. 24.
58. http://www.unccd.int/knowledge/faq.php#answer5, accessed on 20 June, 2008.
59. Ministry of Forest and Environment (MoFE), Government of India, *National Action Programme to Combat Desertification,* (New Delhi: 1998), p. 43.
60. GACGC, n. 53, p. 97.
61. UNEP, n. 9, p. 489.
62. MoEF, n. 59, p. 43.
63. *Ibid.*, p. 7.
64. Batterbury, S.P.J., *et al.*, "Responding to Desertification at the National Scale: Detection, Explanation, and Responses", in Reynolds, J.F., and D.M. Stafford Smith, eds., *Global Desertification: Do Humans Cause Deserts*? (Dahlem University Press, 2002), p. 379.
65. GACGC, *World in Transition: New Ways towards Global Environmental Solutions*, (New York: Springer, 1995), p. 158.
66. UNCCD Secretariat, n. 26, p. 37.
67. UNEP, n. 2, p. 39.
68. UNEP, *Global Environmental Outlook, 2000*, (Nairobi: UNEP, 2000), p. 159.
69. *Ibid.*
70. ESCWA, *Governance for Sustainable Development in the Arab Region: Institutions and Instruments for Moving beyond an Environmental Management Culture* (New York: ESCWA, 2003), p. 20.
71. *Ibid.*
72. Arab Centre for the Studies of Arid Zones and Dry Lands (ACSAD), *Inventory Study and Regional Database on Sustainable Vegetation Cover Management in West Asia (TN2)*, Prepared for the Sub-Regional Action Programme (SRAP) to Combat Desertification and Drought in West Asia, (Damascus: ACSAD, 2003), p. 38.
73. MWA, n. 38, pp. 21-22.
74. ESCWA, n. 70, p. 20.
75. ACSAD, n. 72, p. 61.
76. UNCCD Secretariat, n. 26, p. 43.
77. ACSAD, n. 72, p. 72.
78. MRMEWR, n. 40, p. 96
79. ACSAD, n. 72, p. 72.
80. MRMEWR, n. 40, p. 70.
81. ESCWA, n. 70. p. 20.
82. *Ibid.*
83. UNCCD Secretariat, n. 43, p. 11.
84. ACSAD, n. 72, p. 70.

85. UNCCD Secretariat, n. 43, p. 12.
86. ESCWA, n. 70, p. 20.
87. ACSAD, n. 72, p. 57.
88. UNCCD Secretariat, n. 41, p. 3.
89. ESCWA, n. 70, p. 20.
90. UAE is unique in relation to other countries on matters related to strategies and plans dealing with combating desertification. UAE opposes the term 'combating desertification' and it uses the term 'Greening the Desert', for further see UNCCD Secretariat, no. 42, p. 1. and GRC, *Green Gulf Report* (Dubai: GRC, 2006), p. 16.
91. ACSAD, n. 72, p. 94.
92. UNCCD Secretariat, n. 42, p. 4.
93. UNEP, n. 27, p. 315.
94. UNCCD Secretariat, n. 24.
95. UNEP, n. 2, p. 18.
96. UNEP, *Global Environmental Outlook 1997* (Nairobi: UNEP, 1997), p. 202.
97. *Ibid.*, p. 203.
98. UNCCD Secretariat, *Report of the Committee to Review the Implementation of Convention*, First Session, 2003, [Online: web] Accessed on 28th June, 2008. URL:http://www.unccd.int/cop/officialdocs/cric5/pdf/2add1 eng.pdf.
99. ACSAD, n. 72, p. 38.
100. MWA, n. 38, p. 14.
101. UNCCD Secretariat, n. 26, p. 3.
102. ACSAD, n. 72, pp. 61-62.
103. UNCCD Secretariat, n. 26, p. 42.
104. *Ibid.*
105. MRMEWR, n. 40, p. 103.
106. UNCCD Secretariat, *Report of the Conference of Parties*, [Online: web] Accessed on 25th June, 2008 URL: http://www.unccd.int/cop/officialdocs/cop4/pdf/3add1(b)eng.pdf, p. 17.
107. ACSAD, n. 72, p. 70.
108. *Ibid.*, p. 57.
109. UNCCD Secretariat, *The Third National Report for the Kingdom of Saudi Arabia about the Implementation of the United Nations Convention to Combat Desertification (UNCCD): Executive Summary*, (Bonn, 2006), p. 3.
110. ACSAD, n. 72, p. 94.
111. Ryding, Sven-Olof, *Environmental Management Handbook*, (Amsterdam: IOS Press, 1998), p. 631.
112. Hans, n. 13, p. 205.
113. Knill, Christoph and Andrea Lenschow, "Introduction: New Approaches to reach effective Implementation-Political Rhetoric or Sound Concepts?" in Knill, Christoph and Andrea Lenschow, eds.,

Implementing EU Environmental Policy: New Direction and Old Problems (New York, Manchester University Press, 2000), p. 4.

114. Boyer, n. 30, p. 7. Maria Carmen Lemos and Arun Agrawal argues that "(t)he fragmentary nature of the sources of complex environmental problems... and the reluctance or inability of nation states to regulate the sources of these problems, means that nonstate actors and organizations may be able to play an essential role in mobilizing public opinion and generating innovative solutions."(Lemos, Maria Carmen and Arun Agrawal, "Environmental Governance," *Annual Review of Environment Resources,* vol. 31, 2006, p. 301).
115. Bäckstrand, Karin, "Democratizing Global Environmental Governance? Stakeholder Democracy after the World Summit on Sustainable Development", *European Journal of International Relations,* vol. 12, no. 4, 2006, p. 470.
116. *Ibid.*
117. UNEP, n. 9, p. 530.
118. Milton-Edwards, Beverley, *Contemporary Politics of the Middle East* (Cambridge: Polity Press, 2006), p. 170.
119. UNEP, n. 9, p. 192.
120. Thomas, Alan, "NGOs and their Influence on Environmental Policies in Africa: A Framework" in Thomas, Alan, *et al.*, eds, *Environmental Policies and NGOs' Influence* (London: Routledge, 2001), p. 2.
121. UNEP, n. 9, p. 160.
122. Adeel, Zafar, "Overcoming One of the Greatest Environmental Challenges of Our Times: Re-thinking Policies to Cope with Desertification", A Policy Brief based on the Joint International Conference on Desertification and the International Policy Imperative Algiers, Algeria, 17-19th December, 2006, p. 16.
123. http://www.unccd.int/cop/officialdocs/cop4/pdf/3eng.pdf, p. 3, accessed on 20th June, 2008. According to Lindsay C Stringer, "(s)everal articles of the UNCCD's text advocate a people centred approach towards combating desertification. Indeed, more than 50 references are made to local populations, communities and NGOs in conjunction with participation and participatory activities." (Stringer, Lindsay C., *et al.*, "Implementing the UNCCD: Participatory challenges", *Natural Resources Forum,* vol. 31, 2007, p. 199).
124. The UN Charter permits the creation of suitable arrangements for consultation with NGOs, both international organizations, and, where appropriate, with national organizations after consultation with the member of the UN concerned. The criteria for accreditation are not detailed, except that the home state of any group holds a veto over participation. Accreditation is the first gateways for NGO participation in international meetings. Given the lack of transparency in the accreditation process, it is not surprising that many have called for a

vast overhaul on the procedures and criteria for accreditation of NGOs. While accreditation allows for a limited role for NGOs in the UN cooperative process, many recent Multilateral environmental treaties have gone much further by formally mandating or permitting, NGOs to actively participate in some of their continuing activities (Raustiala, Kal, "States, NGOs and International Environmental Institutions", *International Studies Quarterly*, vol. 41, 1997, pp. 721-722).

125. United Nations Development Programme (UNDP), *The Arab Human Development Report 2002*, (New York: UNDP, 2002), p. 50.
126. The text of the declaration is available at http://www.un.int/uae/E-10-07-02.htm, accessed on 24th June, 2008.
127. Regional Office for West Asia/United Nations Environment Programme (ROWA/UNEP), *State of Environment in the Arab Region: A Progress Report*, (Manama: ROWA/UNEP, 2003), p. 2.
128. UNEP, n. 27, p. 255.
129. Article 11 of UNCCD, n. 24.
130. ROWA/UNEP, *Integrated Natural Resource Management for Combating Desertification in West Asia: UNCCD/SRAP Pilot Projects in Jordan, Lebanon, Syria and Yemen 2003-2006, Final Report*, (Manama: ROWA, 2006), p. 2.
131. ROWA/UNEP, n. 127, pp. 16-17.
132. Some literature on this subject say that the first meeting was held in Manama in 1995. (see GRC, no. 62, p. 17, and UNEP, *Global Environmental Outlook 2000*,(Nairobi: UNEP, 2000), p. 314). It is not clear whether that meeting was intended to prepare Sub-Regional Action Programme or for some other purposes, given the fact that in 1995 except Kuwait, none of the GCC countries were party to the UNCCD. Even Kuwait signed the Convention in 1995, but it ratified it in 1997. See Table 5.3 of this chapter. The only reference available about this Bahrain meeting is the report of the Conference of Parties (CoPs). It says that the UNCCD Secretariat "responded to the demand for an SRAP in West Asia by assisting in and facilitating the organization of preparatory meetings. These meetings, initiated by an awareness-raising forum in Bahrain, were followed by consultations on programme matters that took place at Abu Dhabi, Damascus, and Muscat, (http://www.unccd.int/cop/officialdocs/cop4/pdf/3add1(d)eng.pdf, p. 22, accessed on 10th June, 2008)
133. ROWA/UNEP, *Sub-Regional Action Programme for West Asia*, (Manama: ROWA/UNEP, 2002) p. 6.
134. UNCCD Secretariat, n. 26, p. 22.
135. ROWA/UNEP, n. 133, p. 6.
136. ICARDA, ICARDA Involvement in The United National Convention to Combat Desertification, p. 2, [Online: web] Accessed on 23rd June, 2008 URL:http://www.unccd.int/cop/reports/igo/2002/icarda-eng.pdf, p. 2.

137. ROWA/UNEP, n. 133, p. 6.
138. *Ibid.*
139. *Ibid.*, p. 7
140. *Ibid.*
141. UNCCD Secretariat, n. 26, p. 23.
142. The text of SRAP says, it was in Dubai that the Programme was adopted. However the UNCCD Secretariat mentions it was "in the *Abu Dhabi* meeting, held on 16th February, 2000, which sought the approval and subsequent endorsement of the reformulated framework by country Parties of the SRAP."(Emphasis added), See UNCCD Secretariat, no. 26, p. 23. This is resulted in confusion as to whether the meeting was held in Abu Dhabi or Dubai.
143. Ahmed Ali Ghosn, the Natural Resource Programme Officer of ROWA became the Regional Coordinator for UNCCD, SRAP-WA. This author had a meeting with Ghosn at ROWA in Manama in June 2007 to understand the various challenges involved in implementing the UNCCD in the GCC countries.
144. UNEP/ROWA, n. 127, p. 16-17.
145. UNEP/ROWA, n. 130, p. 3.
146. International Centre for Agricultural Research in the Dry Areas and Arab Centre for the Study of Arid Zones and Dry Lands,(ICARDA) *Integrated Natural Resource Management for Combating Desertification in West Asia, Pilot Projects Proposal*, Prepared for the Sub-Regional Action Programme (SRAP) for West Asia of the UN Convention to Combat Desertification (UNCCD), (Manama: ROWA/UNEP, 2003), p. 5.
147. ICARDA, *Inventory Study and Regional Database on Sustainable Management of Water Resources and Drought Mitigation in West Asia TN1, Prepared for the Sub-Regional Action Programme (SRAP) to Combat Desertification and Drought in West Asia 2003*, (UNEP/ROWA, 2003), p. 19.
148. Drought, overgrazing, collecting and uprooting woody species for use as fuel, ploughing and the mismanagement of water resources are the principal causes of rangeland deterioration. Desirable range species have been slowly disappearing and several important medicinal and forage plant species have been destroyed. More than 30 per cent of grazing land in Saudi Arabia is deteriorating as a result of overgrazing, the gathering of woody plants and dryland farming. Sheep density on some rangelands is more than one mature head per hectare, some four times the natural carrying capacity. This is made possible by heavily subsidized complementary feeding but leads to impoverished rangelands which become invaded by unpalatable species. Dust storms, sand dunes, desert pavements and various forms of wind and water erosion follow. Deterioration of rangelands and the increasing dependency of the sheep industry on the world grain market could have serious long-term effects, jeopardizing food security in the region.

149. ICARDA, n. 146, p. 10.
150. *Ibid.*, p. 11.
151. The Pilot project proposal says that "ten countries have responded positively to the invitation to identify a priority site and to characterize the state of the land in terms of degradation, as follows: (i) Iran, Lebanon, Oman and Yemen for the mountainous priority areas, (ii) Jordan, Saudi Arabia and Syria for the rangeland improvement (and) (iii) Bahrain, Kuwait and Qatar for coping with salinity problems" see ICARDA, no. 109, p. 5. Interestingly by repeating Oman twice, this document mentions total number of members as twelve. However it is eleven. See Table 5.10. Of the eleven participating countries, UAE also member, therefore it can be assumed that UAE did not send the priority site. In the project proposal, there were no detailed studies for any site in the UAE as it was done for other countries to start pilot projects. However the implementation report of the first phase of pilot projects included UAE without giving the selected site.
152. ACSAD, n. 72, p. 21.
153. ACSAD, n. 72, p. 22.
154. ACSAD, n. 72, p. 22.
155. ACSAD, n. 72, p. 23.
156. ACSAD, n. 72, p. 69.
157. *Ibid.*, p. 22.
158. UNEP/ROWA, n. 127, pp. 16-17.
159. UNEP/ROWA, n. 130, p. 3.
160. *Ibid.*, pp. 67-68.
161. Global Mechanism, *UNCCD Implementation and the Global Mechanism: Information Note on the Global Mechanism and its Change Agenda* (Rome: Global Mechanism of the UNCCD, 2006), pp. 27-28.
162. Global Mechanism, "Sustainable Arid Land Management Programme"
[Online: web] Accessed on 23rd June, 2008
URL:http://www.global-mechanism.org/dynamic/documents/document_file/salam-programmebriefeng.pdf.8.
163. This is quoted from the e-mail response dated on 21st November, 2007, received from Walid Nasr, Adviser, Asia and Pacific, Global Mechanism of UNCCD.
164. UNCCD Secretariat, no. 24.
165. *Ibid.*, Article 15 of UNCCD.
166. UNEP, n. 5, p. 50.
167. UNEP, *The State of Environment 1972-2002*, (Nairobi: UNEP, 2002), p. 299.
168. UNCCD Secretariat, "Fact Sheet," [Online: web] Accessed on 23 June 2008 URL:http://www.unccd.int/publicinfo/factsheets/showFS.php?number=4.

169. MoEF, n. 59, p. 174.
170. *Ibid.*
171. *Ibid.*
172. A provisional agreement was reached between the UNCCD Secretariat and ESCAP on the secondment of the regional coordinator. Furthermore, in 1999, UNEP contributed to its running costs.
173. UNCCD Secretariat, n. 109, p. 1.
174. UNCCD Secretariat, *Report of the Conference of Parties/Report of the Committee to Review the Implementation of Convention (CRIC-4),* [Online: web] Accessed on 23rd June, 2008 URL: http://www.unccd.int/cop/officialdocs/cric4/pdf/3eng.pdf., p. 19.
175. *Ibid.*, p. 50.
176. UNCCD Secretariat, *Report of the Conference of Parties (CoP-5)*[Online: web] Accessed on 23d June, 2008 URL: http://www.unccd.int/cop/officialdocs/cop5/pdf/4eng.pdf, p. 51.
177. Global Mechanism, [Online: web] Accessed on 28th June, 2008 URL http://www.global-mechanism.org/dynamic/documents/document_file/gm-facilitated-regional-programme-for-sd-in-wana.pdf, accessed on 10th June, 2008.
178. *Ibid.*
179. *Ibid.*
180. Adeel, n. 122, p. 16.

VI

The GCC Countries' Compliance with the UNCCD

Multilateral Environmental Agreements (MEAs) are an intergovernmental document intended as legally binding with a primary stated objective of preventing or managing human impacts on natural resources. These "MEAs vary considerably, both in terms of their number of participants, geographical scale, target issues and policy requirements. Yet common to the majority of agreements are a set of obligations, actions and constraints, which states consent to follow."[1]

Over the past few decades governments adopted a large number of MEAs. These address a broad range of substantive and procedural issues, from atmospheric protection to the disposal of hazardous wastes, from environmental impact assessment to citizen participation in decision-making.[2] With intensified use of international treatises as a means to address global environmental problems, "concerns have arisen regarding the compliance of States with commitments to which they agreed"[3] under a MEA. "The effectiveness of any international agreement ultimately depends on the extent to which parties comply with their obligations. In most cases, compliance with international agreements needs to take place at the national level..."[4]

Basically the global environmental agreements are "only as effective as the parties make them. Effectiveness is the result of not only how government implement accords (the formal legislation or regulations that countries adopt ...) but also of compliance (the observance of these regulations and commitments contained in the international accords)."[5] For example, weak legislations can produce weak compliance. Similarly, the poorly enforced strong legislations can have a poor impact on natural resource management which will lead to inadequate compliance. Therefore, one cannot simply read domestic legislation to determine whether countries are complying with the provisions of a global treaty. While it is observed "that most States comply with most international treaties most of the time, there are reasons to believe that national implementation of and compliance with international accords is not only imperfect but often inadequate."

Accordingly, States need to ensure sustainable development and initiate efforts to protect the critical ecosystems. "Balancing these goals and meeting basic needs requires the rule of law and good governance, and requires a focus on ensuring effective enforcement and compliance"[7] of global environmental agreements. However, there are "only a few systematic studies of factors affecting compliance with international environmental accords into which countries have already entered."[8] Among them, surprisingly, there are "even fewer studies that focus on factors at the national level (that) affect compliance."[9]

> "...(D)eveloping countries that lack technology and resources may demand assistance from developed countries to deal with global environmental problems. Success in protecting the global environment thus depends crucially on the ability of international institutions to design effective International Environmental Agreements (IEAs) to engage developing countries. But to do so effectively requires better understanding of *how developing countries comply with international environmental treaties*. To date, *there has been little research on this topic*."[10] (Emphasis added).

Compliance with UNCCD became further complicated, because "there is a lack of both concrete commitments with specified schedules, and sufficiently accurate base line data and monitoring systems for observing and assessing soil and land degradation in arid regions."[11]

In this context, this chapter underlines the importance of national compliance with an international treaty, besides elucidating the differences between implementation and compliance with respect to MEAs. It critically analyses the efforts of the Gulf Cooperation Council (GCC) countries to comply with the provisions of the United

Nations Convention to Combat Desertification (UNCCD). It also examines the various indicators used to measure effective compliance with the UNCCD with reference to the GCC countries.

I. Importance of Compliance

In a world of increasing interdependence—among people and societies, and with nature—new approaches to governance must be developed at the local, national, regional, and global levels. Ensuring compliance with existing legal mechanisms also must play a central role. The past few decades witnessed a remarkable increase in the breadth and depth of international environmental cooperation and led to a proliferation of MEAs at an unprecedented level. "There are more than 1000 legal instruments with environmental provisions among 33000 international environmental agreements registered with the United Nations. These agreements have resulted in the rapid growth of international environmental institutions to deal with environmental problems."[12]

> Despite a growing body of environmental law both at the national and international levels, environmental quality and some other important social indicators has been declining around the world. One reason for these trends is the inadequate investment in assuring effective compliance and enforcement, at both the national and international levels. International and national donor agencies should expand their efforts on good governance and rule of law to include an explicit focus on compliance and enforcement.[13]

Indeed, judged by the number of MEAs, the period since the Second World War was a spectacular success for proponents of multilateralism. "Less successful, however, has been the implementation of these agreements. While many governments have been willing to join MEAs, evidence suggests that they have not always fully honoured their legal obligations to put supranational commitments into practice, i.e. by incorporating treaties into domestic law, promulgating regulations, and establishing an adequate monitoring and enforcement infrastructure."[14] The result was a complex geography of legal compliance, characterised by spatial and temporal variations in the implementation of multilateral environmental policies.

While cooperation among nation-states is obviously necessary to address many transboundary environmental problems, virtually all policies must be implemented at the national or local level. One important liberalist argument in the debate about implementation of and compliance with international agreement is that negotiations do not end with the conclusions of a treaty, but are a continuous aspect of living under the agreement.[15] In other words "(i)t is obviously not sufficient for States to agree to take action to protect the global environment if they do not then put these regulations into practice."[16] To achieve the objectives of MEA, compliance is a critical one. As Kofi Annan rightly mentioned in the UNEP's *Annual Report 2000*:

> "There is no shortage of ideas on what should be done... Nor is there a shortage of specific programmes of action.... What we need is a better understanding of how to translate our values into practice, and how to make new instruments and institutions work more effectively."[17]

Whether it is vague and declaratory or explicit and binding international commitments, there are generally some sort of behavioural changes at national level that need to be initiated, which will ideally lead to the fulfilment of those global obligations.[18] Therefore, "successfully addressing the complex and interrelated issues of sustainable development requires designing and implementing appropriate governance systems, which in turn must be built on the foundation of good governance, the rule of law, and compliance."[19]

According to Phillipe Sands and Jan Lineham, three factors appear to be catalyzing concern about compliance with MEAs. First, the extent of international environmental obligations that need to be complied transformed in an unprecedented level in recent years as States take more environmental commitments under MEAs. These impose an increasingly onerous burden on the States. Secondly, the growing demand for access to natural resources, coupled with a finite, perhaps even shrinking, available resources base provide the conditions for increasing conflict over environmental resources. Thirdly, as global environmental obligations increasingly address fundamental economic interests and needs, States which do not comply with their environmental obligations are perceived to gain unfair and perhaps unlawful, advantages (in particular economic advantages) from their environmentally harmful activities.[20] They are "perceived of as 'free riders', obtaining unfair economic advantage in relation to complying states."[21]

Therefore, in recent years the global community realised to shift the focus and efforts "from treaty-making which preoccupied the international community since the 1970s to compliance and enforcement and implementation of existing treaties."[22] "Non-compliance with treaty obligations includes failure to give effect to substantive norms, failure to fulfil procedural requirements and failure to fulfil an obligation to an institution (e.g. submit an annual report)."[23]

II. Implementation and Compliance

Implementation and compliance are different with respect to a MEA. Implementation of an international environmental agreement refers "to the specific actions (including legislative, organizational and practical actions) that States take to make international treatises operative in their national legal system."[24] On the other hand compliance can be defined as "a state of conformity or identity between an actor's behaviour and a specified rule, regardless of the motivations, circumstances, or causes that lead to that conformity. In other words, an actor is in compliance if the actor is doing what the law says the actor must be doing."[25] It also can be generally said that compliance refers to the extent to which the party "actually conforms to the conditions set out in a particular international treaty."[26] Equally, compliance refers to whether countries in fact adhere to the provisions of the agreement and to the implementing measures that they instituted. Measuring compliance is more difficult than measuring implementation.

A State is said to implement a Global Convention at the national level "when it adopts appropriate domestic measures for the purpose of meeting its obligations under the international treaty norm. Such measures might include enacting legislation, formulating policies or allocating resources."[27] "The mere fact that an implementation measure is taken does not mean that it is adequate to meet a treaty obligation nor that the State is necessarily compliant with its obligation."[28]

Therefore implementation of global environmental accords at the national level is just "the process of putting ... commitments into practice, whether those are international commitments, domestic rules, or other sources of law that are not self-executing. Compliance can happen without implementation (as when the commitment reflects current practice or when external factors result in compliance), and implementation may not lead to compliance (as when external factors outweigh the implementation efforts). However, implementation is generally an essential predicate for compliance."[29]

In this regard implementation establishes the link between the national legal and institutional arrangements and the international obligations agreed under a specific global treaty.[30] The prime aim of establishing this link is to ensure compliance with a MEA. Compliance is also interchangeably used with enforcement. However, "compliance is brought into play in the international framework while enforcement is a concept to be used in national perspectives."[31]

III. New Approach to Compliance

Due to globalization and advancement of information and communication technologies and the emergence of non-State actors, "the traditional view of compliance problems is now being abandoned."[32] This was based on imposing sanctions on non-compliance. To meet the emerging challenges, new approaches were developed in recent years to ensure effective compliance of MEAs. These new approaches are employed in drafting, adoption, implementation, operation and enforcement of international environmental treaties.[33]

The compliance record of the State is influenced by a large number of factors in which the wilful desire to violate rules plays only a minor role. Often it is rather practical obstacles, outside the will or control of the State that make compliance difficult.[34] The MEAs generally impose increasing onerous obligations, with growing impacts on a wide range of economic activities.[35] Therefore, the "traditional sanction mechanisms, based on the notion that States intentionally do not comply, have proven largely ineffective."[36]

On the other hand the new approaches to compliance problems now take into account the actual abilities and availability of adequate resources at the disposal of States to comply with the provisions of a global treaty. "(M)ost instances of non-compliance are attributable more to incapacity than to a lack of will, bring cooperative avenues to the fore."[37] Therefore the new strategies are "based on what is referred to as a managerial approach, rather than on a more traditional enforcement approach."[38]

The main purposes of the new approach are "not so much to

designate the acts of a party as wrong and impose sanctions, but more to assist violating parties to return to compliance. Furthermore compliance procedures focus on confidence building and cooperation between the parties to a treaty rather than on authoritative or confrontational means. A compliance regime therefore not only prescribes the methods that can be used to impose sanctions in the event of non-compliance, but also prescribes the means that can be applied to avoid violations and to facilitate compliance."[39]

The changing nature of the compliance mechanism "goes hand in hand with new approach to sovereignty. States are no longer seen as completely sovereign entities but have to accept limitations on their originally sovereign rights, for the benefit of the environment, future generations or the international community as a whole."[40] The emergence of international regimes as tools to address multi-dimensional global problems changed the very locus of the State's power.

Today the international community is increasingly organised in regimes. These regimes consist of a framework of a relatively well developed set of rules and unwritten norms concerning a specific subject matter. The development of regimes can be placed between the traditional concepts of sovereignty, leaving the States unbound and a comprehensive world order, placing the States within a new world governance.[41] According to Vig, the "regimes are arrangements for cooperation in specific areas of international laws or policy that include all relevant actors—member-states, international organizations and officials, and non-official participants such as INGOs (International NGOs) and groups of experts together with various relevant documents such as treaties, conventions, or declarations that established the rules and expectations."[42]

Stephen D. Krasner, eminent political scientist, defines an international regime as principles, norms, rules and decision-making procedures around which actor expectations converge in a given issue area. There are several important aspects of this definition including the paradigm shift in the process of governance.[43] While the sovereign State certainly continues as the principal actor, its freedom to make decisions unilaterally is restricted more and more, and non-State entities are performing increasingly complex tasks.[44] With the development of these regimes "sovereignty no longer consists in the freedom of the States to act independently, in their perceived self-interest, but in membership in reasonably good standing in the regimes that make up the substances of international life. States' interests are increasingly determined by their membership in but also good reputation under, these regimes."[45]

In this more complex perception of compliance, the actors at the international level can no longer be seen as utilitarian decision-makers weighing the benefits and costs of compliance. The new approach to compliance tries to place compliance problems in this increasingly complicated international context with a multitude of regimes, interdependent actions, and different interests and obligations.[46] This is almost similar to the strategy adopted, and measures taken by the governments at the national level to regulate environmental affairs within their jurisdiction. According to Oran R. Young, "(a) striking feature of the debate over environmental protection in recent years has been a rising interest in the introduction of policy instruments featuring incentive mechanisms in contrast to more conventional command-and-control regulations and practices."[47]

IV. Compliance with the UNCCD

> Of all multilateral environmental agreements, the UNCCD is uniquely comprehensive in its scope. It seeks not only to resolve global environmental problems but also to ease global poverty. But despite—or perhaps because of—its broad commitment to development, the Convention is beset by ill-defined policy objectives and uncertainty over its implementation. ...This might explain the acute problems—especially the under-funding and lack of political enforceability—that the Convention faces.[48]

Before analyzing the affected parties' compliance with the UNCCD, it is necessary to take into account two aspects related with this Convention. These are the constraints imposed by the institutionalization process of the UNCCD on the national governments in their efforts to comply with the provisions of this convention and the recommendations of experts to use the weaker definition of success to determine the implementation of the UNCCD instead of the rigorous one.

i. Constraints Imposed by the Institutionalization Process of the UNCCD

Limited bargaining power in the South and low priority in the North notwithstanding, considerable achievements were made "in the institutionalization of the UNCCD as well as in furthering its implementation in affected regions."[49] However these institutionalization processes affected the governments' efforts directly or indirectly in effectively addressing the issue of desertification. After six Conferences of the Parties (CoPs), the building of the institutions of the UNCCD was regarded as largely complete and the implementation phase began.[50] The Situational Analysis Report of the UNCCD clearly summarizes this.

> In its first decade, the UNCCD record in facilitating cooperation and effective implementation has been mixed. This situation can be attributed in part to the sub-optimal performance of its governance structure and institutions. For example, the CoP has focused much of its attention on process-related issues, thereby limiting its effectiveness in addressing substantive implementation issues. The creation of structures and processes at the international level (for example, review or science committees) is an essential component of an efficient governance system, but governing bodies should ensure that procedural issues are not too resource intensive.[51]

A number of measures were taken to build the structure of the UNCCD. Among them, the following two needs special mention, not because they are important, but because they consumed lot of time and energy in the formative years of the UNCCD.

A. Financial Mechanism

"In many instances, international negotiations produce agreements with ambitious goals, but without realistic means of implementing or financing them."[52] The developing countries "face special challenges in meeting their obligations under MEAs. Even with best intentions, these countries can still fall short of full compliance and enforcement, due to insufficient financial resources, lack of scientific or technical knowledge, an underdeveloped legal and enforcement infrastructure and related problems."[53] In the case of financial arrangements the UNCCD "defines no criteria for the level of the financial commitment of the North."[54] Indeed, the UNCCD "embodies the principles of sustainable development better than any other and is, in many ways, best suited as a framework for effective poverty reduction programming"[55] But still it was not provided a dedicated fund to finance desertification related programmes. Therefore the UNCCD "differs from the other two regimes (UNFCCC and CBD) in having no specific multilateral fund for its implementation." [56]

> Unlike its two 'sister conventions' the (UN)CCD is mainly dependent on the use of existing funds from bilateral and multilateral development cooperation. Although there is theoretically greater potential for financing as a result of bundling and better focusing of bilateral and multilateral development cooperation according to the 'multi-source' funding principle, the tangible increase of funds for combating desertification expected by the developing countries has not yet emerged.[57]

Similarly the developed countries which cope with desertification in their landmass in one way or another, "do not perceive of land degradation occurring elsewhere as a threat. Consequently, the bargaining power of developing countries is limited and the convention of little priority to developed countries."[58] The developed countries "felt they bore no responsibility for the problem of desertification worldwide, unlike the issues of ozone depletion and climate change, and were therefore unwilling to incur any obligation to increase their financial assistance to affected countries."[59] A review conducted by the UN Joint Inspection Units (JIU) clearly shows this trend.

> The Inspectors are of the view that the financial resources made available so far to UNCCD cannot be described as substantial; neither can they be considered adequate, timely or predictable.[60]

"Of the three 'Rio Conventions' the Desertification Convention is the most important in terms of development policy."[61] However, UNEP's *Global Environmental Outlook 2003* "described (it) as a 'Rio stepchild' because it did not get as much attention as the UNFCCC (United Nations Framework Convention on Climate Change) and

CBD (Convention on Biological Diversity)."[62] In the words of Klaus Töpfer, Former Director of the United Nations Environment Programme (UNEP), UNCCD "has failed to excite the sort of political and public interest enjoyed by the other two (CBD and UNFCCC)."[63] The JIU report indicates the prevailing discriminatory nature of funding towards the UNCCD comparing other MEAs.

> The Inspectors have concluded that in terms of financial and human resources, UNCCD is undernourished as compared with the other two sister Conventions. They strongly believe that the Parties to the Convention should attach more importance and provide timely policy guidance and adequate financial support to the activities of the UNCCD Secretariat in facilitating the implementation of the Convention.[64]

During the negotiation, as discussed in the fourth chapter, the developing countries demanded a separate financial mechanism. However, the developed countries opposed and finally it resulted in the form of a brokering institution, i.e. Global Mechanism, which could not perform much. The developing countries might have achieved much better than what they had if the UNCCD had a separate financial arrangement like other MEAs. The UNEP report clearly acknowledges that "inadequate resource mobilization is hampering the affected developing countries' efforts to fulfil their commitments under the convention."[65]

The UNCCD contains "the substances of the MDGs, not only in terms of food security, nutrition and health, but also in relation to correcting inequalities and achieving environmental sustainability. Arguably, the low level of attention paid to the UNCCD may be due to its association to the field of environmental agreements, which have in the past often been relegated to low political priority."[66] The lack of specific and dedicated financial mechanism in fact "slowed progress in its implementation."[67] Therefore, the "(d)onors and aid recipients should abandon the mindset of the last ten years and take a fresh look at ways to adjust the Convention (UNCCD) to the new fundamentals of development cooperation."[68]

B. Institutional Mechanism to Review Implementation

Review includes not only the efforts of developing countries to implement the UNCCD but also the commitments made by the developed ones to provide financial resources and transfer environmental friendly technologies to the South. As discussed in the fourth chapter, the developed countries opposed creating a separate institution to review the implementation of the UNCCD.

Since the demand was raised by the developing countries in 1997, it took more than five years to establish the Committee for the Review of the Implementation of the Convention (CRIC). It is widely believed that the developed countries vehemently opposed such a reviewing body because they were in apprehension that their inaction or failure to adhere the obligations under UNCCD would come under scrutiny.

ii. Rigorous Vs. Weaker Definition of UNCCD Implementation

Success in combating desertification is interpreted in different ways by experts. Firstly, quite a rigorous definition was applied in some studies which developed and used comprehensive lists of indicators. For example the United Nations Environment Programme used a framework that included 25 criteria grouped under land use, social and economic aspects and policy related issues.[69] Mortimore proposed a framework of criteria for success grouped into four domains: ecosystem management, land investments, productivity and income and welfare.[70] Although useful, long lists are always difficult to deal with. Presumably some indicators are more important than others. Unfortunately rigorous studies that provide sufficient information to test this type of success are rather few in number.[71]

On the other hand John McDonagh and Yuelai Lu recommended using a weaker definition of success that is much less exacting though much easier to find reported. It requires some progress in controlling land degradation or rehabilitation without much empirical evidence or concern about the size of the area, extent of external support, self-sustainability, spread between land-users and regions etc.[72]

While analyzing the implementation of desertification related activities in Africa, it was found that "almost all of these projects are too young to attempt to apply...(the) more rigorous definition of success."[73] Similarly, the only reliable and important sources of information available to analyze the implementation of the UNCCD are the reports submitted by the governments. However "(t)here is little evidence in any of the reports that would allow the more rigorous definition of success. ... These reports appear to be more brief summaries for publicity purposes, not really adequate for a serious examination of success. As many of the projects had only been in existence for 2-3 years at the time of reporting it is also likely that it was too early in most cases to tell whether they were successful."[74] Therefore, it is easier to find examples of the weaker rather than the more rigorous one.[75]

V. GCC Countries' Compliance with the UNCCD

The UNCCD is an instrument of international cooperation that seeks to address desertification through the implementation of a common policy framework. There are two interrelated elements to this framework: first is the adoption of effective strategies, programmes and measures to implement the Convention. Second is the creation of an enabling environment to facilitate action, which involves the integration of UNCCD objectives and approaches into the broader policy framework.[76]

"(A)lthough being an issue-specific convention that addresses the problem of desertification, the contents of the UNCCD expand to rather elusive complex of issues. The negotiating parties have thus created a problem structure that is rather vague. This vagueness provides those who seek to implement the convention with considerable leeway as to how to go about it."[77] In other words "(t)he inclusion of socio-economic aspects in the definition of desertification has made it more difficult to measure progress through scientific indicators or other quantitative or qualitative measures, which is how the success of other instruments of environmental governance are measured. It becomes more complex when trying to link the impacts between climate change, biodiversity and desertification."[78]

According to Lynn Wagner, the UNCCD "lacks specific mechanisms to put its goals into practice."[79] There are no precise base line data or monitoring systems for the observation and evaluation of land degradation in drylands. Similarly, the UNCCD "also contains no concrete reduction commitments with specified time tables, for instance for soil and land degradation"[80] unlike the UNFCCC which clearly provides specific guidelines to reduce greenhouse gases emission to a certain percentage. In other words,

> "(i)n contrast to the Framework Convention on Climate Change and the Montreal Protocol on ozone, the

> Desertification Convention has *not (yet) specified quantitative and verifiable reduction and conservation goals for a specific time period*."[81] (Emphasis added)

Durwood J. Zaelke, an eminent expert on MEAs, says compliance with, and enforcement of, any MEA, starts with three international obligations:

> The first is your obligation to the entire international community to implement the treaty that you, as a state, have signed and ratified. The second is to ensure that your national laws comply with it. And the third is to do your reporting back to the relevant treaty body. *Even if these obligations are not clearly and precisely stated in the MEA—as is the case with the (UN)CCD—you can still progressively clarify and specify them.*[82] (Emphasis added)

"The institutionalisation of the desertification issue has offered an opportunity for many dryland nations to garner international attention and support for combating desertification… that would not have happened otherwise. However the uncertainties about the scientific basis of understanding of the process made it difficult to define a clear course of actions, paving the way to multiple interpretations and policy orientations."[83] The comprehensive and all-inclusive character of UNCD makes it difficult to define the course of action and to measure the success of its implementation. Since desertification is a complex process, involving a mix of causes and effects, no single indicator alone can adequately reflect the interaction of its several components.[84] Therefore, applying certain kind of environmental indicators will be useful to identify the factors that involved in successful implementation of the UNCCD.

i. Environmental Indicators

Environmental indicators are scientific measurements that track environmental conditions over time.[85] Indicators provide information about the functioning of a specific system, for a specific purpose—to support decision-making and management. An indicator quantifies and aggregates data that can be measured and monitored to determine whether change is taking place, understand the process of change, and facilitate decision-makers to understand why change is taking place.[86] Comprehensive and reliable information on the nation's environment and natural resources is a cornerstone of effective environmental management and an integral part of a national strategy to address problems.[87]

Environmental indicators are essential tools for tracking environmental progress, supporting policy evaluation and informing the public. Since the early 1990s, such indicators gained larger importance for communicating information to decision-makers and the public.[88] There is a growing interest in measuring the environmental performance and evaluating the progress in addressing environmental degradation. Environmental indicators thus became an instrument to chart, monitor, and evaluate success towards sustainable development.[89]

Whereas definitions of an 'environmental indicator' vary, most of them emphasize that an environmental indicator is a selected quantifiable variable that describes, analyses, and presents scientific information and its significance.[90] Under Global Environmental Governance (GEG), even the non-quantifiable and not purely scientific factors can be used as indicators given the comprehensive and all-inclusive nature of GEG.

ii. Application of the UNCCD Secretariat's Indicators in the GCC Countries

A more recent UNCCD Secretariat's publication compiles experiences learned from ten African countries on the implementation of the UNCCD.[91] A framework is applied for reviewing progress and success in each country using seven indicators. These indicators include participatory processes, institutional and legislative frameworks, resource mobilization and coordination, linkages and synergies with other MEAs, rehabilitation of degraded land, drought and desertification monitoring and assessment and access to appropriate technology.[92] All the measures taken by the GCC countries to implement the UNCCD are analyzed using the following seven indicators to determine their compliance with this global treaty.

A. Participatory Processes

"Public participation was not highlighted in the Stockholm

Declaration or emphasized formally by the international community during the 1970s. However, the concept quickly developed during the 1980s and 1990s and was highlighted in the Rio Declaration and Agenda 21. Indeed, public consultation and civil society institutions play key and effective roles in operationalizing governance for sustainable development."[93] In the new global environmental governance arrangements, "the role of non-state actors is a more direct and robust one. Decision-making—governance itself—occurs in and through collaborations among states and non-state actors working side by-side as co-participants, co-authors, and co-executors of policy, roughly as formal equals although certainly often of unequal capacity and resources."[94]

> "(T)he sectoral and technology-oriented approach taken during the early years of efforts to Combat Desertification.... resulted in limited success and inadequate results. The sectoral approaches generally did not involve the local populations and disregarded their needs and perspectives. This presented major obstacles for addressing problems of land degradation and poverty."[95]

The international community rightly realized "that, despite efforts in the past, progress in combating desertification ... has not met expectations and that a new and more effective approach is needed at all levels within the framework of sustainable development."[96] Accordingly, the UNCCD adopted the participatory approach to address desertification related problems. The UNCCD is "the only international convention to date that specifically requires the active participation of the population as a principle of international law."[97] "More recently scientists and decision-makers involved in combating desertification have come to realize that little can be done to reverse desertification processes without the complete involvement of farmers, pastoralists and other natural resource users experiencing and being directly affected by desertification in its many forms."[98]

The preamble of UNCCD emphasizes "the special role of Non-Governmental Organizations and other major groups in programmes to Combat Desertification..." It also clearly "recognizes the fact that in traditional development planning, programmes have often failed because they were designed with too little reference to the perceptions and capacities of local communities."[99] Therefore, the UNCCD attempts to integrate all the elements relating to land resources, land-use and land degradation. It calls for effective action of people at all levels, particularly the local people—the land-users, including civil society.

People's participation with respect to the UNCCD takes place at two levels. These are at the national level and the international level. At the national, the UNCCD mandates the affected developing countries "to involve civil society in the elaboration, implementation and evaluation of National Action Programmes. While under the ozone regime NGOs have no participation rights. However, in the UNCCD, NGOs are a component of the official programme and an essential catalyst of implementation. Thus the NGOs, which already played a part in the negotiation of the UNCCD, are integrated more comprehensively than in any other convention."[100] The National Coordination Bodies (NCBs) set up by the governments provide the forum for people's participation.

Under Article 10(2.f) governments should "provide for effective participation at the local, national and regional levels of non-governmental organizations and local populations, both women and men, particularly resource users, including farmers and pastoralists and their representative organizations, in policy planning, decision-making, and implementation and review of national action programmes."[101]

Similarly the governments under Article 4 (1.b) of the Asian annex of the UNCCD should "involve affected populations, including local communities, in the elaboration, coordination and implementation of their action programmes through a locally driven consultative process, with the cooperation of local authorities and relevant national and Non-Governmental Organizations."[102]

Despite their importance, the civil society's participation in the UNCCD implementation process in the GCC countries is inadequate. Significantly there is no representation of NGOs at the NCBs of the GCC countries. As discussed in the fifth chapter, it is the NCB which formulates and implements the national action programmes in coordination with other stakeholders including NGOs.

The analysis of the composition of NCBs of Saudi Arabia and UAE shows the trend of poor public participation in the UNCCD implementation. Saudi Arabia's NCB "consists of representatives from all Government ministries and agencies pertinent to desertification and renewable natural resources and was mandated to prepare the

Kingdom's national action programme to combat Desertification. The members of this committee include: The Ministries of Agriculture and Water, Interior, Finance and National Economy, Higher Education, Planning, Municipality and Rural Affairs, Communication and Ministry of Information. Specialized institutions such as King Abdulaziz City for Science and Technology, General Council for Meteorology and Environmental protection, National Commission for Wildlife Conservation and Development and Prince Sultan Centre for Environment, Water and Desert Research (King Saud University) are also members of the national committee."[103] Except few research institutes, there is no representation from civil society.

Similarly in the UAE "the Federal Environmental Agency (FEA) established the National Committee for the Follow-up of the UNCCD on 17th June, 2001. The Committee consists of 25 members representing 17 bodies working in the fields related to the UNCCD."[104] The details of the members were not given in the report. However during this author's visit to UAE, it was learned that only few academic institutions were included in the NCB.

For example, on the other hand, India's NCB specifically mentions the NGOs. "India's National Policy and Coordination Committee (NPCC) under chairpersonship of Secretary, Ministry of Environment of Forests would have representatives from related Ministries, departments, state governments, academic institutions, NGOs etc."[105] Even though the GCC countries, technically implemented the provision related with NCBs, by excluding the NGOs, they did not fully comply with the convention.

At the international level, the accredited NGOs influence the policy decisions of the UNCCD's highest policy making body—Conference of Parties (CoPs). The number of accredited NGOs from the GCC countries is negligible. Only Bahrain, Saudi Arabia and UAE have one accredited NGO each. Kuwait, Oman and Qatar do not have even a single accredited NGO. On the other hand the neighbouring countries have a reasonable number of accredited NGOs. For example Egypt has five and Jordan and Lebanon have two each. See Table 6.1.

Although the governments do not have any direct role in this process, but they have indirect responsibilities to encourage NGOs to become UNCCD accredited NGOs.

"(A) nation's ratification of an environmental agreement represents the nation's pledge to create the laws and systems necessary

Table 6.1: Number of UNCCD Accredited NGOs in selected Non-GCC Countries

Sl. No.	Country	No. of NGOs Accredited by the UNCCD Secretariat
1.	Egypt	5
2.	Iran	2
3.	Israel	4
4.	Jordan	2
5.	Lebanon	2
6.	Palestine	1
7.	Syria	2
8.	Turkey	3

Source: UNCCD Secretariat, "Non-Governmental Organisations" [Online: web] Accessed on 20th March, 2010URL: http://www.unccd.int/ngo/accreditationDB/results.php.

to meet the agreements obligations. However, ... there are generally no penalties imposed on parties failing to implement environmental agreements. Instead, the pressure of public opinion is the usual means for ensuring that parties meet their commitments."[106]

In this regard, public awareness of environmental issues is important. The role of the government, the media, educational and research institutions and NGOs is crucial in raising awareness on environmental issues if the public is to understand the problems and participate in resolving them at all levels. Public authorities need effective mechanisms for providing environmental information. The lack of environmental information also affects public participation in decision-making because the public cannot speak out about environmental issues.[107] Public authorities in the GCC countries realized the importance of public awareness about environmental problems and natural resource management.

According to the *Arab Human Development Report 2002*, three factors are critical in mobilizing public opinion with respect to environmental issues.

> One is to integrate environmental awareness into education and training at all levels and in all fields, starting with the earliest stages of education and continuing through graduate studies (engineering, management, economics and law) and research institutes. The second is to mobilize the mass

> media—written, audio and visual—together with artists and writers to draw the public's attention to environmental issues and to enlist their backing. The third is to promote public participation in legislation and in compliance with it once it is passed.[108]

Under Article 5(d) of the UNCCD, the governments have the obligation to "promote awareness and facilitate the participation of local populations, particularly women and youth, with the support of Non-Governmental Organizations, in efforts to combat desertification..."[109] The following are a few selected examples which show the governments' intention to create public awareness on environmental issues in the GCC countries.

When Prince Bandar assumed office as new head of the Saudi's National Commission for Wildlife Conservation and Development (NCWCD) in July 2006 he said that "he has plans to intensify the public awareness programmes ...., to train more local youths in wildlife projects and to obtain foreign expertise to give orientation in various fields of wildlife."[110] Recognising the key role of NGOs Bandar further said that "(h)e would also seek cooperation from foreign Non-Governmental Organizations."[111]

The Public Commission for the Protection of Marine Resources, Environment and Wildlife (PCPMREW) of Bahrain planned to teach students how to properly care for the environment. A series of events were designed to achieve this including interactive workshops on Youth's 'Role in the Environment' and 'Speak Up for a Better Environment.'[112]

The PCPMREW and the Supreme Council for Women of Bahrain jointly organized a two-day workshop on domestic environment and its effects on women and children. According to Zakariya Khonji, Head of Public Relations for the Commission "Women are the main target to create awareness about environmentally-friendly living at home that they can also share with their family. We involved members of women's societies and social workers because they interact with women from various professions including housewives. So, through them, the message of creating awareness for different activities at home that affects humans and environment will reach faster."[113]

Sharjah Electricity and Water Authority launched a year-long power and water conservation campaign to promote the sustainable use of water and energy by targeting all sectors of the community.

Al Waleed Bin Khadem, Director-General of Sharjah Electricity and Water Authority said "(t)hrough the campaign, we intend to change the attitude of residents towards water consumption and educate people not to take this vital natural resource for granted....the campaign's message will reach the public through advertisements in daily newspapers, billboards, utility bills and text messages."[114] To ensure wider reach, he further said, "(b)rochures and publications will also be distributed by Zulal water distributors to all residential, commercial and industrial buildings. Posters will soon be placed in all public areas in Sharjah including shopping centres, government buildings, hospitals, parks and supermarkets."[115]

Secondary Schools in Bahrain started implementing a programme for the support and sponsorship of scientific research in the field of the environment. The Gulf Petrochemical Industries Company Environment Fund, which was launched by the GPIC in co-ordination with the Ministry of Education, aimed to encourage students in Bahrain to develop an interest in scientific research, especially in environment-related topics.[116]

Public awareness and natural resource conservation are effective means of reducing consumption, but conservation campaigns are still lacking in the GCC countries. There are no planned programmes. According to Dr. Al-Rumakhani, eminent expert on water issues, "(t)here are individual efforts, but nothing yet on a national scale."[117]

Dr. Saeed Abdullah[118] of the Bahrain Natural History Society recently won the backing of the Ford Motor Company for an innovative e-learning project that will create an electronic encyclopaedia on Bahrain's biodiversity and to gather all the knowledge about Bahrain's flora, fauna and environment. It is a notable example of an individual effort to generate public awareness and environmental conservation. According to Abdullah "(t)eaching of Bahraini eco-systems and natural history is woefully inadequate in our schools. We hope, through the project, to make our knowledge available to the educators."[119]

Local conservation efforts usually take the form of informative leaflets, books and brochures but these efforts fall short of a well-organized and effective conservation campaign due to lack of consistent support from public authorities.[120] According to Dr. Waleed Zubari, Arabian Gulf University scientist and water expert, there is little cooperation between the government, research centres and universities and very little private sector involvement in water resource management.[121]

The civil society, particularly the NGOs can play a greater complementary role in supporting governments' efforts to conserve natural resources and to create awareness on environment. For example local environmental NGO Environmental Friends Society (EFS) of Bahrain is leading a battle to collect data on turtles in Bahrain waters and record the incidence of deaths among turtles due to environmental negligence.[122] There are a number of similar examples in other GCC countries.

However, the hegemony of the State over economic, social and political aspects of life in the GCC countries marginalized the role of its civil society and retarded their development. For example in Bahrain "the civil society groups involved in biodiversity conservation ... are very limited in number composed primarily of individual university departments, researchers, research institutes and a small number of Non-Governmental Organizations."[123]

"Despite a noisy NGO lobby that focuses on environmental issues, an analysis of Bahrain's environmental track record will show that these NGOs, like other green NGOs in the Arab world, have little or no say in the development plans of the Kingdom (of Bahrain)."[124] Promoting environmental awareness and mobilizing public opinion, is "no easy task in societies where public participation is limited in both law and practice with respect to making and implementing decisions, but it is of critical importance if environmental legislation and action plans are to bear fruit."[125] Consistent and "sustained programmes should also be designed to raise public awareness of the importance of water, the gravity of the current situation and the need to implement the measures needed to deal with it."[126]

B. Institutional and Legislative Frameworks

The governments are expected to "put in place the right structure, systems and tools, skills, incentives, strategies, coordination and partnerships for all stakeholders, and assign roles and responsibility to competent staff members to enforce laws and strengthen the legal and institutional framework for environmental management."[127]

> "The efficiency of the government agencies, Ministries, and departments responsible for implementing an MEA is an absolutely vital element to a State's compliance. States should ensure that all such government bodies have sufficient

> capacity and authority to implement the relevant provisions through such measures as strengthening the laws that provide these bodies' authority and improving their technical capacity. Because implementation is often the responsibility of more than one government body, improving cooperation and coordination among all relevant agencies and departments should be made a priority."[128]

Under the UNCCD, governments have obligations to establish or designate appropriate institutions to implement the convention. Similarly they have commitments to enact necessary legislations and laws to translate the provisions of the convention. The administrative and legislative measures taken by the GCC countries under the UNCCD were listed out in the previous chapter. The following are some of the important decisions made by these countries which have either a direct or an indirect link with the GCC countries' compliance with the UNCCD.

Saudi Arabia secured a fund for human resources development. "A number of the staff concerned with desertification control were trained as well as a number of researches were carried out about sand dune fixation and planting of trees with low water requirements."[129] In Saudi Arabia "several actions are currently underway in the capacity building of the national staff to raise their skills on using modern technologies and methods in the implementation of national action programmes. This will help in meeting national objectives, policies and strategies and (is) in conformity with relevant articles in the convention."[130]

The UAE Ministry of Water and Environment planned to focus on reducing the use of groundwater and shift to alternative sources, such as desalination, over the next three years. UAE "decided to provide modern irrigation systems for about 1,000 farms and a national plan for the maintenance of dams and the development of existing fallows. UAE also planned to increase its groundwater surveillance network to more than 183 wells, increase the number of observation networks by 35 per cent and complete the building of 11 freshwater ducts."[131]

The Ministry of Energy, UAE unveiled a strategic plan 2008-2010, which incorporates sixteen key initiatives including a proposal for a nationwide regulatory framework for the water and electricity sector. The strategy seeks to ensure a balanced sustainable development and high standard of living for the citizens and residents. According to Mohammed ibn Dha'en Al-Hamili, the UAE's Minister for Energy, the "renewable energy research initiatives will be among the Ministry's prime objectives. The Ministry is vigorously pursuing efforts to gather relevant information and statistics to support research programmes. We are keen on promoting alternative energy resources as an essential prerequisite for sustainable development."[132] UAE took an initiative to develop a comprehensive database on oil, mineral, water and power resources in order to assess the country's capabilities and prepare forecasts. The UAE commissioned a project to prepare geological and geo-physical maps and reports, covering an area of 68,500 sq km.[133]

Saudi Arabia planned to establish 60 more protected areas including two marine reserves as per the guidelines of the World Conservation Union. According to Prince Bandar ibn Saud, the Secretary-General of the National Commission for Wildlife Conservation and Development (NCWCD), "currently there are 16 protected areas that cover only four per cent of the Kingdom's land area... the target is to reach 10 per cent in the coming years."[134] He added that the Commission would set up two more marine reserves in Al-Aqaba and Fatul Wajd on the Red Sea in the northwestern part of Saudi Arabia.[135]

"Beginning in the early 1970s, Saudi Arabia adopted a policy with the goal of developing an agricultural sector capable of achieving food self-sufficiency.... Supported by policies that provide up to 1,000 acres of free land as well as machinery and equipment discounts of up to 50 per cent, Saudi farmers have increased agriculture's share of GDP from 1.3 per cent in 1970 to more than 7 per cent in 2002. The area under cultivation has increased from under 400,000 acres in 1976 to more than 9 million acres today."[136]

However, recently, Saudi Arabia decided to abandon its 30-year programme to grow wheat that achieved self-sufficiency[137] but depleted Saudi Arabia's scarce water resources and affected its sustainable development. The government will phase out purchases of wheat from local farmers by 12.5 per cent per year from 2008. Saudi Arabia aims to rely entirely on imports by 2016.[138] The Grain Silos and Flour Mills Organization of Saudi Arabia will buy wheat from abroad to meet domestic demands.[139]

In February 2008 the *Shura* Council of Bahrain discussed elaborately on a comprehensive legislation to address environmental problems. According to Dr. Bahiya Jawad Al Jishi, Council Member,

Bahrain never needed such legislation. Now, however, the contexts changed. In view of the prevailing conditions, a law encompassing air, water, sea, land, soil, micro-organisms, flora and fauna, reefs and even roads and their environment will be considered.[140]

Qatar, with the support of UNESCO, set up its first camel farm. The initiative is part of efforts to combat desertification in Qatar.[141] The farm will be used as an experiment to combat Desertification and restore the ecosystem, ensure viable production of commercial farm products and reduce water demand for fodder production. Intensive camel grazing is the primary reason for the degradation of desert ecosystems and biodiversity loss. For example, "Camel grazing affects over 90 per cent of land on the Arabian Peninsula, of which 44 per cent is severely or very severely degraded."[142] The overpopulation of grazing camels is the major reason. Development of modern farms is an ideal alternative sustainable solution to global warming, growing deserts and increasing scarcity of water and food. The grazing area will be protected from human interference and excessive camel grazing by a fence and daily patrol. The camels will stay in a fenced area where they would feed on indigenous desert plants and halophytes which will be produced adjacent to the farm.[143] The success of camel farms will require strict grazing laws and a sustainable system for fodder production. Governments should allow grazing on rangelands only when it is in tune with the ecological carrying capacity to restore the desert ecosystems.[144] Similarly, the livestock exclosures, reserved places where livestock are not allowed to graze, are started yielding good results. For example, "(i)n Saudi Arabia and Kuwait, livestock exclosures were reported to show a rapid recovery in plant biomass, and similar observations have been made in the United Arab Emirates."[145]

UAE equipped its police force with professionalism and technical expertise to contain any hazardous fallout caused by leaked chemicals, poisonous gas and inflammable liquids.[146] It provided environmental protection equipment which is the first of its kind in the region.

Oman in its report to the UNCCD Secretariat emphasized the need for financial and technical assistance provided by the international organizations and developed countries to implement desertification combating programmes and alleviating the impact of drought. Further it underlined the importance of appropriate support in training Omani technical staff, upgrading and qualifying them to implement desertification combating programmes and to use necessary technologies including remote sensing methodology.[147]

Poor coordination in the GCC countries is mostly visible in all their developmental efforts. For example in Qatar the "national coordination activity of desertification is still in its very infant stages. It has no financial autonomy, separate human resources and logistic or independent entity organization. Even though, most activities could successfully be carried through the very powerful cooperation and harmonic element existing within the Ministry and with other bodies such as the university and its research centres."[148]

Similarly in the water sector, "(m)ost of the GCC Countries have not addressed the tariff, metering and billing as major policy issues, which led to the excessive use and its rapid increase of municipal water."[149]

> While all GCC countries possess significant technical expertise in their ability to carry out hydrogeological surveys, studies, laboratory testing, and numerical modelling, government agencies are relatively weak on areas related to groundwater management planning, monitoring and enforcement of regulations for drilling rigs control, inventory and permits, not to mention pumping volume measurements and charging.[150]

Zubari said "that in terms of legislative and institutional arrangements, the groundwater management was inadequate. There should be a consolidation of all water authorities under one body and the formation of a clear, comprehensive national water policy based on the integrated water resource management framework."[151] He said that the agencies responsible for water supply and management had little coordination among them.

In this context the GCC countries may appropriately follow the model of Jordan for Groundwater Management. In the early 1990s, Jordan established a by-law prohibiting the drilling of new wells in most parts of the country where aquifers were afflicted by depletion and quality degradation. Only new wells for governmental municipal water supply, universities, hospitals and military camps were exempted from this by-law. Furthermore, repairs of existing wells were allowed only if the same specifications of the original wells were used. All drilling companies were notified of the fines against those who violated the regulation under the by-law. If a drilling rig was found at an unlicensed well, the rig would be confiscated and the drilling team would be arrested. They would be released only after paying an appropriate fine and a bail. The regulation has been strictly enforced with very few exceptions.[152]

Jordan commendably undertook a full inventory of wells. Fieldwork was carried out all over the country to register wells and obtain information on depth, water level, year of drilling and water use. As a result, Jordan has files for nearly all wells in the country whether they are licensed or illegal.[153] Jordan also took an important step to install metres on all wells including those used for irrigation.[154]

Even though all the GCC countries established focal points under the UNCCD, they were not given adequate powers and authorities to discharge their responsibilities. Similarly the NCBs were also not adequately represented by all the stakeholders. Some of the GCC countries did not submit their national reports. There was unreasonable delay in formulating National Action Programmes under the UNCCD. For example in Qatar, "(t)he national programme to combat desertification was not yet formally and coherently formulated."[155] In the same way the lack of environmental institutional arrangements was the main reason for GCC countries' poor involvement at the sub-regional and regional level implementation of UNCCD. For example, UAE did not even send the proposals for pilot projects under the Sub-regional Action programme. As discussed in the previous chapter, Oman does not have even a basic framework law related to desertification. These are the clear examples of the GCC countries' inadequate compliance with the UNCCD.

In the GCC countries, while considerable progress has been achieved in managing such natural resources as air quality and water quantity, and in identifying environmental problems in various sectors, particularly industry and agriculture,

> "there has been little improvement in fostering an integrated approach towards environmental, economic and social policy formulation and implementation. This is fundamentally because the prevailing culture in the area of environmental management and its associated institutional arrangements and instruments are inadequate to achieving integrated and participatory sustainable development."[156]

Although considerable national efforts have been undertaken by the countries in the region, and by international organizations, regional and sub-regional institutions, the problem of continuing desertification is "still a serious threat to the livelihoods of the people of Arab region. It also has serious environmental, economic and social implications that could negatively affect the social and political stability of the region."[157]

"To organize and administer measures for the protection and improvement of the human environment will require the enlargement of national as well as international capabilities. Adaptation and innovation of organizational structures and administrative procedures will be necessary if emerging objectives of environmental protection and enhancement are to be realized."[158] Therefore the GCC Countries should initiate appropriate administrative reorganization processes to bring "the environmental effort into dynamic and mutually beneficial relationships with national development efforts and facilitate mutual cooperation and reinforcement among all political levels."[159]

C. Resource Mobilization and Coordination

Under the UNCCD, the technological and financial transfer mechanisms are demand driven. In other words, governments should prepare detailed plans and proposals on the specific requirements of financial and technical needs with intended targets and expected benefits. Developmental assistance in the form of financial and technical means would be extended by the donor countries and the international and regional financial institutions as per the demand. The UN invited the "affected developing countries to place the implementation of their action programmes to combat desertification high among their priorities in their dialogue with their development partners."[160]

On 17th June, 2005 Ekmeleddin Ihsanoglu, Secretary-General of the Organization of the Islamic Conference (OIC) appealed to donor countries and international financial institutions to extend further support to regional networks in the OIC member States hit by desertification and drought. According to Ihsanoglu, "the OIC countries affected by desertification and drought cannot bear by themselves the growing burden of anti-drought and desertification programmes and the implementation of related major projects."[161]

Under Article 12 of the UNCCD, the desertification affected countries, "in collaboration with other Parties and the international community, should cooperate to ensure the promotion of an enabling international environment in the implementation of the Convention. Such cooperation should also cover fields of technology transfer as well as scientific research and development, information collection and dissemination and financial resources."[162]

Similarly the governments of the desertification affected regions make efforts "to promote, finance and/or facilitate the financing of the transfer, acquisition, adaptation and development of environmentally sound, economically viable and socially acceptable technologies relevant to combating desertification ..., with a view to contributing to the achievement of sustainable development in affected areas. Such cooperation shall be conducted bilaterally or multilaterally, as appropriate, making full use of the expertise of intergovernmental and Non-Governmental Organizations."[163]

The above obligations can be achieved by the affected countries if they undertake the process of formulating and implementing the national, sub-regional and regional action programmes. The efforts at the sub-regional and regional level strengthen the efforts at the national level. Under Article 5 of the Asia Annex of UNCCD, the governments "may mutually agree to consult and cooperate with other Parties, as appropriate, to prepare and implement sub-regional or joint action programmes, as appropriate, in order to complement, and increase effectiveness in the implementation of, national action programmes."[164]

"Sub-regional or joint action programmes may include ... coordination and other activities in the fields of capacity building, scientific and technical cooperation, particularly drought early warning systems and information sharing, and means of strengthening the relevant subregional and other organizations or institutions."[165]

The GCC countries' failure to actively involve at the regional and sub-regional level and delay in preparing national action programmes affected the adequate mobilisation of financial and technical resources to address desertification. For example, after waiting for many years, Qatar's national report says that

> "representation of the government in regional and international relevant events *(is) now undertaken* very actively. The government expects to share experience and benefit from such participation in evolving strengthening and implementation of its relevant national programmes."[166] (Emphasis added).

The UNCCD offers an appropriate frame for democratic and participative action to Combat Desertification. Nevertheless, much needs to be done to strengthen relations between donors and affected countries and among national actors to ensure concerted and effective action. Strengthened regional coordination would more effectively secure external cooperation and effective support.[167] Under Article 9 (3) of UNCCD, the governments must "encourage organs, funds and programmes of the United Nations system and other relevant intergovernmental organizations, academic institutions, the scientific community and Non-Governmental Organizations in a position to cooperate, in accordance with their mandates and capabilities, to support the elaboration, implementation and follow-up of action programmes."[168]

Equally to implement the pilot projects of the Sub-Regional Action Programme for West Asia, the Global Mechanism (GM) mobilized US$ 350,000 committed by the Organization of Petroleum Exporting Countries (OPEC) Fund for International Development. These funds, however, were not sufficient to support activities in all participating member countries. Therefore, it was agreed to implement the projects in phases as funds become available. The GCC countries mostly relied on GM for mobilization of resources. It had its own limitations.

> "While the GM has begun to demonstrate success in some cases, it may be too little too late where developing countries are concerned. For example, while it has assisted several countries in brokering partnerships, and in assisting some in mainstreaming desertification into national policies, the number of countries it has assisted is limited, compared to demand. This could be due to a lack of human and financial resources, which has restricted the GM in the initiatives upon which it can embark."[169]

If the GCC countries used their political influence, they could have mobilized more resources from other regional and international financial institutions including the Islamic Development Bank. Even the World Bank agreed earlier to support the sub-regional action programme, but later withdrew. Despite the best efforts, the reasons remain untraceable. Although the GCC countries, by becoming a party to the Sub-regional Action Programme, implemented the provisions of the UNCCD, by showing lack of interest in mobilizing adequate resources to implement the convention, failed to comply with it.

D. Linkages and Synergies with other MEAs

The social systems' interactions with land resources make the problem much more complex, requiring an integrated approach to the planning and management of land resources. Administrative changes of how the conventions relate to each other are essential. At the Secretariat level, "each convention has its own constitution, set of priorities and procedures and is at its own stage of evolution and progress, making it difficult to focus sufficiently on the important synergies and interdependencies between poverty reduction, desertification, climate change and biodiversity loss. Proactive, cross-linked environmental management is called for as a way to directly engage in broader problem-solving."[170] In the GCC countries data are available only on the implementation of various MEAs. The information on the linkages among these conventions with respect to the UNCCD in the GCC countries are not available.

According to *the State of Environment in the Arab Region*, "(d)eveloping a linkage between the global agreement secretariats and the UN specialized agencies is necessary in order to support the efforts of developing countries, including Arab countries, towards achieving sustainable development. If clustering of the large number of MEAs is to be considered, it should not affect the benefits that current MEAs offer to developing countries. An effort is underway to implement a pilot project in West Asia (in cooperation with ACSAD), in which 3-4 countries will be selected to carry out case studies on the development of an integrated approach towards the implementation and compliance with the biological conventions."[171] Addressing the chemical conventions (POPs, Basel and PIC) was suggested as another area where a linkage is possible.[172]

E. Rehabilitation of Degraded Land

The costs of rehabilitating degraded land include both the costs incurred to prevent further degradation and to restore the land to its original, or at least to an improved condition. Drylands slightly affected by desertification require certain corrective measures to prevent further degradation and to sustain their productivity. Severely or very severely degraded drylands require serious efforts and expense to rehabilitate and return to productive use.[173] Therefore rehabilitation of degraded land is an important component of the global strategy to address the issue of desertification.

Article 1(b) defines 'combating desertification' as the "activities which are part of the integrated development of land in arid, semi-arid and dry sub-humid areas for sustainable development which are aimed at: (i) prevention and/or reduction of land degradation; (ii) rehabilitation of partly degraded land; and (iii) reclamation of desertified land."[174]

In order to achieve the objectives of UNCCD, the governments should adopt "long-term integrated strategies that focus simultaneously, in affected areas, on improved productivity of land, and the rehabilitation, conservation and sustainable management of land and water resources, leading to improved living conditions, in particular at the community level."[175]

In Saudi Arabia, a number of degraded forest and range sites were rehabilitated through protection and seed broadcasting and by stepping up of the abilities of seed production centres distributing seeds and seedlings to the farmers. Rehabilitation activities were undertaken to the windbreaks of the sand dune fixation project in Al Ahsa and fixation of sand creeping in a number of different sites. A project for rehabilitation of Wadi Hanifah in Riyadh area started recently. In addition, a project was formulated to specify the deteriorated agricultural lands comprising production of a general soil and land resources maps. Green belts were established in mining sites.[176] A study was commissioned recently to examine the effects of urban expansion towards the forests in Asir and Najran areas.

Saudi Arabia also carried out accelerated afforestation and reforestation programmes, using drought-resistant, fast-growing species, in particular native ones, including legumes and other species, combined with community-based agro-forestry schemes. "In Saudi Arabia it was announced in 2006 that the country will start an ambitious project to induce artificial rain at the cost of 20 million US dollars."[177] A successful test run was carried out in the Asir province in 2005 which encouraged the authorities to design a national artificial rain project to cover all regions of the Kingdom.[178]

UAE also experimented with artificial rain in May 2005 "(u)sing the latest technology, the rainmaking effort—which continued for four days—brought moderate rain, mainly in the Abu Dhabi Emirate and the Northern Emirates."[179] Except Saudi Arabia, no other GCC countries specified their efforts to rehabilitate the degraded drylands in their respective countries. However in Bahrain, Qatar, and Saudi Arabia, "a systematic inter-linkage has been established between urbanization problems, agricultural development, coastal zone management and environmental management. It is increasingly evident that national plans are based on intensive surveys, assessments and GIS tools to implement upgrading and rehabilitation, or clearance in limited cases, of designated areas, according to transparent criteria, prioritisation process, timely and financially secured arrangements."[180]

Since rehabilitation of degraded lands is a part of the national efforts to address desertification, the failure of most of the GCC countries to initiate measures to rehabilitate their degraded lands reflect their poor compliance with the provisions of the UNCCD.

F. Drought and Desertification Monitoring and Assessment

Formulating effective global, regional and national policies on the environment requires the assessment capability to make accurate, long-term projections of global trends and their interactions in areas such as population, natural resources and environmental quality. It also requires a structure to link the results of such projections to decision-making. The early warning and assessment function brings better information into the policy-making process in order to link analysis with decisions and to obtain the best available description of the implications of policy choices. Early warning and assessment gives substance to the ecological insight that 'everything is connected.'[181]

Adequate environmental information is a prerequisite for identifying environmental concerns, root causes, impacts, trends, consequences, as well as emerging environmental problems. Sufficient and reliable information is also essential for formulating effective strategies, policy responses and action plans and programmes to integrate environment and development. Hence, governments at the appropriate level, with the support of the relevant international and regional organizations, should develop the technical and professional skills of people engaged in monitoring and assessing the impact of desertification.

The scientific and technical cooperation involves information collection, analysis, and exchange; technological research and development; and technology transfer. Under Article 16 of UNCCD, governments should make efforts to integrate and coordinate the collection, analysis and exchange of relevant short-term and long-term data and information to ensure systematic observation of land degradation in affected areas and to understand better and assess the processes and effects of drought and desertification. These arrangements would help accomplish, *inter alia*, early warning and advance planning for periods of adverse climatic variation in a form suited for practical application by users at all levels, including especially local populations.

> Although modernization of observation facilities using satellite imagery and computers to analyse data are widely used at present, there are still many uncertainties at the global, regional and national levels on the causes, the extent and the seriousness of desertification. These uncertainties make it difficult to plan properly. They also introduce constraints on the operation of early warning systems with regard to drought, agricultural production and disasters.[182]

Early-warning systems to forecast drought will make possible the implementation of drought-preparedness schemes. Integrated packages at the farm and watershed level, such as alternative cropping strategies, soil and water conservation and promotion of water harvesting techniques, could enhance the capacity of land to cope with drought and provide basic necessities.

In Saudi Arabia monitoring and impact assessment was carried out. "The monitoring and evaluation exercise was useful in establishing database relevant to desertification at both the national, sub-regional and regional level. The result was also used in the preparation of new legislations and regulations for conservation, proper utilization of renewable natural resources and protection of the environment. This was also used in updating of previous regulations."[183] As discussed in the previous chapter, UAE also established a vast network of institutions in the field of early warning system.

In the GCC countries information and data on desertification monitoring and assessment may be available but are "limited and scattered, as there is often no specific database dedicated to UNCCD at the national level. Existing environmental monitoring and evaluation mechanisms in land use changes are in place in most countries, but are limited in scope both in resolution and spatial coverage. Equally, quality data and capability to interpret and convert data into understandable formats like Geographical Information System (GIS) to support policy decision-making are also lacking."[184]

For example in Qatar "(n)o certain comprehensive databases would have been referable at this point. Other data resources such as reports, books and research studies are vastly available, systematically kept and are very easily accessible. An information centre had been formulated which started and (is) still in process of acquiring all informations necessary for agricultural development in some sorts of databases."[185]

Article 19(4) of the UNCCD calls upon the governments to "establish and/or strengthen networks of regional education and training centres to combat desertification... These networks shall be coordinated by an institution created or designated for that purpose, in order to train scientific, technical and management personnel and to strengthen existing institutions responsible for education and training ...with a view to harmonizing programmes and to organizing exchanges of experience among them. These networks shall cooperate closely with relevant intergovernmental and Non-Governmental Organizations to avoid duplication of effort."[186]

Ministers in charge of Environmental Affairs in the GCC countries in March 2005 decided to set up a Regional Centre for Environmental Disasters and Crises. They also agreed to establish several other projects aimed at ensuring a healthier and safer environment in the region including a specialized Regional Environmental Laboratory, an Environmental Database and Regional Centre for Training and Technology Transfer specialized in Hazardous Waste Management.[187] However, there is no progress on setting up these institutions to address the environmental problems in the GCC countries.

In 2007 the Arab officials rejected a UN proposal to set up a Regional Environmental Training Centre in West Asia because it would include Israel. Prince Turki bin Nasser, Saudi official in charge of Environmental Affairs said "the United Nations should establish an Arab—only environment training centre instead. He further said that the Arabs do not need training from Israel."[188] He added that the Arab Governments would discuss the proposal further with the UN Secretary-General Ban Ki-moon. The delay to establish relevant technical research and training institution due to inactions and political reasons shows the GCC countries' failure to comply with the UNCCD.

G. Access to Appropriate Technology

"Environmental issues involve a degree of scientific and technical uncertainty that hinder effective decision-making and require detailed and lengthy research from varied geographical scales."[189] Technology transfer is a critical component for achieving concrete environmental improvements. All the MEAs contain provisions related to technology transfer as part of the incentive packages for developing countries to meet their obligations under the conventions. Agenda 21 also underscores the importance of technology transfer to sustainable development.[190] The UNCCD "includes a number of innovations in the field of international law, in particular the notion of *"demand-oriented technology transfer"*, i.e. countries concerned define by themselves, in the context of national action programmes, what the best way to combat desertification is for their specific situation."[191]

> A strategy for cleaner production covers a wide range of topics, including radically and tangibly reducing the consumption of natural resources, avoiding the use of highly toxic or environmentally harmful substances, and improving product design and manufacturing so as to reduce emissions, refuse and waste and encourage recycling. It also considers the system of social values and the conditions under which social demand for products or services has been generated. It then tries to adjust this system to reduce unnecessary luxury consumption that wastes resources and harms the environment.[192]

Insufficient dissemination and use of sound scientific knowledge to formulate and implement policies, laws, regulations and action programmes *vis-à-vis* environmental issues remains an ongoing challenge to the developing countries.

However, "the process of selecting and operating environmentally sound technologies is not as simple and straightforward process as is sometimes believed. Selecting a technology that is suitable for local needs, adapting it to local conditions, and maintaining it requires substantial skills and information. Yet, the recipients of technology transfers have limited access to information and limited technical capacity, underscoring the need for an information clearing house on various abatement technologies."[193]

The GCC countries introduced a number of technical innovations in different fields ranging from agriculture to transport. These have substantial influence on the process of combating Desertification.

In Bahrain more than 75 per cent of the irrigated area is under flood irrigation which is resulting in huge losses through deep percolation and seepage. "Modern irrigation systems such as sprinklers, centre pivot, drip bubbler system, piping network to replace unlined channels, are introduced on developing farms. As of present, about 300 ha is under sprinkler/centre pivot and 580 ha under drip/bubbler systems. In order to encourage farmers to install improved methods, Bahrain supplies irrigation equipment on subsidized prices. It is expected that a saving of 13 million cubic metres/year will result from converting the traditional irrigation systems into the modern methods."[194]

Bahrain initiated a programme to replace Alfalfa with other suitable crops, like Rhodes grass, Barley, Oats, Rye grass, Sudan grass, and others, requiring not only less volumes and frequency of irrigation but also those which could withstand higher salinity and adverse drainage situation. By replacing alfalfa with other forage crops, a saving of 15 million cubic metres per year is anticipated.[195]

UAE took a number of scientific and technological initiatives to greening deserts, afforestration, planting nutritious productions for human being and animal feed.[196] Many experiments were undertaken to plant different types of fruits and vegetables using modern technologies to increase production and to enhance quality. These experiments produced good results.[197]

There was a proposal from the Arab countries to establish a West Asia Centre of Excellence in Energy for Sustainable Development in the region (as a part of the Global Network on Energy for Sustainable Development).[198] The Abu Dhabi Municipality was successful in rationalizing the use of water by introducing advanced technology. It produced good results with regard to the programme for rationalization of water consumption by tapping the modern technology of drop and sprinkle irrigation system.[199]

Qatar became the first country in the region to have an environmentally-friendly public transport system of solar cars and battery-powered buses. In order to reduce air pollution Mowasalat, a government-owned public transport company planned to replace combustion engines with alternative vehicles propelled by photovoltaic cells and electricity. This will make Qatar a green country, the first to use clean energy for its entire transportation system.[200] This will go a long way in reducing the green house gas emissions and minimize the impact of climate change.

The Arid Land Research Centre, Tottori University (Japan) and the Faculty of Meteorology, Environment and Arid Land Agriculture, King Abdul Aziz University (Saudi Arabia) are jointly working to develop new technologies aimed at establishing a network of oases based on a water circulating system. This joint programme includes biological production by aquaculture and hydroponics using properly treated seawater, waste water, and saline underground water, creation of gardens and parks as a living space by effective use of water resources, establishment of greening methodology using organic materials for low input and low human management by efficient use of harvested water derived from rainfalls and fogs in mountainous areas.[201]

In February 2008, the Supreme Council for the Environment and Natural Reserves (SCENR) of Qatar signed a Memorandum of Understanding (MoU) with the United Nations Environment Programme (UNEP) to enhance understanding, coordination and technical assistance for implementing the Qatar National Environment Plan (QNEP). This MoU was planned in order to get the technical support from the UNEP. The objectives of the MoU include conservation of natural resources (water and biodiversity), waste management and pollution, energy, health, commerce and trade, ecology emergency, eco-evaluation, early warning signals and education and public awareness.[202] The MoU is subject to review annually for updating and modification of its programmes and priorities according to the time-frame.

Saudi Arabia proposed an Environment Fund at the OPEC Summit held in Riyadh in November 2007. It contributed $300 million towards the fund, which aims at establishing an international programme for scientific research in the field of energy, the environment and climate change. Kuwait, Qatar and the UAE also contributed $150 million each bringing the total funds collected for the initiative at $750 million.[203]

In order to strengthen the scientific base of the country, Saudi Arabia decided to spend over SR32 billion ($8.6 billion) on research and development as part of its 20-year National Science and Technology Plan. According to Saleh Al-Athel, President of King Abdul Aziz City for Science and Technology (KACST), the allocation represents 2.5 per cent of the Saudi Arabia's GDP of SR1.3 trillion ($347 billion), up from 0.25-0.50 per cent at present (2006). The Saudi Government also decided to install in the near future the so-called "technology incubators" at five Saudi Universities as part of its programme to promote applied research in the Kingdom.[204]

Prince Abdul Aziz of Saudi Arabia said that the "oil industry in the GCC states are in need of building partnership with research institutions in order to find solutions in the field of geological storage and increase oil production as well as to reduce the cost of separating carbon dioxide from immovable resources."[205]

Refineries in Bahrain, Kuwait, Saudi Arabia and UAE use new technologies to reduce sulphur emissions, gas flaring and other hydrocarbon releases as part of their efforts towards environmentally-friendly production.[206] Similarly the industrial establishments in the GCC countries adopted a number of new technologies to reduce pollution, keeping in view the increasing threats of climate change. The Arab Cement and Building Materials Industry (through the AUCBM's Board Council) adopted the new international initiative on Sustainable Building and Construction (SBC). The Arab Oil and Gas and Refining Industry adopted the WSSD Clean Fuel Initiative (CFI). About 70 companies from the Arab countries were recently trained on the ISO 14001, and the majority is committed to pursue the ISO certification.[207]

"The Arab world spends far too little on research and development of new technology and does not use its political and economic clout effectively enough to force the developed world partners to share their technology and research with it. On the other hand governments in the industrial world invest about a quarter to half of the R&D expenditure directly or indirectly through small and medium enterprises which are consequently more innovative, better financed and highly productive."[208]

Science and Technology (S&T) in General and Research and Development (R&D) in particular "are not institutionalized.... Ongoing research lacks a solid infrastructure of basic science on which to draw. It is scattered, plagued by redundancy, duplication, and absence of serious and effective coordination. It is often neither published or disseminated, nor circulated within a process where researchers and research institutions can exchange, dialogue, build on knowledge, or adjust to changing development requirements and priorities."[209] Similarly, "(t)he link between research and practices of economic, scientific, and social development is very weak and action-oriented research not well articulated."[210] The main reasons include lack of well defined public, national and regional research strategies, problems associated with the dispersion of research, inadequate national funding, weak research management, weak scientific and research capacity and restrictions in terms of independent inquiry and data access and collection.[211]

Despite having a number of common environmental challenges, there is a poor coordination among the Arab countries at the sub-regional and regional level. According to *Arab Human Development Report 2002*, "(e)nvironmental research and study are still scattered among a number of Arab States. This has weakened research in important areas linked to protecting the environment in Arab countries, such as use of solar energy, particularly in water desalination. Establishing new agencies is not necessarily the best way to boost joint Arab scientific efforts, but it is advisable to divide tasks and exchange expertise and information."[212]

Table 6.2: Major Factors for Poor Implementation of UNCCD in Asia

Sl. No.	*Major factors for Poor Implementation of UNCCD*	
1.	Lack of awareness and access to relevant information	• Weak knowledge by the population on the basic ideas of UNCCD and how they can contribute to halt and/or reverse desertification and other forms of land degradation • Insufficient explanatory work with local population • Shortage of the literature on UNCCD in the national languages
2.	Shortage of funds and support	• Insufficient attention from the international organizations • Insufficient financing
3.	Lack of integration and coordination of effort	• Weak coordination between the national bodies which deal with various problems of desertification • Absence of monitoring and evaluation • Lack of opportunities for rational use of natural resources, such as forests and mines, by the local population—leading to irrational use of natural resources by those who exploit the resource
4.	Lack of capacity in government agencies	• Weak development of the technical base and reliance on obsolete technologies • Disregard for traditional methods of preventing desertification

Source: ESCAP, n. 184, p. 11.

The analysis of the UNCCD Secretariat's indicator on the GCC countries' efforts to combat desertification reveals the poor compliance of these countries under the provisions of this convention. In 2007 a study undertaken by the United Nations Economic and Social Commission for Asia and the Pacific listed out the major factors for poor implementation of UNCCD.[213] See Table 6.2. This work also finds the existence of similar factors in the GCC countries.

According to Hama Arba Diallo, the then Secretary-General of UNCCD, "Arab participation in implementing the terms of this convention was still limited, as rich countries were expected to extend bigger assistance to help their less fortunate neighbours in significant programmes to combat Desertification. He noted that oil-rich Gulf countries should extend their reforestation efforts beyond urban areas and beautification projects, to cover genuine rural development in remote regions, which is the only sustainable approach to combat Desertification."[214]

VI. Integrated Development Projects of the GCC Countries

The UNCCD mandates the governments under Article 4 (2.a), to "adopt an integrated approach addressing the physical, biological and socio-economic aspects of the processes of desertification." The GCC countries undertook the following three integrated development projects which have huge potential to conserve energy and natural resources in this region.

i. The GCC Railway Network

The proposed GCC rail network will run along Eastern Coast of the Arabian Peninsula linking all the GCC countries, from Kuwait to Muscat, running in particular through the industrial ports. The railway project complements other major integrated projects such the GCC power grid and water linkage. Two holy cities, Makkah and Madinah in Saudi Arabia will also be connected. The revenues of the project were estimated in a 2004 study at 7 per cent, but this will change in the light of the new feasibility study and the increasing economic growth and development in the region. The other neighbouring countries including Iraq, Turkey and Yemen are also expected to join this project at the later stage.[215]

This regional railway network will be useful for trade purposes, especially the import of food, water and agricultural products. According to transport expert, P.A. Koushki, also Professor at the Department of Civil Engineering, Kuwait University, a regional rail system can transfer passengers and freight speedily, efficiently, and economically especially over long distances. It is environmentally-safe (electric trains), and causes fewer accidents, compared with other modes of land transportation.

Heavy reliance on road transportation in the GCC region also resulted in a major negative side-effect: the growing problem of road accidents. According to Koushki, there is a tremendous potential for high-speed railway which can be used to connect cities like Riyadh, Kuwait City, Manama, Dubai and Sharjah and link regional airports and sea ports. High-speed rail system can also attract a portion of air traffic and road traffic. High-speed rail system can also be connected to Trans-Asian Railway System and Trans-European High Speed Railway Network.[216]

ii. The GCC Power Grid

The proposed GCC power grid will be carried out in three phases. In the first phase it will link Bahrain, Kuwait, Qatar and Saudi Arabia. The other GCC countries will be connected in the next phases. According to Saleh Alawaji, Saudi Deputy Minister for Electricity Affairs, who is also Chairman of the GCC Interconnection Authority (GCCIA), the project will reduce the cost of power generation in member countries. The GCC countries gave the go-ahead for the power grid project in 2004 after the project was declared technically feasible. Regarding the economic viability of the project, Alawaji said the benefit to cost ratio for Phase-I is 1:5 and that the payback period for the investment is less than four years. Upon completion of Phase-I and the reduction of generation capacity, the total cost savings rate of return after four years of operations would be $2.5 billion. The total cost saving rate of return after three years of operations is projected at $3.35 billion.[217]

The project aimed at ensuring an adequate supply of electricity in the GCC countries would be completed by the end of 2009. The GCC Interconnection Authority, which supervises the project, signed 13 contracts with six companies in October 2005 at a cost of $1.079 billion for the implementation of Phase-I. Phase-I includes a double-circuit 400 kV, 50Hz line from Al-Zour in Kuwait to Ghunan in Saudi

Arabia with an intermediate connection at Fadhili in the Kingdom and associated substations and a back-to-back HVDC inter-connection to the 380 kV, 60Hz system at Fadhili.[218]

iii. The GCC Water Link

In 2007 Oman proposed a project to establish a water link among the GCC countries underscoring the vital importance of conserving water. According to Sultan Qaboos, who in fact mooted the idea, the 'water link' "was not meant to cater to the public requirements, but would be used only in emergency situations". An in-depth and comprehensive study on this project is on track. There are no concrete proposals on this project approved."[219]

If these three projects are implemented effectively, subject to the environmental norms, will go long way in ensuring optimum utilization of limited natural resources.

VII. Overseas Agricultural Projects: Saudi's Changing Food Security Strategy

Saudi Arabia's recoverable water reserves are dwindling rapidly, with estimates that existing supplies are only sufficient to last ten years or fewer. Agriculture is the largest user of water in the Kingdom and the government plans to cut back farming production drastically, announcing plans in January 2008 to totally phase out its wheat growing programme by 2016 and import all of the country's needs. In a bid to ensure long-term food security, Saudi Arabia is looking at plans to invest in farms in Thailand, the world's largest exporter of rice.

According to media reports in May 2008, "both private sector companies and Saudi officials have held talks with Thai investors about setting up joint ventures to buy up or develop rice farms in Thailand. Under the proposed partnerships, production would be exported to Saudi Arabia, with any surplus shipped on to neighbouring countries in the Gulf region."[220]

However, Thailand Agriculture Minister Somsak Prissananantakul said "the Ministry had no policy of allowing foreigners to invest in farming or to use the country's land for any agricultural purpose. Foreigners are barred from land ownership and rice farming under the Foreign Business Act."[221]

In June 2008, Saudi Arabia unveiled plans to develop large-scale overseas agricultural projects in Ukraine, Pakistan, Sudan, Turkey and Egypt to secure food supplies. According to Abdullah al-Obaid, the Deputy Agriculture Minister, "the government was planning to set up projects of at least 100,000 hectares in several countries to grow crops such as wheat, corn, rice, soyabean and alfalfa, a feed for livestock."[222] The move, which is also aimed at building up strategic reserves, comes as food prices doubled over the past two years and a series of trade restrictions by exporting countries limited the oil-rich kingdom's ability to secure supplies.

Obaid said the plan to set up agricultural projects was driven by the rise in food prices, the need to secure future food sources and the desire to offer opportunities to the Saudi private sector. Although no deals had been finalised, government officials had been discussing the plans with numerous countries on the basis of some key 'principles.'[223]

Any attempt to increase the agriculture protection using excessive fertilisers and chemicals will lead to land degradation in these countries where Saudi Arabia plans to set up agricultural projects. Therefore, efforts should be made to adopt sustainable agriculture practices. Similarly, the degraded lands in these countries need to be rehabilitated to ensure availability of adequate lands for agriculture purposes. Secondly, Saudi's food security policy aimed at not only increase agricultural production, but to redistribute oil wealth. In the changing nature of food security strategy, the Saudi Government now will invest in overseas agricultural fields. It has to be seen how the redistribution aspects will be compensated as far as farming community in Saudi Arabia are concerned.

Conclusion

Over the past few decades governments adopted a large number of MEAs to protect environment and to ensure sustainable development within the framework of global environmental governance. With intensified use of international treatises as a means to address global environmental problems, concerns were raised regarding the compliance of States with commitments to which they agreed under a MEA.

Implementation and compliance are different with respect to a MEA. Implementation of an international environmental agreement refers to the specific actions (including legislative, organizational and practical actions) that States take to make international treatises operative in their national legal system. On the other hand, compliance refers to whether countries in fact adhere to the provisions of the accord and to the implementing measures that they instituted. Measuring compliance is more difficult than measuring implementation.

While the GCC countries implemented the UNCCD by initiating a number of administrative and legislative measures, their compliance with this convention is poor and inadequate. In many cases the spirit of the convention was not followed including in the areas of people participation and mobilization of adequate resources to combat Desertification. Even though the GCC countries, technically implemented the provision related with NCBs, by excluding the NGOs, they did not fully comply with the convention.

There was unreasonable delay in formulating National Action Programmes under the UNCCD. Similarly, the lack of environmental institutional arrangements was the main reason for GCC countries' poor involvement at the sub-regional and regional level implementation of UNCCD. For example, UAE did not send the proposals for pilot projects under the Sub-regional Action Programme. Oman does not have even a basic framework law related to combating desertification. These are the clear examples of the GCC countries' inadequate and poor compliance with the UNCCD.

References

1. Perkins, Richard and Eric Neumayer, "Implementing Multilateral Environmental Agreements: An Analysis of EU Directives", *Global Environmental Politics* (MIT Press), vol. 7, no. 3, 2007, p. 16. "Generally, a treaty is understood to be an agreement between states that is intended to create obligations for those states under international law."(Wiersema, Annecoos, "The New International Law-Makers? Conferences of the Parties to Multilateral Environmental Agreements", *Michigan Journal of International Law,* vol. 31, no. 231, 2009, p. 247).
2. Sands, Phillipe and Jan Lineham, "Compliance with Multilateral Agreements: the Climatic Change Regime" in Luck, Edward C., and Michael W. Doyle, eds., *International Law and Organization: Closing the Compliance Gap* (Oxford: Rowman and Littlefield Publishers, 2004), p. 93.
3. Faure, Michael and Jurgen Lefevere, "Compliance with international

Environment Agreements" in Vig, Norman J., and Regina S. Axelrod, *The Global Environment: Institutions, Law and Policy*, (London: Earthscan, 1999), p. 138. Alexander Gillespie observes that "the gap between the burgeoning hundreds of international environmental laws and the actual condition of the environment—[is] perhaps one of the largest contradictions of our time." (Quoted in Crossen, Teall E., "Multilateral Environmental Agreements and the Compliance Continuum", Berkeley Electronic Press, bepress Legal Series, paper 36, University of Calgary, 2003, p. 2).

4. Ivanova, Maria, "Environmental Crime and Punishment in Russia: Law as Reason for Breach", in Biermann, Frank, *et al.*, eds., *Global Environmental Change and the Nation State*, (Potsdam, Germany: Potsdam Institute for Climate Impact Research, 2002), p. 77.
5. Jacobson, Harold and Edith Brown Weiss, "A Framework for Analysis" in Weiss, Edith Brown and Harold K. Jacobson, eds., *Strengthening Compliance with International Environmental Accords* (Cambridge: MIT Press, 2000), p. 1. According to Beth A. Simmons, "(w)hile compliance may be necessary for effectiveness, there is no reason to consider it sufficient. The literature reviewed... is almost exclusively concerned with the conformity of behaviour to rules, rather than the ultimate outcome of such conformity." (Quoted in Simmons, Beth A., "Compliance with International Agreements", *Annual Review of Political Science*, vol. 1, 1998, p. 78). Securing compliance, however, does not guarantee the effectiveness of the international agreement; effectiveness goes beyond adherence to legal obligations....Ehrmann suggests that in the MEA context effectiveness refers to, "whether the condition of the environment is improved." ....although compliance and effectiveness are conceptually distinct, Mitchell observes, "compliance can provide a valuable proxy for effectiveness..." (Crossen, Teall E., *Multilateral Environmental Agreements and the Compliance Continuum*, Berkeley Electronic Press, bepress Legal Series, paper 36, University of Calgary, 2003, p. 8).
6. *Ibid.*, p. 2.
7. Zaelke, Durwood *et al.*, eds., *Making Law Work: Environmental Compliance and Sustainable Development* (London: Cameron May Ltd., International Law Publishers, 2005), p. 36.
8. Jacobson, n. 5, p. 2.
9. Faure, n. 3, p. 154.
10. Zhao, Jimin, "Implementing International Environmental Treaties in Developing Countries: China's Compliance with the Montreal Protocol", *Global Environmental Politics*, vol. 5, no. 1, 2005, p. 58.
11. German Advisory Council on Global Change (GACGC), *New Structures for Global Environmental Policy*, (London: Earthscan, 2001), p. 97.

12. Vig, Norman J., "Introduction: Governing the International Environment", in Vig, n. 3, p. 2.
13. Zaelke, n. 7, p. 47.
14. Perkins, n. 1, p. 13.
15. Honneland, Geir, and Anne-Kristin Jorgensen, *Implementing International Environment Agreements in Russia* (NewYork: Manchestor University Press, 2003), p. 28.
16. Desombre, Elizabeth R., *The Global Environment and World Politics* (London: Continuum, 2005), p. 20. "A state that has consented to be bound by an MEA that is in force is, under international law, bound to comply with it....This principle—known as *pacta sunt servanda*—is elaborated in Article 26 of the Vienna Convention on the Law of Treaties (VCLT), which states that "[e]very treaty in force is binding upon the parties to it and must be performed by them in good faith."...the principle of pacta sunt servanda is regarded as "the fundamental principle of the law of treaties")." (Wiersema, Annecoos, "The New International Law-Makers? Conferences of the Parties to Multilateral Environmental Agreements", *Michigan Journal of International Law,* vol. 31, no. 231, 2009, p. 234).
17. UNEP, *Annual Report 2000*, (Nairobi:UNEP, 2000), p. 1.
18. Honneland, n. 15, p. 29.
19. Zaelke, n. 7, p. 29.
20. Sands, n. 2, p. 94.
21. Sampford, Charles., "Environmental Governance for Biodiversity", *Environmental Science and Policy*, vol. 5, 2002, p. 83.
22. UNEP, *Training Manual on International Environmental Law*, (Nairobi: UNEP, 2006), p. 40.
23. Swanson, T., Johnston, S., *Global Environmental Problems and International Environmental Agreements: The Economics of International Institution Building*, (Edward Elgar, Northampton Mass., 1999), p. 247.
24. Faure, n. 3, p. 139. "Implementation is typically a critical step toward compliance, but compliance can occur without implementation; that is, without any effort or action by a government or regulated entity. If an international commitment matches current practice, for instance, implementation is unnecessary and compliance is automatic.... Thus implementation is conceptually neither a necessary nor a sufficient condition for compliance, but in practice is frequently critical." (Raustiala, Kal and Anne-Marie Slaughter, "International Law, International Relations and Compliance", in Carlsnaes, Walter, *et al.*, eds, *Handbook of International Relations,* (London: Sage Publications, 2002), p. 539).
25. Zaelke, n. 7, p. 22. According to Oran Young, "Compliance can be said to occur when the actual behaviour of a given subject conforms to prescribed behaviour, and Non-Compliance or violation occurs when actual behaviour departs significantly from prescribed

behaviour." (Quoted in Simmons, Beth A., "Compliance with International Agreements", *Annual Review of Political Science*, vol. 1, 1998, pp. 77-78). According to Teall E Crossen, "Compliance refers to whether states meet their obligations in an accord, or put another way, whether their behaviour conforms with legal rules. These obligations can be both procedural, such as a requirement to report, and substantive, such as an undertaking to control an activity. Additionally, some scholars extend the concept of compliance to incorporate whether the spirit or intent of the treaty has been met." (Crossen, Teall E., "Multilateral Environmental Agreements and the Compliance Continuum", Berkeley Electronic Press, bepress Legal Series, paper 36, University of Calgary, 2003, p. 6).

26. Faure, n. 3, p. 139.
27. UNEP, *Compliance Mechanisms under Selected Multilateral Environmental Agreements*, (Nairobi: UNEP, 2006), p. 21.
28. *Ibid.*
29. Zaelke, n. 7, p. 22. The definition on compliance given by Oran Young "distinguishes compliance behaviour from treaty implementation (the adoption of domestic rules or regulations that are meant to facilitate, but do not in themselves constitute, compliance with international agreements). It also distinguishes compliance from effectiveness; a poorly designed agreement could achieve high levels of compliance without much impact on the phenomenon of concern (pollution levels for example)." (Quoted in Simmons, Beth A., "Compliance with International Agreements", *Annual Review of Political Science,* vol. 1, 1998, pp. 77-78).
30. Faure, n. 3, p. 139.
31. UNEP, *Negotiating and Implementing Multilateral Environmental Agreements (MEAs): A Manual For NGOs*,(Nairobi: UNEP, 2007), p. 127.
32. Faure, n. 3, p. 140.
33. *Ibid.*, p. 138.
34. *Ibid.*, p. 140.
35. Sands, n. 2, p. 93.
36. Faure, n. 3, p. 141.
37. GACGC, n. 11, p. 97. "The current framework of international environmental governance is undermined by the absence of a holistic approach to environmental issues and lack of clear operational linkages between development assistance on the one hand, and compliance and capacity-building assistance for environmental protection in developing countries, on the other." (Inomata, Tadanori, *Management Review of Environmental Governance within the United Nations System*, Joint Inspection Unit, United Nations, Geneva 2008, p. 7).
38. Faure, n. 3, p. 141.
39. Jagt Juliette, Van Der, "Elaborating an International Compliance Regime under the Kyoto Protocol" in Ierland, Ekko C. Van, *et al.*,

eds., *Issues in International Climate Policy: Theory and Practice* (Chelterham (U.K): Edward Elgar, 2003), p. 225.

40. Faure, n. 3, p. 140.
41. *Ibid.*
42. Vig, n. 12, p. 11.
43. First, it directs attention to a large variety of functional regimes designed to address specific issues, such as global warming or biological loss. Second it emphasizes the acceptance of substantive principles, norms, rules, and procedures rather than formal organizations and laws. Third, it leaves the door open to non-State actors of all kinds; indeed a convergence of expectations involves the development of consensus among broad range of participants. Finally, since regimes are not equated with static texts or laws, they can evolve over time as knowledge advances or as the parties' expectations change.
44. Weiss, Edith Brown, "The Emerging Structure of International Environmental Law", in Vig, n. 3, p. 99.
45. Faure, n. 3, p. 140. "International legal theorists use reputation to refer to both (1) the extent to which a state is considered to be an honourable member of the international community and (2) the degree to which a state reliably upholds its international commitments."(Downs, George W. and Michael A. Jones, "Reputation, Compliance, and International Law", *Journal of Legal Studies*, vol. 31, 2002, p. S96.)
46. Faure, n. 3, p. 140.
47. Young, Oran R., "Environmental Governance: The Role of Institutions in Causing and Confronting Environmental Problems", *International Environmental Agreements: Politics, Law and Economics,* vol. 3, 2003, p. 385.
48. Federal Ministry for Economic Cooperation and Development (Germany), *The Role of Governance in Combating Desertification,* (Berlin: GTZ Haus, 2006), p. 26.
49. Bauer, Steffen, Per-Olof Busch and Bernd Siebenhüner, *Administering International Governance: What Role for Treaty Secretariats?*, Global Governance Working Paper No. 29, (Amsterdam: Vrije Universiteit, Global Governance Project, 2006), p. 18.
50. GACGC, *World in Transition: Fighting Poverty through Environmental Policy,* (London: Earthscan, 2005), p. 128.
51. UNCCD Secretariat, *Situational Analysis of UNCCD,* (Bonn: UNCCD Secretariat, 2007), p. 8.
52. United Nations Development Programme (UNDP), *et al.*, *World Resources 2002-04, Decisions for Earth: Balance, Voice and Power,* (Washington, D.C: World Resource Institute, 2003), p. 138. "Financial instruments can provide incentives to achieve compliance with environmental rules."(Dietz, Thomas, *et al.*, "The Struggle to Govern the Commons", *Science,* vol. 302, 2003, p. 1909.)

53. UNEP, *Manual on Compliance with and Enforcement of Multilateral Environmental Agreements* (Nairobi: UNEP, 2006), p. 208. "Although the Desertification Convention acknowledges that desertification requires substantial resources, such financial dependence... makes the Convention vulnerable. The refusal to make appropriations and investments under many available favourable options may create an absence of resources, putting enforcement measures of the Convention at risk. (Krasnova, Irina O., "Post-Rio Treaties: Implementation Challenges", *Pace Environmental Law Review*, vol. 13, no. 1, 1995, p. 109).
54. GACGC, n. 11, p. 91.
55. Bassett, Charles and Joana Talafre, "Implementing the UNCCD: Towards a Recipe for Success", *Reciel*, vol. 12, no. 2, 2003, p. 134.
56. Grainger, Alan, *et al.*, "Desertification and Climate Change: The Case for Greater Convergence", *Mitigation and Adaptation Strategies for Global Change*, vol. 5, 2000, p. 371.
57. GACGC, *World in Transition: Conservation and Sustainable Use of the Biosphere* (London: Earthscan Publication, 2001), p. 160.
58. Bauer, n. 49, p. 17.
59. Jokela, Minna, "European Union as a Global Policy Actor: The Case of Desertification" in Biermann, Frank, Rainer Brohm and Klaus Dingwerth, eds., *Global Environmental Change and the Nation State*, (Potsdam, Germany: Potsdam Institute for Climate Impact Research, 2002), p. 309.
60. Ortiz, Even Fontaine and Guangting Tang, *Review of the Management, Administration and Activities of the Secretariat of the United Nations Convention to Combat Desertification (UNCCD)*, (Geneva: Joint Inspection Unit (United Nations), 2005), p. 13.
61. GACGC, n. 57, p. 160.
62. UNEP, *Global Environmental Outlook 2003*, (Nairobi: UNEP, 2003), p. 18. "By contrast to the issue of desertification, both biodiversity and climate change topics enjoyed a solid consensus related to their environmental and global nature, a *sine qua non* requisite for access to GEF that was granted to them and denied to UNCCD, in the first instance." (Ortiz, Even Fontaine and Tadanori Inomata, "Assessment of the Global Mechanism of the United Nations Convention to Combat Desertification", Report prepared by the Joint Inspection Unit, the United Nations, Geneva, 2009, p. 3). "These last two (CBD and UNFCCC), although not without their problems with individual countries, have been seen as far more effective in promoting their mandate to the international community." (Gisladottir, G. and M. Stocking, "Land Degradation Control and Its Global Environmental Benefits", *Land Degradation and Development*, vol. 16, 2005, p. 104).
63. Töpfer, Klaus, "Controlling Desertification: An Essential Element of Global Governance", in FMECD, no. 48, p. 7.

64. Ortiz, n. 60, p. 13.
65. UNEP, n. 62, p. 65. "...uncertainties exist in deciding which country Parties would be primarily responsible for providing support to other affected countries. (Krasnova, Irina O., "Post-Rio Treaties: Implementation Challenges", *Pace Environmental Law Review*, vol. 13, no. 1, 1995, p. 110). G. Gisladottir and M. Stocking observes that "(d)eveloped-country parties to the Convention were to commit themselves to providing assistance to developing-country parties to implement National Action Plans, to provide financing, and to mobilize new resources. But very little of this support materialized and the GM (Global Mechanism) limped on, with the reputation in some quarters as an ineffective lobbiest and beggar among the environmental conventions. The UNCCD was, therefore, the laggard among the three global environmental conventions at Rio, and remained so until at least 2002. Even since the Beijing Second GEF (Global Environmental Facility) Assembly in October 2002, when US$250 million was immediately pledged to support the new focal area of land degradation in the GEF, the promised doubling of allocated funds has not materialized. Prejudice against the global institutions tasked with land degradation runs deep among the donor countries." (Gisladottir, G. and M. Stocking, "Land Degradation Control and Its Global Environmental Benefits", *Land Degradation and Development,* vol. 16, 2005, p. 104).
66. Bassett, n. 55, p. 137.
67. Ayton-Shanker, Diana, ed, *A Global Agenda: Issues before the 57th General Assembly of the United Nations* (New York: Rowman and Littlefield Publishers, 2002), p. 170.
68. Hoven, Ingrid-Gabriela, "The New Development Architecture", in FMECD, n. 48, p. 30. The UNCCD "does not impose clearly defined obligations of the Parties, and provisions for liability are acutely absent. The lack of liability provisions in the Desertification Convention probably stems from the minor short-term economic effects countries experience due to desertification." (Krasnova, Irina O., "Post-Rio Treaties: Implementation Challenges", *Pace Environmental Law Review*, vol. 13, no. 1, 1995, p. 103).
69. Cited in McDonagh, John and Yuelai Lu, "Success Stories in Reversing Land Degradation and the Role of UNCCD," Technical Paper 2 produced for UK Department for International Development (DFID), (University of East Anglia: Overseas Development Group, 2007), p. 21.
70. *Ibid.*
71. *Ibid.*, p. 4.
72. *Ibid.*
73. *Ibid.*, p. 9.
74. *Ibid.*, pp. 11-12.
75. *Ibid.*, p. 5.

76. Ministry of Forest and Environment, Government of India, *National Action Programme to Combat Desertification*, (New Delhi: 1998), p. 43.
77. Bauer, n. 49, p. 17.
78. Adeel, Zafar, "Overcoming One of the Greatest Environmental Challenges of Our Times: Re-thinking Policies to Cope with Desertification", A Policy Brief based on the Joint International Conference on Desertification and the International Policy Imperative Algiers, Algeria, 17-19 December, 2006, p. 21.
79. Lynn Wagner, "The Way to Success: Where should UNCCD go now?" in FMECD, n. 48, p. 22. Equally, "(t)he lack of clear boundaries to the concept of desertification itself and what exactly is to be covered by the Convention has subsequently generated a debate among the Parties on this matter that is consuming of time and resources and that compromises more focused and coherent action." (Ortiz, Even Fontaine and Tadanori Inomata, "Assessment of the Global Mechanism of the United Nations Convention to Combat Desertification", Report prepared by the Joint Inspection Unit, the United Nations, Geneva, 2009, p. 3).
80. GACGC, n. 11, p. 90.
81. GACGC, n. 50, p. 73.
82. Zaelke, Durwood J., "Alternatives for Compliance and Enforcement in Global Environmental Policies" in FMECD, n. 48, p. 7.
83. Herrmann, Stefarie M. and Charles F. Hutchinson, "The Scientific Basis." Links between Land Degradation, Drought, and Desertification" in Johnson, P.M., K. Mayrand and M. Paquin, (eds.), *Governing Global Desertification: Linking Environmental Degradation, Poverty and Participation* (Aldershot: Ashgate Publishing Limited, 2006), p. 22.
84. Nasr, M., "Assessing Desertification and Water Harvesting in the Middle East and North Africa: Policy Implications", Policy Paper no. 10, Centre for Development Research, Bonn University, Germany, p. 16.
85. Ali Abahussain, Asma, *et al.*, *Priority Environmental Indicators in West Asia, Arab Africa Regions* (Manama: Arabian Gulf University, n.a.), p. 9.
86. Ali Abahussain, n. 85, p. 9. "Indicators usually describe one or more aspects of desertification and provide data on threshold levels, status and evolution of relevant physical, chemical, biological and anthropogenic processes. However, there is a clear distinction between the indicators that are useful to have and those which are practical to obtain" (Symeonakis, E. and N. Drake, "Monitoring desertification and land degradation over sub-Saharan Africa," *International Journal of Remote Sensing*, vol. 25, no. 3, 2004, p. 575).
87. *Environmental Indicators*, Report to Congressional Requesters,

(Washington, D.C.: United States Government Accountability Office, 2004), p. 1.

88. OECD Environment Directorate, *OECD Key Environmental Indicators* (Paris: OECD Environment Directorate, 2004), p. 3.
89. Ali Abahussain, n. 85, p. 8.
90. *Environmental Indicators*, n. 87, p. 8.
91. *Ten Africa Experiences: Implementing the UNCCD in Africa* published by the Secretariat of UNCCD, in 2006, a collection which gives some fruitful experience from various African sub-regions, and highlights a need for a multi-faceted approach that can and must be adopted in order to ensure sustainable development.
92. McDonagh, n. 69, p. 12.
93. Economic and Social Commission for West Asia (ESCWA), *Governance for Sustainable Development in the Arab Region: Institutions and Instruments for Moving beyond an Environmental Management Culture* (New York: ESCWA, 2003), p. 32. According to Raustiala, "(e)arly international environmental treaties rarely contained provisions for NGOs. For example, the 1933 Convention Relative to the Preservation of Fauna and Flora in Their Natural state, typical of many early conservation agreements, says nothing about non-state actors... The International Convention for the Regulation of Whaling, established in 1946, did not initially permit NGOs access, though from 1977 onward NGOs were permitted to participate as observers." (Raustiala, Kal, "States, NGOs and International Environmental Institutions", *International Studies Quarterly,* vol. 41, 1997, p. 722.)
94. Karkkainen, Bradley C., "Post-Sovereign Environmental Governance: The Collaborative Problem-Solving Model" in Biermann, Frank, *et al.,* n. 4, p. 207.
95. Adeel, n. 78, p. 11.
96. UNCCD Secretariat, "The United Nations Convention to Combat Desertification" [Online: web] Accessed on 23rd June, 2008 URL: http://www.unccd.int/convention/text/convention.php.
97. GACGC, *Ways toward Global Environmental Solutions,* (New York: Springer, 1995), p. 160.
98. Seely, M.K., "Can Science and Community Action connect to combat Desertification?", *Journal of Arid Environments,* vol. 39, 1998, p. 267.
99. UNEP, n. 22, p. 83. The UNCCD is "one of the first international environmental agreements to follow Agenda 21's lead and advocate an explicitly participatory and inclusive approach to address global problems of desertification, land degradation and drought." (Stringer, Lindsay C., *et al.*, "Implementing the UNCCD: Participatory challenges", *Natural Resources Forum,* vol. 31, 2007, p. 198).
100. GACGC, n. 11, p. 90.
101. Article 10 (2.f), n. 96.
102. Article 4 (1.b) of Asian Annex of UNCCD, n. 76.

103. UNCCD Secretariat, *Summary of the Second National Report of the Kingdom of Saudi Arabia on the Implementation of the United Nation's Convention to Combat Desertification* (Bonn, 2002), p. 3.
104. UNCCD Secretariat, *Summary of the Second United Arab Emirates National Report to the UNCCD* (Bonn, 2002), p. 4.
105. MEF, Volume 2, no. 76, p. 20.
106. Leonard, Barry, ed., *International Environment: International Agreements Are Not Well Monitored, Report to Congressional Requesters*, (Darby (U.S.A.): Diane Publishing Company, 1992), p. 10.
107. UNEP, n. 22, p. 86.
108. United Nations Development Programme (UNDP), *The Arab Human Development Report 2002,* (New York: UNDP, 2002), p. 48.
109. Article 5(d), n. 96.
110. Rasooldeen, Mohammed, "Kingdom Seeks to Expand Green Zones" *Arab News*, 29th July, 2006, [Online: web] Accessed on 23rd June, 2008 URL:http://www.arabnews.com/?page=1&section= 0&article= 81497&d=29&m=7&y=2006.
111. *Ibid.*
112. "Role of Youth in Eco Protection to be highlighted", *Bahrain Tribune*, 9th September, 2004, [Online: web] Accessed on 23rd June, 2008 URL: http://www.bahraintribune.com/ArticleDetail.asp accessed on 24th June, 2008.
113. "Bahraini Women urged to preserve Environment", *Bahrain Tribune*, 17th March, 2004, [Online: web] Accessed on 23rd June, 2008 URL: http://www.bahraintribune.com/ArticleDetail.asp.
114. Al Serkal, Mariam M., "Sharjah to Promote Sustainable Use of Water and Energy", *Gulf News*, 4th March, 2008, [Online: web] Accessed on 23rd June, 2008.
URL: http://www.gulfnews.com/nation/environment/10194758.html.
115. *Ibid.*
116. "Call for investment in Water Research: Move ensures Sustainability in Future", *Bahrain Tribune*, 18th October, 2004, [Online: web] Accessed on 23rd June, 2008 URL: http://www.bahraintribune.com/ArticleDetail.asp.
117. Ali, Muniza, "Education and Awareness Can Help Boost Conservation." *Arab News*, 2nd July, 2003, [Online: web] Accessed on 23rd June, 2008 URL: http://www.arabnews.com/?page=1&section =0&article=28266&d=2&m=7&y=2003.
118. In June 2007, this author had a meeting with Dr. Saeed at Manama in Bahrain. Dr. Saeed listed out various initiatives taken by the NGOs in Bahrain to protect environment and the challenges they face.
119. Ravi, Meera, "Green NGOs lack Muscle: Depleting Water and Coastal Resources Alarming", *Bahrain Tribune*, 7th April, 2006, [Online: web] Accessed on 23rd June, 2008. URL: http://www.bahraintribune.com/ArticleDetail.asp.

120. http://www.arabnews.com/?page=1&section=0&article= 28266&d=2&m=7&y=2003., accessed on 24th June, 2008.
121. Ravi, Meera, "Conserve water call", *Bahrain Tribune*, 23rd Mach, 2006 [Online: web] Accessed on 23rd June, 2008 URL: http://www.bahraintribune.com/ArticleDetail.asp.
122. Ravi, Meera, "NGO to collect data on turtles in Bahrain", *Bahrain Tribune*, 8th September, 2005, [Online: web] Accessed on 23rd June, 2008 URL: http://www.bahraintribune.com/ArticleDetail.asp.
123. Fuller, Stephan, *Towards A Bahrain National Report to the Convention on Biological Diversity*, Prepared for the General Directorate of Environment and Wildlife Protection, Bahrain and United Nations Development Programme, Bahrain Country Office, (Manama, 2005), p. 88.
124. Ravi, n. 119.
125. UNDP, n. 108, p. 48.
126. *Ibid.*
127. UNEP, n. 22, p. 18.
128. UNEP, n. 53, p. 203.
129. UNCCD Secretariat, *The Third National Report for the Kingdom of Saudi Arabia about the Implementation of the United Nations Convention to Combat Desertification (UNCCD): Executive Summary*, (Bonn, 2006), p. 3.
130. UNCCD, n. 79, p. 2.
131. Abdurabb, K.T., "UAE Focuses on Reducing the Use of Groundwater," *Arab News*, 22nd August, 2007, [Online: web] Accessed on 23rd June, 2008. URL: http://www.arabnews.com/?page=4&section=0&article= 100281&d=22&m=8&y=2007.
132. Abdurabb, K.T., "UAE Ministry of Energy Unveils Strategic Plan", *Arab News*, 2 August 2007, [Online: web] Accessed on 23rd June, 2008 URL http://www.arabnews.com/?page=6&section=0&article=99216&d=2&m=8&y=2007, accessed on 24th June, 2008.
133. *Ibid.*
134. Rasooldeen, n. 110.
135. *Ibid.*
136. *Ray, Daryll E.*, "Income-rich Saudi Arabia prefers grow-their-own food security." *MidAmerica Farmer Grower*, vol. 20, no. 12, March 21, 2003, p. 1.
137. According to Abdulrahman Al-Qahtani, a Saudi agriculture expert, Saudi Arabia produces 2.5 million tons a year of durum and soft wheat, enough to meet domestic demand. In the 1970s, the government started a programme to encourage farmers to produce wheat, guaranteeing them at the time a massive SR3,500 ($933.5) for every ton. Saudi Arabia even ended up with a large enough surpluses in the early 1990s to export some to the ex-Soviet Union and donated a portion of it to Syria. The government gradually cut the price to SR1,000 per ton. A surge in input costs, such as pesticides, fertilizers and transport,

drastically eroded farmers' margins. According to Samir Qabbani, Deputy Chairman of the National Committee of Agriculture, farming in Saudi Arabia relies totally on underground water resources. It is possible to save 1,300-1,500 cubic metres of water for every ton of wheat produced.

138. "Kingdom to End Wheat Growing" *Arab News*, 9nd January, 2008, [Online: web] Accessed on 23th June, 2008 URL:http://www.arabnews.com/?page=6&section=0&article=105447&d=9&m=1&y=2008.
139. "Saudi Arabia Plans to Import Wheat" *Arab News,* 29th January, 2008, [Online: web] Accessed on 23rd June, 2008 URL: http://www.arabnews.com/?page=6&section=0&article=106225&d=29&m=1&y=2008.
140. Arrackal, Alexander M., "Environment to hold the Stage: *Shura* discusses Comprehensive Bill today", *The Bahrain Tribune*, 4th February, 2008, http://www.bahraintribune.com/ArticleDetail.asp, accessed on 25th June, 2008.
141. According to Benno Boer, Ecologist and Programme Specialist at the UNESCO's Regional Office in Qatar, "A modern camel farm could fight desertification. The number of camels in the Arabian Peninsula rangelands must be reduced and overgrazing stopped to allow the desert ecosystems to recover. But the recovery depends on the soil and the degree of degradation". *Source*: no. 144. http://www.bahraintribune.com/ArticleDetail.asp. accessed on 24 June 2008.
142. Gallacher, D.J. and J.P. Hill, "Effects of camel grazing on the ecology of small perennial plants in the Dubai (UAE) inland desert", *Journal of Arid Environments,* vol. 66, 2006, p. 738.
143. "Qatar to set up first Camel Farm", *Bahrain Tribune,* 2nd December, 2007, [Online: web] Accessed on 23rd June, 2008 URL: http://www.bahraintribune.com/ArticleDetail.asp.
144. "Camel farms Proposed to stop Desertification", *Bahrain Tribune*, 29th September, 2007, [Online: web] Accessed on 23rd June, 2008 URL: http://www.bahraintribune.com/ArticleDetail.asp.
145. Gallacher, n. 142, p. 739.
146. "Police on alert for Environmental Danger", *Gulf News*, 17th February, 2008, [Online: web] Accessed on 23rd June, 2008 URL: http://www.gulfnews.com/nation/Environment/10190420.html.
147. UNCCD Secretariat, *National Report of Oman on the UNCCD Implementation* (Bonn, 2000), p. 9.
148. UNCCD Secretariat, *The National Report of the State of Qatar on the UNCCD Implementation*, (Bonn, 2000), p. 12.
149. World Bank, *A Water Sector Assessment Report on the Countries of the Cooperation Council of the Arab States of the Gulf* (Washington, D.C.: World Bank, 2005), p. 22.

150. *Ibid.*, p. 28
151. Ravi, n. 121.
152. World Bank, n. 149, p. 37.
153. In 1998, a new regulation was issued, charging a price for all extracted groundwater for municipal, industrial and commercial uses, excluding irrigation. The charge was a flat rate of US$ 0.15 per cubic metre. All wells were metered on a regular basis by the MWI, which collected fees based on the abstraction volume. In 1999, the charge was raised to $0.37 per cubic metre. Despite strong protests from consumers, the MWI did not give in and advised industrial users to install water saving and recycling devices. It turned out that those industrial plants succeeded in saving around 10 per cent of water use and found the devices worth the investment. Now, the enforcement rate is about 95 per cent. Farmers were also asked to pay for the amount of water exceeding the limits in the licenses. As a result, farmers gradually stopped selling water to others. Prior to this, they would frequently extract water not included in the licences for trade. In 2002, the Cabinet of Ministers approved a new pricing policy on irrigation water—even on amounts already granted in existing licences—with a block tariff system, where charges increase in relation to the amounts of water extracted.
154. World Bank, n. 149, p. 37.
155. UNCCD Secretariat, n. 148, p. 14.
156. ESCWA, n. 93, p. 1.
157. Regional Office for West Asia/United Nations Environment Programme (ROWA/UNEP), *State of Environment in the Arab Region: A Progress Report,* (Manama: ROWA/UNEP, 2003), pp. 15-16.
158. Caldwell, Lynton K. "Management of Resources and the Environment: A Problem in Administrative Coordination," *International Review of Administrative Sciences*,(Sage Publications Ltd.), vol. 38, 1972, p. 115.
159. *Ibid.*
160. UN, *UN General Assembly Resolution 196*, adopted at the 56th Session on 21st December, 2001.
161. Shaikh, Habib, "Donors Asked to Help Fight Drought", *Arab News*, [Online: web] Accessed on 23 June 2008. URL: http://www.arabnews.com/?page=1&section=0&article= 65524&d=17&m=6&y=2005.
162. Article 12 of UNCCD, n. 96.
163. Article 18 of UNCCD, n. 96.
164. Article 5 of Asia regional Annex, n. 96.
165. *Ibid.*
166. UNCCD Secretariat, n. 148, p. 12.
167. Adeel n. 78, p. 4.
168. Article 9(3) of UNCCD, n. 96.
169. Bassett, n. 55, p. 136.

170. Adeel, n. 78, p. 4.
171. ROWA/UNEP, n. 157, p. 29.
172. *Ibid.*
173. Nasr, n. 84, p. 20.
174. Article 1(b) of UNCCD, n. 96.
175. Article 2(2) of UNCCD, n. 96.
176. UNCCD, n. 129, p. 3.
177. Magola, Christopher, "Tanzania braces for Artificial Rain," *IPP Media*, 16rd January, 2008 [Online: web] Accessed on 23rd June, 2008 URL: http://www.ippmedia.com/ipp/guardian/2008/01/16/106394.html,
178. Ali Khan, M. Ghazanfar, "Project Under Way to Induce Artificial Rains Nationwide", *Arab News*, 22nd August, 2005,[Online: web] Accessed on 23rd June, 2008 URL: http://www.arabnews.com/?page=1&section=0&article=68806&d=22&m=8&y=2005.
179. "Capital, N. Emirates get rain, artificially", *Khaleej Times*, 2nd May, 2005, [Online: web] Accessed on 23rd June, 2008 URL: http://www.khaleejtimes.com/DisplayArticle.asp?xfile=data/theuae/2005/May/theuae_May38.xml&section=theuae.
180. ROWA/UNEP, n. 157, p. 4.
181. UNEP, *Annual Report 2000*, (Nairobi: UNEP, 2000), p. 11.
182. Ali Abahussain, Asma *et al.*, "Desertification in the Arab Region: Analysis of Current Status and Trends" *Journal of Arid Environments* (Amsterdam), vol. 51, 2002, p. 523. "Traditional centralized assessment efforts used to address global change, however, are generally insensitive to the multi-level nature of environmental problems...In response to this shortcoming, a new paradigm for environmental assessment and management has begun to emerge, paralleling and complementing the centralized committee-and-report approach: distributed assessment systems. These integrated networks of research, assessment, and management bridge numerous levels, and include sustained, long-term interactions between scientists, decision-makers, and stakeholders." (Cash, David W., "Distributed Assessment Systems: An Emerging Paradigm of Research, Assessment and Decision-making for Environmental Change." Belfer Centre for Science and International Affairs (BCSIA) Discussion Paper 2000-06, Kennedy School of Government, Harvard University, 2000, p. 1.)
183. UNCCD Secretariat, n. 103, p. 2.
184. United Nations Economic and Social Commission for Asia and the Pacific, *Assessment of Progress on Mitigating and Reversing Desertification and Land Degradation Processes, and Implications for Land Management in the Changing Context of the ESCAP Region with Special Reference to the Asia Pacific Countries*,(Bangkok: ESCAP, 2007), p. 20.
185. UNCCD Secretariat, n. 148, p. 12.
186. Article 19(4) of UNCCD, n. 96.

187. "GCC Environment Centre agreed," *Khaleej Times*, 26 May 2005, [Online: web] Accessed on 23 June 2008, URL:http://www.khaleej times.com/DisplayArticleNew.asp?section= theuae& xfile=data/ theuae/2005/may/theuae_may738.xml.
188. "Arabs against UN Regional Centre that includes Israel", *Bahrain Tribune*, 6th December, 2007, [Online: web] Accessed on 23rd June, 2008 URL: http://www.bahraintribune.com/ArticleDetail.asp.
189. Sampford, n. 21, p. 85.
190. Esty, Daniel C. and Maria H. Ivanova, "Revitalising Global Environmental Governance: A New Function-Driven Approach" in Esty, Daniel, *et al.*, *Global Environmental Institutions: Perspectives on Reform* (London: Royal Institute of International Affairs, 2002), p. 13.
191. GACGA, n. 97, p. 158.
192. UNDP, n. 108, p. 47.
193. Esty, n. 190, p. 13.
194. Ministry of Works and Agriculture (MWA), Government of Bahrain, *National Report on the Implementation of the United Nations Convention to Combat Desertification* (Manama, April 2000), p. 15.
195. *Ibid.*, p. 16. Alfalfa is "extremely water-demanding. It requires 700 to 1000 kg of water to produce 1 kg of dry fodder, while other fodder crops may use only 25 to 30 per cent of that for the same yield. They include millet, barley, saltbushes and cacti, and in the case of agave much less (10-15%) is required... Again, winter crops consume much less water than summer crops as PET in winter is only a fraction of the summer amount" (Le Hou'erou, Henry N., "Climate change, Drought and Desertification," *Journal of Arid Environments*, vol. 34, 1996, p. 167).
196. UNCCD Secretariat, n. 104, p. 3.
197. *Ibid.*
198. ROWA/UNEP, n. 157, p. 8.
199. "New Technology used to save Water in Capital," *Khaleej Times*, 15th September, 2006, [Online: web] Accessed on 23rd June, 2008 URL:http://www.khaleejtimes.com/DisplayArticleNew.asp?section= theuae&xfile=data/theuae/2006/september/theuae_ september475. xml.
200. Bibbo, Barbara, "Green Public Transport System comes to Qatar in Regional First", *Gulf News*, 3rd March, 2008, [Online: web] Accessed on 23rd June, 2008 URL: http://www.gulfnews.com/news/ gulf/qatar/10194692.html.
201. Al-Ghalib, Essam, "Workshop Discusses Desert Greening," *Arab News*, 18th September, 2003 [Online:web] Accessed on 23rd June, 2008 URL: http://www.arabnews.com/?page=1&section=0&article= 32149&d= 18&m=9&y=2003.
202. UNEP "News Briefs" 26th February, 2008[Online: web].

Accessed on 23rd June, 2008 URL: www.unep.org/cpi/briefs/2008Feb26.doc.

203. Al-Mazroei, Faiz, "Kingdom Encourages Use of High-Tech on Climate Change," *Arab News*, 29th January, 2008, [Online: web] Accessed on 23rd June, 2008 URL: http://www.arabnews.com/?page=6&section=0&article= 106207&d=29&m=1&y=2008.
204. Hassan, Javid and Ali Al-Zahrani, "Kingdom to Spend SR32bn on Scientific Research and Development," *Arab News*, 22nd December, 2006 [Online: web] Accessed on 24th June, 2008 URL:http://www.arabnews.com/?page=1&section=0&article =90282&d=22&m=12&y=2006.
205. Al-Mazroei, n. 203.
206. UNEP, *Global Environmental Outlook 2000* (Nairobi: UNEP, 2000), p. 320.
207. ROWA/UNEP, n. 157, p. 7.
208. "Arab World urged to strive for Technological Edge", *Bahrain Tribune*, 23rd September, 2003, [Online: web] Accessed on 23rd June, 2008 URL: http://www.bahraintribune.com/ArticleDetail.asp.
209. Rached, Eglal, and Dina Craissat, eds., *Research for Development in the Middle East and North Africa*, (Ottawa: International Development Centre, 2000), p. 2.
210. *Ibid.*, p. 3.
211. *Ibid.*, p. viii.
212. UNDP, n. 108, p. 50.
213. ESCAP, n. 184, p. 11.
214. Saab, Najib, "Arab Environment Institutions in Coma", *Mectat,* March 2001, [Online: web] Accessed on 23rd June, 2008 URL: http://www.mectat.com.lb/contents/page36.htm, accessed on 28th June, 2008. It has to be noted that Hama Arba Diallo made this comment while he was serving as Secretary-General of UNCCD Secretariat.
215. "Grand Railway Network Project for GCC mooted," *Khaleej Times*, 5 August 2007, [Online: web] Accessed on 23rd June, 2008. URL:http://www.khaleejtimes.com/DisplayArticleNew.asp?section=theuae&xfile=data/theuae/2007/august/theuae_august114.xml.
216. "Railway Network will help boost GCC Development," *Bahrain Tribune*, 24th July 2005, [Online: web] Accessed on 23rd June, 2008 URL: http://www.bahraintribune.com/ArticleDetail.asp.
217. Rafique, Mahmood, "Power Grid to connect GCC Countries on way," *Bahrain Tribune*, 8th January, 2008[Online: web] Accessed on 23rd June, 2008 URL: http://www.bahraintribune.com/ArticleDetail.asp
218. Shaikh, Habib "GCC Power Grid in 3 Phases," *Khaleej Times*, 27th January, 2008, [Online: web] Accessed on 23rd June, 2008 URL:http://www.khaleejtimes.com/DisplayArticle.asp?xfile=/data/business/2008/January/business_January725.xml&section=business.

219. Nath, Ravindra, "GCC Water Link Project Moving as Per Plan: Qaboos", *Khaleej Times*, 27th February, 2007, [Online: web] Accessed on 23rd June, 2008 URL: http://www.khaleejtimes.com/DisplayArticleNew.asp?section=middleeast&xfile=data/middleeast/2007/february/middleeast_february449.xml.
220. "Saudi Arabia: Going With the Grain", *Arab Finance,* 19th May, 2008 [Online: web] Accessed on 23rd June, 2008 URL: https://www.arabfinance.com/news/DefaultDetails.aspx?Id= 5949&Type= Commentary
221. Arunmas, Phusadee, "Saudi Arabia looking to invest in Rice", *Bangkok Post*, 16th May, 2008 [Online: web] Accessed on 23rd June, 2008. URL: http://www.bangkokpost.com/160508_Business/16th May, 2008_biz34.php
222. England, Andrew, "Saudis Plan to grow Crops Overseas," *Financial Times*, 13th June, 2008 [Online: web] Accessed on 16th June, 2008 URL: http://www.bilaterals.org/article.php3?id_article=12416.
223. *Ibid.*

VII
Conclusion

Globalization, the advancement of information and communication technologies and the emergence of non-State actors played a crucial role in shifting the focus from government to governance. The traditional models of administration failed to comprehensively address many global problems. In the emerging web of transnational links, old forms of unilateral, hierarchical and top down decision-making patterns weakened and new forms became possible.

Governance, broader than government is a new process of governing or the new method by which society is governed. It consists of formal institutional arrangements and informal interactions. As a comprehensive and inclusive concept, governance is an all-encompassing, highly participatory, dynamic and engaging process. It seeks solutions to global problems including environmental challenges through dialogue, exchange and communicative action.

Humanity in the twenty-first century faces a new generation of environmental problems which are interlinked across institutional, thematic and geographic boundaries through rapidly changing socio-economic processes. These differ significantly from past environmental problems. These new environmental issues share several common features. They are global in scope, transcending national boundaries and affecting all, or substantial portions of, the world's population and natural resources. Their long-term consequences are irreversible and far reaching. The growing complexity and interconnectedness of environmental threats makes it more difficult to get an overview of a specific problem in all its dimensions-ecological, economic, sociological and political.

Historically, States did not easily accept environmental responsibility. As globalisation continued apace, environmental problems became increasingly complex, in some cases threatening the sustainability of human livelihoods in both rich and poor countries. With the help of new technologies, the governments gradually realized that environmental challenges experienced at any given political level frequently have their origins at locations other than where their impact is most acutely felt. This ramifying and ever changing character of environmental problems and the inability of governments solely by their own efforts to fully protect their natural resources made environmental policy a subject for international action. Nevertheless, it is at the national level where the principal tasks of environmental protection must be performed.

At the national level it is the Public administration which represents the authority system for governments in action, and is expected to carry out politically determined objectives, goals and values. Therefore, the most critical attribute of public administration is its place in the political system and the paramount influence it has on the implementation of sustainable development policies and programmes at the national level.

In the era of globalisation, the winds of change amended the context within which governments operate. Policy makers now find themselves working in international environment, consequently they have to take into consideration the global implications of their domestic policies. Significantly, the complex nature of environmental problems are characterized by considerable degree of scientific uncertainties concerning their causes, impacts, feedbacks, and the interrelationships among complex natural and social parameters. In other words the national public administration must engage and work with a wide range of actors and institutions at different levels.

Today the processes of public policy formulation and its implementation are made up of these diverse, overlapping and integrated networks. These actors bring their own specific sets of powers, roles and responsibilities as determined by values, skills and organizational resources into the network arena. These emerging new patterns of interaction between government and society at various levels can be observed in areas such as social welfare, environmental protection, education and physical planning. This changing nature of collaboration and partnership is apparently aimed at discovering other ways of coping with complex global problems or of creating new possibilities for governing. Therefore, the effectiveness of international agreements and the regime embodying them will depend on the extent to which national policy efforts and initiatives actually comply with the international obligations.

Despite the increasing importance of other actors in the international environmental process, States remain the dominant players in both the development and implementation of international environmental accords. The international organizations, lack the authority and capacity to implement international norms directly, and hence the role of State administrative arrangements is essential and critical to translate policies into actions.

Global Environmental Governance (GEG) is the establishment and operation of a set of rules of conduct that define practice, assign roles and guide interaction so as to enable State and non-State actors to address environmental problems across national boundaries. Growing recognition of the complexity, pervasiveness, and mutual interdependence of environmental problems reshaped environmental regulation and natural resource management through multi-level coordination and engagement. It provides an effective and comprehensive framework to address the complex and highly interconnected nature of environmental problems through participation and partnership of both State and non-State actors.

GEG began to emerge in a significant way only in the late 1960s and 1970s, as part of a growing concern about environmental problems. The Stockholm Conference in 1972 launched global efforts to protect, preserve and enhance the environment. International environmental accords, treaties and agreements were the core of these structured collective efforts. These global environmental instruments, collectively known as Multilateral Environmental Agreements (MEAs) are the legal framework for GEG and constitute a very substantial part of international legal arrangements. They are the official expression of the collective determination of governments to protect the environment.

Standing at the intersection between domestic, international, and global pressures, the State is the preeminent institution with the requisite political authority and steering capacity to address environmental problems through MEAs and national legislations. The past few decades witnessed a remarkable increase in the breadth and depth of international environmental cooperation and led to a proliferation of MEAs at an unprecedented level. With intensified use of international treatises as a means to address global environmental problems, concerns were expressed regarding the compliance of States with obligations to which they agreed under a MEA.

Implementation of these international instruments occurs at the national level through the enactment of legislation, promulgation of regulations, and enforcement of rules and procedures. Implementation is what transforms an MEA from a legal document to a functioning regime. Therefore, it is typically a critical step towards compliance of a global treaty.

Basically the global environmental instruments are only as effective as the parties make them. Effectiveness is the result of not only how government implement accords (the formal legislation or regulations that countries adopt) but also of compliance (the observance of these regulations and commitments contained in the international accords). In other words compliance goes beyond the implementation stage. Therefore, implementation is generally an essential predicate for compliance. However, effective implementation of MEAs at the national level often meets significant challenges, especially in countries with weak governance structures and poor institutional capacity.

While it has been observed that most States comply with most international treaties most of the time, there are reasons to believe that national implementation of and compliance with global accords is not only imperfect but often inadequate. However, there are only a few systematic studies of factors affecting compliance with international environmental accords into which countries have already entered. Among them, there are even fewer studies that focus on factors at the national level affect compliance. Within this framework of GEG, this study analyzed the implementation of United Nations Convention to Combat Desertification (UNCCD) in the Gulf Cooperation Council (GCC) countries and their compliance with the same.

The UNCCD is the newest link in the evolving international institutional arrangements for environmental governance. In linking serious environmental issues with socio-economic developmental concerns, this convention can be viewed as a significant step towards building a multilateral framework for sustainable development. This Convention also recognizes desertification primarily as a problem of sustainable development, poverty and human well-being, and environmental protection. Therefore, it is a much more comprehensive treaty than earlier efforts to address desertification.

Desertification is a problem of global magnitude with far-reaching environmental and socio-economic consequences. It is a complex issue, which arises not from a single, identifiable cause, but from complex interactions among physical, biological, political, social, cultural and economic factors. The process of desertification affects almost every region, but it is most destructive in the drylands of the America, Asia and Africa. The countries most seriously affected by desertification usually are developing countries which do not have the adequate technical and financial means of coping with a problem of such magnitude.

The GCC countries are situated in extremely arid zones. These countries are endowed with natural resources in the form of combined oil and natural gas reserves, but they are less fortunate in the critical resources of productive land and accessible renewable water resources. The source, nature and intensity of environmental degradation differentiate this region from the rest of the world. This is not because of the interaction between man-made and natural environmental problems but because of the magnitude and speed with which this interaction takes place.

The GCC countries have various degrees of economic potential but all are severely affected by desertification. Over the past few decades, all the GCC countries witnessed an unprecedented economic and social transformation. The enormous oil wealth created modern physical and social infrastructures and substantially raised the standard of living of the population. These included the provision of such expensive services. However, the large scale industrialization, inefficient use of limited resources, unplanned urbanization, large-scale consumption, higher population growth and lack of regulatory mechanism produced a critical environmental situation in the GCC countries. These unprecedented levels of socio-economic transformation coupled with limited natural resources created a number of major environmental issues.

The public administration in the GCC countries, which is expected to carry out the developmental objectives, goals and values, faces a tough challenge. The administrative system in these countries, although simple until recently, is being steadily inflated due to an unclear vision of future objectives and the abundance of financial resources. It is suffering from structural and behavioural defects of both external and internal origin. Bureaucratic dysfunctions are rampant in these countries with excessive powers and unrestrained habits of intervention in every aspect of society.

During the past few decades public administration was saddled with socio-economic development that did not serve the cause of equity and social justice in the society. The list of bureaucratic deficiencies incorporates adjectives such as lethargic, apathetic, arrogant, corrupt, insensitive to the masses, non-innovative, venal and incompetent. Governments in the GCC countries never learned the lessons of sharing responsibility and control with citizens, local authorities, or the private sector.

The existing environmental organizations were not designed to address complex cross-sectoral and transboundary issues. The national environmental governance landscape evolved in a largely linear, sectoral fashion to provide specific services. These institutional arrangements are inadequate and insufficient to keep up with the fast pace at which economic growth is generating cumulative environmental degradation. These are critical issues in the GCC countries, where governments often feel overburdened with various international commitments. They also lack the required capacity and adequate financial and human resources to pursue these cross-sectoral, integrated strategies for ensuring sustainable development. In this background, this study critically analyzed the role of the administrative system in the GCC countries in implementing the UNCCD.

Despite governmental efforts to prevent and reduce land degradation at the national, sub-regional and regional levels, only limited success was achieved. The progress made so far is not sufficient to reverse the trends. Inadequate land resource policies, centralized governance, lack of public participation, low-profile expertise, and lack of comprehensive approach to planning and management of natural resources affected effective implementation of the UNCCD.

The first hypothesis of this study was that large-scale socio-economic developmental activities and the harsh climatic conditions accelerated the intensity and magnitude of desertification in GCC countries. This has been validated through the following findings.

The unprecedented levels of socio-economic transformation coupled with limited natural resources created a number of major environmental issues in these countries including desertification. The percentages of desertified land are high in the GCC countries ranging from 89 per cent in Oman to 100 per cent in Bahrain, Kuwait, UAE and Qatar. Fertile agricultural land around major cities was lost to urbanization, industrial establishments and transportation infrastructure. Similarly, the deterioration of rangeland and farm productivity is forcing farmers to abandon agricultural land and migrate to cities, increasing pressure on services and infrastructure.

In the GCC countries agriculture accounts for a small portion of the GDP and does not constitute an important source of employment, except in Oman and, to a lesser extent, Saudi Arabia. However geopolitical instability in and around the countries of West Asia persuaded governments of the GCC countries to adopt policies aimed at achieving national food security. These policies were accompanied by agricultural protectionism, the erection of trade barriers and provision of subsidies for agricultural inputs in several forms, including wells, fuel, energy, inputs, price support programmes, trade protection, and free access to unlimited amounts of groundwater, most of which is non-renewable. This led to large-scale expansion of agricultural activities in the GCC countries.

Without exception, all of the GCC countries are extracting groundwater resources in an unsustainable manner. In Oman, Bahrain, Kuwait, Qatar, and the UAE, this represents a level of extraction in excess of the natural recharge of the aquifers. In the case of Saudi Arabia, this represents the accelerated extraction of non-renewable resources without adequate knowledge of the finite life of water supplies within the aquifers. Over-extraction of water resources affected the quantity and quality of groundwater. This led to seawater intrusion along the shoreline, causing salinisation of coastal agricultural lands. About 2 million ha of irrigated land area in Saudi Arabia and 33.6 per cent of the cultivated land of Bahrain are moderately salinised. For example in Qatar around 30 per cent of irrigated agricultural land is salinised. Similarly about 68 farms went out of production due to salinisation (in Qatar). The yield in state farms decreased by 30 per cent or about 1500 ha from irrigated soil degraded due to salinisation.

Pollution from agriculture, including fertilizers and pesticides runoff and increased salts, added to increasing amounts of industrial and toxic waste and urban pollutants, combine to lower the quality of water. Marine biodiversity in the GCC countries is under severe stress, primarily from oil spillage. Indigenous plants and animals in this region are under increasing threat due to the impact of development. Urban transportation also increased the pollution level in cities.

The second hypothesis was that political and economic issues remain top on the agenda of the GCC countries rather than environmental issues. This has been validated through the following findings. Only Kuwait signed the UNCCD when it was opened for signature, i.e. before the convention came into force. All the other GCC countries became Party to the Convention after it came into force in 1996.

Ministers in charge of Environmental Affairs in the GCC countries in March 2005 decided to set up a Regional Centre for Environmental Disasters and Crises. They also agreed to establish several other projects aimed at ensuring a healthier and safer environment in the region including a specialized Regional Environmental Laboratory, an Environmental Database and Regional Centre for Training and Technology Transfer specialized in Hazardous Waste Management. However, there is no progress on setting up these institutions to address the environmental problems in the GCC countries.

In 2007, the Arab officials rejected a UN proposal to set up a Regional Environmental Training Centre in West Asia because it would include Israel. The delay to establish relevant technical research and training institutions due to inaction and political reasons shows that environment is not in the agenda of the GCC countries.

Another example is the Sustainable Arid Land Management (SALAM) Project which was announced in 2006. The Global Mechanism proposed to develop a multi-country programme that brings the GCC countries together with the neighbouring Arab States in a partnership for Sustainable Land Management practices to facilitate improved livelihoods and ecological services. This programme aimed at responding to the special requirement of the region with regard to the respective countries' different development trajectories and unique ecological context. Beyond the borders of the GCC countries, the region also includes countries with economies in transition that face challenging socio-economic, political and environmental hurdles. However, this project is still in the preparatory phase and is not launched yet.

The GCC countries failed to use this Convention as a framework for international solidarity to bring about more scientific, technical and financial cooperation and partnership. For example, in order to implement the pilot projects of the Sub-Regional Action Programme for West Asia, the Global Mechanism mobilized US$ 350,000 committed by the Organization of Petroleum Exporting Countries (OPEC) Fund for International Development. These funds, however, were not sufficient to support activities in all participating member countries. Therefore, it was agreed to implement the projects in phases as funds become available. If the GCC countries used their political influence, they could have mobilized more resources from other regional and international financial institutions including the Islamic Development Bank. Even the World Bank agreed earlier to support the sub-regional action programme, but later withdrew. Although the GCC countries, by becoming a party to the Sub-regional Action Programme, implemented the provisions of the UNCCD, by showing lack of interest in mobilizing adequate resources to implement the convention, failed to comply with it.

The GCC governments consistently recognized the valuable role of the scientific and academic communities in efforts to combat desertification through their ongoing technical research programmes and studies. However, they spend far too little on research and development of new technology and do not use their political and economic clout effectively enough to force the developed world to share their technology and research with it. Similarly Science and Technology (S&T) in general and Research and Development (R & D) in particular are not institutionalized in these countries. The ongoing research lacks a solid infrastructure of basic science. It is scattered, plagued by redundancy, duplication, and absence of serious and effective coordination. The research works are often neither published or disseminated, nor circulated within a process where researchers and research institutions can exchange, dialogue, build on knowledge, or adjust to changing development requirements and priorities. Similarly, the link between research and practices of economic, scientific, and social development is very weak and action-oriented research not well articulated.

The third hypothesis of this work was that the administrative machineries in the GCC countries are not adequately equipped to tackle environmental problems in general and desertification in particular. This hypothesis is also validated. The GCC countries lag behind the rest of the world in the core domestic institutions that make basic environmental governance possible, and in their contributions to global processes of shared environmental management. State environmental authorities are generally young, inadequately staffed and short of the expertise needed not only to address current issues but also a substantial backlog of environmental problems, both in depleting natural resources and in polluting the environment. Poor coordination among various administrative units in the GCC countries is mostly visible in all their developmental efforts.

Even though all the GCC countries established focal points under the UNCCD, they were not given adequate powers and authorities to discharge their responsibilities. Similarly the NCBs were also not adequately represented by all the stakeholders, especially NGOs. Despite the creation of such bodies in some of the GCC countries, the problems of effectively implementing the NAPs persist. The mechanisms and arrangements for coordinating the various sectoral policies are still inadequate. The NCBs function on an *ad hoc* basis with no certainty as to what specific mandate they are to perform in the long term.

Some of the GCC countries did not submit their national reports. There was unreasonable delay in formulating National Action Programmes under the UNCCD. Only Oman, Saudi Arabia and UAE formulated the national action programmes. The lack of environmental institutional arrangements was the main reason for GCC countries' poor involvement at the sub-regional and regional level implementation of the UNCCD. For example, UAE did not even send the proposals for pilot projects under the Sub-regional Action programme. Same is the case with Oman; it does not have even a basic framework law related to desertification.

Rehabilitation of degraded land is an important component of the global strategy to address the issue of desertification. Except Saudi Arabia, no other GCC country made efforts to rehabilitate the degraded drylands in their respective countries. Since rehabilitation of degraded lands is a part of the national efforts to address desertification, the failure of most of the GCC countries to initiate measures to rehabilitate their degraded lands reflect their poor compliance with the provisions of the UNCCD.

The fourth hypothesis was that only limited provisions of the UNCCD were implemented in these countries. This has been validated. Among the GCC countries, there was no reporting from Bahrain and Oman since 2000. Only Saudi Arabia and UAE submitted all the reports. Secondly, Parties are required to communicate their reports in one of the official languages of the CoP. Parties are also encouraged to submit their reports, or at least their summary, in English in order to disseminate them widely. However, Bahrain (2000), Kuwait (2002 and 2004), Saudi Arabia (2000) and UAE (2006) submitted their reports in Arabic without summary in English (Table 5.6). This affects the wider circulation of the details of the status of desertification-related activities in the GCC countries. Qatar did not establish the national coordination bodies to implement the convention. Even the composition of National Coordination Committees, in other GCC countries shows lack of people's participation, especially NGOs. Only a few research institutes are included in these committees. Lack of people's participation in the UNCCD related activities is in contrast with the very spirit of UNCCD principles and objectives.

Instead of establishing new research institutes, the GCC countries mostly rely on the regional specialized agencies or academic institutes on an *ad hoc* basis for consultation on desertification-related issues. In the GCC countries a comprehensive assessment of the indigenous knowledge is still a weak point.

At the sub-regional level due to lack of financial resources the pilot projects were not able to start. There was a poor response from the GCC countries in mobilizing adequate resources. At the regional level, only Saudi Arabia participated in four Asian Thematic Programme Networks (TPNs), out of six. Qatar was involved in two and Oman in one. The other GCC countries did not show any interest to participate at the regional level. This reflects two things. Firstly, the majority of the GCC countries failed to fulfil the commitments under the UNCCD to cooperate at the regional level. Secondly, the GCC countries also failed to obtain the benefits they could have received if the participated in these programmes. In Asia, the initiatives taken at various levels (national, sub-regional and regional) resulted in large databases being set up, and the work of harmonizing the desertification monitoring/assessment procedures is very well advanced. Discussions are in progress to establish a frame of reference that can be used as a kind of control panel, so as to monitor progress combating desertification.

Despite having similar physical and natural features and closer geographical proximity, except Oman, none of the GCC countries showed interest to get involved in the WANA regional programme.

The fifth hypothesis was that lack of an effective mechanism for people's participation is a major constraint in addressing the desertification problem in the GCC countries. Public participation brings legitimacy, credibility, and effectiveness to the policy making process and its implementation. Civil society plays an important role in bringing emerging environmental issues to the attention of policy makers, raising public awareness, promoting innovative ideas and approaches in environmental decision-making at different levels.

Historically the overall model of governance in the GCC countries is State-led, State-centred, and State-regulated. The rental State which emerged out of natural sources of wealth controlled by the state, together with a political structure which took the form of traditional monarchies dominated by one family gave rise to public governance that minimizes the role and participation of its civil society, magnifies the role of the state in the area of social welfare and distribution of rent.

Despite their importance, the civil society's participation in the UNCCD implementation process in the GCC countries is inadequate. Even though all the GCC countries, except Qatar established National Coordination Committees, the composition shows a lack of people's participation, especially NGOs. Only a few research institutes are included in these committees. Lack of people's participation in the UNCCD related activities is in contrast with the very spirit of UNCCD principles and objectives.

The number of accredited NGOs from the GCC countries is negligible. Only Bahrain, Saudi Arabia and UAE have one accredited NGO each. Kuwait, Oman and Qatar do not have even a single accredited NGO. On the other hand the neighbouring countries have a reasonable number of accredited NGOs. For example Egypt has five and Jordan and Lebanon have two each.

The sixth and last hypothesis of this study was that in GCC countries radical reform measures are required in the areas of recruitment, training and administrative procedures. Bureaucracies in these countries substituted routine work, self-serving behaviour, and survival techniques to risk-taking management. Such bureaucratic behaviours are a major obstacle to numerous campaigns for administrative reform, generally decreed by the political leaders. Thus, avoidance of responsibility, apathy, or inaction became among the survival techniques frequently employed by bureaucrats. The weak capacity for innovation coupled with clerkism in administration hampers effective implementation of development goals.

Even though this work established the need for reforms in environmental administration in these countries, the relevant and suitable methods of recruitment, training and administrative procedure could not be provided due to non-availability of data. Therefore, this hypothesis remains inconclusive.

The GCC countries undertook a number of measures individually as well as collectively. These initiatives have either a direct or an indirect impact on the efforts to Combat Desertification. However, theses are at the early stage which makes it difficult to draw conclusion. The following are some of the important individual efforts. Saudi Arabia decided to abandon wheat cultivation to protect depleting ground-water. It also planned to increase the plan allocation for R&D as part of its 20-year National Science and Technology Plan and the number of bio reserves to protect the environment.

Qatar is in the process of introducing an environment-friendly public transport system of solar cars and battery-powered buses to reduce pollution and save energy. It also approved to set up camel farms to Combat Desertification. It also signed an MoU with the UNEP to enhance understanding, coordination and technical assistance for implementing the Qatar National Environment Plan (QNEP).

Oman adopted a master plan to regulate water management. Bahrain enacted legislation to strictly monitor the use of groundwater and drilling of wells and improving irrigation techniques including sprinkler irrigation system. Bahrain initiated a programme to replace Alfalfa with other suitable crops, like Rhodes grass, Barley, Oats, Rye grass, Sudan grass, and others, requiring not only less volumes and frequency of irrigation but also those which could withstand higher salinity and adverse drainage situation. By replacing alfalfa with other forage crops, a saving of 15 million cubic metres per year is anticipated.

UAE unveiled a strategic plan to save groundwater and solar energy. These are the few examples of the GCC countries' individual efforts to protect natural resources in their countries.

Similarly, the GCC countries took several measures collectively which will go a long way in ensuring the sustainable development of this region. These significant measures include adoption of the Gulf Green Initiative 2007 which focuses on unifying all environmental legislations among the GCC countries and the formulation of three integrated development projects—GCC rail network, GCC power grid and GCC water link. These three integrated development projects have huge potential to conserve energy and natural resources in this region. For example, the rail network is expected to reduce the GCC countries, heavy reliance on road transportation which resulted in a major negative side-effect: the growing problem of road accidents.

However, lack of centralized databases on desertification issues, inadequate monitoring and assessment, poor capacity-building for focal points and NGOs affect the sustainable development in these countries. Furthermore, in the GCC countries, there is no comprehensive assessment of the degradation of irrigated land, rain-fed cropland or rangeland. Given the economic potential of these countries and the threatening extent to which desertification is impeding sustainable growth, more extensive cooperative and participatory efforts are necessary. Adequate and reliable financial resources are necessary to address these shortcomings. The information base on the current magnitude of and trends in desertification both at the national and the sub-regional level needs substantial improvement. New technologies, techniques, methods, approaches, skills, ideas and systems will facilitate the efficient and effective use of limited and scarce natural resources in these countries.

The GCC countries may appropriately adopt the recommendations proposed in the implementation report of the first phase of pilot projects, while launching the next phase of the SRAP pilot projects in their countries.

It is found that not only many of the provisions related with the UNCCD were not implemented, but the implemented provisions were not fully complied. The initiatives taken by the GCC countries in recent years will go a long way in bridging this gap.

References

Reports

Arab Centre for the Studies of Arid Zones and Dry Lands (ACSAD), *The State of Desertification in the Arab World*, (Damascus: ACSAD, 2000).

ACSAD, *Inventory Study and Regional Database on Sustainable Vegetation Cover Management in West Asia (TN2)*, Prepared for the Sub-Regional Action Programme (SRAP) to Combat Desertification and Drought in West Asia (UNEP/ROWA, 2003).

Commission on Global Governance, *Our Global Neighbourhood,* the Report of the Commission on Global Governance, (New York: Oxford University Press, 1995).

Economic and Social Commission for Asia and the Pacific (ESCAP), *Assessment of Progress on Mitigating and Reversing Desertification and Land Degradation Processes, and Implications for Land Management in the Changing Context of the ESCAP Region with Special Reference to the Asia Pacific Countries*, (Bangkok: ESCAP, 2007).

Economic Social Commission for West Asia (ESCWA), *The Role of ESCWA in Agricultural Resource Management and Conservation in Combating Desertification in the Region,* (Beirut: ESCWA, 1993).

————, *Survey of Economic and Social Development in the ESCWA Region 1998-1999,* (New York, 1999).

————, *Application of Sustainable Development Indicators in the ESCWA Member Countries: Analysis of Results,* (New York: ESCWA, 2000).

————, *Governance for Sustainable Development in the Arab Region: Institutions and Instruments for Moving beyond an Environmental Management Culture* (New York,: ESCWA, 2003).

Federal Foreign Office (Government of Germany), *Desertification: A Security Threat?đAnalysis of Risks and Challenges* (Berlin: Technische Zusammenarbeit (GTZ), 2007).

German Advisory Council on Global Change (GACGC), *New Ways to Global Environmental Solutions*, (New York: Springer, 1995).

———, *World in Transition: Conservation and Sustainable Use of the Biosphere* (London: Earthscan, 2001).

———, *New Structures for Global Environmental Policy*, (London: Earthscan, 2001).

———, *World in Transition: Fighting Poverty through Environmental Policy*, (London: Earthscan, 2005).

Global Mechanism, *UNCCD Implementation and the Global Mechanism: Information Note on the Global Mechanism and its Change Agenda* (Rome: Global Mechanism of the UNCCD, 2006).

Inomata, Tadanori, *Management Review of Environmental Governance within the United Nations System*, Report of the Joint Inspection Unit, United Nations, Geneva, 2008.

International Centre for Agricultural Research in the Dry Areas and Arab Centre for the Study of Arid Zones and Dry Lands,(ICARDA), *Inventory Study and Regional Database on Sustainable Management of Water Resources and Drought Mitigation in West Asia* (TN1), Prepared for the Sub-Regional Action Programme (SRAP) to Combat Desertification and Drought in West Asia 2003, (UNEP/ROWA, 2003).

———, *Integrated Natural Resource Management for Combating Desertification in West Asia: Pilot Projects Proposal*, Prepared for the Sub-Regional Action Programme (SRAP) for West Asia of the UN Convention to Combat Desertification (UNCCD), (Manama: ROWA/UNEP, 2003).

Ministry of Forest and Environment (MoFE), Government of India, *National Action Programme to Combat Desertification*, (New Delhi: MoFE, 1998).

Ministry of Works and Agriculture (MWA), Government of Bahrain, *National Report on the Implementation of the United Nations Convention to Combat Desertification* (Manama: MWA, 2000).

OECD Environment Directorate, *OECD Key Environmental Indicators* (Paris: OECD Environment Directorate, 2004).

Regional Office for West Asia/United Nations Environment Programme (ROWA/UNEP) *Sub-Regional Action Programme for West Asia*, (Manama: ROWA/UNEP, 2002).

———, *State of Environment in the Arab Region: A Progress Report*, (Manama: ROWA/UNEP, 2003).

———, *State of Desertification in the Arab World*, (Manama: UNEP/ROWA, 2004).

———, *Integrated Natural Resource Management for Combating Desertification in West Asia: UNCCD/SRAP Pilot Projects in Jordan, Lebanon, Syria and Yemen 2003-2006: Final Report*, (Manama: ROWA, 2006).

Report of World Commission on Environment and Development, *Our Common Future,* (Oxford: Oxford University Press, 1987).

United Nations, *A Handbook of Public Administration* (New York: UN, 1961).

UNCCD Secretariat, *Regional Implementation Annex for Asia National Reports on the UNCCD Implementation: Help Guide*, (Bonn: UNCCD Secretariat, 1999).

————, *National Report of Oman on the UNCCD Implementation* (Bonn: UNCCD Secretariat, 2000).

————, *The National Report of the State of Qatar on the UNCCD Implementation,* (Bonn: UNCCD Secretariat, 2000).

————, *Summary of the Second United Arab Emirates National Report to the UNCCD* (Bonn: UNCCD Secretariat, 2002).

————, *Summary of the Second National Report of the Kingdom of Saudi Arabia on the Implementation of the United Nation's Convention to Combat Desertification* (Bonn: UNCCD Secretariat, 2002).

————, *The Role of Governance in Combating Desertification,* (Bonn: UNCCD Secretariat, 2006).

————, *The Third National Report for the Kingdom of Saudi Arabia about the Implementation of the United Nations Convention to Combat Desertification (UNCCD): Executive Summary*, (Bonn: UNCCD Secretariat, 2006).

————, *Situational Analysis of UNCCD*, (Bonn: UNCCD Secretariat, 2007).

United Nations Development Programme (UNDP), *The Arab Human Development Report 2002*,(New York: UNDP, 2002).

————, *et al.*, *World Resources 2002-04, Decisions for Earth: Balance, Voice and Power,* (Washington, D.C.: World Resource Institute, 2003).

United Nations Environment Programme (UNEP), *The Plan of Action of the United Nations Conference on Desertification* (Nairobi: UNEP, 1977).

————, *The Status of Desertification and the Implementation of the United Nations Plan of Action to Combat Desertification,* The Report of the Executive Director (Nairobi: UNEP, 1992).

————, *Twenty Years since Stockholm* (Nairobi: UNEP, 1993).

————, *Global Environmental Outlook 1997* (Nairobi: UNEP, 1997).

————, *Global Environmental Outlook 2000* (Nairobi: UNEP, 2000).

————, *The State of Environment 1972-2002*, (Nairobi: UNEP, 2002).

————, *Success Stories in the Struggle against Desertification: A Holistic and Integrated Approach to Environmental Conservation and Sustainable Livelihoods* (Nairobi: UNEP, 2002).

————, *Ecosystems and Human Well-being: Desertification Synthesis,* A Report of the Millennium Ecosystem Assessment, (Nairobi: 2005).

————, *Manual on Compliance with and Enforcement of Multilateral Environment Agreement* (Nairobi: UNEP, 2006).

————, *Training Manual on International Environmental Law,* (Nairobi: UNEP, 2006).

————, *One Planet and Many People: Atlas of Our Changing Environment,* (UNEP: Nairobi, 2006).

————, *Multilateral Environmental Agreement Negotiator's Handbook,* (Nairobi: UNEP, 2007).

————, *Global Environmental Outlook 2007* (Nairobi: UNEP, 2007).

UNESCO, *Trends in Research and Application of Science and Technology for Arid Zone Development* (Paris: UNESCO, 1979).

World Bank, World Development Report, 1992: *Development and Environment* (New York: Oxford University Press, 1992).

————, *A Strategy for Managing Water in the Middle East and North Africa,* (Washington D.C.,: World Bank, September, 1993).

————, *Desertification: Implementing the Convention, a World Bank View,* (Washington, D.C.: World Bank, 1994).

————, *New Opportunities for Development: The Desertification Convention,* (Washington D.C.: World Bank, 1998).

————, *A Water Sector Assessment Report on the Countries of the Cooperation Council of the Arab States of the Gulf,* (Washington D.C.: World Bank, 2005.

Books

Adams, William Mark, *Green Development: Environment and Sustainability in the Third World* (New York: Routledge, 2001).

Anderson, James E., *Public Policy Making: An Introduction* (Boston; Houghton Mifflin Co., 2000)

Andersson, Magnus, *Change and Continuity in Poland's Environmental Policy,* (London: Kluwer Academic Publishers, 1999).

Ansari, Shahid Jamal, *Political Modernization in the Gulf,* (New Delhi: Northern Book Centre, 1998).

Arts, B., *The Political Influence of Global NGOs: Case Studies on the Climate and Biodiversity Conventions,* (Utrecht: International Books, 1998).

Ayton-Shanker, Diana, ed., *A Global Agenda: Issues before the 57th General Assembly of the United Nations,* (New York: Rowman and Littlefield Publishers, 2002).

Ayre, Georgina and Rosalie Callway, eds., *Governance for Sustainable Development: A Foundation for the Future,* (London: Earthscan, 2005).

Ayubi, Nazih N., *Over-Stating the Arab State: Politics and Society in the Middle East,* (London: I.B. Tauris, 1995).

Baker, Susan, *Sustainable Development*, (New York: Routledge, 2006).

Barry, John and Robyn Eckersley, eds., *The State and the Global Ecological Crisis*, (Cambridge: MIT Press, 2005).

Barrett, S., *Environment and Statecraft: the Strategy of Environmental Treaty-Making,* (New York: Oxford University Press, 2002).

Barrow, C.J., *Developing the Environment: Problems and Management*, (London: Longman, 1995).

Bearumont, P., *et al.*, *The Middle East: A Geographical Study,* (London: David Fulton, 1988).

————, P., *Drylands: Environmental Management and Development*, (London: Routledge, 1993).

Beltrán, J. Martínez and S. Koo-Oshima, eds., *Water Desalination for Agricultural Applications* (Rome: FAO, 2006).

Blaikie, P. and Brookfield H., *Land Degradation and Society*, (London: Routledge, 1987).

Blowers, Andrew and Pieter Glasberger, eds, *Environment Policy in an International Context*, (London: Arnold, 1996).

Boczeck, Boleslaw Adam, *International Law: A Dictionary,* (Lanham, Maryland: Scarecrow Press, 2005).

Boyer, Brook, *et al., Synergies and Coordination among MEAs: Regional and National Approaches,* (United Nations University: Tokyo, 2002).

Caldwell, Lyndon K., *International Environmental Policy: Emergence and Dimensions,* (New Delhi: Affiliated East-West Press Private Limited, 1991)

————, *Environment Policy: From the Twentieth to Twenty-First Century,* (London: Duke University, 1996).

Conor, Robin and Stephen Dovers, *Institutional Change for Sustainable Development* (Cheltenham, U.K.: Edwar Elgar, 2004).

Cordier, Andrew W. and Harrelson, Max, *Public Papers of the Secretaries-General of the United Nations, Volume VIII, U Thant 1968-1971*, (New York: Columbia University Press, 1977).

Corell, Elisabeth, *The Negotiable Desert: Expert Knowledge in the Negotiations of the Convention to Combat Desertification,* (Linköping: Department of Water and Environmental Studies, Linköping University, 1999).

Cramer, Phillip F., *Rethinking Environmental Protection: A Natural Approach to Nature,* (Lanham (USA): Lexington Books, 2000).

Cullet, Phillippe, *Differential Treatment in International Environmental Law* (Aldershot: Ashgate Publishers, 2005).

Darkoh, Michael and Apollo Rwomire, *Human Impact on Environment and Sustainable Development in Africa,* (Aldershot: Ashgate Publishers, 2003).

Desombre, Elizabeth R., *The Global Environment and World Politics* (London: Continuum, 2005).

Dregne, H.E., *Desertification of Arid Lands,* (London: Hardwood Academic Press, 1983).

Drysdale, Alasdair, and Gerald H. Blake, *The Middle East and North Africa: A Political Geography,* (New York: Oxford University Press, 1985).

Esty, Daniel C. and Maria H. Ivanova, eds., *Global Envirormental Governance Options and Opportunities,* (New Haven (USA): Yale School of Forestry and Environmental Studies, 2002).

Farazmand, Ali and Pinkowski, eds., *Handbook of Globalisation, Governance and Public Administrations* (New York: CRC Press, 2006).

Frederic Launay, *Environmental Situational Assessment for the GCC Countries,* (Dubai: Gulf Research Centre, 2006).

Gause, F. Gregory, *Oil Monarchies: Domestic and Security Challenges in the Arab Gulf States,* (New York: Council of Foreign Relations, 1994).

Gerald E. Caiden, *Administraive Reform* (Chicago: Aldine Publishing Company, 1969).

Glantz, Michael H., ed., *Desertification: Environmental Degradation in and around Arid Lands* (Boulder: West View Press, 1977).

Gulf Research Centre and the Energy Research Institute, *Green Gulf* (Dubai: GRC, 2006).

Hajer, M.A., *The Politics of Environmental Discourse: Ecological Modernization and the Policy Process,* (Oxford: Oxford University Press, 1995).

Hewson, M. and T. Sinclair, eds., *Approaches to Global Governance Theory.* (Albany: State University of New York Press, 1999).

Honneland, Geir, and Anne-Kristin Jorgensen, *Implementing International Environment Agreements in Russia,* (New York: Manchester University Press, 2003).

Horta, Korinna, *et al.*, *The Global Environmental Facility: First Ten Years-Growing Pains or Inherent Flaws?* (Washington, D.C.: Environmental Defense, 2002).

Hyvarinen, Joy and Duncan Brack, *Global Environmental Institutions: Analysis and Options for Change,* (London: Royal Institute of International Affairs, 2000).

Ierland, Ekko C. Van, *et al.*, eds., *Issues in International Climate Policy: Theory and Practice,* (Chelterham (U.K.): Edward Elgar, 2003).

Ivanova, Maria, *Can the Anchor Hold? Rethinking the United Nations Environment Programme for the 21st Century* (New Haven (USA): Yale Center for Environmental Law and Policy, 2005).

James Gustave Speth and Peter M. Haas, *Global Environmental Governance: Foundations of Contemporary Environmental Studies,* (Washington, D.C.: Island Press, 2006).

Johnson, P.M., K. Mayrand and M. Paquin (eds.), *Governing Global Desertification: Linking Environmental Degradation, Poverty and Participation* (Aldershot: Ashgate Publishing Limited, 2006).

Jordan, Andrew, *et al.* (eds.), *New Instruments of Environmental Governance: National Experiences and Prospects* (London: Frank Cass, 2003).

Jreisat, Jamil E., *Politics without Process: Administering Development in the Arab World* (London: Lynne Rienner Publishers, 1997).

Kamrava, Mehran, *The Modern Middle: A Political History since the First World War,* (London: University of California Press, 2005).

Keck, Margaret E., and Kathryn Sikkink, *Activists Beyond Borders: Advocacy Networks in International Politics,* (Cornell, NY: Cornell University Press, 1998).

Kemp, David D., *The Environment Dictionary* (London: Routledge, 1998).

Kemp, R., *Global Environmental Issues: A Climatological Approach* (London: Routledge, 1991).

Kiren Aziz Chaudhry, *The Price of Wealth: Economies and Institutions in the Middle East* (Ithaca, NY: Cornell University Press, 1997).

Koning, H.W., *Setting Environmental Issues and Themes* (New Delhi: APH Public Corporation, 1997).

Kooiman, Jan, ed., *Modern Governance: New Government-Society Interactions*, (New Delhi: Sage Publications, 1993).

Kumar, H.D., *Environmental Science: Economic, Social and Political Dimensions* (Delhi: Daya Publishing House, 2003).

Kutting, Gabriela, *Environment, Society and International Relations* (London: Routledge, 2000).

Leonard, Barry, ed., *International Environment: International Agreements Are Not Well Monitored,* Report to Congressional Requesters, (Darby (U.S.A.): Diane Publishing Company, 1992).

Leonard, H. Jeffrey, *Environment and the Poor: Development Strategies for a Common Agenda* (Oxford (U.K.): Transaction Books, 1989).

Levin, Simon Asher, *Encyclopedia of Biodiversity*, (London: Academic Press, 2001).

Lipschutz, Ronnie, and Judith Mayer, *Global Civil Society and Global Environmental Governance: The Politics of Nature from Place to Planet*, (New York, NY: State University of New York, 1996)

Lovan, W. Robert, *et al.*, "Participatory Governance in a Changing World" in Lovan, W. Robert, *et al., Participatory Governance: Planning, Conflict Mediation and Public Decision Making in Civil Society,* (Aldershot (UK): Ashgate Publishing Ltd., 2004).

Luck, Edward C., and Michael W. Doyle, eds., *International Law and Organisation: Closing the Compliance Gap,* (Oxford: Rowman and Littlefield Publishers, 2004).

Mainguet, Monique, *Desertification: Natural Background and Human Management,* (London: Springer, 1991)

Mairota, P., *et al.*, (eds.), *Atlas of Mediterranean Environment: The Desertification Context* (Chichester: John Wiley & Sons, 1998).

Malabed, Rizalino Noble, *Global Civil Society and the Environmental Discourse*, (Tokyo: UNU/Global Environmental Outreach Centre (GEOC), 2000).

Martin-Mehers, Gillian, *et al.*, (eds.), *Achieving Environmental Objectives,* (Cambridge (UK): IUCN (World Conservation Union), 2004).

Mayer, W.B. and Tuner II, B.L. (eds.), *Changes in Land Use and Land Cover: A Global Perspective,* (Cambridge: Cambridge University Press, 1994).

McCormick, John, *Reclaiming Paradise: The Global Environmental Movement,* (Bloomington: Indiana University Press, 1989).

Milton-Edwards, Beverley, *Contemporary Politics of the Middle East,* (Cambridge: Polity Press, 2006).

Mudacumera, Gedeon M., eds, *Sustainable Development and Administration,* (London: Taylor and Francis, 2006).

Mun, Ted, *Encyclopedia of Global Environmental Change* (Chichester: John Wiley & Sons, 2002).

Murakami, Masahiro, *Managing Water for Peace in the Middle East: Alternative Strategies* (Tokyo: United Nations University Press, 1995).

Najam, Adil, *et al.*, *Global Environmental Governance: A Reform Agenda,* (Winnipeg (Canada): International Institute for Sustainable Development (IISD), 2006).

Nierenberg, William A., *Encyclopaedia of Environmental Biology*, Vol. I, (New York: Academic Press, 1995).

Oberthiir, Sebastian, and Gehring, Thomas, eds., *Institutional Interaction in Global Environmental Governance,* (London: MIT Press, 2006).

Ortiz, Even Fontaine and Guangting Tang, *Review of the Management, Administration and Activities of the Secretariat of the United Nations Convention to Combat Desertification (UNCCD),* (Geneva: Joint Inspection Unit (United Nations), 2005).

Ortiz, Even Fontaine and Tadanori Inomata, *Assessment of the Global Mechanism of the United Nations Convention to Combat Desertification*, Report prepared by the Joint Inspection Unit, the United Nations, Geneva, 2009.

Ostrum, Vincent, *The Intellectual Crisis in American Public Administration,* (London: The University of Alabama Press, 1989).

Owen, Roger and Sevket Pamuk, *A History of Middle East Economies in the Twentieth Century,* (London: I.B. Tauris Publication, 1988).

Paehlke, Robert and Douglas Torgerson, eds., *Managing Leviathan: Environmental Politics and the Administrative State,* (Ontario: Broadview Press, 2005).

Presly, John R., *A Guide to the Saudi Arabian Economy,* (Hong Kong: Macmillan, 1984).

Rached, Eglal, and Dina Craissat, eds., *Research for Development in the Middle East and North Africa* (Ottawa: International Development Centre, 2000).

Rajan, M.G., *Global Environmental Politics* (Oxford: Oxford University Press, 1997).

Rechkemmer, Andreas, *Global Environmental Governance: the United Nations Convention to Combat Desertification,* (Berlin: Wissenschaftszentrum Berlin für Sozialforschung (WZB), 2004).

Rowland, Wade, *The Plot to Save the World*, (Toronto and Vancouver: Clarke, Irwin & Company Limited, 1973).

Ryding, Sven-Olof, *Environmental Management Handbook*, (Amsterdam: IOS Press, 1998).

Saad Eddin Ibrahim, *New Arab Social Order: A Study of the Social Impact of Oil Wealth*, (Boulder: Westview Press, 1982).

Saunier, Richard E. and Richard A. Meganck, *Dictionary and Introduction to Global Environmental Governance* (London: Earthscan, 2007).

Schrijver, Nico, *Sovereignty over Natural Resources*, (Cambridge: Cambridge University Press, 1997).

Sen, A.K. and Kar, Amal, eds., *Land Degradation and Desertification in Asia and Pacific Regions,* (Jodhpur: Scientific Publisher, 1995).

Sherbinin, Alex de, *A CIESIN Thematic Guide to Land-Use and Land-Cover Change (LUCC),* (Centre for International Earth Science Information Network (CIESIN): Columbia University, 2002).

Shine, Clare and Cyrille de Klemm, *Wetlands, Water and the Law* (Bonn: International Union for Conservation of Nature, 1999).

Speth, James Gustave, ed., *Worlds Apart: Globalization and the Environment*, (Washington, DC: Island Press, 2003).

Swanson, T., Johnston, S., *Global Environmental Problems and International Environmental Agreements: The Economics of International Institution Building*, (Edward Elgar, Northampton Mass., 1999).

Thomas, David, *Desertification and the CCD: Issues and Links to Poverty, Natural Resources and Policies* (Sheffield (U.K.): University of Sheffield, 1998).

Timagenis, G.R.J., *International Control of Marine Pollution* (New York: Ocean Publication, 1980).

Tolba, M.K., *Global Environmental Diplomacy: Negotiating Environmental Agreements for the World, 1973-1992*, (Cambridge: MIT Press, 1998).

Verma, S.K. (ed.), *Priorities of Research for Development of Arid Regions,* (Jodhpur: Scientific Publisher, 2001).

Vig, Norman J. and Michael E. Kraft, eds, *Environmental Policy: New Directions For the Twenty-First Century*, (Washington D.C.,: CQ Press: 2005).

Vig, Norman J., and Regina S. Axelrod, *The Global Environment: Institutions, Law and Policy,* (London: Earthscan, 1999).

Warren A. and Agnew C., *An Assessment of Desertification and Land Degradation in Arid and Semi-arid Areas,* (London: International Institute of Environmental Development, 1998).

Weiss, Edith Brown and Harold K Jacobson, eds., *Strengthening Compliance with International Environmental Accords,* (Cambridge: MIT Press, 2000).

Wijen, Frank Kees Zoeteman, and Jan Pieters, eds., *A Handbook of Globalisation and Environmental Policy: Interventions of National Government in a Global Arena,* (Cheltenham: Edward Elgar, 2005).

William G. Kepner, ed., *Desertification in the Mediterranean Region: A Security Issue,* (London: Springer, 2005).

Winckler, Onn, *Arab Political Economy,* (Brighton: Sussex Academic Press, 2005).

Witte, Jan Martin, Charlotte Streck, and Thorsten Benner, eds., *Progress or Peril? Partnerships and Networks in Global Environmental Governance: The Post-Johannesburg Agenda,* (Washington, D.C.: Global Public Policy Institute, 2003).

Wolfrum, Rudiger, and Nele Matz, *Conflicts in International Environmental Law* (London: Springer, 2003).

Young, Oran R., *International Governance: Protecting the Environment in a Stateless Society,* (Ithaca, New York: Cornell University Press, 1994).

Zaelke, Durwood *et al.*, (eds.), *Making Law Work: Environmental Compliance and Sustainable Development,* (London: Cameron May Ltd., International Law Publishers, 2005).

Articles

Abahussain, Asma Ali, *et al.*, "Desertification in the Arab Region: Analysis of Current Status and Trends," *Journal of Arid Environments,* vol. 51, 2002.

Abu-Laban, Baha, *et al.*, "Introduction: Development and the Arab World" in Abu-Laban, Baha, *et al.*, eds., *The Arab World: Dynamics of Development* (Leiden, the Netherlands: E.J. Brill, 1986).

Adeel, Zafar, "Overcoming One of the Greatest Environmental Challenges of Our Times: Rethinking Policies to cope with Desertification", A Policy brief based on the Joint International Conference on Desertification and the International Policy Imperative, Algiers, Algeria, 17-19 December, 2006.

Adger, W. Neil., *et al.*, "Advancing Political Ecology of Global Environmental Discourses", *Development and Change,*(Oxford), vol. 32, 2001.

Agnew, Clive and Andrew Warren, "A Framework for Tackling Drought and Land Degradation", *Journal of Arid Environments*, vol. 33, 1996.

Alagappa, Muthiah., "Environmental Governance: the Potential of Regional Organisations" in Chase, Pamela S., ed., *The Global Environment in the Twenty-First Century: Prospects for International Cooperation* (New Delhi: Mana Publication, 2004).

Al-Awaji, Ibrahim, "Bureaucracy and Development in Saudi Arabia: the Case of Local Administration" in Jabbra, Joseph G., *Bureaucracy and Development in the Arab World,* (New York: E.J. Brill, 1989).

Al-Hegelan, Abdelrahman and Palmer, Monte, "Bureaucracy and Development in Saudi Arabia", *Middle East Journal* (Washington D.C.), vol. 39, no. 1, 1985.

Ammar A. Amin, "The Extent of Desertification on Saudi Arabia" *Environmental Geology*, vol. 4, 2004.

Andrese, Steinar and Ellen Hey, "The Effectiveness and Legitimacy of International Environmental Institutions", *International Environmental Agreements*, vol. 5, 2005.

Åström, Sverker "Global Consensus or Global Catastrophe?" *Ambio*, vol. 1, no. 1,1972.

Ayubi, Nazih, "Bureaucracy as Development: Administrative Development and Development Administration in the Arab World", *International Review of Administrative Sciences* (Brussels), vol. 52, 1986.

————, "Policy Developments and Administrative Changes in the Arab World", in Dwivedi, O.P. and Hederson, Keaith M., eds., *Public Administration in World Perspective* (Ames: Iowa State University Press, 1990).

————, "Arab Bureaucracies: Expanding Size, Changing Roles" in Luciani, Giacomo, ed., *The Arab State* (London: Routledge, 1990).

————, "The Structure and Performance of Arab Administration: New Challenges; Old Constraints" in Niblock, Tim and Wilson, Rodney, eds., *The Political Economy of the Middle East,* Vol. V (Northampton (USA): Edward Elger Publisher, 1999).

Bäckstrand, Karin, "Democratizing Global Environmental Governance? Stakeholder Democracy after the World Summit on Sustainable Development", *European Journal of International Relations*, vol. 12, no. 4, 2006.

Baehr, Peter, "The Netherlands and the United Nations: the Future lies in the Past" in Alger, Chadwick F., *et al.*, (eds.), *The United Nations System: the Policies of Member States*, (Tokyo: United Nations University Press, 1995).

Baker, R., "The Administrative Trap", *The Ecologist*, vol. 6, no. 7, 1976.

————, "Institutional Innovations, Development and Environment: An Administrative Trap Revisited", *Public Administration and Development,* vol. 9, nos. 1 & 2, 1989.

Barrett, Scott, and Robert N. Stavins. "Increasing Participation and Compliance in International Climate Change Agreements," *International Environmental Agreements: Politics, Law and Economics,* vol. 3, 2003.

Bassett, Charles and Joana Talafre, "Implementing the UNCCD: Towards a Recipe for Success", *Reciel,* vol. 12, no. 2, 2003.

Bassow, Whitman, "The Third World: Changing Attitudes Toward Environmental Protection", *The ANNALS of the American Academy of Political and Social Science,* vol. 444, no. 112, 1979.

Batabyal, Amitrajeet, "On the Design of International Environmental Agreements for Identical and Heterogeneous Developing Countries", *Oxford Economic Papers,* vol. 52, 2000.

Batterbury, S.P.J., *et al.*, "Responding to Desertification at the National Scale: Detection, Explanation, and Responses", in Reynolds, J.F., and D.M. Stafford Smith, eds., *Global Desertification: Do Humans Cause Deserts?* (Dahlem University Press, 2002).

Bauer, Steffen, Per-Olof Busch and Bernd Siebenhüner, "Administering International Governance: What Role for Treaty Secretariats?," Global Governance Working Paper No. 29, (Amsterdam: Vrije Universiteit, Global Governance Project, 2006).

Bernstein, Steven, "Legitimacy in Global Environmental Governance," *Journal of International Law & International Relations* vol. 1, nos.1-2, 2005.

Bertrand Charrier, "Water, Conflict Resolution and Environmental Sustainability in the Middle East", *Arid Lands News Letters,* no. 44, 1998.

Betsill, Michele M. and H. Bulkeley, "Transnational Networks and Global Environmental Governance: The Cities for Climate Protection Programme" *International Studies Quarterly,* vol. 48, 2004.

Biermann, F., "Strengthening Green Global Governance in a Disparate World Society. Would a World Environment Organisation Benefit the South?", *International Environmental Agreements,* vol. 2, 2002.

Biermann, Frank and Klaus Dingwerth, "Global Environmental Change and the Nation State", *Global Environmental Politics,* vol. 4, no. 1, 2004.

Boere, Gerard and Douglas Taylor, "Global and Regional Governmental Policy and Treaties as tools towards the mitigation of the effect of Climate Change on Waterbirds", *Ibis* (British Ornithologists' Union), vol. 146 (suppl.1), 2004.

Boon, Emmanuel K., "Environmental Planning" in Nath, Bhaskar, ed., *Environmental Management in Practice: Instruments for Environmental Management*, (London: Routledge, 1998).

Brookfield, H.C., "Development and the Environment: Politics, Production and Pollution", *Pacific Affairs*, vol. 53, no. 4, Winter 1980-1981.

Bulkeley, Harriet, and Arthur P.J. Mol, "Participation and Environmental Governance: Consensus, Ambivalence and Debate", *Environmental Values*, vol. 12, no. 2, 2003.

Burns, W.C., "The International Convention to Combat Desertification: Drawing a Line in the Sand?," *Michigan Journal of International Law*, vol. 16, no. 3, 1995.

Caldwell, Lynton K. "Management of Resources and the Environment: A Problem in Administrative Coordination," *International Review of Administrative Sciences*, (Sage Publications Ltd), vol. 38, 1972.

Camilla Toulmin, "Combating Desertification: Encouraging Local Action within a Global Framework", in Helge Ole Bergesen and Georg Parmann, eds., *Green Globe Yearbook of International Co-operation on Environment and Development*, (Oxford: Oxford University Press, 1994).

Campbell, Tim E.J. "The Political Meaning of Stockholm: Third World Participation in the Environment Conference Process", *Stanford Journal of International Studies*, vol. 8, 1973.

Campbell, Tim, "Urban Development in the Third World: Environmental Dilemmas and the Urban Poor" in Leonard, H. Jefferey, *et al.*, (eds.), *Environment and the Poor: Development Strategies for Common Agenda*, (Oxford: Transaction Book,1989).

Carr, Susan and Roger M. Pande, "Does the Definition of Issue Matters: NGO Influence and the International Convention to Combat Desertification" in Potter, David, ed., *NGOs and Environmental Policies: Asia and Pacific*, (London: Routledge, 1996).

Cash, David W., "Distributed Assessment Systems: An Emerging Paradigm of Research, Assessment and Decision-making for Environmental Change." Belfer Centre for Science and International Affairs (BCSIA) Discussion Paper 2000-06, Kennedy School of Government, Harvard University, 2000.

Chasek, Pamela S., and Elisabeth Corell, "Addressing Desertification at the International Level: The Institutional System," in J.F. Reynolds and D.M. Stafford Smith, eds., *Global Desertification: Do Humans Cause Deserts?*, (Dahlem: Dahlem University Press, 2002).

Chasek, Pamela, "An Interim Report on the INC for the Elaboration of an International Convention to Combat Desertification", *Earth Negotiation Bulletin*, vol. 4, no. 56, 1994.

———, "The Convention to Combat Desertification: Lessons Learned for Sustainable Development", *Journal of Environment and Development*, vol. 6, no. 2, 1997.

Churchill, Robin R. and Geir Ulfstein, "Autonomous Institutional Arrangements in Multilateral Environmental Agreements: A Little-Noticed Phenomenon in International Law", *The American Journal of International Law*, vol. 94, no. 4, 2000.

Churie, Angela, "Summary of the Fourth Conference of the Parties to the Convention to Combat Desertification: 11-22 December 2000", *Earth Negotiations Bulletin*, vol. 4, no. 149, 2000.

Common, Richard, "Administrative Change in the Gulf: Modernization in Bahrain and Oman", *International Review of Administrative Sciences*, vol. 74, no. 2, 2008.

Corell, Elisabeth, "North-South Financial Tensions: Desertification after UNGASS" *Environmental Politics*, vol. 7, no. 1, 1998.

———, "Drylands Degradation-Africa's Main Environmental Challenge" in Chaytor, Beatrice and Kevin R. Gray, eds., *International Environmental Law and Policy in Africa* (London: Kluwer Academic Publishers, 2003).

Cowie, Annette, *et al.*, "Potential synergies between existing Multilateral Environmental Agreements in the implementation of land use, land-use change and forestry activities", *Environmental Science & Policy*, vol. 10, 2007.

Crossen, Teall E., "Multilateral Environmental Agreements and the Compliance Continuum", Berkeley Electronic Press, bepress Legal Series, paper 36, University of Calgary, 2003.

Darkoh, M.B.K., "The Nature, Causes and Consequences of Desertification in the Drylands of Africa", *Land Degradation & Development*, vol. 9, 1998.

———, "The Nature, Causes and Consequences of Desertification in the Drylands of Africa" in Darkoh, Michael and Apollo Rwomire, *Human Impact on Environment and Sustainable Development in Africa* (Aldershot: Ashgate Publishers, 2003).

Desai, Bharat H., "International Environmental Institutions: An Overview" in Dolzer, Rudolf and Joseph Thesing, eds., *Protecting Our Environment*, (Sankt Augustin: Konard-Adenauer-Stiftung, 2000).

———, "Revitalizing International Environmental Institutions: The UN Task Force Report and Beyond", *Indian Journal of International Law* (New Delhi), vol. 40, no. 3, 2000.

Desai, Uday, "Institutions and Environmental Policy in Developed Countries" in Desai, Uday, ed., *Environmental Politics and Policy in Industrial Countries*, (London: MIT Press, 2002).

Dietz, Thomas, *et al.*, "The Struggle to Govern the Commons", *Science*, vol. 302, 2003.

Djamchid Momtaz, "The United Nations and the Protection of the Environment: from Stockholm to Rio de Janeiro", *Political Geography*, vol. 15. no. 3/4,1996.

Downs, George W. and Michael A. Jones, "Reputation, Compliance, and International Law", *Journal of Legal Studies*, vol. 31, 2002.

Drake, Christine, "Water Resource Conflicts in the Middle East, *Journal of Geography*, (Indiana University of Pennsylvania), vol. 96, no. 1, 1997.

Dregne, H.E., Kassas, N. and Roznov, B., "A New Assessment of the World state of Desertification", *Desertification Control Bulletin*, vol. 19, 1991.

———— "Desertification: Problems and Challenges", *Annals of Arid Zone* (Jodhpur), vol. 34, no. 3, 2000.

Ecchia, Giulio and Marco Mariotti, "Coalition Formation in International Environmental Agreements and the Role of Institutions", University of Bologna, Bologna, Italy, 1997.

Ehteshami, Anoushiravan., "Reform from Above: the Politics of Participation in the Oil Monarchies", *International Affairs* (Blackwell Publishers, Oxford), vol. 79, 2003.

El-Sherbini, A.A., "Recent Trends in Agricultural Development in the Middle East" in Kedourie, Elie and Sylvia G. Haim, eds. *Economic History of the Middle East,* (London: Frank Cass, 1988).

El-Tantawi, Attia Mahmoud Mohamed, "Climate Change in Libya and Desertification of Jifara Plain: Using Geographical Information System and Remote Sensing Techniques," Dissertation submitted in der Johannes Gutenberg-Universität in Mainz (Germany), 2005.

Esty, Daniel C. and Maria H. Ivanova, "Revitalising Global Environmental Governance: A New Function-Driven Approach" in Esty, Daniel, *et al.*, *Global Environmental Institutions: Perspectives on Reform* (London: Royal Institute of International Affairs, 2002).

Ewalt, Jo Ann G., "Alternative Governance Structures of Welfare Provider Networks" in Ingraham, Patricia W. and Lawrence E. Lynn, Jr., eds., *The Art of Governance: Analyzing Management and Administration,* (Washington D.C.: Gorgetown University Press, 2004).

Farazmand, Ali, "Globalisation and Governance: A Theoretical Analysis" in Farazmand, Ali, ed., *Sound Governance: Policy and Administrative Innovations* (Westport: Praeger, 2004).

Faruqi, Atiq Ahmad and Afrazul Hasan, "Oil Development in the Gulf", *Political Science Review*, vol. 22, no. 4, 1983.

Fasano, Ugo and Zubair Iqbal, "GCC Countries: From Oil Dependence to Diversification", International Monetary Fund Working Paper, (Washington: IMF, 2003).

Fathaly, Omar and Chackerain, Richard, "Administration: The Forgotten Issue in Arab Development" in Ibrahim, I., ed., *Arab Resources: The Transformation of a Society,* (London: Croom Helm, 1983).

Fisher, Dana R. and Jessica F. Green, Understanding Disenfranchisement: Civil Society and Developing Countries' Influence and Participation in Global Governance for Sustainable Development, *Global Environmental Politics*, vol. 4, no. 3, 2004.

Fitzpatrick, Donald, "The United Nations General Assembly and the Security Council" in Werksman, Jacob, ed., *Greening International Institutions*, (London: Earthscan, 1996).

French, Duncan, "Developing States and International Environmental Law: The Importance of Differentiated Responsibilities," *International and Comparative Law Quarterly*, vol. 49, 2000.

Fuller, Stephan, *Towards A Bahrain National Report to the Convention on Biolocial Diversity,* Prepared for the General Directorate of Environment and Wildlife Protection, Bahrain and United Nations Development Programme, Bahrain Country Office, (Manama, 2005).

Giacomo Luciani, 'The Oil rent, the Fiscal Crisis of the State and Democratization', in Ghassan Salame, ed., *Democracy without Democrats: the Renewal of Politics in the Muslim World* (London: I.B. Tauris, 1994).

———— 'Resources, revenues, and authoritarianism in the Arab world: beyond the rentier state?', in Rex Brynen, Bahgat Korany and Paul Noble, eds., *Political Liberalization and Democratization in the Arab World: Theoretical Perspectives* (Boulder, CO: Lynne Rienner, 1995).

Giannini, Alessandra, "A Climate Model-based Review of Drought in the Sahel: Desertification, the Re-greening and Climate Change", *Global and Planetary Change*, vol. 64, 2008.

Gisladottir, G. and M. Stocking, "Land Degradation Control and Its Global Environmental Benefits", *Land Degradation & Development,* vol. 16, 2005.

Glantz, M.H., and Orlousky, N., "Desertification: A Review of the Concept", *Desertification Control Bulletin*, no. 3, 1983.

Glenn E., *et al.*, "On Our Failure to Control Desertification: Implications for Global Change Issues, and a Research Agenda for the Future", *Environmental Science and Policy,* vol. 1, 1998.

Grainger, Alan, *et al.*, "Desertification and Climate Change: The Case for Greater Convergence", *Mitigation and Adaptation Strategies for Global Change*, vol. 5, 2000.

Hamid Mohtadi, "Environmentally Sustainable Development in the Middle East and North Africa" in Nemat Shafik, ed., *Prospects For Middle Eastern North African Economies: From Boom to Bust and Back?,* (Houndmills: Macmillan,1998).

Hans, Kenneth, "Implementing International Environmental Policies" in Blowers, Andrew and Pieter Glasberger, eds., *Environment Policy in an International Context,* (London: Arnold, 1996).

Harashima, Yohei, "Environmental Governance in Selected Asian Developing Countries", *International Review for Environmental Strategies,* vol. 1, no. 1, 2000.

Hartshorw, G.S., "Key Environmental Issues for Developing Countries", *Journal of International Affairs,* (Columbia University), vol. 44, no. 2, 1991.

Haas, Peter M., "Addressing the Global Governance Deficit," *Global Environmental Politics,* vol. 4, no. 4, 2004.

Herrmann, S.M., and C.F. Hutchinson, "The Changing Contexts of the Desertification Debate," *Journal of Arid Environments,* vol. 63, 2005.

Holtz, Uwe, "The United Nations Convention to Combat Desertification (UNCCD) and its Political Dimension", Paper was prepared for the fifth Parliamentary Round Table in the Context of the Implementation of the United Nations Convention to Combat Desertification (UNCCD), (Bonn, 26th May, 2003).

Humphreys, David and Susan Carr, "Land Degradation and Sustainable Resource Management in an African Context" in Thomas, Alan, *et al.*, eds., *Environmental Policies and NGO Influence: Land Degradation and Sustainable Resource Management in Sub-Saharan Africa* (London: Routledge, 2001).

Israel, Arturo, "The Changing Role of the State in Development", *Finance and Development,* (Washington D.C.), June 1991.

Issawi, Charles, "Growth and Structural Change in the Middle East", *The Middle East Journal,* vol. 25, no. 3, 1971.

Ivanova, Maria "Designing the United Nations Environment Programme: A Story of Compromise and Confrontation," *International Environmental Agreements: Politics, Economics and Law,* vol. 7, no. 3, 2007.

————, "Environmental Crime and Punishment in Russia: Law as Reason for Breach", in Biermann, Frank, *et al.*, eds., *Global Environmental Change and the Nation State,* (Potsdam, Germany: Potsdam Institute for Climate Impact Research, 2002).

Ivanova, Maria and Jennifer Roy, "The Architecture of Global Environmental Governance: Pros and Cons of Multiplicity" in Swart, Lydia and Estelle Perry, *Global Environmental Governance: Perspectives on Current Debates,* (New York: Centre for UN Reform, 2007).

Jabbra, Joseph G. and Nancy W. Jabbra, "Governmental Response to Environmental Challenges in the Middle East" in Jebbra, Joseph and O.P. Dwivedi, eds., *Governmental Response to Environmental Challenges in Global Perspective,* (Oxford: OIS Press, 1998).

Jacobson, Harold and Edith Brown Weiss, "Compliance with International Environmental Accords: Achievements and Strategies" in Rolen, Mats, *et al.*, eds., *International Governance on Environmental Issues,* (London: Kluwer Academic Publishers, 1997).

Jagt Juliette, Van Der, "Elaborating an International Compliance Regime under the Kyoto Protocol" in Ierland, Ekko C. Van, *et al.*, (eds.), *Issues in International Climate Policy: Theory and Practice* (Chelterham (U.K.): Edward Elgar, 2003).

Jamal, Alia, "The United Nations Convention to Combat Desertification in those Countries Experiencing Serious Drought and/or Desertification, Particularly in Africa: Implementing Agenda 21", *Reciel*, vol. 6, no. 1, 1997.

Jänicke, Martin, "No Withering Away of the Nation State: Ten Theses on Environmental Policy", in Biermann, Frank, Rainer Brohm and Klaus Dingwerth, eds., *Global Environmental Change and the Nation State,* (Potsdam, Germany: Potsdam Institute for Climate Impact Research, 2002).

Johnels, A., "Conference on Environmental Resources and Management for the 1980s", *Ambio*, vol. 12, no. 1, 1983.

Jokela, Minna, "European Union as a Global Policy Actor: The Case of Desertification" in Biermann, Frank, Rainer Brohm and Klaus Dingwerth, eds., *Global Environmental Change and the Nation State,* (Potsdam, Germany: Potsdam Institute for Climate Impact Research, 2002).

Jones, Tom, "Policy Coherence, Global Environmental Governance, and Poverty Reduction", *International Environmental Agreements: Politics, Law and Economics*, vol. 2, 2002.

Jreisat, Jamil, "Managing National Development in the Arab States", *Arab Studies Quarterly,* (Association of Arab-American University Graduates, New York), vol. 14, nos. 2/3, 1992.

———, "Bureaucratization of Arab World: Incomplete Influence" in Farazmand, Ali, ed., *Handbook of Comparative and Development Public Administration,* (New York: Marcel, Dekker, 2001).

———, "The Predicament of Administrative Reform in the Arab States" in Farazmand, Ali, *Administrative Reform in Developing Nations*, (London: Praeger, 2002).

Juma, C., "The Global Sustainability Challenge: from Agreement to Action", *International Journal of Global Environmental Issues*, vol. 2, no. 1/2, 2002.

Kalbermatten, Grégoire de "Reviewing the Options", in UNCCD, *The Role of Governance in Combating Desertification,* (Bonn: UNCCD Secretariat, 2006).

Kamal al-Sayyid, Mustapha, "The Concept of Civil Society and the Arab World" in Brynen, Rex, *et al.*, (eds.), *Political Liberalization and Democratization in the Arab World,* (London: Lynne Rienner Publishers, 1995).

Kamieniecki, Sheldom, "Emerging Forces in Global Environmental Politics" In: Kamieniecki, Sheldom, ed., *Environmental Politics in the International Arena: Movements, Organizations and Parties* (Albany: State University of New York Press, 1993).

Kamrava, Mehran and Mora, Frank, 'Civil Society and Democratisation in Comparative Perspective: Latin America and the Middle East', *Third World Quarterly*, vol. 19, no. 5, 1998.

Kaniaru, Donald and Lal Kurukulasurya, "Capacity Building in Environmental Law" in Lin, Sun, ed., *UNEP's New Way Forward: Environmental Law and Sustainable Development* (Nairobi: UNEP, 1995).

Karkkainen, Bradley C., "Post-Sovereign Environmental Governance: The Collaborative Problem-Solving Model" in Biermann, Frank, *et al.*, (eds.), *Global Environmental Change and the Nation State*, (Potsdam, Germany: Potsdam Institute for Climate Impact Research, 2002).

Kassas, M., "Negotiations for the International Convention to Combating Desertification (1993-1994)", *International Environmental Affairs*, vol. 7, no. 2, 1995.

Kassas, M., "Desertification: A General Review", *Journal of Arid Environments*, vol. 30, 1995.

Katyal, Jagdish C. and Paul L.G. Vlek, "Desertification: Concept, Causes and Amelioration", Discussion Papers on Development Policy, Centre for Development Research, Bonn, October 2000.

Kelly, Michael J., "Overcoming obstacles to the Effective Implementation of International Environmental Agreements", *Georgetown International Environmental Review*, vol. 9, 1997.

Kelsey, Elin, "Implications of the Nation-State System on Public Involvement in Environmental Problem-Solving" in Biermann, Frank, Rainer Brohm and Klaus Dingwerth, eds., *Global Environmental Change and the Nation State*, (Potsdam, Germany: Potsdam Institute for Climate Impact Research, 2002).

Kimball, L.A., 'Institutional Linkages between the Convention on Biological Diversity and Other International Conventions', *Reciel,* vol. 6, no. 3, 1997.

Kjellen, Bo., "The Desertification Convention: Towards creating a Multilateral Framework for Coping with Global Threats" in Rolen, Mats, *et al.*, (eds)., *International Governance on Environmental Issues,* (London: Kluwer Academic Publishers, 1997).

Kjellën, Bo., "The Saga of the Convention to Combat Desertification: the Rio/Johannesburg Process and the Global Responsibility for the Drylands", *Reciel*, vol. 12, no. 2, 20.

Kline, Karen and Kal Raustiala, "International Environmental Agreements and Remote Sensing Technologies", Background paper prepared for the Workshop on Remote Sensing and Environmental Treaties: Building More Effective Linkages, 4-5 December 2000, sponsored by the Centre for International Earth Science Information Network, Columbia University, New York.

Knauerhase, Ramon "The Oil Producing Middle East States" *Current History,* (Philadelphia), vol. 76, no. 443, 1979.

Knill, Christoph and Andrea Lenschow, "Introduction: New Approaches to reach Effective Implementation: Political Rhetoric or Sound Concepts?" in Knill, Christoph and Andrea Lenschow, eds., *Implementing EU Environmental Policy: New Direction and Old Problems* (New York, Manchester University Press, 2000).

Kooiman, Jan, "Social-Political Governance: Introduction" in Kooiman, J., ed., *Modern Governance: New Government-Society Interactions,* (New Delhi: Sage Publications, 1993).

Krasnova, Irina O., "Post-Rio Treaties: Implementation Challenges", *Pace Environmental Law Review,* vol. 13, no. 1, 1995.

Lamprey, H.F., *Report on the Desert Encroachment Reconnaissance in Northern Sudan, 21 October to 10 November 1975,* Report of 1975 published as an article in 1988 in *Desertification Control Bulletin,* vol. 17, 1975.

Lavranos, N., 'Multilateral Environmental Agreements: Who Makes the Binding Decisions?,' *European Environmental Law Review,* vol. 11, no. 2, 2002.

Le Hou'erou, Henry N. "Climate change, drought and desertification", *Journal of Arid Environments,* vol. 34, 1996.

Lemos, Maria Carmen and Arun Agrawal, "Environmental Governance," *Annual Review of Environment Resources,* vol. 31, 2006.

Lucas, Russell, "Monarchical Authoritarianism: Survival and Political Liberalization in a Middle Eastern Regime Type", *International Journal of Middle East Studies,* (Cambridge), vol. 36, no. 1, 2004.

Makdisi, Karim and Carol Chouchani Cherfane, "Southern Agenda on Trade and Environment Phase II: Arab Region", Resource Paper, (Winnipeg (Canada): International Institute for Sustainable Development, 2005).

Mandel, Jenny, "Summary of the Fifth Conference of the Parties to the Convention to Combat Desertification: 1-13 October 2001", *Earth Negotiations Bulletin,* vol. 4, no. 160, 2001.

Mann, M.S., Desertification: An Overview", *Annals of Arid Zone* (Jodhpur), vol. 17, no. 3, 1977, pp. 1-3.

Marauhn, Thilo, "The Changing Role of State" in Bodansky, Daniel, *et al.*, (eds.), *The Oxford Handbook of International Environmental Law* (Oxford: Oxford University Press, 2007).

Mark, Allan Gray, "The United Nations Environment Programme: An Assessment", *Journal Environmental Law*, (Oxford University Press), vol. 20, no. 2, 1990.

Martello, Marybeth Long, 'Expert Advice and Desertification Policy: Past Experience and Current Challenges", *Global Environmental Politics*, vol. 4, no. 3, 2004.

Mahmoud H. Fouad, "Petrodollars and Economic Development in the Middle East", *The Middle East Journal,* vol. 32, no. 3, 1978, p. 307.

Mayrand, Karel, *et al.* "Agricultural Trade Liberalization, Poverty, and Desertification in Rural Drylands: The Role of UNCCD", (Unisféra International Centre, 2005).

McDonagh, John and Yuelai Lu, "Success Stories in Reversing Land Degradation and the Role of UNCCD," Technical Paper 2 produced for UK Department for International Development (DFID), (University of East Anglia: Overseas Development Group, 2007).

Meadowcroft, James., "From Welfare State to Ecostate" in Barry, John and Robyn Eckersle,. eds., *The State and the Global Ecological Crisis*, (Cambridge: MIT Press, 2005).

Mische, Patricia M., *et al.*, "Ecological Security and the United Nations System", in Alger, Chadwick F., *The Future of the United Nations System: Potential for the Twenty-First Century,* (Tokyo: United Nations University Press, 1998).

Momtaz, Djamchid, "The United Nations and the Protection of the Environment: from Stockholm to Rio de Janeiro, *Political Geography*, vol. 15, nos. 3/4, 1996.

Mortimore, M., "Shifting Sands and Human Sorrow: Social Response to Drought and Desertification", *Desertification Control Bulletin*, vol. 14, 1987.

Munro, R.D., "Environmental Resources and Management for the 1980s", *Ambio*, vol. 12, no. 1, 1983.

Najam, Adil, "An Environmental Negotiation Strategy for the South", *International Environmental Affairs,* vol. 7, no. 3, 1995.

Najam, Adil, and Nick Robins, "Seizing the Future: The South, Sustainable Development and International Trade". *International Affairs*, vol. 77, no. 1, 2001.

Najam, Adil, "Dynamics of the Southern Collective: Developing Countries in Desertification Negotiations", *Global Environmental Politics* (Massachusetts Institute of Technology), vol. 4, no. 3, 2004.

Najam, Adil, "Developing Countries and Global Environmental Governance: From Contestation to Participation to Engagement," *International Environmental Agreements: Law, Politics and Economics* (SpringerLink), vol. 5, 2005.

————, "The Case Against GEO, WEO, or Whatever-else-EO", in Esty, Daniel, *et al.*, *Global Environmental Institutions: Perspectives on Reform* (London: Royal Institute of International Affairs, 2002).

————, "The View from the South: Developing Countries in Global Environmental Politics" in Regina S. *et al.*, (eds.), *Global Environmental Policy: Institutions, Law and Policy*, (Washington D.C.: CQ Press, 2004).

————, *et al.*, "The Emergent "System" of Global Environmental Governance", *Global Environmental Politics*, vol. 4, no. 4, 2004.

————, "Unravelling of the Rio Bargain", *Politics and the Life Sciences*, vol. 21, no. 2, 2002.

Nasr, M., "Assessing Desertification and Water Harvesting in the Middle East and North Africa: Policy Implications", Policy Paper no. 10, Centre for Development Research, Bonn University, Germany, 1999.

Nicholson, S.E. *et al.*, "Desertification, Drought, and Surface Vegetation: An Example from the West African Sahel," *Bulletin of the American Meteorological Society*, vol. 79, no. 5, 1998.

Nielsen, T.T. and H.K. Adriansen, "Government Policies and Land Degradation in the Middle East", *Land Degradation & Development*, vol. 16, 2005.

Odingo, R.S., "The Definition of Desertification and its Programmatic Consequences for UNEP and the International Community", *Desertification Control Bulletin,* vol. 18, 1991.

————, "Review of UNEP's Definition of Desertification and its Programmatic Implications", in Odingo R., ed., *Desertification Revisited: Proceeding of an Ad-Hoc Consultative Meeting on the Assessment of Desertification*, (Nairobi: UNEP, 1990).

Onchere, Naftali Maddy, "The United Nations Convention to Combat Desertification in Eastern Africa" In: Arnalds, Olafur and Steve Archer, eds., *Rangeland Desertification* (London: Springer, 1999).

Ostrum, Vincent and Ostrum, Elinor, "Public Choice: A Different Approach to Study of Public Administration", *Public Administrative Review* (Washington D.C.), vol. 31, 1971.

Ottinger, Richard L., "Legislation and the Environment: Individual Rights and Government Accountability", *Pace Law Faculty Publications*, Paper 538, 1970.

Oza, G.M., "Towards an Effective and Operational International Convention on Desertification," *Environmental Awareness,* vol. 7, no. 4, 1984.

Pagaza, Ignacio Pichardo, "Environmental Protection and Public Administration in Latin America", *International Review of Administrative Sciences,* vol. 72, no. 1, 2006.

Perkins, Richard and Eric Neumayer, "Implementing Multilateral Environmental Agreements: An Analysis of EU Directives", *Global Environmental Politics* (MIT Press), vol. 7, no. 3, 2007.

Persson, Linn, *et al.*, "Multilateral Environmental Agreements on the Ground—Lessons from Supporting Implementation of the Montreal Protocol", Policy & Institutions Programme-Working Paper, Stockholm Environment Institute, Stockholm, 2007.

Peterson, J.E., "The Arab Gulf States: Further Steps towards Political Participation", GRC Gulf papers series, Gulf Research Centre, Dubai, 2006.

Raustiala, Kal, "States, NGOs and International Environmental Institutions", *International Studies Quarterly,* vol. 41, 1997.

Raustiala, Kal and Anne-Marie Slaughter, "International Law, International Relations and Compliance", in Carlsnaes, Walter, *et al.*, (eds.), *Handbook of International Relations* (London: Sage Publications, 2002).

Redcliff, M., "A Framework for Improving Environment Management: Beyond Market Mchanism", *World Development,* (London), vol. 20, 1992.

Renner, Michael, "Environmental Security: the Policy Agenda", *Conflict, Security & Development*, vol. 4, no. 3, 2004.

Richards, J.F., "Land Transformation", in Turner, B.L., *et al.*, (eds.), *The Earth as Transformed by Human Action* (Cambridge, UK: Cambridge University Press, 1990).

Roberts J. Timmons, *et al.*, "Who Ratifies Environmental Treaties and Why? Institutionalism, Structuralism and Participation by 192 Nations in 22 Treaties", *Global Environmental Politics*, vol. 4, no. 3, August 2004.

Rosenau, J.N., "Governance, Order, and Change in World Politics" in Rosenau, James N. and Ernst-Otto Czempiel, eds., *Governance without Government: Order and Change in World Politics*, (Cambridge: Cambridge University Press, 1992).

Roy, Delwin A., "Management Education and Training in the Arab World: A Review of Issues and Problems", *International Review of Administrative Sciences*, vol. 43, 1977.

Sampford, Charles, "Environmental Governance for Biodiversity", *Environmental Science and Policy*, vol. 5, 2002.

Sand, "Environment: Nature Conservation" in Managing P. Simmons and C. Oudraat, eds., *Global Issues: Lessons Learned*, (Washington, DC: Carnegie Endowment for International Peace, 2001).

Sand, Peter H., "The Evolution of International Environmental Law" in Bodansky, Daniel, *et al.*, (eds.), *The Oxford Handbook of International Environmental Law* (Oxford: Oxford University Press, 2007).

————, "International Environmental Law after Rio", *European Journal of International Law*, vol. 4, no. 1, 1993.

Sandford, Rosemary, "International Environmental Treaty Secretariats: Stage-Hands or Actors?", in Helge Ole Bergesen and Georg Parmann, eds., *Green Globe Yearbook of International Co-operation on Environment and Development 1994* (Oxford: Oxford University Press, 1994).

Sathaye, J., *et al.*, "Sustainable Development and Mitigation", in Metz, B. *et al.*, (eds.), *Climate Change 2007: Mitigation, Contribution of Working Group III to the Fourth Assessment Report of the Intergovernmental Panel on Climate Change* (Cambridge: Cambridge University Press, 2007).

Sayigh, Yosif A., "Problems and Prospects of Development in the Arabian Peninsula", *International Journal of Middle East Studies*, vol. 2, no. 1, 1971.

Scoging, H., "Desertification and its Management", in Bennet, R., and Estall, R., eds., *Global Change and Challenges: Geography for the 1990s* (London: Rutledge, 1991).

Segger, Marie-Claire Cordonier, "Significant Developments in Sustainable Development Law and Governance: A Proposal", *Natural Research Forum*, vol. 28, 2004.

Selin, Henrik and Björn-Ola Linnér, "The Quest for Global Sustainability: International Efforts on Linking Environment and Development," Working Paper No. 5, Centre for International Development, Harvard University, 2005.

Seong-lin Na and Hyun Song Shinf, "International Environmental Agreements under Uncertainty", *Oxford Economic Papers*, vol. 50, 1998.

Simmons, Beth A., "Compliance with International Agreements", *Annual Review of Political Science*, vol. 1, 1998.

Sivakumar, M.V.K., *et al.*, "Agrometeorology and Sustainable Agriculture", *Agricultural and Forest Meteorology,* vol. 103, 2000.

Sjoberg, Helen, "The Challenge of Global Environmental Governance" in Rolen, Mats, *et al.*, eds., *International Governance on Environmental Issues*. (Dordrecht, the Netherlands: Kluwer Academic Press, 1997).

Snider, Lewis W., "Comparing the Strength of Nations: The Arab Gulf States and Political Change," *Comparative Politics*, vol. 20, no. 4, 1988.

Steiner, Achim, *et al.*, "Global governance for the environment and the role of Multilateral Environmental Agreements in conservation", *Oryx,* vol. 37 no. 2, 2003.

Steinar Andresen and Ellen Hey, "The Effectiveness and Legitimacy of International Environmental Institutions" *International Environmental Agreements*, vol. 5, 2005.

Stringer, Lindsay C., *et al.*, "Implementing the UNCCD: Participatory challenges", *Natural Resources Forum*, vol. 31, 2007.

Strong, Maurice, "One Year after Stockholm: An Ecological Approach to Management", *Foreign Affairs*, vol. 51, no. 4, 1973.

Symeonakis, E. and N. Drake, "Monitoring desertification and land degradation over sub-Saharan Africa," *International Journal of Remote Sensing*, vol. 25, no. 3, 2004.

Thomas, Alan, "NGOs and their Influence on Environmental Policies in Africa: A Framework" in Thomas, Alan *et al.*, eds., *Environmental Policies and NGOs' Influence* (London: Routledge, 2001).

Thomas, David S.G., "Science and the Desertification Debate", *Journal of Arid Environments,* vol. 37, 1997.

Toulmin, Camilla, "The Desertification Convention" in Dodds, Felix, ed., *The Way Forward: Beyond Agenda 21* (London: Earthscan, 1997).

United Nations Non-Governmental Liaison Service, "The International Convention to Combat Desertification in Countries Experiencing Serious Drought and/or Desertification, Particularly in Africa", *The Sustainable Development Treaty Series,* vol. I, no. 1, 1994.

Untawale, Mukund G., "Global Environmental Degradation and International Organizations", *International Political Science Review*, vol. 11, no. 3, 1990.

Vero´n, S.R. *et al.*, "Assessing Desertification", *Journal of Arid Environments*, vol. 66, 2006.

Vogler, John and Andrew Jordan, "Governance and Environment" in Berkhout, Frans, *et al.*, eds., *Negotiating Environmental Change: New Perspectives from Social Science* (Cheltenham, JK: Edward Elger, 2003).

Wang, Xunming, *et al.*, "The Relative Role of Climatic and Human factors in Desertification in semi-arid China." *Global Environmental Change*, vol. 16, 2006.

Wiersema, Annecoos, "The New International Law-Makers? Conferences of the Parties to Multilateral Environmental Agreements", *Michigan Journal of International Law*, vol. 31, no. 231, 2009.

Williams, Martin A.J., "Interactions of desertification and climate: Present understanding and future research imperatives", *Arid Lands News Letter*, vol. 49, May/June 2001.

Winckler, Onn, "The Demographic Dilemma of the Arab World: the Employment Aspect", *Journal of Contemporary History*, vol. 37, no. 4, 2002.

Winslow, M., *et al.*, "Desertification, Drought, Poverty and Agriculture: Research Lessons and Opportunities", (Aleppo, Syria: Centre for Agricultural Research in the Dry Areas, (ICARDA), 2004).

Yencken, David, Governance for Sustainability", *Australian Journal of Public Administration,* vol. 61, no. 2, 2002.
Young, Oran R., "Environmental Governance: The Role of Institutions in Causing and Confronting Environmental Problems", *International Environmental Agreements: Politics, Law and Economics,* vol. 3, 2003.
Zeidler, Juliane and Kalemani Jo Mulongoy, "The Dry and Sub-humid Lands Programme of Work of the Convention of Biological Diversity: Connecting the CBD and UN Convention to Combat Desertification", *Receil,* vol. 12, no. 2, 2003.
Zhao, Jimin, "Implementing International Environmental Treaties in Developing Countries: China's Compliance with the Montreal Protocol", *Global Environmental Politics,* vol. 5, no. 1, 2005.
Zoeteman, Kees and Eric Harkink, "Collaboration of National Governments and Global Corporations in Environmental Management" in Wijen, Frank, *et al.*, (eds.), *A Handbook of Globalisation and Environment Policy: National Government Intervening in a Global Arena,* (Cheltenham: Edward Elgar Publishing, 2005).

Internet Sources

"Arabs against UN Regional Centre that includes Israel", *Bahrain Tribune,* 6th December, 2007, [Online: web] Accessed on 23rd June, 2008 URL: http://www.bahraintribune.com/ArticleDetail.asp.
"Arab World urged to strive for Technological Edge", *Bahrain Tribune,* 23rd September, 2003, [Online: web] Accessed on 23rd June, 2008 URL: http://www.bahraintribune.com/ArticleDetail.asp.
"Call for investment in Water Research: Move ensures Sustainability in Future", *Bahrain Tribune,* 18th October, 2004, [Online: web] Accessed on 23rd June, 2008 URL: http://www.bahraintribune.com/ArticleDetail.asp
"Bahraini Women urged to preserve Environment", *Bahrain Tribune,* 17th March, 2004, [Online: web] Accessed on 23rd June, 2008 URL: http://www.bahraintribune.com/ArticleDetail.asp
"Camel farms Proposed to stop Desertification", *Bahrain Tribune,* 29th September, 2007, [Online: web] Accessed on 23rd June, 2008 URL: http://www.bahraintribune.com/ArticleDetail.asp
"Capital, N. Emirates get rain, artificially", *Knaleej Times,* 2nd May, 2005, [Online: web] Accessed on 23rd June, 2008 URL: http://www.khaleejtimes.com/DisplayArticle.asp?xfile=data/theuae/2005/May/theuae_May38.xml&section=theuae.
"GCC Environment Centre agreed," *Khaleej Times,* 26th May, 2005, [Online: web] Accessed on 23rd June, 2008 URL:http://

www.khaleejtimes.comDisplayArticleNew.asp?section=theuae&xfile=data/theuae/2005/may/theuae_may738.xml.

"Grand Railway Network Project for GCC mooted," *Khaleej Times*, 5th August, 2007, [Online: web] Accessed on 23rd June, 2008 URL:http://www.khaleejtimes.com/DisplayArticleNew.asp?section=theuae&xfile=data/theuae/2007/august/theuae_august114.xml.

"Kingdom to End Wheat Growing" *Arab News*, 9th January, 2008, [Online: web] Accessed on 23rd June, 2008 URL:http://www.arabnews.com? page=6&section=0&article=105447&d=9&m=1&y=2008. "New Technology used to save Water in Capital," *Khaleej Times*, 15th September, 2006, [Online: web] Accessed on 23rd June, 2008 URL: http://www.khaleejtimes.com DisplayArticleNew.asp?section=theuae&xfile=data/theuae/2006/september/theuae_september 475.xml.

"Police on alert for Environmental Danger", *Gulf News*, 17th February, 2008, [Online: web] Accessed on 23rd June, 2008 URL: http://www.gulfnews.com/nation/Environment/10190420.html

"Qatar to set up first Camel Farm", *Bahrain Tribune*, 2nd December, 2007, [Online: web] Accessed on 23rd June, 2008 URL: http://www.bahraintribune.com/ArticleDetail.asp.

"Railway Network will help boost GCC Development," *Bahrain Tribune*, 24th July, 2005, [Online: web] Accessed on 23rd June, 2008 URL: http://www.bahraintribune.com/ArticleDetail.asp.

"Role of Youth in Eco Protection to be highlighted", *Bahrain Tribune*, 9th September, 2004, [Online: web] Accessed on 23rd June, 2008 URL: http://www.bahraintribune.com/ArticleDetail.asp accessed on 24th June, 2008.

"Saudi Arabia Plans to Import Wheat" *Arab News*, 29th January, 2008, [Online: web] Accessed on 23rd June, 2008 URL: http://www.arabnews.com/?page=6&section=0&article=106225&d=29&m=1&y=2008.

"Saudi Arabia: Going With the Grain", *Arab Finance*, 19th May, 2008 [Online: web] Accessed on 23rd June, 2008 URL: https://www.arabfinance.com/news/DefaultDetails.aspx?Id=5949&Type=Commentary.

Sustainable Agriculture in Developing Countries", *Bio.org* [Online: web] Accessed on 23rd June, 2008 URL:http://www.bio.org/foodag/background/developingc.asp

Arrackal, Alexander M., "Environment to hold the Stage: Shura discusses Comprehensive Bill today", *The Bahrain Tribune*, 4th February, 2008, [Online: web] Accessed on 23rd June, 2008 URL: http://www.bahraintribune.com/ArticleDetail.asp.

Abdurabb, K.T., "UAE Focuses on Reducing the Use of Groundwater," *Arab News,* 22 August 2007, [Online: web] Accessed on 23rd June, 2008 URL:http://www.arabnews.com/?page=4&section=0&article=100281&d=22&m=8&y=2007.

————, "UAE Ministry of Energy Unveils Strategic Plan", *Arab News*, 2nd August, 2007, [Online: web] Accessed on 23rd June, 2008 URLhttp://www.arabnews.com/?page=6&section=0&article=99216&d=2&m=8&y=2007, accessed on 24th June, 2008.

Al-Ghalib, Essam, "Workshop Discusses Desert Greening," *Arab News*, 18th September, 2003 [Online: web] Accessed on 23rd June, 2008 URL: http://www.arabnews.com/?page=1&section=0&article=32149&d=18&m=9&y=2003

Al-Mazroei, Faiz, "Kingdom Encourages Use of High-Tech on Climate Change," *Arab News*, 29th January, 2008, [Online: web] Accessed on 23rd June, 2008 URL: http://www.arabnews.com/?page=6&section=0&article=106207&d=29&m=1&y=2008.

Ali Khan, M. Ghazanfar, "Project Under Way to Induce Artificial Rains Nationwide", *Arab News*, 22nd August, 2005,[Online: web] Accessed on 23rd June, 2008 URL: http://www.arabnews.com/?page=1&section= 0&article=68806&d=22&m=8&y=2005

Ali, Muniza, "Education & Awareness Can Help Boost Conservation" *Arab News*, 2nd July, 2003, [Online: web] Accessed on 23rd June, 2008 URL:http://www.arabnews.com/?page=1&section=0&article=28266&d=2&m=7&y=2003

Al Serkal, Mariam M., "Sharjah to Promote Sustainable Use of Water and Energy", *Gulf News*, 4th March, 2008, [Online: web] Accessed on 23rd June, 2008 URL: http://www.gulfnews.com/nation/environment/10194758.html.

Arab Centre for the Studies of Arid Zones and Dry Lands (ACSAD), [Online: web] Accessed on 23rd June, 2008 URL: http://www.acsad.org/aboutACSAD.htm.

Arab Organisation for Agriculture Development (AOAD), [Online: web] Accessed on 23rd June, 2008 URL: http://www.aoad.org/about_en.htm.

Arunmas, Phusadee, "Saudi Arabia looking to invest in Rice", *Bangkok Post*, 16th May, 2008 [Online: web] Accessed on 23rd June, 2008 URL: http://www.bangkokpost.com/160508_Business/16th May, 2008_biz34.php.

Ashour, Ahmed Sakr, "Development-Driven Public Governance Reform in the Arab Countries", Conceptual Paper (Draft), 2005, [Online: web] Accessed on 23rd June, 2008 URL: http://www.arabgov-initiative.org/publications/egov/admin-reform-e.pdf

Bibbo, Barbara, "GCC Plans for Green Development", *Gulf News* (Dubai), 29th December, 2007[Online: web] Accessed on 23rd June, 2008 URL: http://archive.gulfnews.com/articles/07/12/29/10177981.html.

————, "Green Public Transport System comes to Qatar in Regional First" *Gulf News*, 03rd March, 2008, [Online: web] Accessed on 23rd June, 2008 URL: http://www.gulfnews.com/news/gulf/qatar/10194692.html.

Centre for Environment and Development in the Arab Region and Europe (CEDARE), [Online: web] Accessed on 23rd June, 2008 URL: http://land.cedare.int/

England, Andrew, "Saudis Plan to grow Crops Overseas," *Financial Times*, 13th June, 2008 [Online: web] Accessed on 16th June, 2008 URL: http://www.bilaterals.org/article.php3?id_article=12416

ESCWA, *The Role of ESCWA in Resources Conservation and Management and the Combat of Desertification*, [Online: web] Accessed on 23rd June, 2008 URL: http://www.fao.org/docrep/x5322e/x5322e00.HTM.

Esty, Daniel C., *et al.*, "Environmental Sustainability in the Arab World" [Online: web] Accessed on 20th June, 2008 URL:http://www.yemenembassy.org/economic/Reports/WEF/Page_236_248 Environment.pdf.

Global Forest Watch. "Frequently Asked Questions" [Online: web] Accessed on 23rd June, 2008 URL:http:/ www.globalforestwatch.org/english/faqs.html

Global Mechanism, "Sustainable Arid Land Management Programme" [Online: web] Accessed on 23rd June, 2008, URL:http://www.global-mechanism.org/dynamic/documents/document_file/salam-programmebriefeng.pdf.

Gulf Cooperation Council, [Online: web] Accessed on 23rd June, 2008 URL: http://www.gcc-sg.org/cooperation.html

Hassan, Javid and Ali Al-Zahrani, "Kingdom to Spend SR32bn on Scientific Research and Development," *Arab News*, 22nd December, 2006 [Online: web] Accessed on 24th June, 2008 URL:http://www.arabnews.com/?page=1&section=0&article=90282&d=22&m=12&y=2006.

International Centre for Agricultural Research in the Dry Areas (ICARDA), [Online: web] Accessed on 23rd June, 2008 URL: http://www.icarda.cgiar.org/AboutICARDA.htm.

Magola, Christopher, "Tanzania braces for Artificial Rain," *IPP Media*, 16th January, 2008 [Online: web] Accessed on 23rd June, 2008 URL: http://www.ippmedia.com/ipp/guardian/2008/01/16/106394.html

Nath, Ravindra, "GCC Water Link Project Moving as Per Plan: Qaboos", *Khaleej Times*, 27th February, 2007, [Online: web] Accessed on 23rd June, 2008 URL: http://www.khaleejtimes.com/DisplayArticleNew.asp? section=middleeast&xfile=data/middleeast/2007/february/middleeast_february449.xml

Rafique, Mahmood, "Power Grid to connect GCC Countries on way," *Bahrain Tribune*, 8th January, 2008[Online: web] Accessed on 23rd June, 2008 URL: http://www.bahraintribune.com/ArticleDetail.asp

Rasooldeen, Mohammed, "Kingdom Seeks to Expand Green Zones" *Arab News*, 29th July, 2006, [Online: web] Accessed on 23rd June, 2008 URL:http://www.arabnews.com/?page=1&section=0&article=81497&d=29&m=7&y=2006.

Ravi, Meera, "NGO to collect data on turtles in Bahrain", *Bahrain Tribune*, 8th September, 2005, [Online: web] Accessed on 23rd June, 2008 URL: http://www.bahraintribune.com/ArticleDetail.asp.

————, "Conserve water call", *Bahrain Tribune*, 23rd Mach, 2006 [Online: web] Accessed on 23rd June, 2008 URL: http://www.bahraintribune.com/ArticleDetail.asp.

————, "Green NGOs lack Muscle: Depleting Water and Coastal Resources Alarming", *Bahrain Tribune*, 7th April, 2006, [Online: web] Accessed on 23rd June, 2008 URL: http://www.bahraintribune.com/ArticleDetail.asp

Saab, Najib "Arab Environment Institutions in Coma", *Mectat*, March 2001, [Online: web] Accessed on 23rd June, 2008 URL: http://www.mectat.com.lb/contents/page36.htm, accessed on 28th June, 2008.

Shaikh, Habib, "Donors Asked to Help Fight Drought", *Arab News* [Online: web] Accessed on 23rd June, 2008 URL:http://www.arabnews.com/?page=1&section=0&article=65524&d=17&m=6&y=2005.

UNCCD Secretariat, "Fact Sheet," [Online: web] Accessed on 23rd June, 2008 URL:http://www.unccd.int/publicinfo/factsheets/showFS.php?number=3

————, "Focal Points", [Online: web] Accessed on 28 June 2008 URL: http://www.unccd.int/focalpoints/focalpoints.php

————, "Frequently Asked Questions," [Online: web] Accessed on 23 June 2008 URL: http://www.unccd.int/knowledge/faq.php#answer0.

————, "National Action Programmes of the Asian Countries" [Online:web] Accessed on 21st June, 2008 URL: http://www.unccd.int/actionprogrammes/asia/asia.php

————, "Non-Governmental Organisations" [Online: web] Accessed on 23rd June, 2008 URL: http://www.unccd.int/ngo/accreditationDB/results.php.

———, "Regional Profile-Asia" [Online: web] Accessed on 23rd June, 2008 URL: http://www.unccd.int/regional/asia/menu.php

———, "Reports of the Asian Countries" [Online: web] Accessed on 27th June, 2008 URL: http://www.unccd.int/cop/reports/asia/asia.php

———, *Report of the Conference of Parties*, [Online: web] Accessed on 23rd June, 2008 URL: http://www.unccd.int/cop/officialdocs/cop4/pdf/3add1(a)eng.pdf

———, *Report of the Committee to Review the Implementation of Convention*, First Session, 2003, [Online: web] Accessed on 28th June, 2008 URL: http://www.unccd.int/cop/officialdocs/cric1/pdf/10eng.pdf.

———, "Secretariat" [Online: web] Accessed on 23rd June, 2008 URL:http://www.unccd.int/secretariat/menu.php

———, "The United Nations Convention to Combat Desertification" [Online: web] Accessed on 23rd June, 2008 URL: http://www.unccd.int/convention/text/convention.php

UNEP "News Briefs" 26 February 2008[Online: web] Accessed on 23rd June, 2008
URL: www.unep.org/cpi/briefs/2008Feb26.doc.

News Papers

1. Arab News
2. Bahrain Tribune
3. Bangkok Post
3. Gulf Times
4. Khaleej Times

Index